The Official Rules
and Explanations

Paul Dickson

The Official Rules and Explanations

The Original Guide
to Surviving the Electronic Age
with Wit, Wisdom, and Laughter

FEDERAL
STREET
PRESS

A Division of Merriam-Webster, Incorporated
Springfield, Massachusetts

To Andrew and Alexander—may they figure out the rules quicker
than their old man—and to the late H. Allen Smith, a hero of mine
who I would like to think would have enjoyed all of this.

Text copyright © 1978, 1980, 1999 by Paul Dickson

Federal Street Press is a trademark of Federal Street Press,
a division of Merriam-Webster, Incorporated.

This edition published by
Federal Street Press
A Division of Merriam-Webster, Incorporated
P.O. Box 281
Springfield, MA 01102

Federal Street Press books are available for bulk purchase for sales promotion
and premium use. For details, write the manager of special sales,
Federal Street Press, P.O. Box 281, Springfield, MA 01102.

Library of Congress Catalog Card Number 99-62656

ISBN 1-892859-10-6

Printed in the United States of America

10 9 8 7 6 5 4 3 2 1

TABLE OF CONTENTS

Y2K FOREWORD TO THE OFFICIAL RULES AND EXPLANATIONS, OR MURPHY AND THE MILLENNIUM

It started simply. In 1976 the author of this omnibus created something called the Murphy Center for the Codification of Human and Organizational Law. He appointed himself its first Director and has been, since 1989, its self-appointed Director for Life. Originally, it amounted to nothing more than a shoe box into which rules and laws were filed.

The Center was created in an effort to collect, test, and make a few bucks from revealed truth, which is often the byproduct of what the Center thinks of fondly as O.F.F.M.& G.C., or Other Folks' Foibles, Misfortunes, and General Confusion. It was inspired mainly by Murphy's Law ("If anything can go wrong, it will") and influenced by the fact that we had put men on the moon but still seemed unable to create shoelaces that didn't break at inopportune moments.

The now-esteemed and verging-on-venerable Murphy Center is alive and well, and enjoying its perverse nature , which means that it thrives on a little turmoil, bad economic times, and the widespread awareness that the universe is flawed. The Center has published seven books of its findings and has now spread out into eight shoe boxes. Great gobs of its early material have been pirated and put onto web pages by folks whose only original idea ever was to get access to a copy machine.

This, then, is the the final volume to serve the needs of the 20th Century, and the Murphy Center is, as of this 1999 writing, ready and willing to become part of the new Millennium, which is expected to revalidate Murphy's Law, starting with those much-heralded Y2K problems. Any century that begins with the worry that one's automatic coffee machine thinks it is 1900 is, in fact, destined to be, *ipso facto*, Murphetic.

The laws that follow appear in the exact language of the person who discovered the phenomenon or universal truth, including his or her name for that discovery. Every attempt has been made to find the original author of each entry, but, sadly, some appear as "origin unknown."

The items were collected over a period of years and are listed alphabetically by the name of the law, effect, or principle. This gives them a sense of categorical and chronological randomness, which approximates the subjects at hand.

The first report from the Murphy Center, *The Official Rules*, appeared in 1978. That book, in turn, attracted thousands of letters—more than 5,000, actually—containing more rules, laws, principles, maxims, and "whatevers." This led to the creation of *The Official Explanations*. Other "Official" books have followed, and there will be still more: The Director is faithfully collecting new items at P.O. Box 80, Garrett Park, MD 20896.

P.S. The Director hereby goes on record as saying that there will be no problems associated with the end of 1999 and the Y2&^%$#@(*&+|||*errormessage*666#$$$*@!23SKiddo.com#@!

The Official Rules

Preface

All things are subject to fixed laws.
—Marcus Manilius, *Astronomica,* I, c. 40 B.C.

Natural laws have no pity.
—Long's 22nd Note, from Robert A. Heinlein's *Time Enough for Love*

For centuries mathematics and the pure sciences held a seem-ingly unbreakable monopoly on natural laws, principles, and named effects. At the gradual pace of a law at a time, researchers and scholars worked to show us that some element of the uni-verse was working in perfect accord with an immutable rule that could be stated without taking a breath.

The *Second Law of Thermodynamics,* for instance, told us that in every energy transaction some of the original energy is changed into heat energy, while *Boyle's Law* informed us that at a constant temperature the volume of a given quantity of gas is inversely proportional to the pressure on the gas. Hundreds and hundreds of laws were created, with most of the great names in science in possessive possession of at least one solid law (e.g., Newton's, Ohm's, Darwin's, Mendel's, Archimedes', Einstein's, and so forth). To get through four years of college (let alone four years of Sunday crossword puzzles) one is forced into contact with a few score such laws, which are liable to range from the *Law of Action and Reaction* to the *Laws of Vibrating Strings.**

---

*The *Law of Action and Reaction* is the one that says for every action there is an equal and opposite reaction. The *Laws of Vibrating Strings* go like this: (1) The frequency of vibration of a wire is inversely proportional to its length. The shorter the string, the higher the pitch. (2) The frequency of vibration varies directly as the square root of tension. (3) The frequency of a vibrating string varies inversely with the square root of its weight per

xi

Yet as new laws were discovered, posted, and accepted by the textbook publishers, people outside the hard sciences increasingly felt that a whopping injustice was in force. Not only were the soft sciences, humanities, and workaday pursuits excluded from the business of lawmaking but—even more to the point— there was a deep and demonstrable prejudice at work as all these big-name scientists were busy describing a perfect Universe when, as everyone else (including not-so-big scientists) was fully aware, it is not all that perfect.

Over the years, there were a few exceptions. Economists were able to gain acceptance for such items as the *Law of Supply and Demand* and *Say's Law* (i.e., "Supply creates its own demand"). But these were exceptions to the rule. Then in the years after World War II, more and more people began hearing series of laws—more often said than written—attached to such names as Murphy, Finagle, and Sod, which had an uncanny ability to describe things as they could be and often were—screwed up. Murphy looked right into our lives and concluded, "If anything can go wrong, it will," and Finagle was able to perceive via his *Fourth Law,* "No matter what occurs, there is always someone who believes it happened according to his pet theory." It cannot be proven, but it has been suggested that Murphy, Finagle, and their disciples (all to be discussed in the pages ahead) have helped more people get through crises, deadlines, bad days, the final phases of projects, and attacks by inanimate objects than either pep talks, uplifting epigrams, or the invocation of traditional rules. It is true that if your paperboy throws your paper in the bushes for five straight days, it can be explained by *Newton's Law of Gravity.* But it takes Murphy to explain why it is happening to *you.*

As these explanations of the perversity of nature grew in popularity and importance, other laws and principles came along to

---

unit of length. Thick, heavy strings vibrate more slowly and hence give tones of lower pitch.

explain how other things worked. In 1955 an obscure historian named C. Northcote Parkinson wrote an article called "Parkinson's Law," in which he showed that "Work expands so as to fill the time available for its completion." Parkinson became famous, and his law has become a permanent tenet of organizational life. Parkinson begat more laws as others brought out their own discoveries. Some were highly successful, such as Dr. Laurence J. Peter and his famous *Peter Principle* (1969), while others created laws that only those in a specific circle could fully appreciate, like the great body of laws created by and for computer programmers. By the early 1970s laws were coming in from all over and showing up everywhere: newspaper columns, books, laboratory walls. . . . What more and more people were discovering in their own lives and jobs are those universal truths which have been begging to be stated scientifically and shared with the rest of the world. In most cases these laws are being discovered by average, not famous men and women —although nothing prevents senators, scientists, press pundits, and other VIPs from getting into the act. Yet, regardless of whether a law is discovered by a Nobel laureate or an insurance company clerk, a good law is a good law and able to move around the country with remarkable speed. Unfortunately, a law often moves so quickly that it is soon separated from the person who discovered and named it. As a result an important new law like *Anthony's Law of Force* (which says, "Don't force it, get a larger hammer") is known far and wide to people who have no idea who Anthony is.

Often a group of a dozen or so new laws are collected and typed out on a sheet of paper. These sheets are drawn to copying machines like metal filings to a magnet, and once copied are posted on bulletin boards, passed out at water coolers, dropped into inter-office mail systems, and swapped at conventions. Whether by jet, teletype, or mail, a list compiled and copied in Boston on a Monday is liable to show up in Santa Monica by the end of the week. The creation and distribution of laws has become full-fledged a cultural phenomenon: a computer-age folk idiom.

What follows is the work of a person who, with the help of many, has been collecting laws in a filing box which (in mock academic style) has been dubbed the Murphy Center for the Codification of Human and Organizational Law. (More on the Murphy Center appears in the "Report from the Center" at the end of the book.)

This collection of new laws is arranged alphabetically, contains special sections on areas of special importance, and is followed by a subject index. To the extent possible each law is accompanied by the identity of the person who discovered it and, when applicable, the person who first collected it. Laws that could not be connected to their discoverers are noted with a *U,* which means "unknown to this collector." There are a number of *U*s, but this is to be expected because the nature of lawgiving is such that a good law is often separated from its owner. More confusing, words taken from the utterings of famous people have been stated as laws and named in their honor. (Conversely, famous people have been known to make up laws and affix bogus names to them. John Kenneth Galbraith has done this on several occasions. See, for instance, *Crump's Law.*) As a result of this, one is liable to come up with a law like *Parker's Law of Parliamentary Procedure* ("A motion to adjourn is always in order") and have no way of knowing if the Parker in question was (a) Dorothy Parker, (b) Charlie Parker, (c) a claims adjuster named Parker who created it at a claim adjusters' convention, or (d) John Kenneth Galbraith.

Similarly, I have tried whenever possible to credit other collections from which laws have been collected. To save space, these have been abbreviated, and a key to these abbreviations appears at the end of the book following the entries for Z. However, six collections have been especially important to this effort, and they deserve mention here. These are the collections belonging to writer Fred Dyer (*FD* in the text), who was instrumental in getting the Center started; *Wall Street Journal* columnist Alan Otten (*AO*), who has done so much to popularize the idiom through his excellent articles on the subject; Jack Womeldorf of the Library of Congress (*JW*); Robert Specht (*RS*) of the RAND Corp.; and two computerized files: the John Erhman file at Stanford University (*J.E*), and the seminally important University of Arizona Computing Center collection, which was begun in January, 1974, by Conrad Schneiker and maintained by Gregg Townsend, Ed Logg, and others (*S.T.L.*).

Finally, one must thank all the people—dozens of them—who have helped with this effort. For their contributions, they have been made Fellows of the Murphy Center, a more than honorary title that might come in handy in a number of situations. For instance, should any of them ever need not to have to explain a nonproductive period in their life, they can simply say they are on a research fellowship from the Murphy Center. A list of Fellows begins on page 467.

Abbott's Admonitions. (1) If you have to ask, you're not entitled to know. (2) If you don't like the answer, you shouldn't have asked the question.

> (Charles C. Abbott, former dean of the Graduate School of Business Administration, University of Virginia. *AO.*)

Abrams's Advice. When eating an elephant take one bite at a time.

> (General Creighton W. Abrams. *HE.*)

Accuracy, Rule of. When working toward the solution of a problem, it always helps if you know the answer. *Advanced's Corollary:* Provided, of course, you know there is a problem.

> (Also known by other titles, such as the *Ultimate Law of Accuracy. AIC.*)

Acheson's Rule of the Bureaucracy. A memorandum is written not to inform the reader but to protect the writer.

> (Dean Acheson, recalled by Harold P. Smith for *AO.*)

Acton's Law. Power tends to corrupt, absolute power corrupts absolutely.

> (Lord Acton. *Co.*)

Ade's Law. Anybody can win—unless there happens to be a second entry.

> (American humorist George Ade. *PQ.*)

- **Advertising Agency Song, The.**

> When your client's hopping mad,
> Put his picture in the ad.
> If he still should prove refractory
> Add a picture of his factory.

(Anonymous, from *Pith and Vinegar,* edited by William Cole, Simon & Schuster, 1969.)

- **Agnes Allen's Law.** Almost anything is easier to get into than out of.

(Agnes Allen was the wife of the famous historian Frederick Lewis Allen. When her husband was teaching at Yale, he encountered an ambitious student named Louis Zahner, who wanted to create and be remembered for a law of his own. Zahner worked on it and finally hit upon one that states: "If you play with anything long enough it will break." Inspired by his student, Allen then went to work on his own and came up with *Allen's Law*: "Everything is more complicated than it looks to most people." Agnes Allen then got into the act and proceeded to outdistance Zahner and her husband by creating the law that to this day carries her full name. Frederick Allen later wrote of his wife's law: ". . . at one stroke human wisdom had been advanced to an unprecedented degree." All of this was revealed in a column by Jack Smith in the *Los Angeles Times* after he had researched the question of who Murphy and Agnes Allen were. Needless to say, he proved Ms. Allen's law in the process.)

- **Airplane Law.** When the plane you are on is late, the plane you want to transfer to is on time.

● **Algren's Precepts.** Never eat at a place called Mom's. Never play cards with a man named Doc. And never lie down with a woman who's got more troubles than you.

(Nelson Algren, on "What Every Young Man Should Know.")

● **Allen's Axiom.** When all else fails, read the instructions. (*U/Scientific Collections*. Sometimes called *Cahn's Axiom*.)

● **Allen's Distinction.** The lion and the calf shall lie down together, but the calf won't get much sleep.
(Woody Allen, from *Without Feathers*, Random House, 1977.)

● **Allen's Law of Civilization.** It is better for civilization to be going down the drain than to be coming up it.
(Henry Allen, *The Washington Post.*)

● **Alley's Axiom.** Justice always prevails . . . three times out of seven!
(*U.* The law itself comes from Michael J. Wagner of Miami.)

● **Allison's Precept.** The best simpleminded test of expertise in a particular area is an ability to win money in a series of bets on future occurrences in that area.
(Graham Allison, the John F. Kennedy School of Government, to *AO.*)

● **Anderson's Law.** I have yet to see any problem, however complicated, which, when you looked at it in the right way, did not become still more complicated.
(Writer Poul Anderson. *JW.*)

● **Andrews's Canoeing Postulate.** No matter which direction you start, it's always against the wind coming back.
(Alfred Andrews. *JE.*)

● **Anthony's Law of Force.** Don't force it, get a larger hammer.

● **Anthony's Law of the Workshop.** Any tool, when dropped, will roll into the least accessible corner of the work-

shop. *Corollary:* On the way to the corner, any dropped tool will first always strike your toes.
(*U/S.T.L.*)

● **Approval Seeker's Law.** Those whose approval you seek the most give you the least.
(This is one of a number of laws created by Washington writer Rozanne Weissman. She is a natural-law writer whose style is characterized by restraint. Note that all of her laws bear situational titles.)

● **Army Axiom.** An order that can be misunderstood will be misunderstood.

● **Army Law.** If it moves, salute it; if it doesn't move, pick it up; and if you can't pick it up, paint it.
(Both of these authentic Army items have been around at least since World War II, if not longer.)

● **Artz's Observation.** You can lead a whore to Vassar, but you can't make her think.
(Frederick B. Artz, noted medieval historian. His observation was recorded in 1955. *JE.* This law is an obvious parody of Dorothy Parker's "You can lead a horticulture but you can't make her think.")

● **Ashley-Perry Statistical Axioms.** (1) Numbers are tools, not rules. (2) Numbers are symbols for things; the number and the thing are not the same. (3) Skill in manipulating numbers is a talent, not evidence of divine guidance. (4) Like other occult techniques of divination, the statistical method has a private jargon deliberately contrived to obscure its methods from nonpractitioners. (5) The product of an arithmetical computation is the answer to an equation; it is not the solution to a problem. (6)

Arithmetical proofs of theorems that do not have arithmetical bases prove nothing.

> (Drawn from Colonel G. O. Ashley's "A Declaration of Independence from the Statistical Method," *Air University Review*, March/April, 1964, and interpreted by R. L. Perry of the RAND Corp. *RS.*)

● **Asimov's Corollary** (to *Clarke's First Law*). When the lay public rallies round an idea that is denounced by distinguished but elderly scientists, and supports that idea with great fervor and emotion—the distinguished but elderly scientists are then, after all, right.

> (Isaac Asimov in his article "Asimov's Law" in the February, 1977, *Fantasy and Science Fiction Magazine*. One should also see *Clarke's Laws* and *Bartz's Law of Hokey Horsepuckery* for comparison. More laws by Asimov appear under *Robotics, The Three Laws of.*)

● **Astrology Law.** It's always the wrong time of the month. (Rozanne Weissman.)

● **Atwood's Fourteenth Corollary.** No books are lost by lending except those you particularly wanted to keep.

> (Alan Atwood, a programmer at the University Computing Center, University of Arizona. *S.T.L.*)

● **Avery, Sayings of.** (1) No ball game is ever much good unless the people involved hate each other. (2) On Monday mornings I am dedicated to the proposition that all men are created jerks. (3) Some performers on television appear to be horrible people, but when you finally get to know them in person, they turn out to be even worse. (4) There's such a thing as too much point on a pencil. (5) When there are two conflicting versions of a story, the wise course is to believe the one in which people appear at their worst.

(These are from the late H. Allen Smith's *Let the Crab-grass Grow,* Bernard Geis Associates, 1960. Avery is Smith's [presumably] fictional neighbor who is also responsible for the next two items. The second Avery item has shown up on various lists and may or may not have come from Smith's Avery.)

● **Avery's Law of Lubrication.** Everything needs a little oil now and then. (This as Smith finds Avery, a destructive do-it-yourselfer, pouring oil into the tiny hinges by which the bows of his glasses are attached to their frames.)

● **Avery's Observation.** It does not matter if you fall down as long as you pick up something from the floor while you get up.

● **Avery's Rule of Three.** Trouble strikes in series of threes, but when working around the house the next job after a series of three is not the fourth job—it's the start of a brand new series of three.

B

● **Baer's Quartet.** What's good politics is bad economics; what's bad politics is good economics; what's good economics is bad politics; what's bad economics is good politics.

> (Eugene W. Baer of Middletown, R.I., to *AO*. Baer also allows that it can all be stated somewhat more compactly as "What's good politics is bad economics and vice versa, vice versa.")

● **Bagdikian's Law of Editor's Speeches.** The splendor of an editor's speech and the splendor of his newspaper are inversely related to the distance between the city in which he makes his speech and the city in which he publishes his paper.

> (Ben Bagdikian, writer and press critic, Berkeley, Cal.)

● **Baker's Law.** Misery no longer loves company. Nowadays it insists on it.

> (Columnist Russell Baker.)

● **Baldy's Law.** Some of it plus the rest of it is all of it.

> (*U*. From the collection of laws assembled by Charles Wolf, Jr., of the RAND Corp.)

● **Barber's Laws of Backpacking.** (1) The integral of the gravitational potential taken around any loop trail you choose to hike always comes out positive. (2) Any stone in your boot always migrates against the pressure gradient to exactly the point of most pressure. (3) The weight of your pack increases in direct proportion to the amount of food you consume from it. If you run out of food, the pack weight goes on increasing anyway. (4) The

8

number of stones in your boot is directly proportional to the number of hours you have been on the trail. (5) The difficulty of finding any given trail marker is directly proportional to the importance of the consequences of failing to find it. (6) The size of each of the stones in your boot is directly proportional to the number of hours you have been on the trail. (7) The remaining distance to your chosen campsite remains constant as twilight approaches. (8) The net weight of your boots is proportional to the cube of the number of hours you have been on the trail. (9)

When you arrive at your campsite, it is full. (10) If you take your boots off, you'll never get them back on again. (11) The local density of mosquitos is inversely proportional to your remaining repellant.

>(Milt Barber, formerly a consultant at the Control Data Corp. *S.T.L.*)

● **Barrett's Laws of Driving.** (1) You can get *anywhere* in ten minutes if you go fast enough. (2) Speed bumps are of negligible effect when the vehicle exceeds triple the desired restraining speed. (3) The vehicle in front of you is traveling slower than you are. (4) This lane ends in 500 feet.

>(*U.* From John L. Shelton, President, Sigma Beta Communications, Inc., Dallas, Texas.)

● **Barr's Comment on Domestic Tranquility.** On a beautiful day like this it's hard to believe anyone can be unhappy— but we'll work on it.

>(Donald Barr, Highland Park, Ill., to *AO.*)

● **Barth's Distinction.** See *Benchley's Distinction.*

● **Bartz's Law of Hokey Horsepuckery.** The more ridiculous a belief system, the higher the probability of its success.

>(Wayne R. Bartz in his article "Keys to Success," *Human Behavior,* May, 1975.)

● **Baruch's Rule for Determining Old Age.** Old age is always fifteen years older than I am.

>(Bernard M. Baruch.)

● **Barzun's Laws of Learning.** (1) The simple but difficult arts of paying attention, copying accurately, following an argument, detecting an ambiguity or a false inference, testing guesses by summoning up contrary instances, organizing one's time and one's thought for study—all these arts . . . cannot be taught in the air but only through the difficulties of a defined subject; they cannot be taught in one course or one year, but must be acquired gradually in dozens of connections. (2) The analogy to athletics must be pressed until all recognize that in the exercise of Intellect those who lack the muscles, coordination, and will power can claim no place at the training table, let alone on the playing field.

> (Jacques Barzun, from *The House of Intellect,* Harper & Row, 1959. Appeared in Martin's *MB* and a number of subsequent lists, including *S.T.L.,* where it appears in conjunction with *Forthoffer's Cynical Summary of Barzun's Laws.* [1] That which has not yet been taught directly can never be taught directly. [2] If at first you don't succeed, you will never succeed.)

● **Beardsley's Warning to Lawyers.** Beware of and eschew pompous prolixity.

> (Charles A. Beardsley, the late president of the American Bar Association.)

● **Beauregard's Law.** When you're up to your nose, keep your mouth shut.

> (Uttered by Henry Fonda in the role of Jack Beauregard in the film, *My Name Is Nobody. MLS.*)

● **Becker's Law.** It is much harder to find a job than to keep one.

> (Jules Becker of Becker and Co., San Francisco, to *AO.* Becker, who claims that his law permeates industry as well as government, goes on to explain, ". . . once a person has been hired, inertia sets in, and the employer would rather settle for the current employee's incompetence and idiosyncrasies than look for a new employee.")

● **Beifeld's Principle.** The probability of a young man meeting a desirable and receptive young female increases by pyramidical progression when he is already in the company of (1) a date, (2) his wife, (3) a better looking and richer male friend.

(Ronald H. Beifeld, Philadelphia attorney, submitted to *AO* with alternative title, *The Law of Inverse Proportion of Social Intercourse.*)

● **Belle's Constant.** The ratio of time involved in work to time available for work is usually about 0.6.

(From a 1977 *JIR* article of the same title by Daniel McIvor and Oslen Belle, in which it is observed that knowledge of this constant is most useful in planning long-range projects. It is based on such things as an analysis of an eight-hour workday in which only 4.8 hours are actually spent working (or 0.6 of the time available), with the rest being spent on coffee breaks, bathroom visits, resting, walking, fiddling around, and trying to determine what to do next.)

● **Benchley's Distinction.** There may be said to be two classes of people in the world; those who constantly divide the people of the world into two classes and those who do not.

(Robert Benchley. This is often listed as *Barth's Distinction* [*S.T.L., JE,* etc.], but the Benchley quote is clearly much older.)

● **Bennett's Beatitudes.** (1) Blessed is he who has reached the point of no return and knows it, for he shall enjoy living. (2) Blessed is he who expects no gratitude, for he shall not be disappointed.

(W. C. Bennett, Trinity Avenue Presbyterian Church, Durham, N.C.)

● **Berkeley's Laws.** (1) The world is more complicated than most of our theories make it out to be. (2) Ignorance is no excuse. (3) Never decide to buy something while listening to the salesman. (4) Most problems have either many answers or no answer. Only a few problems have a single answer. (5) Most general statements are false, including this one. (6) An exception TESTS a rule; it NEVER PROVES it. (7) The moment you have worked out an answer, start checking it—it probably isn't right. (8) If there is an opportunity to make a mistake, sooner or later the mistake will be made. (9) Check the answer you have worked out once more—before you tell it to anybody.

> (Edmund C. Berkeley, "common sense" researcher and former editor of *Computers and Automation*. This is a mere sampling of Berkeley's to-the-point statements. They come from his article "Right Answers—A Short Guide for Obtaining Them," which appeared in the September, 1969, issue of *Computers and Automation*.)

● **Bernstein's Law.** A falling body always rolls to the most inaccessible spot.

> (Theodore M. Bernstein, from *The Careful Writer*, Atheneum, 1965. See also *Anthony's Law of the Workshop*.)

● **Berra's Law.** You can observe a lot just by watching.
> (Yogi Berra. *RS*.)

● **Berson's Corollary of Inverse Distances.** The farther away from the entrance of the market (theater, or any other given location) that you have to park, the closer the space vacated by the car that pulls away as you walk up to the door.

> (Judith deMille Berson, Silver Spring, Md.)

● **Bicycle Law.** All bicycles weigh 50 pounds:
> A 30-pound bicycle needs a 20-pound lock and chain.
> A 40-pound bicycle needs a 10-pound lock and chain.
> A 50-pound bicycle needs no lock and chain.
> (*S.T.L.*)

● **Bicycling, First Law of.** No matter which way you ride, it's uphill and against the wind.
(*S.T.L.*)

● **Bill Babcock's Law.** If it can be borrowed and it can be broken, you will borrow it and you will break it.
(W. W. Chandler, Lyons, Kans., to *AO.*)

● **Billings Phenomenon.** The conclusions of most good operations research studies are obvious.
(Robert E. Machol, from "Principles of Operations Research" [*POR*]. The name refers to a well-known Billings story in which a farmer becomes concerned that his black horses are eating a lot more than his white horses. He does a detailed study of the situation and finds that he has more black horses than white horses. Machol points out that the obvious conclusions are not likely to be obvious a priori but obvious after the results are in. In other words, good research does not have to yield dramatic findings.)

● **Billings's Law.** Live within your income, even if you have to borrow to do so.
(19th Century American humorist Josh Billings. *PQ.*)

● **Blaauw's Law.** Established technology tends to persist in the face of new technology.
(Gerritt A. Blaauw, one of the designers of IBM's System/360. *JE.*)

● **Blanchard's Newspaper Obituary Law.** If you want your name spelled wrong, die.
(Al Blanchard, Washington bureau chief for *The Detroit News. AO.*)

● **Bloom's Law of the Profitable Inertia of Gold.** Certain things shouldn't be moved.

(Writer Murray Teigh Bloom, who first reported his discovery in his first book, *Money of Their Own,* Scribners, 1957. As he explained in a recent letter, "Once the Philadelphia Mint experimented and found $5.00 was lost by abrasion every time a million dollars worth of gold coin was handled. Just lifting the bags—each filled with $5,-000 worth of gold coin—to the truck resulted in a $5.00 loss; transferring them back to the mint caused another $5.00 loss. Letting the stuff rest quietly at Fort Knox instead of moving it around nervously to Sub-Treasuries makes us richer.")

● **Bok's Law.** If you think education is expensive—try ignorance.

(Derek Bok, president, Harvard University, quoted by Ann Landers in her column for March 26, 1978.)

● **Bolton's Law of Ascending Budgets.** Under current practices, both expenditures and revenues rise to meet each other, no matter which one may be in excess.

(Joe Bolton, Fellow of the RAND Graduate Institute. *RS.*)

● **Bombeck's Principles.** ■Any college that would take your son he should be too proud to go to. ■Know that a happy dieter has other problems. ■A man who checks out of the express lane with seven items is the same man who will wear Supp-Hose and park in the Reserved for Handicapped spaces. ■An old car that has served you so well will continue to serve you until you have just put four new tires under it and then will fall apart. ■A pregnancy will never occur when you have a low-paying job which you hate. ■An ugly carpet will last forever.

(Erma Bombeck, from her column of January 10, 1978.)

● **Bombeck's Rule of Medicine.** Never go to a doctor whose office plants have died.

(Erma Bombeck.)

● **Bonafede's Revelation.** The conventional wisdom is that power is an aphrodisiac. In truth, it's exhausting.
(Dom Bonafede in a February, 1977, article in the *Washingtonian* entitled "Surviving in Washington.")

● **Boob's Law.** You always find something the last place you look.
(Arthur Bloch's *Murphy's Law,* Price/Stern/Sloan Publishers Inc.)

● **Booker's Law.** An ounce of application is worth a ton of abstraction.
(*U/S.T.L.*)

● **Boozer's Revision.** A bird in the hand is dead.
(Rhonda Boozer, an elementary school pupil from Baltimore. This was produced when a teacher gave fourth and fifth graders the first half of an old adage and asked them to supply the second half. Other results of the adage improvement project according to an Associated Press report:
—"Don't put all your eggs in your pocket."
[Celestine Clark.]
—"Don't bite the hand that has your allowance in it."
[Lisa Tidler.]
—"If at first you don't succeed, blame it on the teacher."
[Stacey Bass.]

● **Boquist's Exception.** If for every rule there is an exception, then we have established that there is an exception to every rule. If we accept "For every rule there is an exception" as a rule, then we must concede that there may not be an exception after all, since the rule states that there is always the possibility of exception, and if we follow it to its logical end we must agree that there can be an exception to the rule that for every rule there is an exception.

> (Bill Boquist, San Francisco. *HW.*)

● **Boren's Laws of the Bureaucracy.** (1) When in doubt, mumble. (2) When in trouble, delegate. (3) When in charge, ponder.

> (James H. Boren, founder, president, and chairperson of the board of the International Association of Professional Bureaucrats [INATAPROBU].)

● **Borkowski's Law.** You can't guard against the arbitrary.
> (*U//C.*)

● **Boston's Irreversible Law of Clutter.** In any household, junk accumulates to fill the space available for its storage.

> (Bruce O. Boston, Fairfax, Va.)

● **Boultbee's Criterion.** If the converse of a statement is absurd, the original statement is an insult to the intelligence and should never have been said.

> (Arthur H. Boultbee, Greenwich, Conn., to *AO.* The author adds, "It is best applied to statements of politicians and TV pundits.")

● **Bowie's Theorem.** If an experiment works, you must be using the wrong equipment.
> (*U/RS.*)

● **Boyle's Laws.** (1) The success of any venture will be helped by prayer, even in the wrong denomination. (2) When things are going well, someone will inevitably experiment detrimentally. (3) The deficiency will never show itself during the dry runs. (4) Information travels more surely to those with a lesser need to know. (5) An original idea can never emerge from committee in the original. (6) When the product is destined to fail, the delivery system will perform perfectly. (7) The crucial memorandum will be snared in the out-basket by the paper clip of the overlying correspondence and go to file. (8) Success can be insured only by devising a defense against failure of the contingency plan. (9) Performance is directly affected by the perversity of inanimate objects. (10) If not controlled, work will flow to the competent man until he submerges. (11) The lagging activity in a project will invariably be found in the area where the highest overtime rates lie waiting. (12) Talent in staff work or sales will recurringly be interpreted as managerial ability. (13) The "think positive" leader tends to listen to his subordinates' premonitions only during the postmortems. (14) Clearly stated instructions will consistently produce multiple interpretations. (15) On successive charts of the same organization the number of boxes will never decrease.

(Charles P. Boyle, Goddard Space Flight Center, NASA.)

● **Branch's First Law of Crisis.** The spirit of public service will rise, and the bureaucracy will multiply itself much faster, in time of grave national concern.

(Taylor Branch, from his March, 1974, article in *Harper's* entitled "The Sunny Side of the Energy Crisis.")

● **Bribery, Mathematical Formula for.** OG=PLR × AEB: The opportunity for graft equals the plethora of legal requirements multiplied by the number of architects, engineers, and builders.

(Harold Birns, New York buildings commissioner, on the confusion of housing and building laws. *The New York Times,* October 2, 1963.)

● **Bridge, First Law of.** It's always the partner's fault.
(Sig Malek/*S.T.L.*)

● **Brien's First Law.** At some time in the life cycle of virtually every organization, its ability to succeed in spite of itself runs out.

> (Richard H. Brien, "The Managerialization of Higher Education," from *Educational Record,* Summer, 1970. Appears in *MB, S.T.L.,* etc.)

● **Broder's Law.** Anybody that wants the presidency so much that he'll spend two years organizing and campaigning for it is not to be trusted with the office.

> (David Broder in *The Washington Post,* July 19, 1973. *JW.*)

● **Broken Mirror Law.** Everyone breaks more than the seven-year-bad-luck allotment to cover rotten luck throughout an entire lifetime.

> (Rozanne Weissman.)

● **Brontosaurus Principle.** Organizations can grow faster than their brains can manage them in relation to their environment and to their own physiology: when this occurs, they are an endangered species.

> (Thomas K. Connellan, president of The Management Group, Inc. of Ann Arbor, Mich., from his 1976 book *The Brontosaurus Principle: A Manual for Corporate Survival,* Prentice-Hall.)

● **Brooks's Law.** Adding manpower to a late software project makes it later.

> (Frederick P. Brooks, Jr., from *The Mythical Man-Month: Essays on Software Engineering,* Addison-Wesley, 1974. *S.T.L.*)

● **Brown's Law. [J.]** Too often I find that the volume of paper expands to fill the available briefcases.

(Governor Jerry Brown, quoted in *State Government News,* March, 1973. *AO.*)

● **Brown's Law. [S.]** Never offend people with style when you can offend them with substance.
(Sam Brown, from *The Washington Post,* January 26, 1977. *JW.*)

● **Brown's Law of Business Success.** Our customer's paperwork is profit. Our own paperwork is loss.
(Tony Brown, programmer at the Control Data Corp. *S.T.L.*)

● **Bruce-Briggs's Law of Traffic.** At any level of traffic, any delay is intolerable.
(Barry Bruce-Briggs of the Hudson Institute, from his article "Mass Transportation and Minority Transportation" in *The Public Interest.* In explaining his law he adds, "It is amusing for someone accustomed to the traffic in New York to hear residents of places like Houston and Atlanta complain about congestion on the highways. Imagine, in rush hour they have to slow down to 35 miles an hour!")

● **Brumfit's Law.** The critical mass of any do-it-yourself explosive is never less than half a bucketful.
(*ASF* letter from Eric Frank Russell, who explained that the law was first demonstrated by Emmanuel Brumfit. Beginning with a half ounce of homemade gunpowder, Brumfit attempted to see what would happen if he lit it. When nothing happened he went on mixing and adding until, on his fifty-fourth match, he reached exactly a half a bucketful and "went out the window without bothering to open it.")

● **Buchwald's Law.** As the economy gets better, every-thing else gets worse.

(Art Buchwald, *Time,* January, 1972. *JW.*)

● **Bucy's Law.** Nothing is ever accomplished by a reason-able man.

(Fred Bucy, Texas Instruments Inc.)

● **Bugger Factor (sometimes Bouguerre).** See *Finagle.*

● **Bureaucracy, The Second Order Rule of.** The more directives you issue to solve a problem, the worse it gets.

(Jack Robertson, *Electronic News,* quoted in *New Engineer,* November, 1976.)

● **Bureaucratic Cop-Out #1.** You should have seen it when *I* got it.

(Marshall L. Smith, WMAL, Washington, D.C.)

Special Section 1

Bureaucratic Laws, Creeds, and Mottoes. Here is a select collection of items that have been collected in recent years from the halls of the federal government. None is attributed to anyone in particular and all were found hanging from office walls or partitions, where they were presumably placed for their inspirational value:

When you're up to your ass in alligators, it is difficult to keep your mind on the fact that your primary objective is to drain the swamp.

* * *

A. Running a project in this office is like mating elephants—it takes a great deal of time and effort to get on top of things; B. The whole affair is always accompanied by a great deal of noise and confusion, the culmination of which is heralded by loud trumpeting; C. After which, nothing comes of the effort for two years.

* * *

The road to hell is paved with good intentions. And littered with sloppy analysis!

* * *

If you want something done, ask a busy person.

● **Burns's Balance.** If the assumptions are wrong, the conclusions aren't likely to be very good.

(Robert E. Machol, from "Principles of Operations Research." The principle refers to the late radio comedian Robert Burns and his method for weighing hogs. Burns got a perfectly symmetrical plank and balanced it across a sawhorse. He would then put the hog on one end of the plank and began piling rocks on the other end until the plank was again perfectly balanced across the sawhorse. At this point he would carefully guess the weight of the rocks.)

● **Bustlin' Billy's Bogus Beliefs.** (1) The organization of any program reflects the organization of the people who develop it. (2) There is no such thing as a "dirty capitalist," only a capitalist. (3) Anything is possible, but nothing is easy. (4) Capitalism can exist in one of only two states—welfare or warfare. (5) I'd rather go whoring than warring. (6) History proves nothing. (7) There is nothing so unbecoming on the beach as a wet kilt. (8) A little humility is arrogance. (9) A lot of what appears to be progress is just so much technological rococo.

(Bill Gray, formerly of the Control Data Corp., friend of compilers of *S.T.L.*)

● **Butler's Law of Progress.** All progress is based on a universal innate desire on the part of every organism to live beyond its income.

(Samuel Butler, *Note-Books.*)

● **Bye's First Law of Model Railroading.** Any time you wish to demonstrate something, the number of faults is proportional to the number of viewers.

● **Bye's Second Law of Model Railroading.** The desire for modeling a prototype is inversely proportional to the decline of the prototype.

(*U/S.T.L.*)

C

- **Caen's Law.** All American cars are basically Chevrolets. (Herb Caen of the *San Francisco Chronicle*. RS.)

- **Calkins's Law of Menu Language.** The number of adjectives and verbs that are added to the description of a menu item is in inverse proportion to the quality of the resulting dish.
  (John Calkins of Washington, D.C., in a letter to *The Washington Post,* May, 1977. *JW.*)

- **Camp's Law.** A coup that is known in advance is a coup that does not take place.
  (The law that was reported by *AO* was alluded to by former CIA Director William Colby in a briefing for reporters. It is apparently known throughout the intelligence community and, Otten presumes, was named after a secret operation [operator?] named Camp.)

- **Canada Bill Jones's Motto.** It is morally wrong to allow suckers to keep their money.

- **Canada Bill Jones's Supplement.** A Smith and Wesson beats four aces.
  (*U/S.T.L.*)

- **Carson's Consolation.** No experiment is ever a complete failure. It can always be used as a bad example.
  (*U.* From a list entitled "Wisdom from the Giants of Science," found on a wall at National Institutes of Health, *MLS.* This has also been reported as *Carlson's Consolation.*)

● **Chamberlain's Laws.** (1) The big guys always win. (2) Everything tastes more or less like chicken.

> (Jeffery F. Chamberlain, Rochester, N.Y., in a letter to *Verbatim.*)

● **Character and Appearance, Law of.** People don't change; they only become more so.

> (John Bright-Holmes, editor, George Allen & Unwin [Publishers] Ltd., London.)

● **Chatauqua Boulevard Law.** Just when I finally figure out where it's at . . . somebody moves it.

> (Sign in window, Chautauqua Boulevard and Coast Highway, Pacific Palisades, Cal. Collected by *RS.*)

● **Checkbook Balancer's Law.** In matters of dispute, the bank's balance is always smaller than yours.

> (Rozanne Weissman.)

● **Cheops's Law.** Nothing ever gets built on schedule or within budget.

> (*S.T.L.*)

● **Chili Cook's Secret.** If your next pot of chili tastes better, it probably is because of something left out, rather than added.
(Hal John Wimberley, editor and publisher, *The Goat Gap Gazette,* Houston, Texas.)

● **Chinese Fortune Cookie Law.** Inappropriate fortunes always find the right person; and you always want more three hours later.
(Rozanne Weissman.)

● **Chisholm Effect—Basic Laws of Frustration, Mishap, and Delay.** *1st Law of Human Interaction.* If anything can go wrong, it will. *Corollary:* If anything just can't go wrong, it will anyway. *2d Law of Human Interaction.* When things are going well, something will go wrong. *Corollary:* When things just can't get any worse, they will. *Corollary 2:* Anytime things appear to be going better, you have overlooked something. *3rd Law of Human Interaction.* Purposes, as understood by the purposer, will be judged otherwise by others. *Corollary:* If you explain so clearly that nobody can misunderstand, somebody will. *Corollary 2:* If you do something which you are sure will meet with everybody's approval, somebody won't like it. *Corollary 3:* Procedures devised to implement the purpose won't quite work.
(Francis P. Chisholm was professor of English and chairman of the department at Wisconsin State College in River Falls for many years. His original article, "The Chisholm Effect," was published a number of years ago in a magazine called *motive.* Because of their resemblance to *Murphy's* and *Finagle's Laws,* his *1st and 2d Laws* are not well remembered today, but his *3rd,* complete with *Corollaries,* is one of the most quoted of modern laws. Sometimes the *3rd* is quoted with a *Corollary 4*: "No matter how long or how many times you explain, no one is listening." This may have been written by someone other than Chisholm and added after the original article.)

● **Christmas Morning, The First Discovery of.** Batteries not included.

(From the side panel of a toy box. Small print.)

● **Ciardi's Poetry Law.** Whenever in time, and wherever in the universe, any man speaks or writes in any detail about the technical management of a poem, the resulting irascibility of the reader's response is a constant.

(John Ciardi, in his "Manner of Speaking" column in *Saturday Review,* February 13, 1965. He created it in response to the reader outcry over some columns in which he wrote about the technical side of poetry.)

● **Clarke's Laws.** (1) When a distinguished but elderly scientist states that something is possible, he is almost certainly right. When he states that something is impossible, he is very probably wrong. (2) The only way to discover the limits of the possible is to go beyond them to the impossible. (3) Any sufficiently advanced technology is indistinguishable from magic.

(Arthur C. Clarke, from his book *Profiles of the Future,* Harper & Row, 1962. In illustrating the first law he uses the example of Lord Rutherford, who ". . . more than any other man laid bare the internal structure of the atom" but who also made fun of those who predicted the harnessing of atomic power. Clarke also elaborates on the meaning of the word "elderly" in the first law. He says that in physics, astronautics, and mathematics it means over thirty, but that in some fields "senile decay" is postponed into the forties. He adds, "There are, of course, glorious exceptions; but as every good researcher just out of college knows, scientists of over fifty are good for nothing but board meetings, and should at all costs be kept out of the laboratory!")

● **Clark's First Law of Relativity.** No matter how often you trade dinner or other invitations with in-laws, you will lose a small fortune in the exchange. *Corollary 1 on Clark's First:* Don't try it: you cannot drink enough of your in-laws' booze to get even before the liver fails.

(Jackson Clark, Cuero, Texas, to *AO.*)

● **Clark's Law.** It's always darkest just before the lights go out.

(Alex Clark, Lyndon B. Johnson School, Texas, at a RAND Graduate Institute meeting. *RS.*)

● **Cleveland's Highway Law.** Highways in the worst need of repair naturally have low traffic counts, which results in low priority for repair work.

(Named for Representative Jim Cleveland of New Hampshire. Its truth was revealed some years ago during Public Works Appropriations hearings as highway aid to New Hampshire was being reduced. *JMcC.*)

● **Cliff-hanger Theorem.** Each problem solved introduces a new unsolved problem.

(Posted in U.S. Department of Labor. *TO'B.*)

● **Clopton's Law.** For every credibility gap there is a gullibility fill.

(Richard Clopton. *PQ.*)

● **Clyde's Law.** If you have something to do, and you put it off long enough, chances are someone else will do it for you.

(Clyde F. Adams, Auburn, Ala.)

● **Cohen's Choice.** Everybody's gotta be someplace.
(Comedian Myron Cohen. *MLS.*)

● **Cohen's Law. [J.]** What really matters is the name you succeed in imposing on the facts—not the facts themselves.

(Jerome Cohen, Harvard Law School professor, quoted in *Time,* June 7, 1971.)

● **Cohen's Laws of Politics. [M.]** *Cohen's Law of Alienation:* Nothing can so alienate a voter from the political system as backing a winning candidate. *Cohen's Law of Ambition:* At any one time, thousands of borough councilmen, school board members, attorneys, and businessmen—as well as congressmen, senators, and governors—are dreaming of the White House, but few, if any of them, will make it. *Cohen's Law of Attraction:* Power attracts people but it cannot hold them. *Cohen's Law of Competition:* The more qualified candidates who are available, the more likely the compromise will be on the candidate whose main qualification is a nonthreatening incompetence. *Cohen's Law of Inside Dope:* There are many inside dopes in politics and government. *Cohen's Law on Lawmaking:* Those who express random thoughts to legislative committees are often surprised and appalled to find themselves the instigators of law. *Cohen's Law of Permanence:* Political power is as permanent as today's newspaper. Ten years from now, few will know or care who the most powerful man in any state was today. *Cohen's Law of Practicality:* Courses of action which run only to be justified in terms of practicality ultimately prove destructive and impractical. *Cohen's Law of Secrecy:* The best way to publicize a governmental or political action is to attempt to hide it. *Cohen's Law of Wealth:* Victory goes to the candidate with the most accumulated or contributed wealth who has the financial sources to convince the middle class and poor that he will be on their side. *Cohen's Law of Wisdom:* Wisdom is considered a sign of weakness by the powerful because a wise man can lead without power but only a powerful man can lead without wisdom.

(Mark B. Cohen, member, House of Representatives,

Commonwealth of Pennsylvania. Cohen writes his own as well as collects other people's political laws.)

● **Cohn's Law.** The more time you spend in reporting on what you are doing, the less time you have to do anything. Stability is achieved when you spend all your time doing nothing but reporting on the nothing you are doing.
(*U/TO'B.*)

● **Cole's Law.** Thinly sliced cabbage.
(*S.T.L.*)

● **Colson's Law.** If you've got them by the balls, their hearts and minds will follow.
(From a poster *alleged* to have hung in the office of a key Nixon aide. *MLS.*)

● **Comins's Law.** People will accept your idea much more readily if you tell them Benjamin Franklin said it first.
(David H. Comins, Manchester, Conn. *HW.*)

● **Committee Rules.** (1) Never arrive on time, or you will be stamped a beginner. (2) Don't say anything until the meeting is half over; this stamps you as being wise. (3) Be as vague as possible; this prevents irritating the others. (4) When in doubt, suggest that a subcommittee be appointed. (5) Be the first to move for adjournment; this will make you popular—it's what everyone is waiting for.
(Harry Chapman, *Think. FD.*)

● **Commoner's Three Laws of Ecology.** (1) No action is without side effects. (2) Nothing ever goes away. (3) There is no free lunch.
(Barry Commoner. See also *Crane's Law.*)

● **Compensation Corollary.** An experiment may be considered successful if no more than half of the data must be discarded to obtain correspondence with your theory.

(From list, "Wisdom from the Giants of Science," *MLS* collection.)

● **Computability Applied to Social Sciences, Law of.** If at first you don't succeed, transform your data set.

(*U/JE.*)

● **Computer Maxim.** To err is human but to really foul things up requires a computer.

(*The Farmers' Almanac,* 1978 edition.)

● **Computer Programming, Laws of.** (1) Any given program, when running, is obsolete. (2) Any given program costs more and takes longer. (3) If a program is useful, it will have to be changed. (4) If a program is useless, it will have to be documented. (5) Any given program will expand to fill all available memory. (6) The value of a program is proportional to the weight of its output. (7) Program complexity grows until it exceeds the capability of the programmer who must maintain it. (8) Make it possible for programmers to write programs in English, and you will find that programmers cannot write in English.

(*SICPLAN Notices,* Vol. 2, No. 2. *JE.*)

● **Connally's Rule.** Wage and price controls cause inequities, inefficiencies, distortions, and venality, and therefore should be invoked only when necessary.

(John B. Connally. Culled from speech by *JMcC.*)

● **Connolly's Law of Cost Control.** The price of any product produced for a government agency will be not less than the square of the initial Firm Fixed-Price Contract.

(Ray Connolly, Washington bureau manager and columnist, *Electronics* magazine.)

● **Connolly's Rule for Political Incumbents.** Short-term success with voters on any side of a given issue can be guaranteed by creating a long-term special study commission made up of at least three divergent interest groups.
(Ray Connolly, *Electronics.*)

● **Considine's Law.** Whenever one word or letter can change the entire meaning of a sentence, the probability of an error being made will be in direct proportion to the embarrassment it will cause.
(Reporter and author Bob Considine. Recalled by Bill Gold in his *Washington Post* column the day after a reader had written in to report that the paper had stated that a woman was "sex weeks pregnant.")

● **Cooke's Law.** In any decision situation, the amount of relevant information available is inversely proportional to the importance of the decision.
(*U.* Michael T. Minerath, West Haven, Conn.)

● **Coolidge's Immutable Observation.** When more and more people are thrown out of work, unemployment results.
(Calvin Coolidge, from Leonard C. Lewin's *Treasury of American Political Humor,* Dial, 1964.)

● **Coomb's Law.** If you can't measure it, I'm not interested.
(*U* from an article in *Human Behavior* called "Peter's People" by Lawrence J. Peter, August, 1976.)

● **Corcoran's Law of Packrattery.** All files, papers, memos, etc., that you save will never be needed until such time as they are disposed of, when they will become essential and indispensible.

(John Corcoran, Washington writer and television personality. He also wrote the next item, which appeared in the *Washingtonian* magazine, March, 1974.)

● **Corcoroni's Laws of Bus Transportation.** (1) The bus that left the stop just before you got there is your bus. (2) The amount of time you have to wait for a bus is directly proportional to the inclemency of the weather. (3) All buses heading in the opposite direction drive off the face of the earth and never return. (4) If you anticipate bus delays by leaving your house thirty minutes early, your bus will arrive as soon as you reach the bus stop or when you light up a cigarette, whichever comes first. (5) The last rush-hour express bus to your neighborhood leaves five minutes before you get off work. (6) Bus schedules are arranged so your bus will arrive at the transfer point precisely one minute after the connecting bus has left. (7) Any bus that can be the wrong bus will be the wrong bus. All others are out of service or full.

(John Corcoran, aka Corcoroni, *The Washingtonian*, March, 1974.)

● **Cornuelle's Law.** Authority tends to assign jobs to those least able to do them.

(*U/S.T.L.*)

● **Crane's Law.** There ain't no such thing as a free lunch. (Burton Crane, in *The Sophisticated Investor*, Simon and Schuster, 1959. See also *Commoner's Laws, Solis's Amendment to Crane's Law.*)

● **Crane's Rule.** There are three ways to get something done: do it yourself, hire someone, or forbid your kids to do it. (Monta Crane, in *Sunshine Magazine* and requoted in *Reader's Digest,* June, 1977.)

● **Cripp's Law.** When traveling with children on one's holidays, at least one child of any number of children will request a rest room stop exactly half way between any two given rest areas.

> (Mervyn Cripps, St. Catherines, Ontario, in a letter to *Verbatim.*)

● **Culshaw's First Principle of Recorded Sound.** Anything, no matter how bad, will sound good if played back at a very high level for a short time.

> (John Culshaw, in his column for *High Fidelity Magazine,* November, 1977.)

● **Curley's Law.** As long as they spell the name right.
> (Named for the famous Boston mayor. From Vic Gold's *P.R. as in President,* Doubleday, 1977.)

● **Cushman's Law.** A fail-safe circuit will destroy others.
> (*U/S.T.L.*)

● **Cutler Webster's Law.** There are two sides to every argument, unless a person is personally involved, in which case there is only one.
> (*U/RS.*)

● **Czecinski's Conclusion.** There is only one thing worse than dreaming you are at a conference and waking up to find that you are at a conference: and that is the conference where you can't fall asleep.

> (Adapted from a translation of a letter from Tadeusz Czecinski to a Warsaw newspaper. *RS.*)

D

● **Darrow's Observation.** History repeats itself. That's one of the things wrong with history.
(Clarence Darrow.)

● **Darwin's Observation.** Nature will tell you a direct lie if she can.
(Charles Darwin.)

● **Dave's Law of Advice.** Those with the best advice offer no advice.

● **Davidson's Maxim.** Democracy is that form of government where everybody gets what the majority deserves.
(James Dale Davidson, executive director of the National Taxpayer's Union. *JMcC.*)

● **Dave's Rule of Street Survival.** Speak softly and own a big, mean Doberman.
(Dave Miliman, Baltimore.)

● **Davis's Basic Law of Medicine.** Pills to be taken in twos always come out of the bottle in threes.
(Robert Davis. *AO.*)

● **Davis's Laws.** (1) Writers desire to be paid, authors desire recognition. (2) The further an individual is from the poorhouse, the more expert one becomes on the ghetto. (3) In business, price increases as service declines. (4) On soap operas all whites are in personal touch with (a) a doctor and (b) a lawyer.
(James L. Davis, Washington, D.C.)

● **Dawes-Bell Law.** Whereas in many branches of economic activity employment depends on the number of job openings available, in the public service, as also in the advertising business, social science investigation, and university administration, the level of employment regularly depends on the number of men available and devoting their time to the creation of job opportunities.

(First reported in *The McLandress Dimension* by Mark Epernay, Houghton Mifflin, 1962. See also *McLandress Dimension.*)

● **Dean's Law of the District of Columbia.** Washington is a much better place if you are asking questions rather than answering them.

(John Dean, former counsel to President Nixon, on the occasion of beginning his syndicated radio interview show.)

● **DeCaprio's Rule.** Everything takes more time and money.

(Annie DeCaprio, High Bridge, N.J. *HW.* Note similarity to *Cheops's Law.*)

● **Deitz's Law of Ego.** The fury engendered by the misspelling of a name in a column is in direct ratio to the obscurity of the mentionee.

(Alan Deitz of the American Newspaper Publishers Association to *AO* on the misspelling of his name in *The Wall Street Journal.*)

● **Dennis's Principles of Management by Crisis.** (1) To get action out of management, it is necessary to create the illusion of a crisis in the hope it will be acted on. (2) Management will select actions or events and convert them to crises. It will then over-react. (3) Management is incapable of recognizing a true crisis. (4) The squeaky hinge gets the oil.

(Gene Franklin, from his article in *Computers and Automation. JE.*)

● **Dhawan's Laws for the Non-Smoker.** (1) The cigarette smoke always drifts in the direction of the non-smoker regardless of the direction of the breeze. (2) The amount of pleasure derived from a cigarette is directly proportional to the number of the non-smokers in the vicinity. (3) A smoker is always attracted to the non-smoking section. (4) The life of a cigarette is directly proportional to the intensity of the protests from the non-smokers.

(Raj K. Dhawan, West Covina, Cal.)

● **Dibble's First Law of Sociology.** Some do, some don't. (Letter to *Verbatim* from Jeffery F. Chamberlain.)

● **Dieter's Law.** Food that tastes the best has the highest number of calories.

(Rozanne Weissman.)

● **Dijkstra's Prescription for Programming Inertia.** If you don't know what your program is supposed to do, you'd better not start writing it.

(*IF* carries this with the notation: "Stanford Computer Science Colloquium, April 18, 1975.")

● **Dilwether's Law of Delay.** When people have a job to do, particularly a vital but difficult one, they will invariably put it off until the last possible moment, and *most* of them will put it off even longer.

(Gordon L. Becker, counsel, Exxon Corp. *AO.*)

● **Diogenes's First Dictum.** The more heavily a man is supposed to be taxed, the more power he has to escape being taxed.

● **Diogenes's Second Dictum.** If a taxpayer thinks he can cheat safely, he probably will.
  (*S. T. L.*)

● **Dirksen's Three Laws of Politics.** (1) Get elected. (2) Get reelected. (3) Don't get mad, get even.
  (Senator Everett Dirksen. Recalled by Harry N. D. Fisher for *AO*. See also *Johnson's "Prior" Laws of Politics.*)

● **Dirksen's Version of an Old Saw.** The oil can is mightier than the sword.
  (Senator Dirksen again. This was contained in Donald Rumsfeld's collection of laws.)

● **Displaced Hassle, Principle of.** To beat the bureaucracy, make your problem their problem.
  (Marshall L. Smith, who is also law-collector *MLS.*)

● **Distance, Law of.** Happiness is in direct proportion to the distance from the home office. *Contradictory Corollary:* The diner who is furthest from the kitchen is a nervous eater.
  (Stated by Al Blanchard, *The Detroit News,* in his column for September 16, 1977.)

● **Dobbins's Law.** When in doubt, use a bigger hammer.
  (A variation of *Anthony's Law of Force,* probably earlier.)

● **Domino Theory II.** If you disregard the advice of Gen. Douglas MacArthur and go into the quicksand of an Asian country, like a domino you will fall into the quicksand of another Asian country next to it.
  (Representative Andrew Jacobs, Jr., D-Ind., who created it about the time of the U.S. incursion into Cambodia.)

● **Donohue's Law.** What's worth doing is worth doing for money.

(Joseph Donohue. *JW.*)

● **Donsen's Law.** The specialist learns more and more about less and less until, finally, he knows everything about nothing; whereas the generalist learns less and less about more and more until, finally, he knows nothing about everything.

(*U/"LSP."*)

● **Dorm Room Living, Laws of.** (1) The amount of trash accumulated within the space occupied is exponentially proportional to the number of living bodies that enter and leave within any given amount of time. (2) Since no matter can be created or destroyed (excluding nuclear and cafeteria substances), as one attempts to remove unwanted material (i.e., trash) from one's living space, the remaining material mutates so as to occupy 30 to 50 percent more than its original volume. *Corollary:* Dust breeds. (3) The odds are 6:5 that if one has late classes, one's roommate will have the *earliest* possible classes. *Corollary 1*: One's roommate (who has early classes) has an alarm clock that is louder than God's own. *Corollary 2*: When one has an early class, one's roommate will invariably enter the space late at night and suddenly become hyperactive, ill, violent, or all three.

(*U.* Part of a larger collection originating at East Russell Hall, University of Georgia, Athens.)

● **Douglas's Law of Practical Aeronautics.** When the weight of the paperwork equals the weight of the plane, the plane will fly.

(Airplane-builder Donald Douglas, who articulated it for Jerome S. Katzin of La Jolla, Cal., who passed it along to *AO.*)

● **Dow's Law.** In a hierarchical organization, the higher the level, the greater the confusion.
(*U/S.T.L.*)

● **Dror Law, First.** While the difficulties and dangers of problems tend to increase at a geometric rate, the knowledge and manpower qualified to deal with these problems tend to increase at an arithmetic rate.

● **Dror Law, Second.** While human capacities to shape the environment, society, and human beings are rapidly increasing, policymaking capabilities to use those capacities remain the same.
(Yehezkel Dror, Israeli policy analyst at Hebrew University, from "Policy Sciences: Developments and Implications," RAND Corp. Paper P–4321, March, 1970.)

● **Drucker, The Sayings of Chairman Peter.** (1) If you have too many problems, maybe you should go out of business. There is no law that says a company must last forever. (2) As to the idea that advertising motivates people, remember the Edsel. (3) The only things that evolve by themselves in an organization are disorder, friction, and malperformance. (4) We know nothing about motivation. All we can do is write books about it. (5) Marketing is a fashionable term. The sales manager becomes a marketing vice-president. But a gravedigger is still a gravedigger even when he is called a mortician—only the price of burial goes up. (6) Fast personal decisions are likely to be wrong. (7) Strong people always have strong weaknesses. (8) Start with what is right rather than with what is acceptable. (9) We always remember best the irrelevant. (10) When a subject becomes totally obsolete we make it a required course. (11) Medicare and Medicaid are the greatest measures yet devised to make the world safe for clerks. (12) We may now be nearing the end of our hundred-year belief in Free Lunch. (See *Commoner's* and *Crane's Laws.*) (13)

Look at governmental programs for the past fifty years. Every single one—except for warfare—achieved the exact opposite of its announced goal. (14) The computer is a moron. (15) The main impact of the computer has been the provision of unlimited jobs for clerks.

> (Selected by the author from *Drucker: The Man Who Invented the Corporate Society* by John J. Tarrant, Cahners Books, Inc., 1976.)

● **Dude's Law of Duality.** Of two possible events, only the undesired one will occur.

> (This can be expressed mathematically as:

$$A \cap B^u = B \ [1]$$
$$A^u \cap B = A \ [2]$$

> where A and B are possible outcomes, where the superscript u denotes the undesired outcome, and where $\cap$ means either/or.
> ([From Walter Mulé's article, "Beyomd Murphy's Law," in *Northliner*. Mulé says the law was named for Sam Dude, whose genius was cut short by a skydiving accident that occurred just after he was forced to choose between two types of parachute.])

● **Duggan's Law.** To every Ph.D there is an equal and opposite Ph.D.

> (B. Duggan, quoted from one of Robert Specht's quote-laden calendars, *1970 Expectation of Days. RS.* This law helps explain why it is so easy to find expert witnesses to totally contradict each other.)

● **Dunne's Law.** The territory behind rhetoric is too often mined with equivocation.

> (John Gregory Dunne, "To Die Standing," *The Atlantic*, June, 1971.)

● **Dunn's Discovery.** The shortest measurable interval of time is the time between the moment I put a little extra aside for a sudden emergency and the arrival of that emergency.

(Marvin Dunn, quoted in the *Louisville Courier-Journal.*)

● **du Pont's Laws.** A COMPENDIUM OF HELPFUL RULES GOVERNING THE LEGISLATIVE PROCESS NOT TO BE FOUND IN JEFFERSON'S MANUAL OF RULES AND PRACTICES OF THE HOUSE OF REPRESENTATIVES. (1) Vote as an individual; lemmings end up falling off cliffs. Camaraderie is no substitute for common sense, and being your own man will make you sleep better. (2) The speed at which the legislative process seems to work is in inverse proportion to your enthusiasm for the bill. If you want a bill to move quickly, committee hearings, the rules committee, and legislative procedures appear to be roadblocks to democracy. If you do not want the bill to pass, such procedures are essential to furthering representative government, etc., etc. (3) The titles of bills—like those of Marx Brothers movies—often have little to do with the substance of the legislation. Particularly deceptive are bills containing title buzz words such as *emergency, reform, service, relief,* or *special.* Often the *emergency* is of the writer's imagination; the *reform,* a protection of vested interest; the *service,* self-serving; the *relief,* an additional burden on the taxpayer; and the *special,* something that otherwise shouldn't be passed. (4) Sometimes the best law of all is no law at all. Not all the world's ills are susceptible to legislative correction. (5) When voting on appropriations bills, more is not necessarily better. It is as wasteful to have a B–1 bomber in every garage as it is to have a welfare program for every conceivable form of deprivation. (6) The Crusades ended several centuries ago after killing thousands of people. The most important issues arouse intense passions. Earmuffs to block the shouting are inappropriate, but filter the feedback. Joining a cause and leading a constituency are not mutually exclusive, but neither are they necessarily synonymous. Neither welfare nor profits are "obscene." (7) "Beware the [lobbyist], my son, the jaws that bite, the claws that snatch" (with thanks to Lewis Carroll). No matter how noble the cause or well meaning its professional advocates, lobbyists are still paid to get results. They're subject to errors in judgment, shortcomings in motives, and most of them don't even vote in your district. (8) Mirror, mirror on the wall, who's the fairest one of all? The press is hopelessly biased or genuinely fair, depending upon whose views are being misquoted, misrepresented, or misunderstood. (9) If you are concerned about being criticized—you're in the wrong job. However you vote, and whatever you do, somebody will be out there telling you that you are: (a) wrong, (b) insensitive, (c) a bleeding heart, (d) a pawn of somebody else, (e) too wishy-washy, (f) too unwilling to compromise, (g) all of the above—consistency is not required of critics.

> (Governor Pierre S. du Pont of Delaware, who wrote them when he was a congressman. The laws were written for incoming members, about whom he said in his introduction to the laws: "A freshman Congressman trying to do his job properly is similar to a quarterback trying to throw a 60-yard pass with a deflated football. The only difference is the quarterback knows there is no air in the ball—the freshman Congressman doesn't even know what game he is playing." See also *Fifth Rule*.)

● **Durant's Discovery.** One of the lessons of history is that nothing is often a good thing to do and always a clever thing to say.

> (Will Durant, from an item in the November, 1972, *Reader's Digest* quoting Derek Gill's article on Durant in *Modern Maturity*.)

● **Durrell's Parameter.** The faster the plane, the narrower the seats.

> (John H. Durrell of Mason, Ohio, in a letter to the editor, *The Wall Street Journal,* March 15, 1976.)

● **Dyer's Law.** A continuing flow of paper is sufficient to continue the flow of paper.

(Professor John M. Dyer, director, International Finance and Marketing Program, University of Miami, Coral Gables, Fla. *FD.*)

E

- **Ear's Law.** Before a party or a trip, if it can, it will let rip. (From the "Ear" column in the *Washington Star*. It was recalled in print when the Carters' hot-water heater burst on their last day in Plains before leaving for the Inauguration.)

- **Economists' Laws.** (1) What men learn from history is that men do not learn from history. (2) If on an actuarial basis there is a 50/50 chance that something will go wrong, it will actually go wrong nine times in ten.
  (2p.?)

- **Edington's Theory.** Hypotheses multiply so as to fill the gaps in factual knowledge concerning biological phenomena.
  (Named for C. W. Edington, but first explained by James D. Regan in the April, 1963, issue of the *Journal of Irreproducible Results*. Although created for biological phenomena, it was noted in the original article that it applied in other scientific areas as well.)

- **Editorial Correction, Law of.** Anyone nit-picking enough to write a letter of correction to an editor doubtless deserves the error that provoked it.
  (This law was created by Alvin Toffler and published in the *New York Times Magazine* on April 7, 1968. It was written in response to an article by Harold Faber on laws, i.e., "Faber's Law—If There Isn't a Law, There Will Be." Toffler said, in part, that a law credited to Anthony Toffler called the *Law of Raspberry Jam* was originated by Stan-

ley Edgar Hyman. He added, "Not only is my name not Anthony—which I regret—but I heartily disagree with said Law of Raspberry Jam. My book, 'The Culture Consumers,' mentions it, then spends 14 chapters disputing its contention that 'the wider any culture is spread, the thinner it gets.' " *FD.*)

● **Ehrlich's Rule.** The first rule of intelligent tinkering is to save all the parts.

(Environmentalist Paul Ehrlich, *The Saturday Review,* June 5, 1971.)

● **Ehrman's Corollary to Ginsberg's Theorem.** (1) Things will get worse before they get better. (2) Who said things would get better.

(John Ehrman, Stanford Linear Accelerator Center. *JE.* Of course, you should see *Ginsberg's Theorem.*)

● **Einstein's Other Formula.** If A equals success, then the formula is A+X + Y + Z. X is work. Y is play. Z is keep your mouth shut.

(Albert Einstein defining success, news summaries of April 19, 1955, quoted in *Contemporary Quotations,* compiled by J. B. Simpson, Crowell, 1964.)

● **Eliot's Observation.** Nothing is so good as it seems beforehand.

(George Eliot.)

● **Emerson's Insight.** That which we call sin in others is experiment for us.

(Ralph Waldo Emerson.)

● **Engineer's Law, The Old.** The larger the project or job, the less time there is to do it.

(George A. Daher, Philadelphia, to *AO.*)

● **Epstein's Law.** If you think the problem is bad now, just wait until we've solved it.

(*U.* From Arthur Kasspé, Ph.D., New York City.)

● **Err's Laws.** See *Murphy's Law(s).* Err is basically a synonym for Murphy, but those who quote him over the better-known prophet insist he is as real as Murphy. The basis for their argument: (1) his spirit, like Murphy's, is everywhere and (2) Err is human.

● **Eternity Rule.** Nothing is certain except death and taxes. *Bretagna's Corollary*: If anything else is permanent, it is the fact that, given *any* roadway, somewhere upon it there will be someone going slower than you want to go.

(The *Eternity Rule* is one of several names currently being given to various close paraphrases of Benjamin Franklin's line, "In this world, nothing is certain but death and taxes." It first appeared in a letter from Franklin to M. Leroy in 1789. The corollary comes from Nicholas Bretagna II, Orlando, Fla.)

● **Ettorre's Observation.** The other line moves faster.

(Barbara Ettorre, New York City. This first appeared in *Harper's* in August, 1974, and has become a bona fide hit, showing up on almost every list of laws produced since it was first published. The original was longer than what is now commonly known as *Ettorre's Observation.* The full version: "The Other Line moves faster. This applies to all lines—bank, supermarket, tollbooth, customs, and so on. And don't try to change lines. The Other Line—the one you were in originally—will then move faster." HW.)

● **Evans's Law.** Nothing worth a damn is ever done as a matter of principle. (If it is worth doing, it is done because it

is worth doing. If it is not, it's done as a matter of principle.)
(James T. Evans, attorney, Houston.)

● **Evans's Law of Political Perfidy.** When our friends get into power, they aren't our friends anymore.
(M. Stanton Evans, who was until recently the head of the American Conservative Union. *JMcC.*)

● **Evelyn's Rules for Bureaucratic Survival.** (1) A bureaucrat's castle is his desk . . . and parking place. Proceed cautiously when changing either. (2) On the theory that one should never take anything for granted, follow up on everything, but especially those items varying from the norm. The greater the divergence from normal routine and/or the greater the number of offices potentially involved, the better the chance a never-to-be-discovered person will file the problem away in a drawer specifically designed for items requiring a decision. (3) Never say without qualification that your activity has sufficient space, money, staff, etc. (4) Always distrust offices not under your jurisdiction which say that they are there to serve you. "Support" offices in a bureaucracy tend to grow in size and make demands on you out of proportion to their service and in the end require more effort on your part than their service is worth. *Corollary:* Support organizations can always prove success by showing service to someone . . . not necessarily you. (5) Incompetents often hire able assistants.
(Douglas Evelyn, National Portrait Gallery, Washington, D.C.)

● **Everitt's Form of the Second Law of Thermodynamics.** Confusion (entropy) is always increasing in society. Only if someone or something works extremely hard can this confusion be reduced to order in a limited region. Nevertheless, this effort will still result in an increase in the total confusion of society at large.

(Dr. W. L. Everitt, dean emeritus of the College of Engineering at the University of Illinois.)

● **Eve's Discovery.** At a bargain sale, the only suit or dress that you like best and that fits is the one not on sale. *Adam's Corollary*: It's easy to tell when you've got a bargain—it doesn't fit.

(Fred Dyer. *FD.*)

● **Evvie Nef's Law.** There is a solution to every problem; the only difficulty is finding it.

(*Washington Post Potomac,* January, 1972. *JW.*)

● **Expert Advice, The First Law of.** Don't ask the barber whether you need a haircut.

(Science writer-columnist Daniel S. Greenberg first revealed this some years ago in *Saturday Review* and returned to it in late 1977 in his *Washington Post* column. Greenberg attaches the law to ". . . the promotion of a technology by its developers or custodians without any independent check on whether it does what it's supposed to do." He gives several examples, including a chemical shark repellent called Shark Chaser, which the Navy bought in great quantities between World War II and 1974, at which time it was learned that sharks had no aversion to eating Shark Chaser.)

● **Extended Epstein-Heisenberg Principle.** In a research and development orbit, only two of the existing three parameters can be defined simultaneously. The parameters are: task, time and resources ($).

(1) If one knows what the task is, and there is a time limit allowed for the completion of the task, then one cannot guess how much it will cost.

(2) If the time and resources ($) are clearly defined, then it is impossible to know what part of the R&D task will be performed.

(3) If you are given a clearly defined R&D goal and a definite amount of money which has been calculated to be necessary for the completion of the task, one cannot predict if and when the goal will be reached.

(4) If one is lucky enough and can accurately define all three parameters, then what one deals with is not in the realm of R&D.

(From the article "Uncertainty Principle in Research and Development," in *JIR,* January, 1973.)

F

● **Faber's Laws.** (1) If there isn't a law, there will be. (2) The number of errors in any piece of writing rises in proportion to the writer's reliance on secondary sources. (This is also called *The First Law of Historical Research.*)

> (Harold Faber. The first was used as the title of his 1968 *New York Times Magazine* article on laws, and the second was created in response to some errors that appeared in the article—i.e. calling Alvin Toffler, Anthony Toffler. [See *Editorial Correction, Law of.*] At the time the article was written, Faber was editorial director of the Book and Education Division of the *Times.*)

● **Falkland's Rule.** When it is not necessary to make a decision, it is necessary not to make a decision.

> (Lord Falkland.)

● **Farber's Laws.** (1) Give him an inch and he'll screw you. (2) We're all going down the same road in different directions. (3) Necessity is the mother of strange bedfellows.

> (Dave Farber, from a Farberism contest list. *S.T.L.*)

● **Farmer's Law on Junk.** What goes in, comes out. *Corollary 1:* He who sees what comes out, and why, gains wisdom. *Corollary 2:* He who sees only half the problem will be buried in the other half. *Corollary 3:* One man's junk is another's income—and sometimes his priceless antique. *Corollary 4:* Ten thousand years from now, the only story this civilization will tell will be in its junk piles—so observe what is important! *Corollary 5:* Seers and soothsayers read crystal balls to find the future. Less

51

lucky men read junk—with more success. *Corollary 6:* A rose is a rose is a rose, but junk is not junk is not junk. It never is quite what you think it is. *Corollary 7:* Happiness at age ten was finding an empty six pack of returnable Coke bottles. The poor kids these days will never know what they missed, which is why we have a generation gap.

> (Richard N. Farmer, chairperson, International Business School, Indiana University. From his book *Farmer's Law: Junk in a World of Affluence,* Stein & Day Publishers, 1973. One needs to read the whole book to appreciate fully the technique, but the basic law and its corollaries attempt to show you how to read the future, national and international trends, other people's personalities, and competitors' plans—all by reading junk.)

● **Fashion, Law of.** The same dress is indecent 10 years before its time

> daring 1 year before its time
> chic in its time
> dowdy 3 years after its time
> hideous 20 years after its time
> amusing 30 years after its time
> romantic 100 years after its time
> beautiful 150 years after its time

(James Laver. *JW.*)

● **Father Damian Fandal's Rules for [Academic] Deans.** Rule 1—*Hide!!!* Rule 2—*If they find you, lie!!!*
> (Father Damian C. Fandal, O.P., former dean of academic affairs, University of Dallas, Texas.)

● **Fetridge's Law.** Important things that are supposed to happen do not happen, especially when people are looking.
> (Claude Fetridge, an NBC radio engineer in the 1930s. In

1936 he came up with the idea of broadcasting, live of course, the departure of the swallows from their famous roost at Mission San Juan Capistrano. As is well known, the swallows always depart on October 23, St. John's Day. NBC decided that Fetridge's idea was sound and made all due preparations, including sending a crew to the Mission. The sparrows then left a day ahead of schedule.

Fetridge's Law was all but forgotten until H. Allen Smith recalled it in an essay on laws in his classic work *A Short History of Fingers and Other State Papers,* Little Brown, 1963. Smith pointed out that *Fetridge's Law* also has its good points, which are sometimes overlooked. An example from Smith, "In my own case I have often noted that whenever I develop a raging toothache it is a Sunday and the dentists are all on the golf course. Not long ago my toothache hung on through the weekend and Monday morning it was still throbbing and pulsating like a diesel locomotive. I called my dentist and proclaimed an emergency and drove to his office and going up the stairway the ache suddenly vanished altogether.")

● **Fiedler's Forecasting Rules.** (1) *The First Law of Forecasting:* Forecasting is very difficult, especially if it's about the future. (2) *For this reason*: He who lives by the crystal ball soon learns to eat ground glass. (3) *Similarly:* The moment you forecast you know you're going to be wrong, you just don't know when and in which direction. (4) *Nevertheless, always be precise in your forecasts because:* Economists state their GNP growth projections to the nearest tenth of a percentage point to prove they have a sense of humor. (5) *Another basic law:* If the facts don't conform to the theory, they must be disposed of. (6) *If you've always had doubts about the judgment of forecasters, it's quite understandable because:* An economist is a man who would marry Farrah Fawcett-Majors for her money. (7) *By the same* *reasoning, your suspicions about the narrow range of most forecasts are justified:* The herd instinct among forecasters make sheep look like independent thinkers. (8) *Correspondingly:* If a camel is a horse designed by a committee, then a consensus forecast is a camel's behind. (9) *When presenting a forecast:* Give them a number or give them a date, but never both. (10) *When asked to explain your forecast:* Never underestimate the power of a platitude. (11) *And remember Kessel's insight on the value of malarkey:* There must be underinvestment in bulls . . . just look at the rate of return. (12) *Speaking of profits:* Once economists were asked, "If you're so smart, why ain't you rich?" Today they're asked, "Now that you've proved you ain't so smart, how come you got so rich?" (13) *On the use of survey techniques in forecasting:* When you know absolutely nothing about the topic, make your forecast by asking a carefully selected probability sample of 300 others who don't know the answer either. (14) *In a modern economy everything is related to everything else, so:* Forecasters tend to learn less and less about more and more, until in the end they know nothing about everything . . . (15) *The oldest saw about the profession:* If all the economists were laid end to end, they still wouldn't reach a conclusion. (16) *Another oldie:* Ask five economists and you'll get five different explanations (six, if one went to Harvard). (17) *How an economist defines "hard times":* A recession is when my neighbor loses his job. A depression is when I lose my job. A panic is when my wife loses her job. (18) *The boss's supplication:* Lord, please find me a one-armed economist so we won't always hear, "On the other hand . . ." (19) *The forecaster has his own invocation:* Thank God for compensating errors. (20) *Speaking of the Diety:* Most economists think of God as working great multiple regressions in the sky. . . . [Items (21), (22), and (23) are, respectively, *Murphy's Law, O'Toole's Commentary,* and *Finagle's Constant.*] (24) *A forecaster's best defense is a good offense, so:* If you have to forecast, forecast often. (25) *But:* If you're ever right, never let 'em forget it.

(Edgar R. Fiedler, Conference Board economic researcher and vice-president, in the June, 1977, issue of the Conference Board's magazine *Across the Board.*)

● **Fifth Rule.** You have taken yourself too seriously.
(This law comes from Governor du Pont, who uses it to sum up his political laws (see *du Pont's Laws*). He first heard it from NBC's John Chancellor. To quote du Pont:

"A veteran British diplomat had a favorite way to put down a pushy or egotistical junior. The diplomat would call the younger man in for a heart-to-heart talk and quite often at the end of the talk would say, 'Young man, you have broken the Fifth Rule: You have taken yourself too seriously.' That would end the meeting—except that invariably, as the younger man got to the door, he would turn and ask, 'What are the other rules?'

"And the diplomat would smile serenely and answer, 'There *are* no other rules.' ")

Special Section 2

The Finagle File. People had talked about a mysterious scientist named Finagle for many years before November, 1957, when John W. Campbell, Jr., editor of *Astounding Science Fiction,* asked his readers to help him collect and publish Finagle's "famous unwritten laws of science," but after that announcement Finagle became as much a part of scientific lore as Murphy has become to general lore.

The results of Campbell's request were most gratifying; for more than two years the magazine published letters from Finagle's disciples and fans revealing dozens of laws, corollaries, and factors. Here are some of the most important elements of Finaglania:

☐ *Four Basic Rules.*
1. If anything can go wrong in an experiment, it will. 2. No matter what result is anticipated, there is always someone willing to fake it. 3. No matter what the result, there is always someone eager to misinterpret it. 4. No matter what occurs, there is always someone who believes it happened according to his pet theory.

☐ *The Finagle Factor vs. Other Major Factors.*
The Finagle Factor is characterized by changing the Universe to fit the equation.

The Bouguerre Factor changes the equation to fit the Universe.

The Diddle Factor changes things so that the equation and the Universe appear to fit, without requiring any real change in either. This is also known as the "smoothing" or "soothing" factor, mathematically somewhat similar to a damping factor; it has the characteristic of eliminating differences by dropping the subject under discussion to zero importance.

☐ *Finagle's Creed.*
SCIENCE IS TRUTH: DON'T BE MISLED BY FACTS.

☐ *Applied Finaglism.*
The Law of the Too, Too Solid Point. In any collection of data, the figure that is most obviously correct—beyond all need of checking—is the mistake.

>   Corollary 1: No one whom you ask for help will see it either. *Corollary 2:* Everyone who stops by with unsought advice will see it immediately.

Finagle's Very Fundamental Finding. If a string has one end, then it has another end.

Finagle's Fifth Rule. Whenever a system becomes completely defined, some damn fool discovers something that either abolishes the system or expands it beyond recognition.

Delay Formula. After adding two weeks to the schedule for unexpected delays, add two more for the unexpected, unexpected delays.

On Corrections. When an error has been detected and corrected, it will be found to have been correct in the first place.

> *Corollary:* After the correction has been found in error, it will be impossible to fit the original quantity back into the equation.

Travel Axiom. He travels fastest who travels alone . . . but he hasn't anything to do when he gets there.

Law of Social Dynamics. If, in the course of several months, only three worthwhile social events take place, they will all fall on the same evening.

☐ *Finagle's Contributions to the Field of Measurement.*
1. Dimensions will be expressed in the least convenient terms, e.g.: Furlongs per (Fortnight)^2 = Measure of Acceleration.
2. Jiffy—the time it takes for light to go one cm in a vacuum.
3. Protozoa are small, and bacteria are small, but viruses are smaller than the both of 'em put together.

☐ *Finagle's Proofs, Household Examples.*
Any vacuum cleaner would sooner take the nap off a rug than remove white threads from a dark rug.

No dog will knock a vase over unless it has water in it.

☐ *Finagle's Rules for Scientific Research.*
1. Do Not Believe in Miracles—Rely on Them.
2. Experiments Must Be Reproducible—They Should Fail the Same Way.
3. Always Verify Your Witchcraft.
4. First Draw Your Curves—Then Plot Your Readings.
5. Be Sure to Obtain Meteorological Information Before Leaving on Vacation.

6. A Record of Data is Useful—It Indicates That You've Been Working.

7. Experience Is Directly Proportional to Equipment Ruined.

8. To Study a Subject Best—Understand It Thoroughly Before You Start.

9. In Case of Doubt—Make It Sound Convincing.

☐ *Later Findings.*

In the years since the original information on Finagle appeared in *Astounding Science Fiction,* scores of new laws have been discovered and attributed to Finagle. Here is but one example:

Finagle's Laws of Information.

1. The information you have is not what you want.

2. The information you want is not what you need.

3. The information you need is not what you can obtain.

4. The information you can obtain costs more than you want to pay!

☐ *Friends of Finagle and Examples of Their Laws* (from the original *ASF* letters).

Sprinkle's Law: Things fall at right angles.

Stockmayer's Theorem: If it looks easy, it's tough. If it looks tough, it's damn near impossible.

Deadlock's Law: If the law makers make a compromise, the place where it will be felt most is the taxpayer's pocket. *Corollary:* The compromise will always be more expensive than either of the suggestions it is compromising.

☐ *Aliases, Pseudonyms, and aka's for Dr. Finagle.*

Dr. Henri Bouguerre, Dr. Gwen T. Diddle, Bougar T. Factor, Dr. Finnagle, and Dr. von Nagle.

● **First Thesis.** Everything is nothing. Everything is all. All is one. One is inconceivable, infinite. Therefore it is nothing. Therefore everything is nothing.

Everything is matter. Matter is electricity. Electricity is invisible, intangible. Therefore it is nothing. Therefore everything is nothing.

Atoms are made up of electrons and protons (protons are also nothing). Fifty billion electrons placed side by side in a straight line would stretch across the diameter of the period at the end of this sentence. Protons are heavier but take up less space. Such an idea is incapable of absorption by the human mind.

> (From *The Crowning of Technocracy* by Professor John Lardner and Dr. Thomas Sugrue, 1933, published by "Laboratory of Robert M. McBride & Co., NY.")

● **Fischer's Finding.** Sex is hereditary. If your parents never had it, chances are you won't either.
> (Joseph Fischer, W. Melbourno, Fla. *HW.*)

● **Fishbein's Conclusion.** The tire is only flat on the bottom.
> (*U.* From John L. Shelton, Dallas.)

● **Fitz-Gibbon's Law.** Creativity varies inversely with the number of cooks involved with the broth.
> (Bernice Fitz-Gibbon in *Macy's, Gimbels and Me,* Simon and Schuster, 1967. *FL.*)

● **Flap's Law of the Perversity of Inanimate Objects.** Any inanimate object, regardless of its composition or configuration, may be expected to perform at any time in a totally unexpected manner for reasons that are either totally obscure or completely mysterious.
> (Dr. Fyodor Flap, encountered in Walter Mulé's "Beyomd Murphy's Law." From this Flap builds *Mulé's*

Law. Flap's Law is often identified as *Flagle's Law,* but Flap seems more appropriate.)

● **Flip Wilson's Law.** You can't expect to hit the jackpot if you don't put a few nickles in the machine.

(Wilson on his TV show on October 28, 1971. This was recognized as a universal truth by Thomas Martin.)

● **Forthoffer's Cynical Summary of Barzun's Laws.** See *Barzun's Laws.*

● **Foster's Law.** If you cover a congressional committee on a regular basis, they will report the bill on your day off.

(Herb Foster. According to Foster it was created some years ago when he was at UPI [then UP] and the Senate Appropriations Committee reported out the biggest civil works appropriations up to that point in history. "I knew nothing of the places or projects involved, but had to cover it." Compounded by many later situations involving Foster and others.)

● **Fourth Law of Thermodynamics.** If the probability of success is not almost one, then it is damn near zero.

(David Ellis, from his classic 1957 paper, "Some Precise Formulations on the Alleged Perversity of Nature." *RS.*)

● **Fowler's Law.** In a bureaucracy accomplishment is inversely proportional to the volume of paper used.

(Foster L. Fowler, Jackson, Miss. *AO.*)

● **Frankel's Law.** Whatever happens in government could have happened differently and it usually would have been better if it had. *Corollary:* Once things have happened, no matter how accidentally, they will be regarded as manifestations of an unchangeable Higher Reason.

(Professor Charles Frankel of Columbia University, from his book, *High on Foggy Bottom,* Harper & Row, 1969.)

● **Franklin's Law.** Blessed is he who expects nothing, for he shall not be disappointed.
(Gene Franklin, from an article in *Computers and Automation. JE.*)

● **Franklin's Observation.** He that lives upon Hope dies farting.
(Attributed to Benjamin Franklin, *1974 Expectation of Days. RS.*)

● **Freemon's Rule.** Circumstances can force a generalized incompetent to become competent, at least in a specialized field.
(Frank R. Freemon, of the Department of Neurology, Vanderbilt University School of Medicine, from an article of the same title in the *JIR,* March, 1974. *Freemon's Rule* goes beyond the *Peter Principle* and *Godin's Law* (see each) to explain such individuals as Ulysses S. Grant, Harry S Truman, and Winston Churchill, who all reached a level of incompetence [Truman and Grant failed in business, and Churchill fared badly in politics in the 1930s] and then went on to become competent.)

● **Fried's 23rd Law.** Ideas endure and prosper in inverse proportion to their soundness and validity.
(*U//W.*)

● **Friendship, The 17th and 18th Rules of.** (17) A friend will refrain from telling you he picked up the same amount of life insurance coverage you did for half the price and his is noncancelable. (18) A friend will let you hold the ladder while he goes up on the roof to install your new TV antenna, which is the biggest son of a bitch you ever saw.

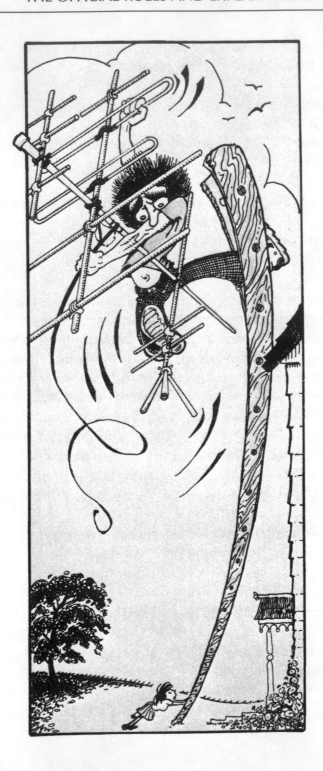

(From "*Esquire*'s 27 Rules of Friendship," which appears in the May, 1977, issue. The items are very clever, but also repetitive. These were picked more or less at random.)

● **Frisbee, The 10 Commandments of the.** (1) The most powerful force in the world is that of a disc straining to land under a car, just beyond reach. (This force is technically termed "car suck.") (2) The higher the quality of a catch or the comment it receives, the greater the probability of a crummy re-throw. (Good catch—bad throw.) (3) One must never precede any maneuver by a comment more predictive than, "Watch this!" (Keep 'em guessing.) (4) The higher the costs of hitting any object, the greater the certainty it will be struck. (Remember—the disc is positive—both cops and old ladies are clearly negative.) (5) The best catches are never seen. ("Did you see that?"—"See what?") (6) The greatest single aid to distance is for the disc to be going in a direction you did not want. (Goes the wrong way = Goes a long way.) (7) The most powerful hex words in the sport are—"I really have this down—watch." (Know it? Blow it!) (8) In any crowd of spectators at least one will suggest that razor blades could be attached to the disc. ("You could maim and kill with that thing.") (9) The greater your need to make a good catch, the greater the probability your partner will deliver his worst throw. (If you can't touch it, you can't trick it.) (10) The single most difficult move with a disc is to put it down. (Just one more.)

> (Dan "The Stork" Roddick, editor of *Frisbee World* and director of the International Frisbee Association. Reprinted with permission from the February, 1975, issue of *Flying Disc World.)*

● **Froben's Law of Publishing.** Never send a letter requesting information to an editor unless you expect to receive a prolix letter in return.

(Froben is the alter ego of Indiana University Press editor Robert Cook.)

● **Froud's Law.** A transistor protected by a fast-acting fuse will protect the fuse by blowing first.
(*U/S.T.L.*)

● **Frustration in the Large, Principle of.** Realization of the expectation total over all events will be as low as possible.
(David Ellis, from "Some Precise Formulations of the Alleged Perversity of Nature," 1957.)

● **Fudd's First Law of Opposition.** If you push something hard enough it will fall over.

● **Fudd's Law of Insertion.** What goes in, must come back out.
(Van Mizzell, Jr., Mobile, Ala.)

● **Fudge Factor.** A physical factor occasionally showing up in experiments as a result of stopping a stopwatch a little early to compensate for reflex error. . . . *Or:* The numerical factor by which experimental results must be multiplied to be in agreement with theory. . . . *Or: Any of a number of other statements used to indicate the conscious addition of a bogus factor or figure.*
(Who was Fudge you ask? Here is the "Fudge" entry from *The Dictionary of Words, Facts and Phrases* by Eliezer Edwards, Chatto & Windus, London, 1901, in its entirety: "*Fudge.* In a 'Collection of some Papers of William Crouch' (8vo. 1712), Crouch, who was a Quaker, says that one Marshall informed him that 'In the year 1664, we were sentenced for banishment to Jamaica by Judges Hyde and Twysden, and our number was 55. We were put on board the ship "Black Eagle," the master's name was *Fudge,* by some called "Lying Fudge." ' Isaac D'Is-

raeli quotes from a pamphlet entitled 'Remarks upon the Navy' (1700), to show that the word originated in a man's name: 'There was, sir, in our time one Captain Fudge, commander of a merchantman, who, upon his return from a voyage, how ill fraught soever his ship was, always brought home his owner a good cargo of lies, so much that now aboard ship the sailors when they hear a great lie told, cry out, "You *fudge* it!" ' ")

- **Fuller's Law of Cosmic Irreversibility.**
$$1 \text{ Pot T} = 1 \text{ Pot P}$$
$$1 \text{ Pot P} \neq 1 \text{ Pot T}$$
(R. Buckminster Fuller.)

- **Funkhouser's Law of the Power of the Press.** The quality of legislation passed to deal with a problem is inversely proportional to the volume of media clamor that brought it on.
(G. Ray Funkhouser, Ph.D., Field Research Corp., San Francisco, *AO.*)

- **Futility Factor.** No experiment is ever a complete failure. It can always serve as a bad example, or the exception that proves the rule (but only if it is the first experiment in the series.)
(Embellished version of *Car[l]son's Consolation.*)

- **Fyffe's Axiom.** The problem-solving process will always break down at the point at which it is possible to determine who caused the problem.
(*U/2p?*)

● **Gadarene Swine Law.** Merely because the group is in formation does not mean that the group is on the right course.

> (Law derived from the passage in the New Testament in which Christ sent the pigs tumbling into the lake [Mark 5:11–13]. Reported by Robert Cook.)

● **Galbraith's Law of Political Wisdom.** Anyone who says he isn't going to resign, four times, definitely will.

● **Galbraith's Law of Prominence.** Getting on the cover of *Time* guarantees the existence of opposition in the future.

> (John Kenneth Galbraith. The first from *AO;* the second, *MBC.* See also *Grump's Law.*)

● **Gall's Principles of Systemantics** (1) *The Primal Scenario or Basic Datum of Experience:* Systems in general work poorly or not at all. (2) *The Fundamental Theorem:* New systems generate new problems. (3) *The Law of Conservation of Anergy:* The total amount of energy in the universe is constant.*(4) *Law of Growth:* Systems tend to grow, and as they grow, they encroach. (5) *The Generalized Uncertainty Principle:* Systems display antics.

> (Dr. John Gall, from his book *Systemantics: How Systems Work and Especially How They Fail,* Quadrangle/ The New York Times Book Company, 1977. The laws quoted above are just an abbreviated sampling from a much

---

*Gall's definition of anergy: "Any state or condition of the Universe, or of any portion of it, that requires the expenditure of human effort or ingenuity to bring it into line with human desires, needs, or pleasures is defined as an ANERGY-STATE."

longer list of axioms and laws revealed and explained in this benchmark book that ranks in importance with *Parkinson's Law* and *The Peter Principle* for anyone trying to understand our modern, technological society. Gall, a professor and practicing physician, has a particular ability to come up with concisely stated truths—e.g., "The dossier is not the person," and "Any large system is going to be operating most of the time in failure mode.")

● **Gallois's Revelation.** If you put tomfoolery into a computer, nothing comes out but tomfoolery. But this tomfoolery, having passed through a very expensive machine, is somehow ennobled, and no one dares to criticize it.

(Pierre Gallois in *Science et Vie,* Paris, reprinted in the *Reader's Digest.*)

● **Gammon's Theory of Bureaucratic Displacement.** In a bureaucratic system an increase in expenditure will be matched by a fall in production. Such systems will act rather like "black holes" in the economic universe, simultaneously sucking in resources and shrinking in terms of "emitted" production. *Or, as restated by Milton Friedman:* In a bureaucratic system, useless work drives out useful work.

(British physician Dr. Max Gammon, on the completion of a five-year study of the British health system. Discussed by Milton Friedman in his November 7, 1977, *Newsweek* column. See also *Parkinson's Law,* of which *Gammon's Theory* is an extension.)

● **Gardening, Laws of.** (1) Other people's tools work only in other people's yards. (2) Fancy gizmos don't work. (3) If nobody uses it, there's a reason. (4) You get the most of what you need the least.

(Jane Bryant Quinn, in her newspaper column syndicated by *The Washington Post,* 1975.)

●   **Gardner's Rule of Society.** The society which scorns
excellence in plumbing because plumbing is a humble activity
and tolerates shoddiness in philosophy because it is an exalted
activity will have neither good plumbing nor good philosophy.
Neither its pipes nor its theories will hold water.

(John W. Gardner, *Forbes,* "Thought" page, August 1, 1977.)

● **G Constant (or Godin's Law).** Generalizedness of incompetence is directly proportional to highestness in hierarchy.

(Guy Godin, from an article with the same title in *JIR,* March, 1972. Godin has found an exception to the *Peter Principle* because he argues that some people are incompetent before they begin to rise. Peter argues that they rise to their level of incompetence. See also *Freemon's Rule.*)

● **Geanangel's Law.** If you want to make an enemy, do someone a favor.

(Charles L. Geanangel, teacher, Winter Haven, Fla. *JMcC.*)

● **Gell-Mann's Dictum.** Whatever isn't forbidden is required. *Corollary:* If there's no reason why something shouldn't exist, then it must exist.

(Murray Gell-Mann. *JW.*)

● **Germond's Law.** When a group of newsmen go out to dinner together, the bill is to be divided evenly among them, regardless of what each one eats and drinks.

(Newsman-columnist Jack Germond. See also *Weaver's Law,* of which Germond's is a corollary. *AO.*)

● **Gerrold's Laws of Infernal Dynamics.** (1) An object in motion will always be headed in the wrong direction. (2) An object at rest will always be in the wrong place. (3) The energy required to change either one of these states will always be more than you wish to expend, but never so much as to make the task totally impossible.

(David Gerrold, writer and columnist for *Starlog* magazine. See *Short's Quotations,* which are also his.)

● **Getty's Reminder.** The meek shall inherit the earth, but *not* its mineral rights.

(J. Paul Getty, quoted by Earl Wilson, among others.)

● **Gilb's Laws of Reliability.** (1) Computers are unreliable, but humans are even more unreliable. *Corollary:* At the source of every error which is blamed on the computer you will find at least two human errors, including the error of blaming it on the computer. (2) Any system which depends on human reliability is unreliable. (3) The only difference between the fool and the criminal who attacks a system is that the fool attacks unpredictably and on a broader front. (4) A system tends to grow in terms of complexity rather than of simplification, until the resulting unreliability becomes intolerable. (5) Self-checking systems tend to have a complexity in proportion to the inherent unreliability of the system in which they are used. (6) The error-detection and correction capabilities of any system will serve as the key to understanding the type of errors which they cannot handle. (7) Undetectable errors are infinite in variety, in contrast to detectable errors, which by definition are limited. (8) All real programs contain errors until proved otherwise—which is impossible. (9) Investment in reliability will increase until it exceeds the probable cost of errors, or somebody insists on getting some useful work done.

(Tom Gilb, "The Laws of Unreliability," *Datamation,* March, 1975. *JE.*)

● **Gilmer's Law of Political Leadership.** Look over your shoulder now and then to be sure someone's following you.

(Uttered by Virginia's State Treasurer Henry Gilmer some 30 years ago and recently quoted in a column by James J. Kilpatrick.)

● **Ginsberg's Theorem.** (1) You can't win. (2) You can't break even. (3) You can't even quit the game.

(*U/S.T.L.* See *Ehrman's Corollary.*)

● **Glasow's Law.** There's something wrong if you're always right.

(Arnold Glasow, quoted on *Forbes's* "Thought" page, March 15, 1977.)

● **Golden Principle.** Nothing will be attempted if all possible objections must first be overcome.

(Posted in Department of Labor. *TO'B.*)

● **Golden Rule of the Arts and Sciences, The (GRASS).** Whoever has the gold makes the rules.

(This important and oft-quoted rule was announced in the *Journal of Irreproducible Results* in 1975 by O. W. Knewittoo—either a pseudonym or an Eskimo scientist.)

● **Gold's Law. [V.]** The candidate who is expected to do well because of experience and reputation (Douglas, Nixon) must do *better* than well, while the candidate expected to fare poorly (Lincoln, Kennedy) can put points on the media board simply by surviving.

(Vic Gold, in *P.R. as in President,* Doubleday, 1977.)

● **Gold's Law. [W.]** A column about errors will contain errors.

(Popular *Washington Post* columnist Bill Gold, who announced this law in May, 1978, after he had done a column on glitches that get into print—i.e., the "not" which disappears from "not guilty." Before it went into print Gold was able to find and rid the column of three errors and his copy editor was able to find two more. After all of this (more than 20 careful readings) a just-for-good-measure final reading was made by still another editor and it was put into type. When the first edition of the paper came out, the three segments of the column [or legs] had been pasted up wrong so that the last section was in the middle and the middle at the end.)

● **Goldwyn's Law of Contracts.** A verbal contract isn't worth the paper it's written on.
(Samuel Goldwyn. *Co.*)

● **Golub's Laws of Computerdom.** (1) Fuzzy project objectives are used to avoid the embarrassment of estimating the corresponding costs. (2) A carelessly planned project takes three times longer to complete than expected; a carefully planned project will take only twice as long. (3) The effort required to correct course increases geometrically with time. (4) Project teams detest weekly progress reporting because it so vividly manifests their lack of progress.
(*U//JE.*)

● **Goodfader's Law.** Under any system a few sharpies will beat the rest of us.
(Al Goodfader, Washington, D.C. *AO.*)

● **Gordon's First Law.** If a research project is not worth doing at all, it is not worth doing well.
(*U//RS.*)

● **Goulden's Axiom of the Bouncing Can (ABC).** If you drop a full can of beer, and remember to rap the top sharply with your knuckle prior to opening, the ensuing gush of foam will be between 89 and 94 percent of the volume that would splatter you if you didn't do a damned thing and went ahead and pulled the top immediately.

● **Goulden's Law of Jury Watching.** If a jury in a criminal trial stays out for more than twenty-four hours, it is certain to vote acquittal, save in those instances where it votes guilty.

(Joseph C. Goulden, writer, developed the second law during twenty-seven months of intensive research as a courts reporter for *The Dallas News.*)

● **Graditor's Laws.** (1) If it can break, it will, but only after the warranty expires. (2) A necessary item only goes on sale after you have purchased it at the regular price.
(Sherry Graditor, Skokie, Ill.)

● **Grandma Soderquist's Conclusion.** A chicken doesn't stop scratching just because the worms are scarce.
(Letter from John Peers of Logical Machine Corp., thanking contributors for laws for that company's law collection.)

● **Gray's Law of Bilateral Asymmetry in Networks.** Information flows efficiently through organizations, except that bad news encounters high impedance in flowing upward.
(Paul Gray to Robert Machol for his *POR* series. Gray also told Machol, ". . . people at the top make decisions as though times were good when people at the bottom know that the organization is collapsing.")

● **Gray's Law of Programming.** $n+1$ trivial tasks are expected to be accomplished in the same time as n trivial tasks.
(*U/S.T.L.* See *Logg's Rebuttal to Gray's Law of Programming.*)

● **Greener's Law.** Never argue with a man who buys ink by the barrel.
(Bill Greener. *AO.*)

● **Greenberg's First Law of Influence.** Usefulness is inversely proportional to reputation for being useful.
(Daniel S. Greenberg, in a column entitled "Debunking

the UTK [Useful to Know] Myth," *The Washington Post,* October 25, 1977. He attacks the conventional wisdom that says there are people who are useful to know in the sense that they possess inordinate influence. He makes many points in favor of his law, including this one: "What must be noted about the many fallen political celebrities of recent years is that salvation eluded them, though they knew all the people in Washington who are useful to know.")

● **Gresham's Law.** Bad money drives out good.
(Sir Thomas Gresham discovered this law in the sixteenth century. It has been generalized, restated, and redirected to a number of fields, so it appears in many forms, including the currently popular version that says, "Trivial matters are handled promptly; important matters are never solved." An example of a specialized application is "Gresham's TV Law," which appeared in a January 2, 1977, article by Frank Mankiewicz in *The Washington Post:* "In a Medium in which a News Piece takes a minute and an 'In-Depth' Piece takes two minutes, the Simple will drive out the Complex.")

● **Grobe's Thought on Memory.** If you can't remember it, it couldn't have been important.
(*U.* John L. Shelton, Dallas.)

● **Grosch's Law.** Computing power increases as the square of the cost. If you want to do it twice as cheaply, you have to do it four times as fast.
(Herb Grosch, editor, *Computerworld. S.T.L.*)

● **Gross's Law.** When two people meet to decide how to spend a third person's money, fraud will result.
(Herman Gross, Great Neck, N.Y. *AO.*)

● **Grump's Law.** If both Alsops say it's true, it can't be so. (From an undated, unauthenticated paper entitled "Great Days for Grump's Law" by John Kenneth Galbraith. He insists that this law is invaluable in American political forecasting but adds, "As a man of more than average caution, I have never felt absolutely secure until Evans and Novak have spoken." The paper appears to have been written in 1972.)

● **Gummidge's Law.** The amount of expertise varies in inverse proportion to the number of statements understood by the general public.

(From an essay in *Time,* December 30, 1966, entitled "Right You Are If You Say You Are—Obscurely." The item opens with a scene at Instant College, where a student is being briefed by key faculty members on the importance of learning jargon on the way to becoming an Expert. Dr. Gummidge, professor of sociology, tells the student, "Remember Gummidge's Law and you will never be Found Out." Gummidge illustrates by telling the student how he would tell the student's mother that he was a lazy, good-for-nothing: "The student in question is performing minimally for his peer group and is an emerging underachiever.")

● **Gumperson's Law.** The probability of anything happening is in inverse ratio to its desirability.

(This very important law first appeared in the November, 1957, issue of *Changing Times* and was credited to Dr. R. F. Gumperson [although we have subsequently learned that the real author is John W. Hazard, now the magazine's executive editor]. The law was announced in conjunction with a long-forgotten article on firewood, to account for a phenomenon known to anyone who has ever lit fires, to wit: ". . . that you can throw a burnt match out the window of your car and start a forest fire while you can use two boxes of matches and a whole edition of the Sunday paper without being able to start a fire under the dry logs in your fireplace."

Gumperson began serious work in 1938 on the *Farmers' Almanac* phenomenon [by which that esteemed annual always does a better job predicting the weather than the official weather bureau] and during World War II went on to develop the procedure for the armed forces ". . . whereby the more a recruit knew about a given subject, the better chance he had of receiving an assignment involving some other subject."

Some of the many real-life examples he was able to derive from his law and his pioneering work as a divicist:*

⭐ That after a raise in salary you will have less money at the end of each month than you had before.

⭐ That children have more energy after a hard day of play than they do after a good night's sleep.

⭐ That the person who buys the most raffle tickets has the least chance of winning.

⭐ That good parking places are always on the other side of the street.

It was further reported that Gumperson met with an untimely death in 1947 while walking down the highway. He was obeying the proper rule of walking on the left facing traffic when he was hit from behind by a Hillman-Minx driven by an Englishman hugging the left.

Over the years Gumperson has picked up many disciples, including the late H. Allen Smith, who wrote that he felt that the law was written just for him. One of Smith's many examples: "I dislike going to the garage with a rattle

---

*One skilled in divicism. Divicism is the science of making predictions according to the law of diverges. A diverge is the opposite of an average.

in my car, because the moment the mechanic begins his inspection, that rattle will vanish.'')

● **Gumperson's Proof.** The most undesirable things are the most certain (e.g., death and taxes).
  (From Martin S. Kottmeyer, Carlyle, Illinois.)

● **Guthman's Law of Media.** Thirty seconds on the evening news is worth a front page headline in every newspaper in the world.
  (Edwin Guthman. *MBC*'s *Laws of Politics.*)

● **Hacker's Law.** The belief that enhanced understanding will necessarily stir a nation or an organization to action is one of mankind's oldest illusions.

● **Hacker's Law of Personnel.** It is never clear just how many hands—or minds—are needed to carry out a particular process. Nevertheless, anyone having supervisory responsibility for the completion of the task will invariably protest that his staff is too small for the assignment.

> (Andrew Hacker, from *The End of the American Dream,* Atheneum, 1970. The *Law of Personnel* has been revised on various lists and is sometimes written as: "Anyone having supervisory responsibility for the completion of a task will invariably protest that more resources are needed.")

● **Hagerty's Law.** If you lose your temper at a newspaper columnist, he'll get rich or famous or both.

> (James C. Hagerty, President Eisenhower's press secretary, who discovered it after blowing his top over a column by humorist Art Buchwald. *FL.* For other press-secretary laws, see *Nessen's Law, Powell's Laws, Ross's Law,* and *Salinger's Law.*)

● **Halberstam's Law of Survival.** Always stay in with the outs.

> (David Halberstam. *MBC*'s *Laws of Politics.*)

● **Haldane's Law.** The universe is not only stranger than we imagine, it is stranger than we *can* imagine.

> (J. B. S. Haldane, British geneticist and Marxist. *JW.*)

● **Hale's Rule.** The sumptuousness of a company's annual report is in inverse proportion to its profitability that year.
(Irving Hale, the Sarvis Group Inc., Denver. *AO.*)

● **Hall's Law.** There is a statistical correlation between the number of initials in an Englishman's name and his social class (the upper class having significantly more than three names, while members of the lower class average 2.6).
(*U//W.*)

● **Halpern's Observation.** That tendency to err that programmers have been noticed to share with other human beings has often been treated as if it were an awkwardness attendant upon programming's adolescence, which like acne would disappear with the craft's coming of age. It has proved otherwise.
(Mark Halpern. *JE.*)

● **Harden's Law. [F.]** Every time you come up with a terrific idea, you find that someone else thought of it first.
(Frank Harden, radio personality, Washington, D.C. *JW.*)

● **Hardin's Law. [G.]** You can never do merely one thing.
(Biologist Garrett Hardin. It applies to any complex system and tells us that even when an action has its intended effect, it also has other, unintended, effects. An editorial in the February, 1974, *Fortune* said, in part, "If a prize were to be awarded for the most illuminating single sentence authored in the past ten years, one of the candidates would surely be Hardin's Law . . ." *Fortune* said examples were common: e.g., New York City's off-track betting system had its intended effect of weaning waging away from illegal bookies, but it also had the unintended effect of creating a new clientele of horseplayers.)

● **Harris's Law.** Any philosophy that can be put "in a nut-shell" belongs there.

● **Harris's Restaurant Paradox.** One of the greatest un-solved riddles of restaurant eating is that the customer usually gets faster service when the restaurant is crowded than when it is half empty; it seems that the less that the staff has to do, the slower they do it.

(Sydney J. Harris, the first from his book *Leaving the Surface,* 1968, and the second from *On the Contrary,* 1964, both published by Houghton Mifflin.)

● **Hartig's How Is Good Old Bill? We're Divorced Law.** If there is a wrong thing to say, one will.

(Betty Hartig, "the Nantucket Kitelady.")

● **Hartig's Sleeve in the Cup, Thumb in the Butter Law.** When one is trying to be elegant and sophisticated, one won't.

● **Hartley's Law.** You can lead a horse to water, but if you can get him to float on his back you've got something.

(Let Conrad Schneiker explain how he acquired this law: "Hartley was a University of Arizona student who wan-dered into my office looking lost, circa 1974." *S.T.I.*)

● **Hartman's Automotive Laws.** (1) Nothing minor ever happens to a car on the weekend. (2) Nothing minor ever hap-pens to a car on a trip. (3) Nothing minor ever happens to a car.

(Charles D. Hartman, Belleair, Fla.)

● **Hart's Law of Observation.** In a country as big as the United States, you can find fifty examples of anything.

(*U.* Jeffery F. Chamberlain letter to *Verbatim.*)

●   **Harvard Law.** Under the most rigorously controlled conditions of pressure, temperature, volume, humidity, and other variables, the organism will do as it damn well pleases.
(*U/Co.*)

●   **Hein's Law.** Problems worthy of attack prove their worth by hitting back.
(Piet Hein, from a group of "Quips" in *Journal of Irreproducible Results,* March, 1971.)

●   **Heller's Myths of Management.** The first myth of management is that it exists. The second myth of management is that success equals skill.
(Robert Heller, *The Great Executive Dream,* Delacorte, 1972. *JE.* See *Johnson's Corollary* to *Heller's Law.*)

●   **Herblock's Law.** If it's good they'll stop making it.
(Conceived by the famous political cartoonist after they stopped making a particular kind of carbon drawing stick that he liked best. Reported on by Sydney J. Harris in his December 28, 1977, syndicated column, "Modern Way: If It's Good, Scrap It." *FD.*)

●   **Herrnstein's Law.** The attention paid to an instructor is a constant regardless of the size of the class. Thus as class size swells, the amount of attention paid per student drops in direct ratio.
(Psychologist Richard J. Herrnstein. *AO.*)

●   **Hersh's Law.** Biochemistry expands so as to fill the space and time available for its completion and publication.
(R. T. Hersh, in a 1962 *American Scientist* article, "Parkinson's Law, the Squid and pU.")

●   **Hildebrand's Law.** The quality of a department is inversely proportional to the number of courses it lists in its catalogue.

(Professor Joel Hildebrand, University of California at Berkeley.)

● **Historian's Rule.** Any event, once it has occurred, can be made to appear inevitable by a competent historian.

(Lee Simonson, from Herbert V. Prochow's *The Public Speaker's Treasure Chest,* Harper & Row, 1977.)

● **Hoare's Law of Large Programs.** Inside every large program is a small program struggling to get out.

(Tony Hoare, computer scientist. *S.T.L.*)

● **Hogg's (Murphy's) Law of Station Wagons.** The amount of junk carried is in direct proportion to the amount of space available. *Baggage Corollary:* If you go on a trip taking two bags with you, one containing everything you need for the trip and the other containing absolutely nothing, the second bag will be completely filled with junk acquired on the trip when you return.

(Tony Hogg, in an *Esquire* article, "The Right Way to Buy a New Small Car," February, 1975.)

● **Hollywood's Iron Law.** Nothing succeeds like failure.

(Discussed and reapplied by Sidney Zion in his article "Hollywood's Iron Law Comes to Washington," *New York,* January 24, 1977. As Zion explains, ". . . if a genius lost a few million on a picture, he was immediately installed in a fancier office with a better title and a bigger budget. . . . Only after nine straight flops was he eligible to become head of the studio.")

● **Horner's Five-Thumb Postulate.** Experience varies directly with equipment ruined.

(Presumably, Little Jack Horner. *A/C.*)

Special Section 3

HOW TO . . .

△ *Kill an Enterprise.*

(1) Do not go to meetings.

(2) If you go, arrive late.

(3) Criticize the work of the organizers and members.

(4) Get mad if you are not a member of the committee, but if you are, make no suggestions.

(5) If the chair asks your opinion on a subject, say you have none. After the meeting say you have learned nothing, or tell everyone what should have happened.

(6) Don't do what has to be done yourself, but when the members roll up their sleeves and do their very best, complain that the group is run by a bunch of ego-trippers.

(7) Pay your dues as late as possible.

(8) Never think of introducing new members.

(9) Complain that nothing is ever published which interests you but never offer to write an article, make a suggestion, or find a writer.

(10) And if the enterprise dies, say you saw it coming ages before.

(Jean-Charles Terrassier, founder of the French Society for Gifted Children, who listed these suggestions in *Quipos,* the international French journal.)

△ *Make Yourself Miserable.*

(1) Forget the good things in life and concentrate on the bad.

(2) Put an excessive value on money.

(3) Think that you are indispensable to your job, your community, and your friends.

(4) Think that you are overburdened with work and that people tend to take advantage of you.

(5) Think that you are exceptional and entitled to special privileges.

(6) Think that you can control your nervous system by sheer willpower.

(7) Forget the feelings and rights of other people.

(8) Cultivate a consistently pessimistic outlook.

(9) Never overlook a slight or forget a grudge.

(10) And don't forget to feel sorry for yourself.
(*U/TO'B.*)

△ *Tell Republicans from Democrats.*

•Democrats buy most of the books that have been banned somewhere. Republicans form censorship committees and read them as a group.

•Republicans consume three-fourths of all the rutabaga produced in this country. The remainder is thrown out.

•Republicans usually wear hats and almost always clean their paint brushes.

•Democrats give their worn-out clothes to those less fortunate. Republicans wear theirs.

•Republicans employ exterminators. Democrats step on the bugs.

•Democrats name their children after currently popular sports figures, politicians, and entertainers. Republican children are named after their parents or grandparents, according to where the money is.

•Democrats keep trying to cut down on smoking but are not successful. Neither are Republicans.

•Republicans tend to keep their shades drawn, although there is seldom any reason why they should. Democrats ought to, but don't.

•Republicans study the financial pages of the newspaper. Democrats put them in the bottom of the bird cage.

•Most of the stuff alongside the road has been thrown out of car windows by Democrats.

•Republicans raise dahlias, Dalmatians, and eyebrows. Democrats raise Airedales, kids, and taxes.

•Democrats eat the fish they catch. Republicans hang them on the wall.

•Republican boys date Democratic girls. They plan to marry Republican girls, but feel they're entitled to a little fun first.

•Democrats make up plans and then do something else. Republicans follow the plans their grandfathers made.

•Republicans sleep in twin beds—some even in separate rooms. That is why there are more Democrats.

> (Document submitted and published in the *Congressional Record,* October 1, 1974, by Representative Craig Hosmer [R-Cal.]. Hosmer said that the author chose to remain anonymous.)

△ *Test Yourself for Paranoia.*

You know you've got it when you can't think of anything that's your fault.

> (Robert Hutchins.)

△ *Work It So That You Get Your Face on a Postage Stamp.*

We cannot put the face of a person on a stamp unless said person is deceased. My suggestion, therefore, is that you drop dead.

> (James Edward Day, postmaster general, in a letter dictated but not mailed to a man who wanted his likeness on a postage stamp. *The New York Times,* March 7, 1962.)

● **Howe's Law.** Every man has a scheme that will not work. (*U/S.T.L.*)

● **Hull's Warning.** Never insult an alligator until after you have crossed the river.

> (Cordell Hull.)

● **Human Rights Articles, A Sampling of Proposed.** *Article I:* All men are born naked. *Article VIII:* All men have the right to wait in line. *Article XV:* Each person has the right to take part in the management of public affairs in his country, provided he has prior experience, a will to succeed, a college degree, influential parents, good looks, a résumé, two 3×4 snapshots, and a good tax record. *Article XVI:* Each person has the right to take the subway. *Article XXI:* Everyone has the right, without exception, to equal pay for equal work. Except women.

(Carlos Eduardo Novaes, columnist for *Jornal do Brasil* of Rio, from a much larger collection that appeared in *Atlas*. It was written after the Organization of American States [OAS] was unable to get anywhere in its 1977 debate on human rights. Novaes created a Universal Declaration on Human Rights that he felt that most members of the OAS and UN could live with.)

● **IBM Pollyanna Principle.** Machines should work. People should think.

(IBM motto, so titled on various computer-oriented lists. *S.T.L., JE,* etc.)

● **Idea Formula.** One man's brain plus one other will produce about one half as many ideas as one man would have produced alone. These two plus two more will produce half again as many ideas. These four plus four more begin to represent a creative meeting, and the ratio changes to one quarter as many. . . .

(Anthony Chevins, vice-president of Cunningham and Walsh, in an *Advertising Age* article entitled "The Positive Power of Lonethink," April 27, 1959. J.B. Simpson's *Contemporary Quotations,* Crowell, 1964.)

● **Imhoff's Law.** The organization of any bureaucracy is very much like a septic tank—the really big chunks always rise to the top.

(This first appeared in Thomas L. Martin's *Malice in Blunderland,* McGraw-Hill, 1971, with the following footnote: "Professor John Imhoff, Head of Industrial Engineering, University of Arkansas. A distant cousin, Karl Imhoff, invented the Imhoff Septic Tank of international fame.)

● **Index of Development.** The degree of a country's development is measured by the ratio of the price of an automobile to that of the cost of a haircut. The lower the ratio, the higher the degree of development.

(Samuel Devons, professor of physics, Columbia University, from Charles P. Issawi's *Issawi's Laws of Social Motion.*)

● **Inertia, Law of.** Given enough time, what you put off doing today will eventually get done by itself.
(G. Gestra, Oregon.)

● **Instant Status, Merrill's Rules and Maxims of.** (1) The early bird catches the worm as a rule, but the guy who comes along later may be having lobster Newburg and crêpes suzette. (2) Genuine status is a rare and precious jewel, and also rather easy to simulate. (3) In a democracy you can be respected though poor, but don't count on it. (4) Society heaps honors on the unique, creative personality, but not until he has been dead for fifty years. (5) Money is not the measure of a man, but it will do quite nicely if you don't have any other yardstick handy. (6) If at first you don't succeed, you must be doing something wrong. (7) Everybody believes in rugged individualism, but you'll do better by pleasing the boss. (8) To those who doubt the importance of careful mate selection, remember how Adam wrecked a promising career. (9) It is nice to be content in a little house by the side of the road, but a split-level in suburbia is a lot more comfortable . . .
(Charles Merrill Smith, from his book *Instant Status, or How to Become a Pillar of the Upper Middle Class,* Doubleday, 1972. These ten rules and maxims come from a longer list of fifteen. All but one of the remaining items are amplifications of the status theme, save for number fourteen, which states, "When God created two sexes, he may have been overdoing it.")

● **Institutional Food, Laws of.** (1) Everything is cold except what should be. (2) Everything, including the cornflakes, is greasy.

(*U.* Part of a collection originating at East Russell Hall, University of Georgia, Athens.)

● **Inverse Appreciation, Law of.** The less there is between you and the environment, the more you appreciate the environment.
(*U//JW.*)

● **Iron Law of Distribution.** Them what has—gets.
(*Co.*)

● **Issawi's Laws of Social Motion** (A Sampling). *Aggression:* At any given moment, a society contains a certain amount of accumulated (stock, ΣA) and accruing (flow, flow,$\Delta A/\Delta T$) aggressiveness. If more than twenty-one years elapse without this aggressiveness being directed outward, in a popular war against other countries, it turns inward, in social unrest, civil disturbances, and political disruption. *Committo-Dynamics, First Law of: Comitas comitatum, omnia comitas. Committo-Dynamics, Second Law of:* The less you enjoy serving on committees, the more likely you are to be pressed to do so. (Explanation: If you do not like committees, you keep quiet, nod your head, and look wise while thinking of something else and thereby acquire the reputation of being a judicious and cooperative colleague; if you enjoy committees, you talk a lot, make many suggestions and are regarded by the other members as a nuisance. *Conservation of Evil, Law of:* The total amount of evil in any system remains constant. Hence any diminution in one direction—for instance a reduction in poverty or unemployment—is accompanied by an increase in another, e.g., crime or air pollution. *Consumption Patterns:* Other people's patterns of expenditure and consumption are highly irrational and slightly immoral. *Cynics:* Cynics are right nine times out of ten; what undoes them is their belief that they are right ten times out of ten. *A Depressing Thought:* One cannot make an omelette without breaking eggs—but it is amazing how many eggs one can break without making a decent omelette. *Dogmatism:* When we call others dogmatic, what we really object to is their holding dogmas that are different from our own. *Factor of Error:* Experts in advanced countries underestimate by a factor of 2 to 4 the ability of people in underdeveloped countries to do anything technical. (Examples: Japanese on warplanes, Russians on the bomb, Iranians on refineries . . . etc.) *Near and Distant Neighbors:* All countries hate their immediate neighbors and like the next but one. (For example, the Poles hate the Germans, Russians, Czechs, and Lithuanians, and they like the French, Hungarians, Italians, and Latvians.) *Operational Definition of Development:* In an underdeveloped country, when you are absent, your job is taken away from you; in a developed country a new one is piled on you. *Path of Progress:* A shortcut is the longest distance between two points. *Petroleum, Law of:* (formulated circa 1951) Where there are Muslims, there is oil; the converse is not true. *Social Science Theories:* By the time a social science theory is formulated in such a way that it can be tested, changing circumstances have already made it obsolete.

> (Professor Charles P. Issawi, Princeton economist and author, from his 1973 book *Issawi's Laws of Social Motion,* Hawthorne Books. Issawi uses the book to attempt for social science what Darwin did for biology and Newton did for physics—to state universal laws. He has succeeded, right down to his "Last Words of Advice," which are: "If you pay your taxes and don't get into debt and go to bed early and never answer the telephone—no harm can befall you.")

J

● **Jacoby's Law.** The more intelligent and competent a woman is in her adult life, the less likely she is to have received an adequate amount of romantic attention in adolescence.

> (Susan Jacoby in *The New York Times.* "If a girl was smart," she goes on to explain, "and if she attended an American high school between 1930 and 1965, chances are that no one paid attention to anything but her brains unless she took the utmost care to conceal them.")

● **Jacquin's Postulate on Democratic Governments.** No man's life, liberty, or property are safe while the legislature is in session.

> (*U/S.T.L.*)

● **Jake's Law.** Anything hit with a big enough hammer will fall apart.

> (Robert A. "Jake" Jackson, Socorro, N.M.)

● **Jaroslovsky's Law.** The distance you have to park from your apartment increases in proportion to the weight of packages you are carrying.

> (*U/AO.*)

● **Jay's Laws of Leadership.** (1) Changing things is central to leadership, and changing them before anyone else is creativeness. (2) To build something that endures, it is of the greatest importance to have a long tenure in office—to rule for many years. You can achieve a quick success in a year or two, but nearly all of the great tycoons have continued their building much longer.

(Antony Jay, from *Management and Machiavelli,* Holt, Rinehart and Winston, 1967.)

● **Jinny's Law.** There is no such thing as a short beer. (As in, "I'm going to stop off at Joe's for a short beer before I meet you.")
(Virginia W. Smith. *MLS.*)

● **John Adams's Law of Erosion.** Once the erosion of power begins, it has a momentum all its own.
(From *MBC*'s *Laws of Politics.*)

● **John Cameron's Law.** No matter how many times you've had it, if it's offered, take it, because it'll never be quite the same again.

● **John's Axiom.** When your opponent is down, kick him.

● **John's Collateral Corollary.** In order to get a loan you must first prove you don't need it.
(All John Cameron, who, says Conrad Schneiker, is "a Kansas farmer and friend of 'Big' Peggy.")

● **Johnson's Corollary to Heller's Law.** Nobody really knows what is going on anywhere within your organization.
(*U/S.T.L.*)

● **Johnson's First Law of Auto Repair.** Any tool dropped while repairing an automobile will roll under the car to the vehicle's exact geographic center.
(*U/S.T.L.* Similar to *Anthony's Law of the Workshop.*)

● **Johnson's "Prior" Laws of Politics.** (1) Pay your dues. (2) Attend the meetings.
(Lyndon B. Johnson. The "prior" in the title refers to the

fact that they precede *Dirksen's Laws of Politics* and must be understood "prior" to understanding Dirksen's Laws. Harry N. D. Fisher to *AO*.)

● **Jones's Law.** The man who can smile when things go wrong has thought of someone he can blame it on.

(*Co.* This item appears in virtually every collection of laws, yet there is no clue as to who Jones is. Nor do we know the identity of the Jones of the next law. See also *Tom Jones's First Law*.)

● **Jones's Principle.** Needs are a function of what other people have.

(*U/JW*.)

● **Journalist's Adage.** Never assume anything except a 4¼ percent mortgage.

(Dave Kindred, from his "This Morning" column in *The Washington Post,* January 14, 1978.)

● **Joyce's Law of Bathroom Hooks.** A bathroom hook will be loaded to capacity immediately upon becoming available.

(John Joyce, Waldie and Briggs Inc., Chicago. *AO*. According to Joyce there is more to this law than immediately meets the eye, as it ". . . applies to freeways, closets, playgrounds, downtown hotels, taxis, parking lots, bookcases, wallets, purses, pockets, pipe racks, basement shelves, and so on. The list is endless." However, he is the first to concede that further research is called for. As he told Otten in a note, "The ultimate test of the law, which I have been postponing, would be to array hooks in a continuous strip around the bathroom to see if the towels, bathrobes, etc., actually meet in the middle of the room preventing opening of the door and entry of would-be bathers.")

- **Kafka's Law.** In the fight between you and the world, back the world.

  (Franz Kafka. *RS*'s *1974 Expectation of Days.*)

- **Kamin's Seventh Law.** Politicians will always inflate when given the opportunity.

  (Identified by Conrad Schneiker as an economist from Ventura, California.)

- **Kaplan's Law of the Instrument.** Give a small boy a hammer and he will find that everything he encounters needs pounding.

  (Abraham Kaplan. *S.T.L.*)

- **Katz's Maxims.** (1) Where are the calculations that go with the calculated risk? (2) Inventing is easy for staff outfits. Stating a problem is much harder. Instead of stating problems, people like to pass out half-accurate statements together with half-available solutions which they can't finish and which they want you to finish. (3) Every organization is self-perpetuating. Don't ever ask an outfit to justify itself, or you'll be covered with facts, figures, and fancy. The criterion should rather be, "What will happen if the outfit stops doing what it's doing?" The value of an organization is easier determined this way. (4) Try to find out who's doing the work, not who's writing about it, controlling it, or summarizing it. (5) Watch out for formal briefings, they often produce an avalanche. (Definition: A high-level snow job of massive and overwhelming proportions.) (6) The difficulty of the coordination task often blinds one to the fact that a fully coordinated piece of paper is not supposed to be either the major or the final product of the organization, but it often turns out that way. (7) Most organizations can't hold more than one idea at a time . . . Thus comlementary ideas are always regarded as competitive. Further, like a quantized pendulum, an organization can jump from one extreme to the other, without ever going through the middle. (8) Try to find the real tense of the report you are reading: Was it done, is it being done, or is it something to be done? Reports are now written in four tenses: past tense, present tense, future tense, and pretense. Watch for novel uses of CONGRAM (CONtractor GRAMmar), defined by the imperfect past, the insufficient present, and the absolutely perfect future.

● **Katz's Other Observations** (A Sampling). (1) Brevity and superficiality are often concomitants. (2) Statements by respected authorities which tend to agree with a writer's viewpoint are always handy. (3) When you are about to do an objective and scientific piece of investigation of a topic, it is well to have the answer firmly in hand, so that you can proceed forthrightly, without being deflected or swayed, directly to the goal.

> (All of these were written by Amrom Katz, senior RAND Corp. staff member and until recently assistant director of the Arms Control and Disarmament Agency. The Maxims first appeared in the November, 1967, *Air Force/Space Digest* as part of a much longer article entitled "A Guide for the Perplexed, or a Minimal/Maxim-al Handbook for Tourists in a Classified Bureaucracy." Katz compiled the first five in the 1950s and added six through eight in the 1960s. The "Other Observations" came from three Katz articles: respectively, "Good Disarmament and Bad," *Air Force/Space Digest,* May, 1963; "On Style in R&D," *Air Force/Space Digest,* February, 1962; "A Tribute to George W. Goddard," *Airpower Historian,* October, 1963. *RS.*)

● **Kauffmann's Law.** Authors (and perhaps columnists) eventually rise to the top of whatever depths they were once able to plumb.

(Critic Stanley Kauffman. *JMcC* to *AO.*)

● **Kelley's Law.** Last guys don't finish nice.

(Princeton professor Stanley Kelley, occasioned by the increasing bitterness of political campaigns. *AO.*)

● **Kelly's Law.** An executive will always return to work from lunch early if no one takes him.

(*U.* "Laws to Live By," *The Farmers' Almanac.*)

● **Kennedy's Law.** Excessive official restraints on information are inevitably self-defeating and productive of headaches for the officials concerned.

(Edward Kennedy, AP correspondent best known for his work during World War II. *JW.*)

● **Kent's Law.** The only way a reporter should look at a politician is down.

(From Vic Gold's *P.R. as in President,* Doubleday, 1977, attributed to the *Baltimore Sun*'s Frank Kent.)

● **Kerr-Martin Law.** In dealing with their own problems, faculty members are the most extreme conservatives. In dealing with other people's problems, they are the world's most extreme liberals.

(Clark Kerr.)

● **Kerr's General Rules of Life, Plus Culpability Clause.** (1) Always run a yellow light. (2) Never say no. (3) The younger, the better. *Culpability Clause:* Never admit anything. Never regret anything. Whatever it is, you're not responsible.

(Kerr is a man who works with Sharon Mathews, of Arlington, Va., who collected laws for this collection. She also got the next item from him.)

● **Kerr's Three Rules for Trying New Foods.** (1) Never try anything with tomatoes in it. (2) Never try anything bigger than your head. (3) Never, *never* try anything that looks like vomit . . . then as he says, he broke all three rules by discovering pizza.

● **Kettering's Laws.** (1) If you want to kill any idea in the world today, get a committee working on it. (2) If you have always done it that way, it is probably wrong.

(Charles F. Kettering, probably the nation's most quotable inventor. *Co.*)

● **Key to Status.** $S = D/K$. S is the status of a person in an organization, D is the number of doors he must open to perform his job and K is the number of keys he carries. A higher number denotes a higher status. Examples: The janitor needs to open 20 doors and has 20 keys ($S = 1$), a secretary has to open two doors with one key ($S = 2$), but the president never has to carry any keys since there is always someone around to open doors for him (with $K = 0$ and a high D, his S reaches infinity).

(Psychologist Robert Sommer, from his paper "Keys, Kings and Kompanies." See also his *No. 3 Pencil Principle.*)

● **Kharasch's Institutional Imperative.** Every action or decision of an institution must be intended to keep the institution machinery working.

(Washington lawyer Robert N. Kharasch, from his book *The Institutional Imperative,* Charterhouse Books, 1973. From the basic principle others follow, such as the *Law of Institutional Expertise,* which says, "The expert judgment of an institution, when the matters involve continuation of the institution's operations, is totally predictable, and hence the finding is totally worthless." See also *Security Office, Special Law of. AO.*)

● **Kirkland's Law.** The usefulness of any meeting is in inverse proportion to the attendance.

(AFL-CIO Secretary-Treasurer Lane Kirkland. *AO.*)

● **Kirkup's Law.** The sun goes down just when you need it the most.

(Jon Kirkup. *RS.*)

● **Kitman's Law.** Pure drivel tends to drive ordinary drivel off the TV screen.

(Marvin Kitman, from his book *You Can't Judge a Book by Its Cover,* Weybright and Talley. This law was created at the beginning of the 1967 season in which *The Flying Nun* began its two-year run. In explaining the law, Kitman wrote, "It is inconceivable that three competing networks, working independently in complete secrecy, could produce by accident twenty-six new series so similar in quality.")

● **Knoll's Law of Media Accuracy.** Everything you read in the newspapers is absolutely true except for that rare story of which you happen to have firsthand knowledge.

(Erwin Knoll, editor, *The Progressive.*)

● **Knowles's Law of Legislative Deliberation.** The length of debate varies inversely with the complexity of the issue. *Corollary:* When the issue is simple, and everyone understands it, debate is almost interminable.

(Robert Knowles. *AO.*)

● **Kohn's Second Law.** An experiment is reproducible until another laboratory tries to repeat it.

(Dr. Alexander Kohn, editor in chief, *JIR,* and Department of Biophysics, Israel Institute for Biological Research. *JIR,* December, 1968.)

● **Koppett's Law.** Whatever creates the greatest inconvenience for the largest number must happen.

(*U.* From a 1977 Red Smith column, "World Series Rhetoric." Smith says it was first promulgated when "baseball teams began flying around like rice at a wedding in pursuit of the championship of North America.")

● **Kriedt's Law.** Sanity and insanity overlap a fine gray line.

(Charles van Kriedt, who, according to Laurence J. Peter, reported on a conversation about a politician in which one participant said, "I don't think they could put him in a mental hospital. On the other hand, if he were already in, I don't believe they'd let him out." From the article "Peter's People" in the August, 1976, *Human Behavior.*)

● **Kristol's Law.** Being frustrated is disagreeable, but the real disasters in life begin when you get what you want.

(Irving Kristol, quoted in George F. Will's *Newsweek* column for November 28, 1977, "Pharaoh in the Promised Land." *JW.*)

● **K Rule.** Words with a *k* in them are funny. If it doesn't have a *k,* it's not funny.

(Willie Clark, explaining to his nephew why certain things are funny, in Neil Simon's *The Sunshine Boys.* Clark goes on to explain that "chicken" and "pickle" are funny, but "tomato" and "roast beef" are not. This rule is discussed in some detail in Thomas H. Middleton's "Light Refractions'' column in *Saturday Review,* November 13, 1976. Middleton, incidentally, finds some exceptions to the *K Rule,* for example, that ''pike'' is not a terribly funny word but that ''herring'' is.)

L

- **Labor Law.** A disagreeable task is its own reward. (Found posted at the Department of Labor. *TO'B.*)

- **Langin's Law.** If things were left to chance, they'd be better.
  (*U.* Unsigned letter to *Playboy.*)

- **Lani's Principles of Economics.** (1) Taxes are not levied for the benefit of the taxed. (2) $100 placed at 7 percent interest compounded quarterly for 200 years will increase to more than $100,000,000, by which time it will be worth nothing. (3) In God we trust, all others pay cash.
  (*U/S.T.L.*)

- **La Rochefoucauld's Law.** It is more shameful to distrust one's friends than to be deceived by them.
  (Duc de La Rochefoucauld. *S.T.L.*)

- **Late-Comers, Law of.** Those who have the shortest distance to travel to a meeting invariably arrive the latest.
  (Carl Thompson, executive vice-president, Hill and Knowlton. *AO.*)

- **Lawyer's Law.** The phone will not ring until you leave your desk and walk to the other end of the building.
  (Linda A. Lawyer, Pittsburgh.)

- **Lawyer's Rule.** When the law is against you, argue the

facts. When the facts are against you, argue the law. When both are against you, call the other lawyer names.

(*U/ JW.*)

● **Leahy's Law.** If a thing is done wrong often enough, it becomes right. *Corollary:* Volume is a defense to error.

(Richard A. Leahy, Boston. *AO.*)

● **Le Chatellier's Law.** If some stress is brought to bear on a system in equilibrium, the equilibrium is displaced in the direction which tends to undo the effect of the stress.

(Traditional law in the physical sciences that tends to get wide application or, as *Esquire* put it when it listed "Scientific Principles for English Majors," "This may not be one of the all-time essential scientific principles, but it has a certain ring to it.")

● **Ledge's Law of Fans.** (Or, why you can't run when there's trouble in the office.) No matter where you stand, no matter how far or fast you flee, when it hits the fan, as much as possible will be propelled in your direction, and almost none will be returned to the source.

(*U.* John L. Shelton, Dallas.)

● **Lenin's Law.** Whenever the cause of the people is entrusted to professors it is lost.

(Nikolai Lenin. *RS.*)

● **Le Pelley's Law.** The bigger the man, the less likely he is to object to caricature.

(Guernsey Le Pelley, editorial cartoonist for the *Christian Science Monitor,* quoted in the Lewiston, Maine, *Daily Sun,* July 18, 1977.)

● **Levian's Lament.** The fault lies not with our technologies but with our systems.

(Roger Levian, the RAND Corp. *RS.*)

● **Levy's Ten Laws of the Disillusionment of the True Liberal.** (1) Large numbers of things are determined, and therefore not subject to change. (2) Anticipated events never live up to expectations. (3) That segment of the community with which one has the greatest sympathy as a liberal inevitably turns out to be one of the most narrow-minded and bigoted segments of the community.* (4) Always pray that your opposition be wicked. In wickedness there is a strong strain toward rationality. Therefore there is always the possibility, in theory, of handling the wicked by outthinking them. *Corollary 1:* Good intentions randomize behavior. *Subcorollary 1:* Good intentions are far more difficult to cope with than malicious behavior. *Corollary 2:* If good intentions are combined with stupidity, it is impossible to outthink them. *Corollary 3:* Any discovery is more likely to be exploited by the wicked than applied by the virtuous. (5) In unanimity there is cowardice and uncritical thinking. (6) To have a sense of humor is to be a tragic figure. (7) To know thyself is the ultimate form of aggression. (8) No amount of genius can overcome a preoccupation with detail. (9) Only God can make a random selection. (10) Eternal boredom is the price of constant vigilance.

> (Marlon J. Levy, Jr., chairman of the East Asian studies department, Princeton University. These oft-quoted laws were only nine until recently, and Dr. Levy says, "I have been toying with an 11th. The 11th, if I decide to add it to the 10th, will read as follows, 'Default is more revolutionary than ideals.' ")

---

*At this point Levy refers to *Kelley's Law* ("Last guys don't finish nice") as a "reformation" of number 3.

● **Lewis's Law.** People will buy anything that's one to a customer.

> (Sinclair Lewis, quoted by Leo Rosten in his "Diversions" column in *Saturday Review,* May 15, 1976.)

● **Liebling's Law.** If you just try long enough and hard enough, you can always manage to boot yourself in the posterior.

> (A. J. Liebling, in *The Press,* Ballantine Books, 1975.)

● **Lincoln, Ten Points He Did Not Make.** (1) You cannot bring about prosperity by discouraging thrift. (2) You cannot strengthen the weak by weakening the strong. (3) You cannot help small men up by tearing big men down. (4) You cannot help the poor by destroying the rich. (5) You cannot lift the wage-earner up by pulling the wage-payer down. (6). You cannot keep out of trouble by spending more than your income. (7) You cannot further the brotherhood of man by inciting class hatred. (8) You cannot establish sound social security on borrowed money. (9) You cannot build character and courage by taking away a man's initiative and independence. (10) You cannot help men permanently by doing for them what they could and should do for themselves.

> (*Not* Abraham Lincoln. This list of admonitions has been published far and wide—almost always attributed to Lincoln. It has shown up in newspapers, Christmas cards, official documents, the *Congressional Record,* and magazines, with one of the more recent appearances being in the October, 1975, issue of the *Saturday Evening Post.* A May 19, 1950, report from the Library of Congress definitely determined that the ten points were not Lincoln's, but concluded, ". . . there seems to be no way of overtaking the rapid pace with which the mistaken identity has been spreading." To be sure.)

● **Lindy's Law.** The life expectancy of a television comedian is proportional to the total amount of his exposure on the medium.

> (Reported on by Albert Goodman in an article, "Lindy's Law," in *The New Republic,* June 13, 1964. Lindy's, of course, refers to the restaurant where comedians traditionally hang out in New York.)

● **Lloyd-Jones's Law of Leftovers.** The amount of litter on the street is proportional to the local rate of unemployment.

> (David Lloyd-Jones, Tokyo. *AO.*)

● **Local Anesthesia, Law of.** Never say "oops" in the operating room.

> (Dr. Leo Troy.)

● **Loevinger's Law.** Bad news drives good news out of the media.

> (Lee Loevinger, partner, Hogen and Hartson, and former Federal Communications Commission member. An analogue of *Gresham's Law. AO.*)

● **Logg's Rebuttal to Gray's Law of Programming.** $n+1$ trivial tasks take twice as long as n trivial tasks for n sufficiently large.

> (Ed Logg of *S.T.L.*)

● **Longfellow's Elevator Rules.** (1) Face forward. (2) Fold hands in front. (3) Do not make eye contact. (4) Watch the numbers. (5) Don't talk to anyone you don't know. (6) Stop talking with anyone you do know when anyone you don't know enters the elevator. (7). Avoid brushing bodies.

> (Psychologist Layne Longfellow, quoted in *New York,* November 21, 1977, in the article "What New Yorkers

Do in Elevators.'' Longfellow says we observe these rules "to protect against the possibility of intimate contact.")

● **Long-Range Planning, The (F)law of.** The longer ahead you plan a special event, and the more special it is, the more likely it is to go wrong.
(David and Jayne Evelyn, Arlington, Va.)

● **Long's Notes** (A Handful). (1) Always store beer in a dark place . . . (6) Small change can often be found under seat cushions. (7) It's amazing how much "mature wisdom" resembles being too tired. (8) Secrecy is the beginning of tyranny. (11) An elephant: a mouse built to government specifications. (14) Waking a person unnecessarily should not be considered a capital crime. For a first offense, that is. (17) Rub her feet . . . (21) Never try to outstubborn a cat. (22) Natural laws have no pity. (23) You can go wrong by being too skeptical as readily as by being too trusting . . . (28) A skunk is better company than a person who prides himself on being "frank" . . .
(The main character of *Time Enough for Love: the Further Adventures of Lazurus Long* by Robert A. Heinlein, Putnam, 1973. Long was the oldest human being in the galaxy and his "Notes" were his collected observations and opinions. The "Notes" section of the book has become widely read, quoted, and imitated, especially among science fiction readers. Also see *Short's Quotations.*)

● **Lowrey's Law.** If it jams . . . force it. If it breaks, it needed replacing anyway.
(*U/Scientific Collections.*)

● **Lowrey's Law of Expertise.** Just when you get really good at something, you don't need to do it anymore.
(William P. Lowrey, Sidney, Ill. *HW.*)

● **Lubin's Law.** If another scientist thought your research was more important than his, he would drop what he is doing and do what you are doing.

> (From the law collection of William K. Wright, administrative officer, Naval Health Research Center, San Diego, Cal.)

● **Luce's Law.** No good deed goes unpunished.
(Clare Boothe Luce.)

● **Luten's Laws.** (1) When properly administered, vacations do not diminish productivity: for every week you're away and get nothing done, there's another when your boss is away and you get twice as much done. (2) It's not so hard to lift yourself by your bootstraps once you're off the ground!
(Daniel B. Luten, Berkeley, Cal. *AO.*)

● **Lynott's Law of the Reverse Learning Curve.** Wisdom and knowledge decrease in inverse proportion to age.

> (William J. Lynott, Abington, Pa. *AO.* The proof of this law, according to its author, comes when you engage in conversation with someone younger than yourself and find that person knows far more about any subject than you do.)

● **Maier's Law.** If facts do not conform to the theory, they must be disposed of.

> (N. R. F. Maier first announced this oft-quoted law in the March, 1960, issue of *American Psychologist.* At that time he also revealed that psychologists commonly obey the law by [a] failing to report the facts, or [b] giving them a new name.)

● **Malek's Law.** Any simple idea will be worded in the most complicated way.

> (*Sig Malek/S.T.L.*)

● **Mankiewicz's Laws.** *Law of Crowds:* The more enthusiastic, unruly, and large the candidate's crowds in the week before the election, the less likely he is to carry the area, cf. JFK in Ohio. *Environmental Law:* People who are excessively concerned about the environment invariably turn out to own a great deal of land. There are damn few unemployed and renters in the ecology movement. *Law of Provincial Hotels:* The amount of quaint, authentic, rustic charm varies inversely with the pounds per square inch of water pressure in the shower. High charm, low pressure. *School Law:* The higher the tuition, the fewer days they spend in school. *Second Law of Politics:* A politician will always tip off his true belief by stating the opposite at the beginning of the sentence. For maximum comprehension, do not start listening until the first clause is concluded. Begin instead at the word "but" which begins the second—or active—clause. This is the way to tell a liberal from a conservative—before they tell you. Thus: "I have always believed in a strong national defense, second to none, but . . . (a liberal, about to propose a $20 billion cut in the defense budget).

> (Frank Mankiewicz, president of National Public Radio and formerly press secretary to the 1972 McGovern campaign. The *Second Law of Politics* originally appeared in the *Washingtonian,* July, 1975. As for his *First Law of Politics,* he explains, "All of my laws of politics are 'second' on the theory that I will find a better one.")

● **Man's Law.** No matter what happens, there is always somebody who knew that it would.

> (*U/"LSP."*)

● **Marcus's Law.** The number of letters written to the editor is inversely proportional to the importance of the article.

> (Robert L. Marcus, Scarsdale, N.Y., in a letter published in *The New York Times* on April 7, 1968. It was in response to the "Faber's Law" article, which had occasioned a number of letters. *FD.*)

● **Marshall's Generalized Iceberg Theorem.** Seven-eighths of everything can't be seen.

> (*U/S.T.L.*)

● **Marshall's Universal Laws of Perpetual Perceptual Obfuscation.** (1) Nobody perceives anything with total accuracy. (2) No two people perceive the same thing identically. (3) Few perceive what difference it makes . . . or care.

> (Jack A. Marshall, Arlington, Mass. *AO.*)

● **Martin's Basic Laws of Instant Analysis.** (1) *The Law of Nondefinition*: If it is generally known what one is supposed to be doing, then someone will expect him to do it. (2) *The Law of Minimum Effort:* In any given group, the most will do the least and the least the most. (3) *The Law of Augmented Complexity:*

There is nothing so simple that it cannot be made difficult. (4) *The Law of Nonresponsibility:* In any given miscalculation, the fault will never be placed if more than one person is involved. (5) *The Law of Prior Menace:* People see what they have been conditioned to see; they refuse to see what they don't expect to see. (6) *The Law of Randomness:* Consistency is the product of small minds. (Paraphrasing Emerson on the "hobgoblin of little minds.") (7) *The Law of Instant Response:* A quick response is worth a thousand logical responses.

> (Merle P. Martin, Anchorage, Alaska, in his 1975 *Journal of Systems Management* article entitled "The Instant Analyst." Martin, a systems analyst, uses the article to reveal the secrets of that profession—or, at least, the instant version. One of the highlights of the piece is the collection of "instant phrases" Martin suggests to use when applying the *Law of Instant Response.* Among others, he sanctions the use of: "Don't stop to stomp ants when the elephants are stampeding," "That's only true because it's true," "That is utterly preposterous," and "Trust me!" RS.)

● **Martin's Definition of Drunkenness.** You're not drunk if you can lie on the floor without holding on.
> (Dean Martin. *S.T.L.*)

● **Martin's Laws, Principles, Effects, Plagiarisms, etc.** *The Martin-Berthelot Principle*: Of all possible committee reactions to any given agenda item, the reaction that will occur is the one which will liberate the greatest amount of hot air. *Martin's Laws of Academia:* (1) The faculty expands its activity to fit whatever space is available, so that more space is always required. (2) Faculty purchases of equipment and supplies always increase to match the funds available, so these funds are never adequate. (3) The professional quality of the faculty tends to be inversely proportional to the importance it attaches to space and equipment. *Martin's Law of Committees:* All committee reports conclude that "it is not prudent to change the policy [or procedure, or organization, or whatever] at this time." *Martin's Exclusion:* Committee reports dealing with wages, salaries, fringe benefits, facilities, computers, employee parking, libraries, coffee breaks, secretarial support, etc., always call for dramatic expenditure increases. *Martin's Law of Communication:* The inevitable result of improved and enlarged communication between different levels in a hierarchy is a vastly increased area of misunderstanding. *Martin's Laws of Hierarchical Function:* (1) All hierarchies contain administrators and managers, and they tend to appear at alternating levels in the hierarchy. (2) Administration maintains the status quo. (3) Management directs and controls change. *Martin's Minimax Maxim:* Everyone knows that the name of the game is to let the other guy have all of the little tats and to keep all of the big tits for yourself. *Martin's Plagiarism of H. L. Mencken:* Those who can—do. Those who cannot—teach. Those who cannot teach become deans.

(Thomas L. Martin, Jr., from *Malice in Blunderland,* McGraw-Hill, 1971.)

● **Matsch's Maxim.** A fool in high station is like a man on the top of a high mountain: everything appears small to him and he appears small to everybody.

(Professor Leader W. Matsch.)

● **May's Mordant Maxim.** A university is a place where men of principle outnumber men of honor.

(Historian Ernest May. *AO.*)

● **McCarthy's Law of Intelligence.** Being in politics is like being a football coach. You have to be smart enough to understand the game and dumb enough to think it's important.

(Eugene McCarthy. *MBC's Laws of Politics.*)

● **McClaughry's Iron Law of Zoning.** When it's not needed, zoning works fine; when it is essential, it always breaks down.

> (John McClaughry, Concord, Vt. The law was born when McClaughry was studying the effects of zoning in the course of the 1974 debate on the Vermont Land Use Plan. As he explains, "A speaker had urged state zoning to 'keep Vermont from turning into Los Angeles.' When it was pointed out that Los Angeles had had zoning in force since 1923, McClaughry's Iron Law rapidly emerged. I was at the time chairman of the Planning Commission of Kirby, Vermont, population 230, which had zoning but absolutely no need for it since there was no development pressure.")

● **McClaughry's Law of Public Policy.** Politicians who vote huge expenditures to alleviate problems get reelected; those who propose structural changes to prevent problems get early retirement.

> (John McClaughry.)

● **McClaughry's Second Law.** Liberals, but not conservatives, can get attention and acclaim for denouncing liberal policies that failed; and liberals will inevitably capture the ensuing agenda for "reform."

> (McClaughry again.)

● **McGovern's Law.** The longer the title, the less important the job.

> (Robert Shrum, who was one of George McGovern's speechwriters, recalled this law for *AO*. McGovern discovered the law in 1960, when President Kennedy tried to persuade him that being director of the Food for Peace Program was a more influential job than secretary of agriculture.)

● **McGurk's Law.** Any improbable event which would create maximum confusion if it did occur, will occur.

> (H. S. Kindler, from *Organizing the Technical Conference,* Reinhold Publishing Co., 1960. McGurk, no doubt, is Murphy's first cousin.)

● **McKenna's Law.** When you are right be logical, when you are wrong be-fuddle.

> (Gerard E. McKenna, president, Gerard E. McKenna & Associates, Middle Grove, N.Y.)

● **McLandress's Theorems of Business Confidence.** (1) The confidence of the business executive in a President is inversely related to the state of business. (2) Government action and inaction both gravely impair business confidence. (3) Reassurance of business by a President has an unfavorable effect on confidence. (4) Unkind words do not enhance business confidence. (5) That politics has a bearing on business confidence is unproven.

> (Mark Epernay, in *The McLandress Dimension,* Houghton Mifflin, 1962. By way of explanation, if one thinks of Herbert Hoover the theorems come into better focus. For example, no modern president enjoyed the level of business confidence that Hoover did [Theorem (1)], and the only time that he did not enjoy that confidence was in 1930 and 1931, after he tried to reassure them [Theorem (3)].
>
> Epernay's book reveals and discusses many other theories first offered by the legendary but mythical Dr. Herschel McLandress. For instance the "Dimension" mentioned in the title is a measure of human behavior determined by finding "the arithmetic mean or average of the intervals of time during which a subject's thoughts remained centered on some substantive phenomenon other than his own personality." Art Buchwald, for in-

stance, has a high score of two hours, Norman Cousins, three minutes, and Richard Nixon, one of the lowest, at three seconds.

In case you have not heard of Epernay, the author of this book, some light was shed on the matter when a Christmas card was found tucked in a used edition of the book:

Dec 16.

Dear ———,

We hope that you both enjoy this "spoof," we have. There is a strong rumor around Cambridge that "Mark Epernay" is a pen name for John Kenneth Galbraith. That seems plausible. This is not what I hoped to be able to send.)

● **McLaughlin's Law.** The length of any meeting is inversely proportional to the length of the agenda for that meeting.
(G. Robert McLaughlin, John Hancock Mutual Life Insurance Co., Boston. *AO.*)

● **McNaughton's Rule.** Any argument worth making within the bureaucracy must be capable of being expressed in a single declarative sentence that is obviously true once stated.
(The late John McNaughton, a government national security expert. It was sent to *AO* by Harvard political scientist Graham Allison.)

● **Meditz Subway Phenomenon.** No matter which train you are waiting for, the wrong one comes first.
(J. R. Meditz, New York City.)

● **Melcher's Law.** In a bureaucracy every routing slip will expand until it contains the maximum number of names that can be typed in a single vertical column, namely, twenty-seven.
(Daniel Melcher. *JW.*)

● **Mencken's Law.** Whenever A annoys or injures B on the pretense of saving or improving X, A is a scoundrel.

(H. L. Mencken. Joe Goulden, writer and student of Mencken, reports that this appeared in Mencken's *Newspaper Days* as "Mencken's Law," but that it was derived from "the Law of the Forgotten Man," found in "The Absurd Effort to Make the World Over," *The Forum,* XVII, 1894, by the Social Darwinist William Graham Sumner, to wit, "When A and B join to make a law to help X, their law always proposes to decide what C shall do for X, and C is the Forgotten Man." Mencken acknowledged his debt to Sumner, but still called his version "Mencken's Law." Goulden adds that Mencken had another version that concludes, ". . . A is a scoundrel, and should be briskly clubbed." Still another variation appeared in a recent column by James J. Kilpatrick where it was termed "Mencken's Working Hypothesis of the Legislative Process" and stated as: "Whenever A attempts by law to impose his moral standards on B, A is most likely a scoundrel.")

● **Mencken's Meta-law.** For every human problem, there is a neat, plain solution—and it is always wrong.

(H. L. Mencken. *AO.*)

● **Merrill's First Corollary.** There are no winners in life; only survivors.

(*U/S.T.L.*)

● **Meskimen's Laws of Bureaucracies.** (1) When they want it bad (in a rush), they get it bad. (2) There's never time to do it right but always time to do it over.

(John K. Meskimen, Falls Church, Va. *AO.*)

● **Mesmerisms of Review and Control, The Twelve.** (1) First, in order to keep engineers and scientists cognizant of the importance of progress, load them down with forms, multiple reports, and frequent meetings. (2) Remember, the more engineering projects there are, the more products there will be. (3) . . . the less management demands of engineers and scientists, the greater their productivity. (4) Computer-based management information systems will cure most review and control problems. (5) The greater the number of professionals (advanced degrees preferred) assigned to a project, the greater the progress. (6) . . . cost consciousness and sophisticated design are basically incompatible. (7) If enough reports are prepared and technical reviews are held, negative information will always filter its way to senior management. (8) . . . high salaries equals happiness equals project progress. (9) The expenditure of funds is critical—engineers and scientists should not be permitted to authorize any purchase. (10) Scientists and engineers set high performance standards for themselves; therefore, performance appraisal and career planning are perfunctory. (11) Since blue-sky projects are targeted for major breakthroughs, they are relatively immune from effective planning and control. (12) Vastly improved review and control will result by promoting the most productive engineers and scientists to management positions.

(Richard F. Moore, the National Cash Register Co., Dayton, Ohio. *JIR*, January, 1973.)

● **Metz's Rules of Golf for Good Players** (Whose Scores Would Reflect Their True Ability If Only They Got an Even Break Once in Awhile) (1) On beginning play, as many balls as may be required to obtain a satisfactory result may be played from the first tee. Everyone recognizes a good player needs to "loosen up" but does not not have time for the practice tee. (2) A ball sliced or hooked into the rough shall be lifted and placed in the fairway at a point equal to the distance it carried or rolled in the rough. Such veering right or left frequently results from friction between the face of the club and the cover of the ball, and the player should not be penalized for erratic behavior of the ball resulting from such uncontrollable mechanical phenomena. (3) A ball hitting a tree shall be deemed not to have hit the tree. Hitting a tree is simply bad luck and has no place in a scientific game. The player should estimate the distance the ball would have traveled if it had not hit the tree and play the ball from there, preferably from atop a nice firm tuft of grass. (4) There shall be no such thing as a lost ball. The missing ball is on or near the course somewhere and eventually will be found and pocketed by someone else. It thus becomes a stolen ball, and the player should not compound the felony by charging himself with a penalty stroke. (5) When played from a sand trap, a ball which does not clear the trap on being struck maybe hit again on the roll without counting an extra stroke. In no case will more than two strokes be counted in playing from a trap, since it is only reasonable to assume that if the player had time to concentrate on his shot, instead of hurrying it so as not to delay his playing partners, he would be out in two. (6) If a putt passes over the hole without dropping, it is deemed to have dropped. The law of gravity holds that any object attempting to maintain a position in the atmosphere without something to support it must drop. The law of gravity supercedes the law of golf. (7) Same thing goes for a ball that stops at the brink of the hole and hangs there, defying gravity. You cannot defy the law. (8) Same thing goes for a ball that rims the cup. A ball should not go sideways. This violates the laws of physics. (9) A putt that stops close enough to the cup to inspiresuchcommentsas"you could   blow   it   in"   may   be   blown   in. This rule does not apply if the ball is more than three inches from the hole, because no one wants to make a travesty of the game.

(Donald A. Metz, Devon, Pa.)

● **Michehl's Theorem.** Less is more.
  (*U/S.T.L.* See *Pastore's Comment on Michehl's Theorem.*)

● **Miles's Law.** Where you stand depends on where you sit.

(Rufus Miles, former career administrator at the Department of Health, Education and Welfare, to express the fact that your opinion depends on your job. Appeared in *AO*'s column and elsewhere. Has become one of Robert Machol's *POR.*)

● **Miller's Law. [J.]** Unless you put your money to work for you—you work for your money.

(Joe Miller. Fort Myers, Fla.)

● **Miller's Law.[M.]** The yoo-hoo you yoo-hoo into the forest is the yoo-hoo you get back.

(Merle Miller. *RS.*)

● **Miller's Law.[N.]** The corruption in a country is in inverse proportion to its state of development.

(Nathan Miller, Chevy Chase, Md. *AO.*)

● **Miller's Law.[?]** You can't tell how deep a puddle is until you step into it.

(*U/S.T.L.*)

● **Mills's Law of Transportation Logistics.** The distance to the gate from which your flight departs is inversely proportionate to the time remaining before the scheduled departure of the flight.

(Edward S. Mills, National Association of Blue Shield Plans, *AO.*)

● **Money, The Natural Law of.** Anything left over today will be needed tomorrow to pay an unexpected bill.

(Betty Canary, in her *Surviving as a Woman,* Henry Regnery Publishing, 1976.)

● **Montagu's Maxim.** The idea is to die young as late as possible.

(Anthropologist Ashley Montagu. *MLS.*)

● **Morley's Conclusion.** No man is lonely while eating spaghetti.

(Robert Morley.)

● **Mosher's Law.** It's better to retire too soon than too late.

(Representative Charles A. Mosher [R-Ohio], on retiring at seventy after sixteen years in Congress. *JW.*)

● **Mother Sigafoos's Observation.** A man should be greater than some of his parts.

(Uttered by a character of the same name in Peter De Vries's *I Hear America Swinging. RS.*)

● **Moynihan's Law.** If the newspapers of a country are filled with good news, the jails will be filled with good people.

(Senator Daniel P. Moynihan. *JW.*)

● **Mudgeeraba Creek Emu-Riding and Boomerang-Throwing Association, Rule of the.** Decisions of the judges will be final unless shouted down by a really overwhelming majority of the crowd present. Abusive and obscene language may not be used by contestants when addressing members of the judging panel, or, conversely, by members of the judging panel when addressing contestants (unless struck by a boomerang).

(From Benjamin Ruhe's *Many Happy Returns: The Art and Sport of Boomeranging,* Viking, 1977. The rule was created to underscore the informality and casualness of boomerang competition.)

● **Munnecke's Law.** If you don't say it, they can't repeat it.

(Wilbur C. Munnecke, quoted in a letter to Ann Landers from one ''Benton Harbor Ben.'')

● **Murchison's Law of Money.** Money is like manure. If you spread it around, it does a lot of good. But if you pile it up in one place, it stinks like hell.

(Clint Murchison, Jr., Texas financier, repeating his father's advice. *Time,* June 16, 1971.)

Special Section 4

Murphy's Law(s).

The importance of *Murphy's Law(s)* in contemporary American society is such that:

o   In late 1977, when things were not going particularly well at the White House, a set of *Murphy's Laws* was sent to all of the President's aides. According to the *Washingtonian,* which reported it, all the notes were signed J.C.

o   Serious business and scientific periodicals discuss important issues in terms of Murphy (''A Partial Repeal of Murphy's Law'' was a recent *Business Week* article title), and he has become the darling of newspaper columnists, who apply his findings to help explain an altogether imperfect world.

Because of the once and future importance of *Murphy's Law(s),* the subject is worthy of more than passing attention. Therefore, let us examine the Murphy phenomenon by addressing some basic questions.

EXACTLY WHAT ARE MURPHY'S LAWS AND IN WHAT ORDER SHOULD
THEY BE LISTED?

Having examined dozens of printed, typewritten, and
Xeroxed listings of *Murphy's Laws,* we can report that no two are
exactly alike. Even those which at first appear to have been
copied by hand from one another tend to show discrepancies in
order, phrasing, or both. (This is, of course, a direct confirmation
of Murphian theory.) If there is any semblance of consistency, it
is with the first and ninth laws, which are the same on a number
of lists but not all. This confusion is so pervasive and in the spirit
of Murphy that it seems to have mystic overtones—one expects
that if you Xeroxed enough copies of a given list, eventually one
would emerge with a glitch in it.

Lacking an "official" listing, here is the author's collection

Murphy's Laws.

① If anything can go wrong, it will.

② Nothing is ever as simple as it seems.

③ Everything takes longer than you expect.

④ If there is a possibility of several things going wrong,
the one that will go wrong first will be the one that will do the
most damage.

⑤ Left to themselves, all things go from bad to worse.

⑥ If you play with something long enough, you will
surely break it.

⑦ If everything seems to be going well, you have obviously overlooked something.

⑧ If you see that there are four possible ways in which
a procedure can go wrong, and circumvent these, then a fifth
way, unprepared for, will promptly develop.

⑨ Nature always sides with the hidden flaw.

⑩ Mother Nature is a bitch.

⑪ It is impossible to make anything foolproof, because
fools are so ingenious.

⑫ If a great deal of time has been expended seeking the

answer to a problem with the only result being failure, the answer will be immediately obvious to the first unqualified person.

IS THAT ALL? IT SEEMS AS IF I RECALL OTHERS.

Using the basic laws for inspiration, all sorts of corollaries, amendments, and specialized laws follow. A sampling:

> *Murphy's Law of Thermodynamics.* Things get worse under pressure. (*S.T.L.*)

Royster's Refinement of Murphy's Law. When things go wrong somewhere, they are apt to go wrong everywhere. (Vermont Royster, in *The Wall Street Journal.*)

Murphy's Law of Priorities. Whatever you want to do, you have to do something else first. (Art Kosatka, a staff assistant to Rep. John M. Murphy [!] of New York, quoted in Bill Gold's column in *The Washington Post,* March 7, 1978.)

Murphy's Law of the Open Road. When there is a very long road upon which there is a one-way bridge placed at random and there are two cars only on that road, it follows that: (1) the two cars are going in opposite directions and (2) they will always meet at the bridge. (B. D. Firstbrook, Westmount, Quebec. *AO.*)

Barton's Amendment to Murphy's Law. . . . and even if it can't, it might. (A. J. Barton, The National Science Foundation.)

Murphy's Laws of College Publishing. (1) Availability of manuscripts in a given subject area is inversely proportional to the need for books in that area. (2) A manuscript for a market in which no textbooks currently exist will be followed two weeks after contracting by an announcement of an identical book by your closest competitor. (*Computer Science News,* December, 1972.)

Murphy's Law of Copiers. The legibility of a copy is inversely proportional to its importance. (Letter to *AO* from G. H. Brandenburger, Butte, Mont., containing illegible photocopy of *Murphy's Laws.*)

Crowell's Law. Murphy's Law never fail∾ (Walter J. Crowell, Bethpage, N.Y.)

Warren's Law. The likelihood of anything happening is in direct proportion to the amount of trouble it will cause if it does happen. (Sam W. Warren, editor and publisher, *The Northside Sun,* Jackson, Miss.)

The Yulish Additions. ■Persons disagreeing with your facts are always emotional and employ faulty reasoning. ■ Enough research will tend to confirm your conclusions. ■ The more urgent the need for decision, the less apparent becomes the identity of the decision-maker. ■The more complex the idea or technology, the more simpleminded is the opposition. ■Each profession talks to itself in its own unique language. Apparently there is no Rosetta Stone. (From a collection of "Murphy's Fundamental Laws" published by Charles Yulish Associates, Inc., of New York, 1975.)

API Corollary. If things can go wrong, they will—and when they do, blame it on the oil industry. (Law created by an American Petroleum Institute spokesman when the oil industry got blamed for creating snafus associated with delegates checking in for the National Women's Conference in Houston. The API claimed it checked out two days earlier.)

Murphy's Laws of Analysis. (1) In any collection of data, the figures that are obviously correct will contain errors. (2) It is customary for a decimal to be misplaced. (3) An error that can creep into a calculation, will. Also, it will always be in the direction that will cause the most damage to the calculation. (Three of twenty-nine laws that appear in G. C. Beakly's *Introduction to Engineering Design and Graphics,* Macmillan, 1975.)

Murphy's Law and Correlative Collegiate Cabalae. (1) During an exam, the pocket calculator battery will fail. (2) If only one parking space is available it will have a blue curb.* (3) Exams will always contain questions not discussed in class.

(4) All students who obtain a B will feel cheated out of an A. (5) Campus sidewalks never exist as the straightest line between two points. (6) When a pencil point breaks, the nearest sharpener is exactly 1,000 feet away. (7) At five minutes before the hour, a student will ask a question requiring a ten minute answer. (8) If a course requires a prerequisite, a student will not have had it. (9) The office space and salaries of college administrators are in inverse proportion to those of the instructors. (10) Slightly deaf students will have instructors who mumble. (11) The next class is always three buildings away on a rainy day. (12) He who can will. He who can't, will teach. (13) When a student actually does a homework problem, the instructor will not ask for it. (14) All math classes begin at 8 A.M.; also, movies on Federal Government. (15) Students who obtain an A for a course will claim that the instructor is a great teacher. (16) If an instructor says, "It is obvious," it won't be. (17) When wool sweaters are worn, classroom temperatures are 95 degrees Fahrenheit. (18) If a student has to study, he will claim that the course is unfair. (19) Ambidextrous instructors will erase with one hand while writing with the other. (20) An A is easily obtained if a student calls the instructor "Professor." (21) When slides are shown in a darkened room, the instructor will require students to take notes. (22) When . . . then . . . (You fill in the blanks.) (M. M. "Johnny" Johnston, Ormond Beach, Fla.)

WHO WAS MURPHY ANYHOW?

Good question. The Murphy Center devoted considerable time and expense to this question. Various approaches were taken, including, for instance, contacting a fair sampling of Murphys, such as Patrick V. Murphy, former New York City police commissioner and present director of the Police Foundation in Washington. He, along with the other Murphys contacted, had

---

*Not prohibitions against X-rated movies, but curbs painted blue and reserved for "STAFF."

no idea who the original lawmaker was. Nor, for that matter, were any meaningful clues unearthed through a study of famous Murphys, including possibilities as promising as William Lawrence Murphy (1876–1959), the inventor and man who gave his name to the fabled folding bed.

However, some interesting theories and clues emerged from the quest, including the following:

The Kilroy Theory. Like those kingpins of World War II folklore, Kilroy and Murgatroyd the Kluge Maker, one body of thought concludes that somewhere along the line there *may or may not* have been a real Murphy, but that this is beside the point.* The point is that Murphy has come to represent a spirit and presence that transcends one human being. If one accepts this, then virtually any accounting works, whether it be the Edsel Murphy of the engineering magazines or the Finn Cool O'Murphy who allegedly recorded his rules on a runic scroll in the first century A.D.

The Knoll Shul Theory. To quote, "I'm afraid I can only offer you a conjecture about the original Murphy. Thirty years ago, when I lived in the Crown Heights section of Brooklyn, the neighborhood synagogue was widely known (at least among the young hoodlums with whom I consorted) as Murphy's Shul. I have no idea who that Murphy was, or how he happened to lend his name to an orthodox synagogue, but I have always assumed—since first I encountered Murphy's Law—that it must be the same Murphy. Somehow it figures."†

---

*Kilroy was a household name during the war, and the line "Kilroy was here" appeared everywhere from the hulls of battleships to the tattooed chests of sailors. There were many theories as to who he was, but none stuck. He was represented by this: Murgatroyd was a young man who finagled himself a nice billet on a ship as a "Kluge maker." He got away without doing anything for a long time, but finally, on the occasion of an admiral's visit, he was told to make a Kluge to impress the VIP. He worked all night, and just as the admiral arrived he ran up on deck, started to present it, tripped, and it fell overboard. As it sank it went, "Kluge."
†Erwin Knoll, editor of *The Progressive,* in a letter to the author.

The Great Teacher Theory. To quote, "One day a teacher named Murphy wanted to demonstrate the laws of probability to his math class. He had thirty of his students spread peanut butter on slices of bread, then toss the bread into the air to see if half would fall on the dry side and half on the buttered side. As it turned out, twenty-nine of the slices landed peanut-butter side on the floor, while the thirtieth stuck to the ceiling."*

The Yulish Blur Hypothesis. An exhaustive search by a New York consulting firm concluded that Murphy (a) had no first name, (b) could not hold a job, (c) never prepared a résumé. Little else was known about him.†

While all of these theories are worth considering, the real story may have recently come to light without great fanfare. On January 13, 1977, Jack Smith, a columnist for the *Los Angeles Times,* revealed that he had gotten a letter from George E. Nichols of the Jet Propulsion Laboratory in Pasadena stating that he not only knew the origin of the law but the true identity of Murphy. According to the Nichols letter, "The event [that led to the naming of the law] occurred in 1949 at Edwards Air Force Base . . . during Air Force Project MX981 . . . The law [was named after] Capt. Ed Murphy, a development engineer from Wright Field [Ohio] Aircraft Lab. Frustration with a strap transducer that was malfunctioning due to an error in wiring the strain gauge bridges caused him to remark [of the technician who had wired the bridges at the lab], 'If there is any way to do it wrong, he will.' I assigned the name Murphy's Law to that statement and the associated variations."

Nichols went on to point out that the law was off and running after it was alluded to in a press conference a few weeks later. A similar letter appeared in late 1977 in Arthur Bloch's book *Murphy's Law.* Further detail on Project MX981 and Murphy

---

*Letter to William and Mary Morris from Gary M. Klauber of Silver Spring, Md. It appears in their *Dictionary of Word and Phrase Origins,* Vol. III, Harper & Row, 1971. The Morrises solicited theories on Murphy through their newspaper column.
†Press release from the firm of Charles Yulish Associates in New York.

were supplied to the author when he contacted Robert J. Smith, Chief of the History Office at Wright-Patterson Air Force Base. Smith was unable to confirm the actual naming but was able to supply information on Murphy—graduated from West Point in 1940, was a pilot as well as an engineer, worked on a number of research projects and would be sixty years old today. The mysterious-sounding MX981 was intended "to study the factors in human tolerance to high decelerative forces of short duration in order to determine criteria for design of aircraft and protective equipment." As Smith adds, "If this project gave birth to Murphy's Law, hopefully, the consequences were minor."

DO YOU BELIEVE THIS?

Yes, as a matter of fact, but there is still much to be said for the Kilroy theory, which says that if Ed Murphy had not discovered *Murphy's Law,* someone else would have. Then again, one of the many corollaries to *Murphy's Law* states that on the rare occasion on which something is successful, the wrong person gets the credit.

ARE THERE OTHER NAMES FOR MURPHY'S LAW?

Certainly. Other names include "Thermodamnics," "Snafu Theory," and "Klugemanship." One should also be aware of the name D. L. Klipstein, who has worked out several score corollaries for engineers. Also see the entries in this book for Finagle, O'Toole, and Sod.

● **Murstein's Law.** The amount of research devoted to a topic in human behavior is inversely proportional to its importance and interest.

(Bernard I. Murstein. *JW.*)

● **Nader's Law.** The speed of exit of a civil servant is directly proportional to the quality of his service.

(Ralph Nader, from *The Spoiled System,* a study of the Civil Service Commission by a Nader task force. *AO.*)

● **NASA Truisms.** (1) Research is reading two books that have never been read in order to write a third that will never be read. (2) A consultant is an ordinary person a long way from home. (3) Statistics are a highly logical and precise method for saying a half-truth inaccurately.

(From a file in the NASA archives on "Humor and Satire.")

● **Nations, Law of.** In an underdeveloped country, don't drink the water; in a developed country, don't breathe the air.

(An item that originally appeared in *Changing Times* and was quoted in the *Reader's Digest* of June, 1976.)

● **Navy Law.** If you can keep your head when all about you others are losing theirs, maybe you just don't understand the situation.

(Traditional sign that has been showing up on ships and offices of the U.S. Navy for years. It is found elsewhere, too, but is primarily associated with the Navy.)

● **Nessen's Law.** Secret sources are more credible.
(Ron Nessen, President Ford's press secretary, who was quoted in *Newsweek,* January 31, 1977: "Some statements you make in public . . . are reported as . . . an unnamed source . . . Nobody believes the official spokes-

man . . . but everybody trusts an unidentified source."
From the latest version of Martin Krakowski's paper "An-
thropogenic Ills.")

● **Newton's Little-Known Seventh Law.** A bird in the
hand is safer than two overhead.
(*U/S.T.L.*)

● **Nienberg's Law.** Progress is made on alternate Fridays.
(*U/S.T.L.*)

● **Nies's Law.** The effort expended by the bureaucracy in
defending any error is in direct proportion to the size of the error.
(John Nies, Washington patent lawyer and *AO*'s neighbor.)

● **Ninety-Nine Rule of Project Schedules.** The first 90
percent of the task takes 90 percent of the time, the last 10
percent takes the other 90 percent.
(*Co.*)

● **Nixon's Principle.** If two wrongs don't make a right, try
three.
(Lawrence J. Peter. *MLS.*)

● **Nobel Effect.** There is no proposition, no matter how
foolish, for which a dozen Nobel signatures cannot be collected.
Furthermore, any such petition is guaranteed page-one treatment
in *The New York Times.*
(Daniel S. Greenberg, from his *Science and Government
Report,* December, 1976. *RS.*)

● **Noble's Law of Political Imagery.** All other things being
equal, a bald man cannot be elected President of the United
States. *Corollary:* Given a choice between two bald political

candidates, the American people will vote for the less bald of the two.

> (Bald writer Vic Gold in his *Washingtonian* article "Can a Bald Man Be Elected President?" Noble is G. Vance Noble, author of *The Hirsute Tradition in American Politics,* widely believed to be one of Gold's alter egos.)

● **Nofziger's Law of Details.** The American people aren't interested in details.

> (Lyn Nofziger of Ronald Reagan's campaign staff, on such matters as Senator Barry Goldwater giving analyses of such things as the comparative defense capabilities of a General Dynamics prototype aircraft *vs.* Boeing's model. From Vic Gold's *P.R. as in President.* See *Spencer's* [*Contradictory*] *Corollary.*)

● **North Carolina Equine Paradox.** VYARZERZOMANIMOR ORSEZASSEZANZERAREORSES?

> (Sign seen on the walls of print shops in North Carolina, reported to *AO* by Carl Thompson of Hill and Knowlton.)

● **No. 3 Pencil Principle.** Make it sufficiently difficult for people to do something, and most people will stop doing it. *Corollary:* If no one uses something, it isn't needed.

> (Another important discovery from psychologist Robert Sommer. He discovered the principle when he worked for a government agency and his office manager decided to ban soft, comfortable-to-use No. 2 pencils and order No. 3s, which are scratchy and write light. Pencil consumption in the office went down and the office manager was able to prove that No. 3s "last longer." Sommer revealed his finding in the December, 1973, issue of *Worm Runner's Digest.*)

● **Nyquist's Theory of Equilibrium.** Equality is not when a female Einstein gets promoted to assistant professor; equality is when a female schlemiel moves ahead as fast as a male schlemiel.

(Ewald Nyquist. *RS.*)

● **Oaks's Unruly Laws for Lawmakers.** (1) Law expands in proportion to the resources available for its enforcement. (2) Bad law is more likely to be supplemented than repealed. (3) Social legislation cannot repeal physical laws.

> (Dallin B. Oaks, president of Brigham Young University and president of the American Association of Presidents of Independent Colleges and Universities. The laws appeared in an essay, "Unruly Laws for Lawmakers," by Oaks which appeared in *The Congressional Record* for March 17, 1978. Oaks, who makes no effort to hide his bias against lawmaking as the solution to all problems, also uses the essay to list three hypotheses which have come out of his research on the first law: [1] The public is easily fooled by government claims of economizing. [2] An uninformed lawmaker is more likely to produce a complicated law than a simple one. [3] Bad or complicated law tends to drive out good judgment.)

● **O'Brien's First Law of Politics.** The more campaigning, the better.

> (Larry O'Brien, who stated it when he ran John F. Kennedy's campaign in 1960. *FL.*)

● **O'Brien's Law.** If an editor can reject your paper, he will. *Corollary:* If you submit the paper to a second editor, his journal invariably demands an entirely different reference system.

> (Maeve O'Connor of *The British-Medical Journal* on discovering at least 2,632 possible ways of setting out references in scientific articles. Named for O'Brien, who is first cousin to Murphy.)

● **O'Brien's Principle (aka The $357.63 Theory).** Auditors always reject any newsman's expense account with a bottom line divisible by 5 or 10.

(Named for Emmet N. O'Brien and passed along to *AO* by Jake Underhill of the New York Life Insurance Co. Underhill worked for O'Brien, as did Germond of *Germond's Law. O'Brien's, Germond's, and Weaver's laws* form a set that came of research conducted around Albany, New York, in the early 1950s. Underhill terms the experience the "Albany Reportorial School of Economics." See also *O'Doyle's Corollary.*)

● **O'Brien's Rule.** Nothing is ever done for the right reasons.

(*U/"LSP."*)

● **Occam's Electric Razor.** The most difficult light bulb to replace burns out first and most frequently.

(Writer Joe Anderson.)

● **Occam's Razor.** Entities ought not to be multiplied except from necessity.

(William of Occam, a fourteenth-century scholar, whose call to keep things simple has many modern incarnations, including the following:

• "The explanation requiring the fewest assumptions is the most likely to be correct." *JW.*
• "Whenever two hypotheses cover the facts, use the simpler of the two." *Forbes.*
• "Cut the crap." *Esquire.*)

● **O'Doyle's Corollary.** No matter how many reporters share a cab, and no matter who pays, each puts the full fare on his own expense account.

(Edward P. O'Doyle of Melrose Park, Ill., to *AO.* This is

a corollary to *Weaver's Law.* It is sometimes referred to as *Doyle's Corollary.*)

● **Oeser's Law.** There is a tendency for the person in the most powerful position in an organization to spend all his time serving on committees and signing letters.
(*U/Co.*)

● **Office Holders, First Law of.** Get reelected.
(*U/Co.*)

● **Old Childrens' Law.** If it tastes good, you can't have it. If it tastes awful, you'd better clean your plate.
("The Wizard," FM 101, Youngstown, Ohio.)

● **O'Neill's Law of Time Saturation.** The news of the day, no matter how trivial or unimportant, always takes up more time than a married man has. *Corollary:* News stories expand and time contracts, meeting inexorably each day precisely twenty minutes after a man is supposed to be home for dinner.
(Named for Ray O'Neill, who was national affairs editor of *The New York Times.* It was explained in detail in an April 22, 1956, column by James Reston entitled "A Note to Miss Truman." Reston quotes Clifton Daniel as having told reporters that his hours at the *Times* were from 9:30 to 5:30. Countered Reston, "It is not a reporter's working hours that count, but the hours he works." He added, "These are regulated by the news and the news is regulated by a very simple mathematical rule." The rule, of course: *O'Neill's Law.*)

● **Oppenheimer's Observation.** The optimist thinks this is the best of all possible worlds, and the pessimist knows it.
(J. Robert Oppenheimer, in *The Bulletin of the Atomic Scientists,* February, 1951. *RS.*)

● **Optimum Optimorum Principle.** There comes a time when one must stop suggesting and evaluating new solutions, and get on with the job of analyzing and finally implementing one pretty good solution.

(Robert Machol, in his *POR* series. To illustrate the point of this principle, he points out that some years ago an ABM expert said that for optimal protection the entire continental United States could be covered with a mile-thick layer of peanut butter—it would be impenetrable and have the support of the peanut industry. Says Machol, ''The point of this anecdote is that the solutions which may be suggested for a problem are inexhaustible.'')

● **Orben's Packaging Discovery.** For the first time in history, one bag of groceries produces two bags of trash.

(Humorist Robert Orben. See also his *Travel, First Law of.*)

● **Orwell's Bridge Law.** All bridge hands are equally likely, but some are more equally likely than others.

(After George Orwell by Alan Truscott, in his *New York Times* bridge column for December 23, 1974.)

● **Osborn's Law.** Variables won't, constants aren't.
(Don Osborn, associate director, State of Arizona Solar Energy Commission. *S.T.L.*)

● **OSHA's Discovery.** Wet manure is slippery.
(The Occupational Health and Safety Administration [OSHA], in a finding reported in *The Washington Post* of June 18, 1976. This replaces an earlier U.S. Navy finding: ''Classified material is considered lost when it cannot be found.'')

● **O'Toole's Commentary on Murphy's Law.** Murphy was an optimist.

(Perhaps the most quoted of all the laws and corollaries to come in as a result of the *AO* columns, yet the name of the author or discoverer of the commentary is illegible. This unreadable signature could quickly lead to a situation in which O'Toole could raise as many questions as Murphy. Rumor has it that O'Toole was [a] a policeman in Newark during the riots and [b] a White House clerk during the last months of the Nixon Administration.)

●   **Otten's Law of Testimony.** When a person says that in the interest of saving time, he will summarize his prepared statement, he will talk only three times as long as if he had read the statement in the first place.

●   **Otten's Law of Typesetting.** Typesetters always correct intentional errors, but fail to correct unintentional ones.
    (Both Alan Otten originals.)

●   **Ozian Option.** I can't give you brains, but I can give you a diploma.
    (The Wizard of Oz to the Scarecrow. *RS.*)

● **Paige's Six Rules for Life (Guaranteed to Bring Anyone to a Happy Old Age).** (1) Avoid fried foods which angry up the blood. (2) If your stomach disputes you, pacify it with cool thoughts. (3) Keep the juices flowing by jangling around gently as you move. (4) Go very lightly on the vices, such as carrying on in society, as the social ramble ain't restful. (5) Avoid running at all times. (6) Don't look back, something might be gaining on you.

    (Baseball immortal Satchel Paige. *Co.*)

● **Panic Instruction for Industrial Engineers.** When you don't know what to do, walk fast and look worried.

    (Bob Duckles, now with the Department of Commerce, picked this up from a plant engineer who had learned it at the Ford Motor Company.)

● **Paradox of Selective Equality.** All things being equal, all things are never equal.

    (Marshall L. Smith.)

● **Pardee's Law.** There is an inverse relationship between the uniqueness of an observation and the number of investigators who report it simultaneously.

    (A. B. Pardee, in his 1962 *American Scientist* article "pU, a New Quantity in Biochemistry." *FD.*)

● **Pardo's Postulates.** (1) Anything good is either illegal, immoral, or fattening. (2) The three faithful things in life are money, a dog, and an old woman. (3) Don't care if you're rich

or not, as long as you can live comfortably and have everything you want.
   (*U/S.T.L.*)

● **Pareto's Law. (The 20/80 Law.)** 20 percent of the customers account for 80 percent of the turnover, 20 percent of the components account for 80 percent of the cost, and so forth.
   (After Vilfredo Pareto, the Italian economist [1848–1923]. *S.T.L.*)

Special Section 5

The Parkinson Contribution.
   On November 19, 1955, an unsigned article appeared in *The Economist* simply entitled, "Parkinson's Law." As it was put in the first sentences:

> It is a commonplace observation that work expands so as to fill the time available for its completion. Thus, an elderly lady of leisure can spend the entire day in writing and dispatching a postcard to her niece at Bognor Regis. An hour will be spent in finding the postcard, another in hunting for spectacles, half an hour in search for the address . . .

The article went on to point out that the law came with two axiomatic additions that helped relate it to organizations:
   Factor I—An official wants to multiply subordinates not rivals; and

Factor 2—Officials make work for each other.

In proving his contentions, the mysterious Parkinson showed, for example, that between 1914 and 1928 the number of ships in the Royal Navy went down by 67.74 percent, while the number of dockyard officials and clerks went up by 40.28 percent and Admiralty officials by a stunning 78.45 percent.

At first many thought that Parkinson was a fanciful name created by the magazine's editors. He was, in fact, C. Northcote Parkinson, a little-known history professor at the University of Malaya. Within a few years Parkinson became an international celebrity. His book was a best seller on both sides of the Atlantic and found its way into fourteen languages. He became an immensely popular lecturer, visiting professor, and essayist who occasionally added another law to his collection. As *Dun's Review* summed it up in a 1975 article on him, ". . . Parkinson has made a lucrative twenty-seven year career out of [a few] seemingly simple words."

Parkinson, who now lives on the island of Guernsey, has been asked many times why he thinks his law has had such an impact and seems to be as well used and widely quoted today as it was when it was newly coined. He always responds by saying that the main reason is that the law is true. He told *Dun's Review,* "[It] is as valid today as it was twenty years ago, because as a rule of nature it is immutable."

Here is a documented collection of Parkinson's laws:

1. *Parkinson's First Law.* Work expands so as to fill the time available for its completion.

2. *Parkinson's Second Law.* Expenditure rises to meet income.

3. *Parkinson's Third Law.* Expansion means complexity and complexity, decay; or to put it even more plainly—the more complex, the sooner dead.

4. *Parkinson's Law of Delay.* Delay is the deadliest form of denial.

5. *Parkinson's Law of Medical Research.* Successful re-

search attracts the bigger grant which makes further research impossible.

6. *Mrs. Parkinson's Law*. Heat produced by pressure expands to fill the mind available from which it can pass only to a cooler mind.

7. *Parkinson's New Law*. The printed word expands to fill the space available for it.

8. *Parkinson's Principle of Non-Origination*. It is the essence of grantsmanship to persuade the Foundation executives that it was *they* who suggested the research project and that you were a belated convert, agreeing reluctantly to all they had proposed.

9. *Parkinson's Finding on Journals*. The progress of science varies inversely with the number of journals published.

10. *Parkinson's Telephone Law*. The effectiveness of a telephone conversation is in inverse proportion to the time spent on it.

11. *Parkinson's Law of 1000*. An enterprise employing more than 1000 people becomes a self-perpetuating empire, creating so much internal work that it no longer needs any contact with the outside world.

The Parkinson contribution is twofold. First, his law, which is not only noteworthy when an institution shows that it is an exception to it rather than an example of it. A few years ago Anthony Lewis wrote in *The New York Times* that the Supreme Court "alone" among the great institutions did not

1. Book of the same title, Houghton Mifflin, Boston, 1957. 2. Essay of same title from *The Law and the Profits,* Houghton Mifflin, 1960. 3. Essay of same title from *In-Laws and Outlaws,* Houghton Mifflin, 1962. 4. Book of the same title, Houghton Mifflin, 1971. 5. Article of same title, *New Scientist,* 13:193 (1962.) 6. Book of the same title, Houghton Mifflin 1968. 7. Article of same title, *Reader's Digest,* February, 1963. 8. Same source as number 5. 9. *JIR,* Vol. 11/2. 10. Article of same title, *New York Times Magazine,* April 12, 1974. 11. This appears in various locations, including direct quotes from Parkinson that appear in F. P. Adler's "Relationship between Organization Size and Efficiency," *Management Science Journal,* October, 1960. Parkinson also told Adler, "With a research establishment the same point is reached but only after the staff is double that size" (i.e. 2000).

conform to the law. At the end of 1976, *Newsweek* asked if Jimmy Carter could repeal the law during his administration. At this writing, nothing has happened to indicate that he has. Second, Parkinson more than anyone else helped break the stranglehold of the pure sciences and mathematics on immutable laws, principles, and named effects. He paved the way for others and created an atmosphere in which an explanation like this could appear in *The Manchester Guardian:* ". . . much blame must attach itself to the [U.N.] administrative system, which has not only set out to prove Parkinson's Law, but which religiously follows the Peter Principle of promoting mediocrities."*

● **Parliament, Simple Rules for Interpreting Acts of.** Always avoid reading the preamble, which is likely to confuse rather than to enlighten. It sets forth not what the act is to do, but what it undoes, and confuses you with what the law was instead of telling you what it is to be.

When you come to a very long clause, skip it altogether, for it is sure to be unintelligible. If you try to attach one meaning to it, the lawyers are sure to attach another; and, therefore, if you are desirous of obeying an act of Parliament, it will be safer not to look at it, but wait until a few contrary decisions have been come to, and then act upon the latest.

When any clause says either one thing or the other shall be right, you may be sure that both will be wrong.

> (This comes from an old British Comic Almanac and appears in the anthology *Comic Almanac,* edited by Thomas Yoseloff, published by A. S. Barnes and Co., New York, 1963.)

*Hella Pick, *The Manchester Guardian Weekly,* July 25, 1970.

● **Parsons's Laws.** ■If you break a cup or plate, it will not be the one that was already chipped or cracked. ■A place you want to get to is always just off the edge of the map you happen to have handy. ■A meeting lasts at least 1½ hours however short the agenda. ■A piece of electronic equipment is housed in a beautifully designed cabinet, and at the side or on top is a little box containing the components which the designer forgot to make room for.

(Denys Parsons, London.)

● **Pastore's Comment on Michehls's Theorem.** Nothing is ultimate.

● **Pastore's Truths.** (1) Even paranoids have enemies. (2) This job is marginally better than daytime TV. (3) On alcohol: four is one more than more than enough.

(Jim Pastore, former Control Data Corp. manager. *S.T.L.*)

● **Patrick's Theorem.** If the experiment works, you must be using the wrong equipment.

(*U/ Scientific Collections.*)

● **Paturi Principle.** Success is the result of behavior that completely contradicts the usual expectations about the behavior of a successful person. *Reciprocity Theorem:* The amount of success is in inverse proportion to the effort in attaining success.

(Felix R. Paturi, pseudonym for a successful management engineer, who explains his principle and other theories in *The Escalator Effect,* Peter H. Weyden, 1973. The book contains many examples of the principle in operation. Here is just one: a small child who needs to get home quickly begins walking slower. He eventually stops and makes the "inaccurate and therefore inverse statement, 'I just can't anymore.' So then daddy carries him home.")

● **Paul Principle.** People become progressively less competent for jobs they once were well equipped to handle.

(Paul Armer, director of Stanford University's Computation Center, who first described it for a large audience in the June, 1970, issue of *The Futurist.* Armer is very concerned with the occupational hazard of "technological obsolesence" and argues for educational sabbaticals and other forms of continuing education. It was written, in part, in response to the *Peter Principle.*)

● **Peers's Law.** The solution to a problem changes the problem.

(John Peers, president, Logical Machine Corp. [LOMAC.])

● **Perelman's Point.** There is nothing like a good painstaking survey full of decimal points and guarded generalizations to put a glaze like a Sung vase on your eyeball.

(S. J. Perelman, quoted in *RS*'s *1974 Expectation of Days.*)

● **Perversity of Nature, Law of the (aka Mrs. Murphy's Corollary).** You cannot successfully determine beforehand which side of the bread to butter.

(*Co.*)

● **Perversity of Production Precept.** If it works well, they'll stop making it.

(*AO* credits Jane Otten and Russell Baker for this law. See also *Herblock's Law,* which it is close to.)

● **Peter Principle, Corollaries, Inversion, etc.** *Peter Principle:* In every hierarchy, whether it be government or business, each employee tends to rise to his level of incompetence; every post tends to be filled by an employee incompetent to execute its duties. *Corollaries:* (1) Incompetence knows no barriers of

time or place. (2) Work is accomplished by those employees who have not yet reached their level of incompetence. (3) If at first you don't succeed, try something else. *Peter's Inversion:* Internal consistency is valued more highly than efficiency. *Peter's Law:* The unexpected always happens. *Peter's Paradox:* Employees in a hierarchy do not really object to incompetence in their colleagues. *Peter's Placebo:* An ounce of image is worth a pound of performance. *Peter's Theorem:* Incompetence plus incompetence equals incompetence.

(Dr. Laurence J. Peter and Peter Hull, from their *The Peter Principle,* William Morrow and Co., 1969, with the exception of *Peter's Law,* which is from *PQ.* The *Peter Principle* ranks with *Parkinson's Law* and *Murphy's Law* as one of the most famous and widely applied laws of modern life. The *Peter Principle* is not without its critics, as others have attempted to revise or amend it [see, for instance, the *Paul Principle*], and no less an authority than Parkinson has remarked that it does not always work out in real life. Parkinson says that we get on an airplane with a fairly high level of confidence that the pilot and navigator will be able to find their destination. He concluded, however, that Peter had a right to make the conclusion that he did since he had spent his life in an area where the principle is literally true—institutions of higher education.)

● **Peterson's Law.** History shows that money will multiply in volume and divide in value over the long run. Or expressed differently, the purchasing power of currency will vary inversely with the magnitude of the public debt.

(Economist William H. Peterson, from his article in the November, 1959, issue of *Challenge.*)

● **Phases of a Project.**
1. Exultation.
2. Disenchantment.

3. Confusion.
4. Search for the Guilty.
5. Punishment of the Innocent.
6. Distinction for the Uninvolved.
(Project manager's wall poster, Battelle Memorial Institute, Columbus, Ohio.)

● **Phelps's Laws of Renovation.** (1) Any renovation project on an old house will cost twice as much and take three times as long as originally estimated. (2) Any plumbing pipes you choose to replace during renovation will prove to be in excellent condition; those you decide to leave in place will be rotten.
(Lew Phelps, Chicago. *AO.*)

● **Phelps's Law of Retributive Statistics.** An unexpectedly easy-to-handle sequence of events will be immediately followed by an equally long sequence of trouble.
(Charles Phelps, RAND Corp. economist. *AO.*)

● **Pierson's Law.** If you're coasting, you're going downhill.
(L. R. Pierson, from *Rumsfeld's Rules.*)

● **Pike's Law of Punditry.** Success provides more opportunities to say things than the number of things the pundit has worth saying.
(Writer and radio commentator Douglas Pike, Washington, D.C. Pike is an up-and-coming pundit whose producer understands the law and only lets him air his opinions once or twice every two weeks.)

● **Pipe, Axiom of the (aka Trischmann's Paradox).** A pipe gives a wise man time to think and a fool something to stick in his mouth.
(*Ed Trischmann/S.T.L.*)

● **Plotnick's Third Law.** The time of departure will be delayed by the square of the number of people involved. Simply stated, if I wish to leave the city at 5 P.M., I will most likely depart at 5:01. If I am to meet a friend, the time of departure becomes 5:04. If we were to meet another couple, we won't be on our way before 5:16, and so on.

(Paul D. Plotnick, Stamford, Conn., in a letter to *The New York Times,* April 7, 1968. *FD.*)

● **Politicians' Rules.** (1) When the polls are in your favor, flaunt them. (2) When the polls are overwhelmingly unfavorable, (a) ridicule and dismiss them or (b) stress the volatility of public opinion. (3) When the polls are slightly unfavorable, play for sympathy as a struggling underdog. (4) When too close to call, be surprised at your own strength.

(*U/JW.*)

● **Potter's Law.** The amount of flak received on any subject is inversely proportional to the subject's true value.

(*U/S.T.L.*)

● **Powell's Law. [A.C.]** Never tell them what you wouldn't do.

(Adam Clayton Powell, cited by Julian Bond in a radio interview.)

● **Powell's Laws. [J.]** (1) Bad news does not improve with age. *Corollary:* When in doubt, get it out. (2) [For handling professional baiters at daily briefings and other appropriate problems of life.] Indifference is the only sure defense.

(Jody Powell, President Carter's press secretary.)

● **Pratt, The Rules of.** (1) If an apparently severe problem manifests itself, no solution is acceptable unless it is involved, expensive, and time-consuming. (2)(a) Completion of any task within the allocated time and budget does not bring credit upon the performing personnel—it merely proves the task was easier than expected; (b) failure to complete any task within the allocated time and budget proves the task was more difficult than expected and requires promotion for those in charge. (3) Sufficient monies to do the job correctly the first time are usually not available; however, ample funds are much more easily obtained for repeated major redesigns.

(From an undated clipping from *IEEE Spectrum.*)

● **Price's Law of Politics.** It's easier to be a liberal a long way from home.

(Don Price, dean of Harvard's Graduate School of Government, who discovered this when working with foundations that were more willing to undertake controversial projects overseas than in the United States. *AO.*)

● **Price's Law of Science.** Scientists who dislike the restraints of highly organized research like to remark that a truly great research worker needs only three pieces of equipment: a pencil, a piece of paper, and a brain. . . . But they quote this maxim more often at academic banquets than at budget hearings.

(Don Price. *RS's 1978 Expectation of Days.*)

● **Probable Dispersal, Law of.** Whatever hits the fan will not be evenly distributed. (Sometimes called *The How Come It All Landed on Me Law.*)

(Logical Machine Corp. ad, *The New Yorker,* 1976.)

● **Professional's Law.** Doctors, dentists, and lawyers are only on time for appointments when you're not.

(Rozanne Weissman.)

● **Professor Gordon's Rule of Evolving Bryographic Systems.** While bryographic plants are typically encountered in substrata of earthly or mineral matter in concreted state, discrete substrata elements occasionally display a roughly spherical configuration which, in presence of suitable gravitational and other effects, lends itself to combined translatory and rotational motion. One notices in such cases an absence of the otherwise typical accretion of bryophyta. We therefore conclude that a rolling stone gathers no moss.

> *(U/ S.T.L.)*

● **Proverbial Law.** For every proverb that so confidently asserts its little bit of wisdom, there is usually an equal and opposite proverb that contradicts it.

> (Writer Richard Boston in a review of *The Oxford Dictionary of English Proverbs* which appeared in *The New Statesman* for October 9, 1970. "Though many hands make light work, too many cooks spoil the broth," is just one example of Boston's discovery.)

● **Public Relations, Prime Rules of Political.** (1) Experts do not like surprises. It makes them look bad at the home office (e.g., JFK picking LBJ, Nixon picking Agnew, Reagan picking Schweiker). (2) Never say maybe in the same circulation area where you just said never.

> (Both Vic Gold, from his *P.R. as in President*. The second was written relative to candidate Jimmy Carter saying no embargoes on grain shipments at the Iowa State Fair and then telling newspaper editors in Des Moines that he would make exceptions in times of national emergency.)

● **Public Relations Client Turnover Law.** The minute you sign a client is the minute you start to lose him.

> (James L. Blankenship, senior vice-president, the public relations firm of R. C. Auletta and Co. Inc., New York.)

● **Public Speaking, First Rule of.** Nice guys finish fast.
> (*Reader's Digest,* June, 1976.)

●   **Pudder's Law.** Anything that begins well ends badly. Anything that begins badly ends worse.
     (*U/S.T.L.*)

●   **Purina Paradox.** You don't need to fly to have more fun with wings.
     (Writer Joe Anderson discovered this law when he covered a story for *The Daily Oklahoman* in 1949. Let him explain: "In the late forties, a midwestern university and a manufacturer of chicken feed collaborated in breeding a wingless chicken which would prove meatier and more tender because it didn't flop around as much. It has never reached the market, however, because a rooster uses his wings to balance himself while in the process of impregnating a hen.")

●   **Putney's Law.** If the people of a democracy are allowed to do so, they will vote away the freedoms which are essential to that democracy.
     (Snell Putney in *The Conquest of Society,* Wadsworth Publishing, 1972. *JW.*)

R

● **Rakove's Laws of Politics.** (1) The amount of effort put into a campaign by a worker expands in proportion to the personal benefits that he will derive from his party's victory. (2) The citizen is influenced by principle in direct proportion to his distance from the political situation.

> (Milton Rakove of the University of Illinois, who first spelled them out in *The Virginia Quarterly Review,* Summer, 1965. *FL.*)

● **Randolph's Cardinal Principle of Statecraft.** Never needlessly disturb a thing at rest.

> (Early American statesman John Randolph of Richmond. Cited in a recent column by James J. Kilpatrick.)

● **Rapoport's Rule of the Roller-Skate Key.** Certain items which are crucial to a given activity will show up with uncommon regularity until the day when that activity is planned, at which point the item in question will disappear from the face of the earth.

> (Dan Rapoport, Washington writer.)

● **Raskin's Zero Law.** The more zeros found in the price tag for a government program, the less Congressional scrutiny it will receive.

> (Marcus Raskin, the Institute for Policy Studies, Washington, D.C. Collected by Barbara Raskin, novelist.)

● **Raspberry Jam, Law of.** The wider any culture is spread, the thinner it gets.

(Stanley Edgar Hyman. This was incorrectly attributed to Alvin Toffler in a *New York Times* article, which in turn gave birth to *Toffler's Law of Editorial Correction* [See *Editorial Correction, Law of*]. Toffler had reason to dispute it, as he had spent fourteen chapters of his book *The Culture Consumers* arguing that the *Law of Raspberry Jam* was wrong.)

● **Rather's Rule.** In dealing with the press do yourself a favor. Stick with one of three responses: (a) I know and I can tell you. (b) I know and I can't tell you, or (c) I don't know.
(Dan Rather, CBS. These were originally stated some years ago and appear in a collection of rules put together by Donald Rumsfeld.)

● **Rayburn's Rule.** If you want to get along, go along.
(House Speaker Sam Rayburn. *Co.*)

● **Rebecca's House Rules—** At Least One Fits Any Occasion.
1. Throw it on the bed.
2. Fry onions.
3. Call Jenny's mother.
4. No one's got the corner on suffering.
5. Run it under the cold tap.
6. Everything takes practice, except being born.
(Sharon Mathews, Arlington, Va.)

● **Reform, Fundamental Tenet of.** Reforms come from below. No man with four aces howls for a new deal.
(JohnF.Parker,*If Elected, I Promise,* Doubleday, 1960)

● **Restaurant Acoustics, Law of.** In a restaurant with seats which are close to each other, one will always find the decibel

level of the nearest conversation to be inversely proportional to the quality of the thought going into it.
(Stuart A. Cohn. *AO.*)

● **Richman's Inevitables of Parenthood.** (1) Enough is never enough. (2) The sun always rises in the baby's bedroom window. (3) Birthday parties always end in tears. (4) Whenever you decide to take the kids home, it is always five minutes earlier that they break into fights, tears, hysteria.
(Phyllis C. Richman, writer and restaurant critic for *The Washington Post.*)

● **Riddle's Constant.** There are coexisting elements in frustration phenomena which separate expected results from achieved results.
(*U/Scientific Collections.*)

● **Riesman's Law.** An inexorable upward movement leads administrators to higher salaries and narrower spans of control.
(David Riesman. *JW.*)

● **Riggs's Hypothesis.** Incompetence tends to increase with the level of work performed. And, naturally, the individual's staff needs will increase as his level of incompetence increases.
(Arthur J. Riggs, in his article "Parkinson's Law, the Peter Principle, and the Riggs Hypothesis—A Synthesis," from the *Michigan Business Review,* March 1971. Riggs gives much detail on how his hypothesis fits in with the other principles in the title of his article. He also suggests a typical Riggs progression: ". . . from competent line worker to slightly incompetent foreman to incompetent supervisor." *FD.*)

● **Road Construction, Law of.** After large expenditures of federal, state, and county funds; after much confusion generated by detours and road blocks; after greatly annoying the surrounding population with noise, dust, and fumes, the previously existing traffic jam is relocated by one-half mile.

> (Alan Deitz, American Newspaper Publishers Association. *AO.*)

● **Robertson's Law.** Everything happens at the same time with nothing in between.

> (*U.* From Paul Hebig, Chicago, who adds, "It usually refers to social engagements and business meetings.")

● **Robotics, The Three Laws of.** (1) A robot may not injure a human being or, through inaction, allow a human being to come to harm. (2) A robot must obey the orders given it by human beings except where such orders would conflict with the First Law. (3) A robot must protect its own existence as long as such protection does not conflict with the First or Second.

> (Isaac Asimov, from "The Handbook of Robotics, 56th Edition, 2058 AD," which appears in his *I, Robot,* Doubleday, 1950.)

● **Rodovic's Rule.** In any organization, the potential is much greater for the subordinate to manage his superior than for the superior to manage his subordinate.

> (*U//JW.*)

● **Roemer's Law.** The rate of hospital admissions responds to bed availability. Or, If we insist on installing more beds, they will tend to get filled.

> (Dr. Milton Roemer of UCLA, who first suggested it in 1959. It is an entirely serious statement which, according to Victor R. Fuchs in his book *Who Shall Live?*, Basic Books, 1974, ". . . has received considerable support in recent econometric studies." *RS.*)

● **Rogers's Ratio.** One-third of the people in the United States promote, while the other two-thirds provide.

(Will Rogers, quoted in Leonard C. Lewin's *Treasury of American Political Humor,* Dial, 1964.)

● **Rosenbaum's Rule.** The easiest way to find something lost around the house is to buy a replacement.

(Jack Rosenbaum, in the *San Francisco Examiner and Chronicle.*)

● **Rosenstock-Huessy's Law of Technology.** All technology expands the space, contracts the time, and destroys the working group.

(Eugen Rosenstock-Huessy, the German-American social philosopher and historian.)

● **Ross's Law. [A.]** Bare feet magnetize sharp metal objects so they always point upward from the floor—especially in the dark.

(Al Ross. *JW.*)

● **Ross's Law. [C.]** Never characterize the importance of a statement in advance.

(Charles G. Ross, President Truman's press secretary. This, along with *Hagerty's* and *Salinger's* laws, was collected by Robert Donovan of the *Los Angeles Times* a number of years ago. They have appeared in a number of places, including *FL* and *S.T.L.*)

● **Ross's Law of Public Transportation. [S.]** Scheduled changes always mean cutbacks. *Corollary:* Minor schedule adjustments always affect your bus (train, whatever).

(Steve Ross, editor, *New Engineer.*)

● **Rowe's Rule.** The odds are 6 to 5 that the light at the end of the tunnel is a headlight of an oncoming express train. (*U/"LSP."*)

● **Rudin's Law.** In a crisis that forces a choice to be made among alternative courses of action, most people will choose the worst one possible.

(S. A. Rudin of Atlanta, from a 1961 letter to *The New Republic. FL.*)

● **Rumsfeld's Rules** (A Sampling). ■*On Serving the President*: Don't play President—you're not. The Constitution provides for only one President. Don't forget it and don't be seen by others as not understanding that fact. Where possible, preserve the President's options—he will very likely need them. Never say "The White House wants"—buildings don't "want." Don't speak ill of your predecessors (or successors)—you did not walk in their shoes. ■*On Keeping Your Bearings in the White House:* Keep your sense of humor about your position. Remember the observation (attributed to General Joe Stilwell) that "the higher a monkey climbs, the more you see of his behind"—you will find that it has more than a touch of truth. Don't begin to believe you are indispensible or infallible, and don't let the President, or others, think you are—you're not. It's that simple. Don't forget that the fifty or so invitations you receive a week are sent not because those people are just dying to see you, but because of the position you hold. If you don't believe me, ask one of your predecessors how fast they stop. If you are lost—"Climb, conserve, and confess." (From the SNJ Flight Manual, as I recall from my days as a student naval aviator.) ■*On Doing the Job in the White House:* Read and listen for what is missing. Many advisors —in and out of government—are quite capable of telling the President how to improve what has been proposed, or what's gone wrong. Few seem capable of sensing what isn't there. ■ *On Serving in Government:* When an idea is being pushed because it is "exciting," "new," or "innovative"—beware. An exciting, new, innovative idea can also be foolish. If in doubt, don't. If in doubt, do what is right. Your best question is often, "Why?" ∎*On Politics, the Congress, and the Press:* The First Rule of Politics: You can't win unless you are on the ballot. Politics is human beings. Politics is addition, not subtraction. When someone with a rural accent says, "I don't know anything about politics," zip up your pockets. If you try to please everybody, somebody is not going to like it. With the press, it is safest to assume that there is no "off the record." ∎*On Life (and other things):* It takes everyone to make a happy day. (Marcy Kay Rumsfeld at age seven.) In unanimity there may well be either cowardice or uncritical thinking. ∎If you develop rules, never have more than ten.

> (Donald Rumsfeld, from the rules and observations he created and collected while at the Pentagon and White House. The rules here were excerpted from an article in the February, 1977, *Washingtonian* entitled "Rumsfeld's Rules." The article, in turn, was excerpted from Rumsfeld's original eighteen-page memo on rules.)

● **Runyon's Law.** The race is not always to the swift, nor the battle to the strong, but that's the way to bet.
(Damon Runyon. *PQ.*)

● **Rural Mechanics, First Rule of.** If it works, don't fix it. (From William O'Neill, the National Geographic Society News Service.)

● **Russell's Observation.** In America everybody is of the opinion that he has no social superiors, since all men are equal, but he does not admit that he has no social inferiors, for, from the time of Jefferson onward, the doctrine that all men are equal applies only upwards, not downwards.

(Bertrand Russell, *Unpopular Essays,* Simon and Schuster, 1951. *RS.*)

● **Ryan's Law.** Make three correct guesses consecutively and you will establish yourself as an expert.
(*U/RS.*)

● **Sadat's Reminder.** Those who invented the law of supply and demand have no right to complain when this law works against their interest.

(Anwar Sadat, quoted in *1978 Expectation of Days. RS.*)

● **Salinger's Law.** Quit when you're still behind.

(Pierre Salinger, President Kennedy's press secretary. He discovered it when he protested news reports that a lavish reception the President had held was "expensive." *FL.*)

● **Sam's Axioms.** (1) Any line, however short, is still too long. (2) Work is the crabgrass of life, but money is the water that keeps it green.

(*U/S.T.L.*)

● **Sattingler's Law.** It works better if you plug it in.

(*U/Scientific Collections.*)

● **Sattler's Law.** There are 32 points to the compass, meaning that there are 32 directions in which a spoon can squirt grapefruit; yet, the juice almost invariably flies straight into the human eye.

(Professor Louis Sattler, whose discovery appears in H. Allen Smith's *A Short History of Fingers* in the important essay "Fetridge's Law Explained.")

● **Saunders's Discovery.** Laziness is the mother of nine inventions out of ten.

(Millionaire inventor Philip K. Saunders, quoted by Bennett Cerf in his *Laugh Day,* Doubleday, 1965.)

● **Sayre's Third Law of Politics.** Academic politics is the most vicious and bitter form of politics, because the stakes are so low.

> (The late Wallace Sayre of Columbia University has been given credit for this. A later corollary states: "They're the most vicious form of politics because the fighting is over issues decided five years earlier." *AO.*)

● **Schenk's First Principle of Industrial Market Economics.** Good salesmen and good repairmen will never go hungry.

> (Economist Robert E. Schenk, St. Joseph's College, Rensselaer, Ind. *AO.*)

● **Schickel's TV Theorems.** (1) Any dramatic series the producers want us to take seriously as a representation of contemporary reality cannot be taken seriously as a representation of anything—except a show to be ignored by anyone capable of sitting upright in a chair and chewing gum simultaneously. (2) The only programs a grown-up can possibly stand are those intended for children. Or, more properly, those that cater to those pre-adolescent fantasies that most have never abandoned.

> (Richard Schickel, from his review of the new television season, *Time,* September 22, 1975.)

● **Schuckit's Law.** All interference in human conduct has the potential for causing harm—no matter how innocuous the procedure may be.

> (Schuckit would appear to be a pseudonym. Collected by William K. Wright, San Diego, Cal.)

● **Schultze's Law.** If you can't measure output, then you measure input.

> (Charles Schultze as chairman, Council of Economic Advisors. *JW.*)

● **Schumpeter's Observation of Scientific and Non-scientific Theories.** Any theory can be made to fit any facts by means of appropriate additional assumptions.

> (Submitted by Schenk, of *Schenk's First Principle* . . . above. *AO.*)

● **Science, Two Important Observations from the Collection of Robert D. Specht.** (1) Science is a wonderful thing, but it has not succeeded in maximizing pleasure and minimizing pain, and that's all we asked of it. (2) A stagnant science is at a standstill.

> (The first comes from an unsigned "Notes and Comment" item in the June 13, 1970, issue of *The New Yorker.* The second is from *JIR,* December, 1973.)

● **Scientific Productivity of a Laboratory, Law of.**

$$\text{Productivity} = \frac{\text{Number of Secretaries} \times \text{Average Typing Speed}}{\text{Number of Scientists}}$$

> (From Robert Sommer's *Expertland,* Doubleday, 1963. He explains, "One interesting feature of this equation is that when the number of scientists is zero, productivity becomes infinite.")

● **Screwdriver Syndrome.** Sometimes, where a complex problem can be illuminated by many tools, one can be forgiven for applying the one he knows best.

> (Robert Machol, from his *POR.* It is illuminated by an anecdote in which an operations researcher is at home for the weekend with nothing to do and decides to tighten all the loose screws in the house. When he runs out of screws to tighten, he gets a file and begins filing slots in the heads of nails, which he dutifully begins tightening.)

● **Scriptural Injunctions and Observations** (A Sample). Old Scottish Prayer: O Lord, grant that we may always be right, For Thou knowest we will never change our minds.
(*JE.*)

● **Second-Ratedness, Unfailing Law of.** Never be first to do anything.
(Ken S., Wayland, Mass., in Ann Landers's column, 1978.)

● **Security Office, Special Law of.** Threats to security will be found. *Or, as an Axiom:* The finding of threats to security by a security office is totally predictable, and hence the finding is totally worthless.
(Robert N. Kharasch in *The Institutional Imperative,* Charterhouse Books, 1973. *AO.*)

● **Segal's Law.** A man with one watch knows what time it is; a man with two watches is never sure.
(*U/S.T.L.*)

● **Selective Gravity, Law of.** An object will fall so as to do the most damage. *Jennings's Corollary:* The chance of the bread falling buttered side down is directly proportional to the cost of the carpet.
(The law is common on scientific lists. The corollary was first spotted in a list by Arthur Bloch, "18 Unnatural Laws," which appears in the best-selling *Book of Lists* by David Wallechinsky, Irving Wallace, and Amy Wallace.)

● **Sells's Law.** The first sample is always the best.
(*U.* From William K. Wright.)

● **Serendipity, Laws of.** (1) In order to discover anything you must be looking for something. (2) If you wish to make an improved product, you must already be engaged in making an inferior one.

(These come from William K. Wright's collection. He attributes the first to Harvey Neville and the second to Jacob A. Varela.)

● **Sevareid's Law.** The chief cause of problems is solutions. (Eric Sevareid, on the CBS *News* for December 29, 1970.)

● **Shaffer's Law.** The effectiveness of a politician varies in inverse proportion to his commitment to principle.
(Newsweek reporter Sam Shaffer. *JW.)*

● **Shalit's Law.** The intensity of movie publicity is in inverse ratio to the quality of the movie.
(Gene Shalit, *The Today Show. S.T.L.)*

● **Shanahan's Law.** The length of a meeting rises with the square of the number of people present.
(Eileen Shanahan, when economics reporter for *The New York Times. FL.)*

● **Sharkey's 4th Law of Motion.** Passengers on elevators constantly rearrange their positions as people get on and off so there is at all times an equal distance between all bodies.
(John Sharkey of *The Washington Post.)*

● **Shaw's Principle.** Build a system that even a fool can use, and only a fool will want to use it.
(Christopher J. Shaw. *JE.)*

● **Shelton's Laws of Pocket Calculators.** (1) Rechargeable batteries die at the most critical time of the most complex problem. (2) When a rechargable battery starts to die in the middle of a complex calculation, and the user attempts to connect house current, the calculator will clear itself. (3) The final answer will exceed the magnitude or precision or both of the calculator. (4)

There are not enough storage registers to solve the problem. (5) The user will forget mathematics in proportion to the complexity of the calculator. (6) Thermal paper will run out before the calculation is complete.

   (John L. Shelton, president, Sigma Beta Communications, Inc., Dallas.)

● **Short's Quotations** (Some of many). ■Any great truth can—and eventually will—be expressed as a cliché—a cliché is a sure and certain way to dilute an idea. For instance, my grandmother used to say, "The black cat is always the last one off the fence." I have no idea what she meant, but at one time, it was undoubtedly true. ■Half of being smart is knowing what you're dumb at. ■Malpractice makes malperfect. ■Neurosis is a communicable disease. ■The only winner in the War of 1812 was Tchaikovsky. ■Nature abhors a hero. For one thing, he violates the law of conservation of energy. For another, how can it be the survival of the fittest when the fittest keeps putting himself in situations where he is most likely to be creamed? ■A little ignorance can go a long way. ■Learn to be sincere. Even if you have to fake it. ■There is no such thing as an absolute truth—that is absolutely true. ■Understanding the laws of nature does not mean we are free from obeying them. ■Entropy has us outnumbered. ■The human race never solves any of its problems—it only outlives them. ■TINSTAFL!—There is no such thing as free love. ■Hell hath no fury like a pacifist.

   (David Gerrold, from two of his 1978 columns in *Starlog*. They come from his "Quote-book of Solomon Short"—Short being a first-cousin to Robert A. Heinlein's Lazarus Long. [See *Long's Notes.*] He is also the author of *Gerrold's Three Laws of Infernal Dynamics.*)

● **Simmons's Law.** The desire for racial integration increases with the square of the distance from the actual event.

  (*U/J.W*)

● **Simon's Law.** Everything put together sooner or later falls apart.

(Paul Simon. *S.T.L.*)

● **Sinner's Law of Retaliation.** Do whatever your enemies don't want you to do.

(Gary Novak, Highmore, S. Da.)

● **Skinner's Constant.** That quantity which, when multiplied by, divided by, added to, or subtracted from the answer you get, gives you the answer you should have gotten.

> (*U/AIC.* Sometimes known as *Flannegan's Finagling Factor. FD* says this was called *DeBunk's Universal Variable Constant* in the 1930s.)

● **Skole's Rule of Antique Dealers.** Never simply say, "Sorry, we don't have what you are looking for." Always say, "Too bad, I just sold one the other day."

(Robert Skole, reporter, Stockholm, Sweden.)

● **Slide Presentation, Law of.** In any slide presentation, at least one slide will be upside down or backwards, or both.

> (John Corcoran, whose entry in the *Directory of Washington Independent Writers* reads, in part, "Send for clips to see how I write. If you don't, frogs will sneak into your house and eat your fingers.")

● **Smith's Laws of Politics and Other Things.** ■A politician always abuses his own constituency and placates the opponent's. ■The main beneficiaries of federal aid are those states that most oppose the principle. ■A baseball player who makes a spectacular defensive play always leads off the next inning as batter. ■A person over age 65 who drinks says that his doctor recommends it.

(Bob Smith, Washington, D.C., founder, editor, and publisher of *The Privacy Journal.*)

● **Smith's Principles of Bureaucratic Tinkertoys.** (1) Never use one word when a dozen will suffice. (2) If it can be understood, it's not finished yet. (3) Never do anything for the first time.

(*U.* From Paul Herbig, Chicago, Ill.)

● **Socio-Genetics, First Law of.** Celibacy is not hereditary. (Proposed by Guy Godin in *JIR* in 1975 and quickly questioned. Wrote one reader, "If your parents didn't have any children, the odds are that you won't have any.")

● **Sod's Law.** The degree of failure is in direct proportion to the effort expended and to the need for success.

(Generally speaking, Sod is the British incarnation of Finagle, Gumperson, Murphy, *et al.* One authority on Sod's Law is Richard Boston of London, who has written of it in such periodicals as *The New Statesman* and *The Times Literary Supplement.* Boston does not claim to be its author: on the contrary, he has traced a version of it back to a Lancashire proverb dating from 1871, "The bread never falls but on its buttered side." He also reports that in France it is called *La loi d'emmerdement maximum.*

However, Boston's greatest contribution may be in telling the story of the man whose bread fell and landed buttered side up. He ran straight away to his rabbi to report this deviance from one of the basic rules of the universe. At first the rabbi would not believe him but finally became convinced that it had happened. However, he didn't feel qualified to deal with the question and passed it along to one of world's leading Talmudic scholars. After months of waiting, the scholar finally came up with an answer: "The bread must have been buttered on the wrong side.")

● **Spare Parts Principle.** The accessibility, during recovery of small parts which fall from the work bench, varies directly with the size of the part—and inversely with its importance to the completion of the work underway.
(*AIC.*)

● **Specht's Meta-law.** Under any conditions, anywhere, whatever you are doing, there is some ordinance under which you can be booked.
(Robert D. Specht of the RAND Corp., who is also collector *R.S.*)

● **Spencer's (Contradictory) Corollary (to Nofziger's Law of Detail.** If a political candidate chooses to go into specifics on a program that affects a voter's self-interest, the voter *gets* interested. If the proposal involves money, he gets very interested.
(Stuart Spencer of President Ford's PR staff, *re* Reagan's proposed $90 billion cut in the federal budget. From Vic Gold's *P.R. as in President.*)

● **Sprague's Law.** Satisfaction derived from a trip goes down as Expectation goes up *if* Reality is unchanged $S = R/E$ As Reality becomes more favorable, the chance for Satisfaction goes up *if* Expectation is unchanged.
(Hall T. Sprague, *The New York Times,* Travel section, January 16, 1977. *JW.*)

● **Stamp's Statistical Probability.** The government [is] extremely fond of amassing great quantities of statistics. These are raised to the nth degree, the cube roots are extracted, and the results are arranged into elaborate and impressive displays. What must be kept ever in mind, however, is that in every case, the figures are first put down by a village watchman, and he puts down anything he damn well pleases.

> (Attributed to Sir Josiah Stamp, 1840–1941, H.M. collector of inland revenue. From rules collected by Donald Rumsfeld.)

● **Steele's Plagiarism of Somebody's Philosophy.** Everyone should believe in something—I believe I'll have another drink.

> (Mary Steele. *S.T.L.*)

● **Steinbeck's Law.** When you need towns, they are very far apart.

> (John Steinbeck, on the occasion of coming down with car trouble on a lonely road in Oregon while researching *Travels with Charlie*. Recalled by H. Allen Smith in *A Short History of Fingers*.)

● **Stephens's Soliloquy.** Finality is death. Perfection is finality. Nothing is perfect. There are lumps in it.

> (James Stephens, quoted in *The Public Speaker's Treasure Chest*.)

● **Stockbroker's Declaration.** The market will rally from this or lower levels.

> (Larry W. Sisson, Seattle. *AO.*)

● **Stock Market Axiom.** The public is always wrong.
> (*U/ Co.*)

● **Sturgeon's Law.** 90 percent of everything is crud.
> (Science fiction writer Theodore Sturgeon. This law is widely quoted—from *The Washington Post* to *Harper's*

—with the percentages varying from 90 to 99 percent
and the last word variously "crud" or "crap.")

● **Suhor's Law.** A little ambiguity never hurt anyone.
(Charles Suhor, deputy executive director, National
Council of Teachers of English. He formulated the law
when he discovered "the universe is intractably squiggly.")

● **Survival Formula for Public Office.** (1) Exploit the inevitable (which means, take credit for anything good which happens whether you had anything to do with it or not.) (2) Don't disturb the perimeter (meaning don't stir a mess unless you can be sure of the result.) (3) Stay in with the Outs (the Ins will make so many mistakes you can't afford to alienate the Outs.) (4) Don't permit yourself to get between a dog and a lampost.
(*AO.*)

● **Sutton's Law.** Go where the money is.
(Named after bank robber Willie Sutton who, when asked
why he robbed banks replied, "Because that's where the
money is." It is used regularly in a number of fields today
where, when the question of which direction to take is
asked, it is common to simply say "Let Sutton's Law
apply." Machol uses it as one of his *Principles of Operations Research,* but it is also applied in fields as diverse
as medical research and broadcasting.)

● **Swipple Rule of Order.** He who shouts loudest has the
floor.
(*U/S.T.L.*)

● **Symington's Law.** For every credibility gap there is a
gullibility gap.
(Senator Stuart Symington quoted in a recent Ann Landers
column.)

T

- **Taxi Principle.** Find out the cost before you get in. (Posted in U.S. Department of Labor. *TO'B.*)

- **Technology, Law of.** The very technology that makes our living simpler makes society more complex. The more efficient we get, the more specialized we become and the more dependent.
  (Thomas Griffith, *The Waste-High Culture,* Harper & Row, 1959.)

- **Terman's Law of Innovation.** If you want a track team to win the high jump, you find one person who can jump seven feet, not seven people who can jump one foot.
  (Frederick E. Terman, provost emeritus, Stanford University. See also *Bowker's Law.*)

- **Thermopolitical Rhetoric, Laws of.** (1) Cant produces countercant. *Corollary:* The quantity of rhetoric has been directly proportional to the lack of action. (2) Social groups are generally in disarray. To protect themselves from other groups, especially the groups just below them, groups will attempt to convey an appearance of interior order and purpose they do not possess. (3) Social institutions will change only at the speed required to protect them from attack—slowly or fast to the degree required, but usually slowly. They will put off change as long as possible . . .
  (Arthur Herzog, from his book *The B. S. Factor: The Theory and Technique of Faking It in America,* Simon and Schuster, 1973.)

174

Third Corollary. The difficulty of getting anything started increases with the square of the number of people involved.
(Jim MacGregor. *AO.*)

Thoreau's Law. If you see a man approaching you with the obvious intent of doing you good, you should run for your life.
(Attributed to Thoreau by William H. Whyte, Jr., in *The Organization Man,* Simon and Schuster, 1956, and quoted in *MB, S.T.L.*, etc.)

Thoreau's Rule. Any fool can make a rule, and every fool will mind it.
(Thoreau. *JW.*)

● **Thurber's Conclusion.** There is no safety in numbers, or in anything else.
(James Thurber, *Fables for Our Time*, Harper & Row, 1939. *RS.*)

Tipper's Law. Those who expect the biggest tips provide the worst service.
(Rozanne Weissman.)

‾ **Tishbein's Law.** There are more horses' backsides in the military service of the United States than there are horses.
(*U.* Robert J. Clark of Southampton, N.Y., learned this as a plebe at West Point and passed it along to *AO.*)

Titanic Coincidence. Most accidents in well-designed systems involve two or more events of low probability occurring in the worst possible combination.
(Robert Machol, in *POR.*)

Tom Jones's Law. Friends may come and go, but enemies accumulate.

(Dr. Thomas Jones, president of the University of South Carolina.)

● **Tom Sawyer's Great Laws of Human Action.** (1) In order to make [a person] covet a thing, it is only necessary to make the thing difficult to attain. (2) Work consists of whatever a body is *obliged* to do, and Play consists of whatever a body is not obliged to do.

(Samuel Clemens, *Tom Sawyer.*)

● **Torquemada's Law.** When you are sure you're right, you have a moral duty to impose your will upon anyone who disagrees with you.

(Robert W. Mayer, Champaign, Ill. *AO.*)

● **Transcription Square Law.** The number of errors made is equal to the sum of the "squares" involved.

(*AIC.*)

● **Travel, First Law of.** No matter how many rooms there are in the motel, the fellow who starts up his car at five o'clock in the morning is always parked under your window.

(Comedy writer Bob Orben.)

● **Tribune Tower, Law of.** Elevators traveling in the desired direction are always delayed and on arrival tend to run in pairs, threes of a kind, full houses, etc.

(Pete Maiken, *The Chicago Tribune.*)

● **Truman's Law.** If you can't convince them, confuse them.

(Harry S Truman. *Co.*)

● **Truths of Management.** (1) Think before you act; it's not your money. (2) All good management is the expression of one great idea. (3) No executive devotes effort to proving himself wrong. (4) Cash in must exceed cash out. (5) Management capability is always less than the organization actually needs. (6) Either an executive can do his job or he can't. (7) If sophisticated calculations are needed to justify an action, don't do it. (8) If you are doing something wrong, you will do it badly. (9) If you are attempting the impossible, you will fail. (10) The easiest way of making money is to stop losing it.

(Robert Heller, *The Great Executive Dream,* Delacorte, 1972. *JE.*)

● **Turner's Law.** Nearly all prophecies made in public are wrong.

(Malcolm Turner, Scottish journalist, passed along to *AO* by his son Arthur Campbell Turner, a California political scientist.)

● **Twain's Rule.** Only kings, editors, and people with tapeworm have the right to use the editorial "we."

(Samuel Clemens. *Co.*)

● **Tylk's Law.** Assumption is the mother of all foul-ups.

(*U/"LSP"*)

- **Ubell's Law of Press Luncheons.** At any public relations luncheon, the quality of the food is inversely related to the quality of the information.

    (Earl Ubell, who created it when he was the New York *Herald Tribune*'s science writer. Recalled by Ben Bagdikian.)

- **Uhlmann's Razor.** When stupidity is a sufficient explanation, there is no need to have recourse to any other. *Corollary:* (Also, the *Law of Historical Causation.*) "It seemed like the thing to do at the time."

    (Michael M. Uhlmann, who was assistant attorney general for legislation in the Ford Administration. *AO* and *JMcC.*)

- **Ultimate Law.** All general statements are false.
    (R. H. Grenier, Davenport, Iowa. *AO.*)

- **Ultimate Principle.** By definition, when you are investigating the unknown, you do not know what you will find.
    (*Scientific Collections.*)

- **Umbrella Law.** You will need three umbrellas: one to leave at the office, one to leave at home, and one to leave on the train.

    (James L. Blankenship, R. C. Auletta and Co., New York.)

- **United Law.** If an organization carries the word "united" in its name, it means it isn't, e.g., United Nations, United Arab Republic, United Kingdom, United States.

(Professor Charles I. Issawi, quoting Warner Schilling, professor of political science, who is quoting Professor Harry Rudin. From *Issawi's Laws of Social Motion.*)

● **Universal Field Theory of Perversity (or Mulé's Law).** The probability of an event's occurring varies directly with the perversity of the inanimate object involved and inversely with the product of its desirability and the effort expended to produce it.
(Walter Mulé, from his article "Beyomd Murphy's Law" in *Northliner.* Mulé uses his article as proof of the law, whereas if it had not appeared in print it would have been an example of *Murphy's Law.*)

● **Unnamed Law.** If it happens, it must be possible.
(*RS.*)

● **Unspeakable Law.** As soon as you mention something if it's good, it goes away. . . . If it's bad, it happens.
(From Bloch's list in *The Book of Lists.*)

V

- **Vail's First Axiom.** In any human enterprise, work seeks the lowest hierarchical level.

  (Charles R. Vail, vice-president, Southern Methodist University.)

- **Vance's Rule of 2 ½.** Any military project will take twice as long as planned, cost twice as much, and produce only half of what is wanted.

  (Attributed to Cyrus Vance when he was under secretary of defense. *AO.*)

- **Vique's Law.** A man without religion is like a fish without a bicycle.

  (Semi-*U*. Conrad Schneiker believes Vique is a friend of Edith Folta's in Urbanna, Ill. Gregg Townsend is not sure of this. Nonetheless, it is a popular law that has begun to show up in variant forms, such as at a recent NOW conference, where several delegates were reported to have said, "A woman without a man . . ." etc.)

- **Von Braun's Law of Gravity.** We can lick gravity, but sometimes the paperwork is overwhelming.

  (The late Wernher von Braun, during the early months of the U.S. space program.)

● **Waddell's Law of Equipment Failure.** A component's degree of reliability is directly proportional to its ease of accessibility (i.e., the harder it is to get to, the more often it breaks down.)

(Johnathan Waddell, crew member, *Exxon New Orleans,* oil tanker.)

● **Waffle's Law.** A professor's enthusiasm for teaching the introductory course varies inversely with the likelihood of his having to do it.

(*U.* Quoted in "The Geologic Column" in *Geotimes* for July-August, 1968. The author of the column is Robert L. Bates. *FD.*)

● **Wakefield's Refutation of the Iron Law of Distribution.** Them what gets—has.

(Dexter B. Wakefield of Coral Gables, Fla., in a letter to *The Wall Street Journal,* November 11, 1974.)

● **Waldo's Observation.** One man's red tape is another man's system.

(Dwight Waldo, from his essay "Government by Procedure," which appears in Fritz Morstein Marx's *Elements of Public Administration,* Prentice-Hall, 1946.)

● **Walinsky's Laws.** (1) The intelligence of any discussion diminishes with the square of the number of participants. (2) *His First Law of Political Campaigns:* If there are twelve clowns in a ring, you can jump in the middle and start reciting Shake-

speare, but to the audience, you'll just be the thirteenth clown.
(Adam Walinsky. *AO.*)

● **Walker's Law.** Associate with well-mannered persons
and your manners will improve. Run with decent folk and
your own decent instincts will be strengthened. Keep the
company of bums and you will become a bum. Hang around
with rich people and you will end by picking up the check
and dying broke.

> (Stanley Walker, city editor of the New York *Herald Trib-
> une* during the 1930s. It was rediscovered by Alan Deitz
> of the American Newspaper Publishers Association, who
> passed it along to *AO* with this comment, "Although
> there are no facts to substantiate this, it was probably
> enunciated by Walker after spending an evening with
> Lucius Beebe and Ogden Reid in Jack Bleek's.)

● **Walters's Law of Management.** If you're already in a
hole, there's no use to continue digging.

> (Roy W. Walters, Roy Walters Associates, Glen Rock, N.J.)

● **Washington's Law.** Space expands to house the people
to perform the work that Congress creates.

> (Haynes Johnson, *The Washington Post,* August 14,
> 1977.)

● **Weaver's Law.** When several reporters share a cab on
assignment, the reporter in the front seat pays for all.

> (Named for Warren Weaver of *The New York Times.* See
> also *Doyle's Corollary* and *Germond's Law. AO.*)

● **Weidner's Queries.** (1) The tide comes in and the tide
goes out, and what have you got? (2) They say an elephant never
forgets, but what's he got to remember?

> (*U.* From Dave Miliman, Baltimore, Maryland.)

● **Weight-Watcher's Law.** Better to throw it OUT—than throw it in.

> (Attributed to one Skinny Mitchell in a letter from "Benton Harbor Ben" from Ann Landers's column.)

● **Weiler's Law.** Nothing is impossible for the man who doesn't have to do it himself.

> (A. H. Weiler of *The New York Times. FL.*)

● **Weinberg's Law.** If builders built buildings the way programmers wrote programs, then the first woodpecker that came along would destroy civilization. *Corollary:* An expert is a person who avoids the small errors while sweeping on to the grand fallacy.

> (Gerald Weinberg, computer scientist, University of Nebraska. *JE.*)

● **Weisman's College Exam Law.** If you're confident after you've just finished an exam, it's because you don't know enough to know better.

> (Jay Weisman, Easton, Pa.)

● **Wells's Law.** A parade should have bands *or* horses, not both.

> (Nancy M. Wells, San Pedro [Cal.] High School teacher and representative at large to the National Council of Teachers of English.)

● **Westheimer's Rule.** To estimate the time it takes to do a task: estimate the time you think it should take, multiply by two, and change the unit of measure to the next highest unit. Thus we allocate two days for a one-hour task.

> (*U/S.T.L.*)

● **Whispered Rule.** People will believe anything if you whisper it.

> (*The Farmers' Almanac,* 1978 edition.)

● **White Flag Principle.** A military disaster may produce a better postwar situation than victory.

(Shimon Tzabar, in a book of the same title, Simon and Schuster, 1972. He says that if you can accept the principle, "then there can be a science of military disasters as there is a science of military victories." He adds, "Such a science must comprise a theory and a practice. The practice should provide the armies with handbooks and textbooks for the accomplishment of defeats and surrenders. The fact that the big powers of today are powerful enough to make absurd any effort by lesser powers to overcome them in the traditional way, makes an alternative to victory the more urgent.")

● **White's Statement.** Don't lose heart . . . (*Owen's Comment on White's Statement:* . . . they might want to cut it out . . . *Byrd's Addition to Owen's Comment on White's Statement:* . . . and they want to avoid a lengthy search.)
(*U/S.T.L.*)

● **Wicker's Law.** Government expands to absorb revenue —and then some.
(Tom Wicker, *The New York Times. FL.*)

● **Wilcox's Law.** A pat on the back is only a few centimeters from a kick in the pants.
(*U/RS.*)

● **Will's Rule of Informed Citizenship.** If you want to understand your government, don't begin by reading the Constitution. (It conveys precious little of the flavor of today's statecraft). Instead read selected portions of the Washington telephone directory containing listings for all the organizations with titles beginning with the word "National."
(George Will. *JW.*)

● **Wilson's Law of Demographics. [W.]** The public is not made up of people who get their names in the newspapers.
(Woodrow Wilson. *MBC.*)

● **Wilson's Laws. [J.Q.]** (1) All policy interventions in social problems produce the intended effect—*if* the research is carried out by those implementing the policy or their friends. (2) No policy intervention in social problems produces the intended effect—*if* the research is carried out by independent third parties, especially those skeptical of the policy.
(James Q. Wilson, Harvard political scientist, in his article "On Pettigrew and Armor" in *Public Interest,* Winter, 1973.)

● **Wing-Walking, First Law of.** Never leave hold of what you've got until you've got hold of something else.
(Donald Herzberg, dean of Georgetown University's graduate school, reported to *AO.* It came from the days of the barnstorming pilots and is now applied in situations such as when one quits a job before having another lined up.)

● **Witzenburg's Law of Airplane Travel.** The distance between the ticket counter and your plane is directly proportional to the weight of what you are carrying and inversely proportional to the time remaining before takeoff.
(Gary Witzenburg, Troy, Mich.)

● **Wober's SNIDE Rule.** Ideal goals grow faster than the means of attaining new goals allow.
(Mallory Wober, *JIR,* March, 1971. The acronym SNIDE stands for Satisfied Needs Incite Demand Excesses.)

● **Wolf's Laws.** ■*Historical Lessons:* Those who don't study the past will repeat its errors. Those who do study it, will

find *other* ways to err! ■ *Decision-making:* Major actions are rarely decided by more than four people. If you think a larger meeting you're attending is really "hammering out" a decision, you're probably wrong. Either the decision was agreed to by a smaller group before the meeting began, or the outcome of the larger meeting will be modified later when three or four people get together. ■*Briefings:* In briefings to busy people, summarize at the beginning what you're *going to tell* them, then *tell* them, then summarize at the end what you *have told* them. ■*Good*

Management: The tasks to do immediately are the minor ones; otherwise, you'll forget them. The major ones are often better to defer. They usually need more time for reflection. Besides, if you forget them, they'll remind you. ■*Meetings:* The only important result of a meeting is agreement about next steps. ■*Planning:* A good place to start from is where you are. ■*Wolf's Law* (subtitled, *An Optimistic View of a Pessimistic World):* It isn't that things will necessarily go wrong (*Murphy's Law*), but rather that they will take so much more time and effort than you think, if they are not to. ■*Tactics*: If you can't beat them, have them join you.

(Charles Wolf, Jr., head, economics department, the RAND Corp., and director, RAND Graduate Institute. *RS.* See also *Baldy's Law,* which is also Wolf's.)

● **Woman's Equation.** Whatever women do, they must do twice as well as men to be thought half as good. Luckily, this is not difficult.

(*U/RS.*)

● **Wood's Law.** The more unworkable the urban plan, the greater the probability of implementation.

(Robert Wood, *Ekistics,* October, 1969. *JW.*)

● **Woodward's Law.** A theory is better than its explanation.

(H. P. Woodward, in a letter to Robert L. Bates, who published it in his "Geologic Column" in the July-August, 1968, *Geotimes.*)

Special Section 6

Work Rules. (Found posted in various locations about the working world.)

RULES.

1. THE BOSS IS ALWAYS RIGHT.

2. WHEN THE BOSS IS WRONG, REFER TO *RULE 1*.

THE WORKER'S DILEMMA.

1. No matter how much you do, you'll never do enough.
2. What you don't do is always more important than what you do do.

NEW WORK RULES.

Sickness. No excuses will be acceptable. We will no longer accept your doctor's statement as proof of illness, as we believe that if you are able to go to the doctor, you are able to come to work.

Leave of Absence (for an Operation.) We are no longer allowing this practice. We wish to discourage any thoughts that you may need all of whatever you have, and you should not consider having something removed. We hired you as you are, and to have anything removed would certainly make you less than we bargained for.

Death (Other Than Your Own). This is no excuse. If you can arrange for funeral services to be held late in the afternoon, however, we can let you off an hour early, provided all your work is up to date.

Death (Your Own). This will be accepted as an excuse, but we would like at least two weeks' notice, as we feel it is your duty to teach someone else your job.

Also, entirely too much time is being spent in the washrooms. In the future, you will follow the practice of going in alphabetical order. For instance, those whose surnames begin with "A" will be allowed to go from 9–9:05 A.M., and so on. If you are unable to go at your appointed time, it will be necessary to wait until the next day when your time comes around again.

THE TWO KINDS OF WORK
Work is of two kinds: (1) Altering the position of matter at or near the earth's surface relative to other such matter; (2) Telling other people to do so.

The first is unpleasant and ill paid; the second is pleasant and highly paid.

——*The Rotarian.*

Eat a live toad the first thing in the morning and nothing worse will happen to you the rest of the day.

Our troops advanced today without losing a foot of ground.
——*Spanish Civil War Communiqué.*

Anyone can do any amount of work provided it isn't the work he is supposed to be doing at that moment.
——*Robert Benchley.*

ANNOUNCEMENT.

(These rules were printed in the *Boston Globe* some years ago and were reported to be the rules posted by the owner of a New England carriage works in 1872, as a guide to his office workers.)

1. Office employees will daily sweep the floors, dust the furniture, shelves, and showcases.

2. Each day fill lamps, clean chimneys, and trim wicks. Wash the windows once a week.

3. Each clerk will bring in a bucket of water and scuttle of coal for the day's business.

4. Make your pens carefully. You may whittle nibs to your individual taste.

5. This office will open at 7 A.M. and close at 8 P.M. except on the Sabbath, on which day we will remain closed. Each employee is expected to spend the Sabbath by attending church and contributing liberally to the cause of the Lord.

6. Men employees will be given off each week for courting purposes, or two evenings a week if they go regularly to church.

7. After an employee has spent his 13 hours of labor in the office, he should spend the remaining time reading the Bible and other good books.

8. Every employee should lay aside from each pay a goodly sum of his earnings for his benefit during his declining years, so that he will not become a burden on society or his betters.

9. Any employee who smokes Spanish cigars, uses liquor in any form, or frequents pool and public halls, or gets shaved in a barber shop, will give me good reason to suspect his worth, intentions, integrity and honesty.

10. The employee who has performed his labors faithfully and without a fault for five years, will be given an increase of five cents per day in his pay, providing profits from the business permit it.

● **Wynne's Law.** Negative slack tends to increase. (*U/S.T.L.*)

X

● **Xerces Englebraun's Big Man Syndrome.** The importance of the man and his job, in that relative order, rises in direct proportion to the distance separating his audience from his home office.

> (This Shanghai psychiatrist appears in *For Men With Yen* by Alan Rosenberg and William J. O'Neill, Wayward Press, Tokyo, 1962.)

Y

● **Yapp's Basic Fact.** If a thing cannot be fitted into something smaller than itself some dope will do it.

> (Eric Frank Russell, in a November, 1959, letter to *ASF*. Yapp discovered this fact at an early age when he got his head stuck in a fence and had to be freed by the fire department. *FD.*)

● **Yolen's Law of Self-Praise.** Proclaim yourself "World Champ" of something—tiddly-winks, rope-jumping, whatever—send this notice to newspapers, radio, TV, and wait for challengers to confront you. Avoid challenges as long as possible, but continue to send news of your achievements to all media. Also, develop a newsletter and letterhead for communications.

> (Will Yolen, former PR man and kite VIP, who by now probably owns a suitcase filled with clippings of articles that talk about him and his World Championship.)

Z

● **Zellar's Law.** Every newspaper, no matter how tight the news hole, has room for a story on another newspaper increasing its newsstand price.

(Ed Zellar, Park Ridge, Ill. *AO.*)

● **Zimmerman's Law.** Regardless of whether a mission expands or contracts, administrative overhead continues to grow at a steady rate.

(*"LSP"* list, which identifies him as Charles J. Zimmerman. *C.L.U.*)

● **Zimmerman's Law of Complaints.** Nobody notices when things go right.

(M. Zimmerman. *AO.*)

● **Zusmann's Rule.** A successful symposium depends on the ratio of meeting to eating.

(*U.* From a group of "Quips" in the *JIR*, March, 1971.)

● **Zymurgy's First Law of Evolving System Dynamics.** Once you open a can of worms, the only way to recan them is to use a larger can. (Old worms never die, they just worm their way into larger cans.)

● **Zymurgy's Law on the Availability of Volunteer Labor.** People are always available for work in the past tense.

● **Zymurgy's Seventh Exception to Murphy's Laws.** When it rains it pours.

(The truth can now be told. The oft-quoted Zymurgy is actually Conrad Schneiker.)

ACKNOWLEDGMENTS

"Three Laws of Robotics" by Isaac Asimov: Used by permission of the author.

Berkeley's Laws: Reprinted with permission from "The Notebook on Common Sense, Elementary and Advanced" copyright 1978 by and published by Berkeley Enterprises, Inc., 815 Washington Street, Newtonville, Mass. 02160.

From "At Wit's End" by Erma Bombeck: Copyright 1978 Field Enterprises, Inc. Courtesy of Field Newspaper Syndicate.

From FARMER'S LAW by Richard N. Farmer: Copyright © 1973 by Richard N. Farmer. Reprinted with permission of Stein and Day, Publishers.

Fiedler's Laws: © 1977 Edgar R. Fiedler. First published in *Across the Board*.

"Gilb's Laws": Reprinted with permission of DATAMATION® magazine, © copyright by Technical Publishing Company, a Division of Dun-Donnelley Publishing Corporation, A Dun & Bradstreet Company, 1978—all rights reserved.

"Gerrold's Law" and "Short's Quotation": © 1978 David Gerrold. Used by permission

From "WrapAround": Copyright © 1974 by *Harper's Magazine*. All rights reserved. Excerpted from the August 1974 issue by special permission.

From *The Journal of Irreproducible Results:* Used by permission of the publisher.

"Levy's Laws": Used by special permission of the copyright owner, Marion J. Levy, Jr.

From MALICE IN BLUNDERLAND by Thomas Martin: Used by permission of McGraw-Hill Book Company.

Excerpts from "Faber's Law: If There Isn't a Law, There Will Be" (*New York Times Magazine,* March 17, 1968) and excerpts from *New York Times Magazine,* April 7, 1968: © 1968 by The New York Times Company. Reprinted by permission.

"Parkinson's 1st, 2nd, and 3rd Laws; Law of Delay; Law of Medical Research; Principle of Non-Origination; Finding on Journals; and Mrs. Parkinson's Law" by C. Northcote Parkinson: From PARKINSON'S LAW copyright © 1957 by C. Northcote Parkinson. THE LAW AND THE PROFITS copyright © 1960 by C. Northcote Parkinson, MRS. PARKINSON'S LAW copyright © 1968 by C. Northcote Parkinson, THE LAW OF DELAY copyright © 1970 by C. Northcote Parkinson and INLAWS AND OUTLAWS copyright © 1959, 1960, 1961, 1962 by Roturman, S. A. Used by permission of Houghton Mifflin Co.

"The Peter Principle," "Peter's Corollary," "Peter's Paradox," "Peter's Placebo," and 5 words from entry under "imcompetance" in the Glossary: From THE PETER PRINCIPLE by Dr. Lawrence J. Peter. and Raymond Hull. Copyright © 1969 by William Morrow and Company, Inc. Used by permission of William Morrow & Company, Inc.

"Peter's Law": from PETER'S QUOTATIONS by Dr. Lawrence J. Peter. Copyright © by Lawrence J. Peter. Used by permission of William Morrow & Company, Inc.

"Rumsfeld's Rules": Reprinted with permission. Copyright 1976 Donald H. Rumsfeld. All Rights Reserved.

From INSTANT STATUS OR HOW TO BECOME A PILLAR OF THE UPPER MIDDLE CLASS by Charles Merrill Smith: Copyright © 1972 by Charles Merrill Smith. Reprinted by permission of Doubleday & Company, Inc.

From DRUCKER: The Man Who Invented the Corporate Society by John J. Tarrant: Reprinted by permission of CBI Publishing Company, Inc., 51 Sleeper Street, Boston, MA 02210.

Index

A

Abstraction: *Booker's*
Absurdity: *Boultbee's*
Academia: *Abbott's; Barzun's; Bok's; Bombeck's (Principles); Dawes-Bell; Duggan's; Father; Gummidge's; Herrnstein's; Hildebrand's; Kerr-Martin; Martin's (Laws); May's; Murphy's; Nyquist's; Ozian; Sayre's; Waffle's; Weisman's*
Accidents: *Frankel's; Titanic*
Accomplishment: *Bucy's; Evans's; Golden*
Accuracy: *Accuracy*
Acoustics: *Restaurant*
Adjournment: *Committee*
Advertising: *Advertising; Dawes-Bell; Drucker*
Advice: *Dave's (Law), Expert*
Age: *Baruch's; Lynott's; Paige's*
Aggression: *Issawi's*
Air: *Nations*
Airplanes/Air Transportation/Aviation: *Douglas's; Durrell's; Mills's (Law of Transportation Logistics); Witzenburg's*
Alcohol: *Pastorés.* See also: Drink
Alienation: *Cohen's (Laws of Politics)*
Ambiguity: *Suhor's*
Ambition: *Cohen's (Laws of Politics)*
America: *Russell's*
Analysis: *Martin's (Basic); Murphy's*
Anesthesia: *Local*
Annual Reports: *Hale's*
Antiques: *Skole's*
Appearance: *Character*
Appreciation: *Inverse*
Approval: *Approval*
Architecture: *Cheops's*
Arguments: *Cutler Webster's*
Army: *Army (Axiom); Army (Law); Tishbein's*
Arrogance: *Bustlin'; Fifth*
Arts: *Golden*
Assumptions: *Burns's; Schumpeter's; Tylk's*
Astrology: *Astrology*
Attraction: *Cohen's (Laws of Politics)*
Auditors: *O'Brien's (Principle)*
Authority: *Katz's (Other)*
Authors: *Kauffmann's*
Automobiles/Automotive: *Barrett's; Berson's; Bombeck's (Principles); Bruce-Brigg's; Caen's; Cleveland's; Eternity; Fishbein's; Hartman's; Hogg's; Johnson's (First); Road; Travel*

B

Backpacking: *Barber's*
Bad Luck: *Broken*
Baldness: *Nobel's*
Banks: *Checkbook; Ettorre's; John's (Collateral); Sutton's*
Barbers: *Expert*
Bargains: *Eve's*
Baseball: *Avery (Sayings); Berra's; Smith's (Laws)*
Bathroom Hooks: *Joyce's*
Beer: *Goulden's (Axiom); Jinny's; Long's*
Beliefs: *Bartz's*
Bicycle: *Bicycle; Bicycling*
Biochemistry: *Hersh's*
Biology: *Edington's*
Birthday Parties: *Richman's*
Books: *Atwood's; Joyce's; NASA*
Boomerangs: *Mudgeeraba*
Boredom: *Levy's*
Borrowing: *Bill Babcock's; Billings's (Law)*
Bosses: *Work*
Brains: *Ozian*
Bread and Butter: *Murphy's; Perversity (of Nature); Selective; Sod's*
Brevity: *Katz's (Other)*
Bribery: *Bribery*
Bridge: *Bridge; Orwell's*
Briefings: *Katz's (Maxims)*
Budgets: *Bolton's; Cheops's; Pratt*
Bureaucracy: *Acheson's; Boren's; Branch's; Brown's (J.); Bureaucracy; Bureaucratic Cop-Out; Bureaucratic Laws; Cohn's; Displaced; Evelyn's; Fowler's; Gammon's; Imhoff's; McNaughton's; Melcher's; Meskimen's; Miles's; Mills's (Law); Nies's; Rodovic's; Smith's (Principle)*
Buses: *Corcoroni's; Ross's (S.)*
Business: *Brown's (Law of Business Success); Davis's (Laws); Drucker; McLandress's; Pareto's; Peter Principle; Robertson's*

C

Calculators: *Murphy's; Shelton's*
Campaigns: *O'Brien's (First); Rakove's; Walinsky's*
Candidates: *Gold's (V.); Kelley's; Nobel's; Nofziger's; Prime; Public Relations; Spencer's*
Canoeing: *Andrew's*

198

D

E

Equality: *Nayquist's; Paradox; Russell's*
Equations: *Finagle*
Equilibrium: *Le Chatellier's*
Equipment: *Horner's; Martin's (Laws); Price's (Law of Science)*
Erosion: *John Adams's*
Errors: *Computer; Considine's; Editorial; Err's; Faber's; Fiedler's; Finagle; Fudge; Gilb's; Halpern's; Issawi's; Leahy's; Mills (Law); Murphy's; Nies's; Otten's (Law of Typesetting); Transcription; Wolf's*
Events: *Dude's; Economist's; Gumperson's (Law); Long-Range; McGurk's; Phelps's (Law of Retributive Statistics)*
Exams: *Weisman's*
Exceptions: *Boquist's*
Executives: *Kelly's*
Expansion: *Parkinson's*
Expectations: *Frustration*
Expense Accounts: *O'Brien's (Principle); O'-Doyle's (Corollary)*
Experience: *Horner's*
Experiments: *Bowie's; Carson's; Emerson's; Finagle; Fudge; Futility; Harvard; Kohn's; Parkinson's; Patrick's*
Experts: *Allison's; Expert; Gummidge's; Lowrey's; Prime; Public Relations; Ryan's; Weinberg's*
Explosives: *Brumfit's*

F

Facts: *Cohen's (Law) (J.); Fiedler's; Finagle; Lawyer's (Rule); Maier's; Schumpeter's*
Failure: *Boyle's; Futility; Hollywood's; Sod's; Waddell's*
Falling Bodies: *Bernstein's*
Fans: *Ledges; Probable*
Fashion: *Fashion*
Favors: *Geanangel's*
Files: *Corcoran's*
Finality: *Stephens's*
Food: *Algren's; Calkins's; Chamberlain's; Chili; Chinese; Clark's; Cole's; Dieter's; Distance; Germond's; Institutional; Kelly's; Kerr's; Morley's; Old; Paige's; Three; Ubell's; Zusmann's*
Fools: *Murphy's*
Football: *McCarthy's*
Force: *Jake's; Kaplan's; Lowrey's*
Forecasting: *Allison's; Asimov's; Clarke's; Fiedler's; Grump's; Man's; Ryan's; Turner's*
Fortune Cookie: *Chinese*
Foundations: *Parkinson's*
Frankness: *Long's*
Fraud: *Gross's*
Freedom: *Putney's*
Free Love: *Short's*
Free Lunch: *Commoner's; Crane's (Law); Drucker*
Friendship: *Friendship; LaRochefoucauld's; Tom Jones*
Frisbee: *Frisbee*

Frustration: *Chisholm; Frustration; Kristol's; Riddle's*
Futility: *Futility*

G

Gambling: *Algren's; Allison's; Canada; Flip; Runyon's*
Games: *Bridge; Canada; Orwell's*
Gardening: *Gardening*
Generalists: *Donsen's*
GNP: *Fiedler's*
Goals: *Wober's*
Gold: *Bloom's*
Golf: *Metz's*
Good Deeds: *Luce's*
Good Intentions: *Levy's*
Government: *Branch's; Broder's; Brown's (J.); Bureaucratic Laws; Cohen's (Laws of Politics); Connally's; Connolly's (Law); Davidson's; Drucker; du Pont's; Evans's (Law of Political Perfidy); Frankel's; Human; Jacquin's; Kennedy's; Knowles's; Long's; McGovern's; McNaughton's; Nader's; No. 3; Oaks's; OSHA's; Parkinson's; Parliament; Peter Principle; Raskin's; Rumsfeld's; Security; Stamp's; Survival; Wicker's*
Graft: *Bribery*
Grants: *Parkinson's*
Grapefruit: *Sattler's*
Gratitude: *Bennett's*
Groups: *Gadarene*
Growth: *Gall's*
Guns: *Canada*

H

Hard Times: *Fiedler's*
Harvard: *Fiedler's; Harvard*
Heart: *White's*
Heredity: *Fischer's; Socio-Genetics*
Hero: *Short's*
Hierarchy: *Dow's; G Constant; Martin's (Laws); Peter Principle; Vail's*
High Fidelity: *Culshaw's*
High-Jump: *Terman's*
Highways: *Cleveland's; Eternity; Gumperson's (Law); Murphy's; Road*
History: *Bustlin'; Darrow's; Durant's; Economist's; Historian's; Wolf's*
Hollywood: *Hollywood*
Home Repairs: *Avery's (Law)*
Hope: *Franklin's (Observation)*
Horses: *Hartley's; North; Runyon's; Tishbein's*
Hospitals: *Roemer's*
Hotels: *Mankiewicz's*
Household Laws: *Allen's (Axiom); Avery's (Law); Avery's (Rule); Barr's; Boston's; Chatauqua; Clark's (First Law); Dunn's; Finagle; Gardening; Matsch's; Money; Occam's;*

Orben's; Parsons's; Phelps's (Law of Reno-
vation); Rapoport's; Rebecca's; Ross's (A.);
Sattingler's; Yapp's
Human Condition: Abbott's; Agnes Allen's; Ap-
proval; Army (Axiom); Artz's; Avery's (Ob-
servation); Baker's; Baruch's; Beauregard's;
Benchley's; Bennett's; Boozer's; Borkow-
ski's; Broken; Butler's; Chamberlain's;
Character; Chatauqua; Checkbook; Chi-
sholm; Clark's (Law); Cohen's (Choice);
Cohn's; Colson's; Dibble's; Ehrman's;
Eliot's; Farber's; Fetridge's; Franklin's (Law);
Glasow's; Goodfader's; Hardin's (G.);
Howe's; How To; John's (Axiom); Jones's;
Kafka's; Kettering's; Kirkup's; Koppett's;
Kristol's; Langin's; LaRochefoucauld's;
Leahy's; Ledge's; Levy's; Lewis's; Liebling's;
Lowrey's; Luce's; Man's; Marshall's (Uni-
versal); McGurk's; Mencken's (Law);
Mencken's (Metalaw); Miller's (M.);
Miller's (?); Munnecke's; Murphy's; Mur-
stein's; Navy; Newton's; Nixon's; North;
No. 3; O'Brien's (Rule); Occam's; O'-
Toole's; Paige's; Paradox; Pardo's; Pas-
tore's; Paturi; Peer's; Pierson's; Potter's;
Probable; Professor; Pudder's; Robertson's;
Rowe's; Rudin's; Runyon's; Sattler's;
Schuckit's; Scriptural; Segal's; Simon's; Sin-
ner's; Sprague's; Sturgeon's; Third; Tho-
reau's (Law); Thoreau's (Rule); Uhlmann's;
Unnamed; Unspeakable; Walker's; Weid-
ner's; Weiler's; Wicker's; Wilcox's; Wolf's;
Woman's; Work; Yapp's; Zymurgy's (First);
Zymurgy's (Seventh)
Human Interaction: Chisholm
Human Rights: Human
Humility: Bustlin'
Hypotheses: Edington's

I

Iceberg: Marshall's (Generalized)
Ideas: Boyle's; Fried's; Harden (H.); Idea; Katz's
(Maxims); Kettering's; Malek's; Truths
Ignorance: Short's
Inconvenience: Koppett's
Inertia: Inertia
Infernal Dynamics: Gerrold's
Influence: Greenberg's
Information: Boyle's; Cooke's; Finagle; Gray's
(Law of Bilateral Asymmetry); Kennedy's;
Mesmerisms; Ubell's
Inlaws: Clark's (First Law of Relativity)
Insanity: Kriedt's
Insertion: Fudd's (Law)
Inside Dope: Cohen's (Laws of Politics)
Institutions: Kharasch's
Insurance: Friendship
Intervention: Schuckit's
Invention/Innovation: Katz's (Maxims); Saun-
der's; Terman's

J

Jackpot: Flip
Jobs: Becker's; Cornuelle's; Dawes-Bell;
McGovern's; Wing-Walker
Journals: O'Brien's (Law); Parkinson's
Junk: Boston's; Farmer's; Hogg's; Lloyd-Jones's;
Orben's
Jury: Goulden's (Law)
Justice: Alley's; Goulden's (Law)

K

Keys: Key

L

Labor: Labor
Language: Beardsley's; K' Rule
Late-Comers: Late-Comers
Law/Lawyers: Alley's; Beardsley's; Goulden's
(Law); Lawyer's (Rule); Oaks's; Parliament;
Professionals; Specht's
Lawmaking/Legislation: Cohen's (Laws of Poli-
tics); du Pont's; Finagle; Funkhouser's; Jac-
quin's; Knowles's; Mencken's (Law); Parlia-
ment
Laws: Faber's; Short's
Laziness: Saunder's
Leadership: Boyle's; Jaroslovsky's; Matsch's
Learning: Barzun; Donsen's
Liberals: Kerr-Martin; Levy's; Mankiewicz's;
McClaughry's (Second); Price's (Law of
Politics)
Life: Kerr's (General); Paige's; Rumsfeld's
Light Bulbs: Occam's
Lincoln: Lincoln
Lines: Ettorre's; Sam's
Loans: John's (Collateral)
Lobbying: du Pont's; Will's
Long-Range: Long-Range
Lost Objects: Boob's
Luggage: Hogg's
Lunch: Kelly's

M

Machines: IBM; Rural
Male: Algren's; Beifeld's; Mother
Management: Boyle's; Brien's; Brontosaurus;
Brown's (Law of Business Success); Bureau-
cratic Laws; Dennis's; Dror's (First);
Drucker; Hacker's (Law of Personnel);
Heller's; Jay's; Johnson's (Corollary); Mes-
merisms; Truths; Walters's; Wolf's

Manure: *OHSA's*
Maps: *Parsons's*
Marketing: *Drucker; Lewis's*
Marriage: *O'Neill's*
Mate: *Instant*
Math: *Ashley-Perry*
Measurement: *Coomb's; Finagle; Schultze's; Westheimer's*
Media: *Bagdikian's; Blanchard's; Considine's; Deitz's; du Pont's; Editorial; Foster's; Funkhouser's; Germond's; Gold (V.); Gold (W.); Hagerty's; Kauffmann's; Kent's; Knoll's; Loevinger's; Marcus's; Nessen's; O'Brien's (Principle); O'Doyle's; O'Neill's; Pike's; Rather's; Rumsfeld's; Ubell's; Weaver's; Wilson's (W.)*
Medicare/Medicaid: *Drucker*
Medicine: *Bombeck's (Rule); Davis's (Basic); Drucker; Local; Parkinson; Professionals'; Roemer's*
Meetings: *Czecinski's; Kirkland's; Late-Comers; McLaughlin's; Parson's; Shanahan's; Wolf's*
Memory: *Grobe's*
Memos: *Acheson's; Boyle's; Corcoran's*
Menus: *Calkins's*
Military: *Vance's; White*
Mineral Rights: *Getty's*
Mirrors: *Broken*
Misery: *Baker's; How To*
Mishap: *Chisholm*
Misunderstanding: *Chisholm*
Model Railroading: *Bye's*
Monday: *Avery (Sayings)*
Money: *Billings's (Law); Bolton's; Butler's; Canada; DeCaprio's; Donohue's; Dunn's; Evelyn's; Golden; Gresham's; Gross's; Gumperson's (Law); Instant; John's (Collateral); Lani's; Long's; Miller's (J.); Money; Murchison's; Pardo's; Pratt; Raskin's; Sam's; Sutton's; Truth's; Vance's*
Mortgage: *Journalist's*
Motivation: *Drucker*
Movies: *Shalit's*

N

Names: *Cohen's (J.); Curley's*
Nations: *Hacker's (Law); Index; Issawi's; Miller's (N.); Moynihan's; Nations*
Natural Law: *Long's; Murphy's*
Nature: *Darwin's; Fetridge's; Gumperson's (Law); Harvard; Long's; Murphy's; Perversity (of Nature); Short's*
Necessity: *Farber's*
Neighbors: *Issawi's*
Newspapers: See: Press
New York Times: Nobel
Nobel: *Nobel*
Non-Smokers: *Dhawan's*

O

Obituaries: *Blanchard's*
Objects (Perversity of): *Bernstein's; Boob's; Boyle's; Chatauqua; Chisholm; Cushman's; Ear's; Finagle; Flap's; Fudd's (First); Gerrold's; Murphy's; Perversity (of Nature); Perversity (of Production); Rapoport's; Ross's (A.); Sattler's; Selective; Universal; Waddell's*
Offensiveness: *Brown's (S.)*
Office Holders: *Office Holder's*
Oil: *Dirksen's (Version); Issawi's; Sadat's*
Opposition: *Fudd's (First); Galbraith's (Law of Prominence)*
Optimist/Optimism: *Oppenheimer's; O'Toole's; Wolf's*
Orders: *Army (Axiom)*
Organization: *Boyle's; Brien's; Brontosaurus; Dow's; Drucker; Evelyn's; Gadarene; G Constant; Golub's; Gray's (Law of Bilateral Asymmetry); Hacker's (Law); Hacker's (Law of Personnel); How To; Imhoff's; Johnson's (Corollary); Katz's (Maxims); Kharasch's; Miles's; Navy; No. 3; Oeser's; Parkinson's; Rodovic's; Vail's; Zimmerman's*
Oz: *Ozian*

P

Packaging: *Orben's*
Pain: *Science*
Paperwork: *Brown's (J.); Brown's (Law of Business Success); Corcoran's; Dyer's; Fowler's; Katz's (Maxims); Mesmerisms; Oeser's; Von Braun's*
Parades: *Wells's*
Paranoia: *How To; Pastore's*
Parking: *Jaroslavsky's; Joyce's; Murphy's*
Parliamentary Procedure: *Swipple*
Parties: *Ear's*
Pencils: *Avery (Sayings); Murphy's; No. 3; Price's (Law of Science)*
Perfection: *Stephens's*
Permanence: *Cohen's (Law of Politics)*
Personnel: *Hacker's (Law of Personnel)*
Pessimist/Pessimism: *Oppenheimer's; O'Toole's; Wolf's*
Ph.Ds: *Duggan's*
Philosophy: *Gardener's; Harris's (Law)*
Pills: *Davis's (Basic)*
Pipe: *Pipe*
Pizza: *Kerr's (Three)*
Planning: *Wolf's*
Plants: *Bombeck's (Rule)*
Plumbing: *Gardner's; Phelps's (Law of Renovation)*
Poetry: *Ciardi's*
Policy: *Dror's (First); Dror's (Second); Wilson's (J.Q.)*

Political Incumbent: *Connolly's (Rule)*
Politics: *Acton's; Baer's; Boultbee's; Broder's; Cohen's (Laws of Politics); Connolly's (Rule); Curley's; Dirksen's (Three); Evans's (Law of Political Perfidy); Galbraith's (Law of Political Wisdom); Gilmer's; Gold's (V.); Halberstam's; How To; Jacquin's; John Adams's; Johnson's (Prior); Kamin's; Mankiewicz's; McCarthy's; McClaughry's (Law); Munncke's; Nobel's; Nofziger's; O'Brien's (First); Office; Politician's; Powell's (A.C.); Price's (Law of Politics); Public Relations; Rakove's; Randolph's; Rayburn's; Rumsfeld's; Sayre's; Shaffer's; Smith's (Laws); Spencer's; Symington's; Thermopolitics; Truman's; Wallinsky's; Will's*
Postage Stamp: *How To*
Poverty: *Davis's (Laws)*
Power: *Acton's; Bonafede's; Dirksen's (Version); Drucker; Evans's (Law of Political Perfidy); Grandma, Hein's; John Adams's; Oeser's*
Practical Advice: *Allen's (Axiom); Allen's (Distinction); Baldy's; Bartz's; Beauregard's; Benchley's; Berkeley's; Berra's; Bill Babcock's; Bloom's Boozer's; Dave's (Law); Dave's (Rule); Hartley's; How To; Hull's; Rebecca's; Sattlinger's; Suhor's*
Practicality: *Cohen's (Laws of Politics)*
Pregnancy: *Bombeck's (Principles)*
Presidents: *Broder's; Coolidge's; Johnson's (Prior); Lincoln, McLandress's, Nixon's, Nobel's; Rumsfeld's; Truman's*
Press: *Bagdikian's; Blanchard's; Considine's; Deitz's; du Pont's; Editorial; Foster's; Funkhouser's; Germond's; Gold (V.); Gold (W.); Gray's (Law of Bilateral Asymmetry); Greener's; Gresham's; Grump's; Hagerty's; Journalist's; Kauffmann's; Kent's; Knoll's; Loevinger's; Marcus's; Moynihan's; Nessen's; Nobel; O'Brien's (Principle); O'Doyle's; O'Neill's; Otten's (Law of Typesetting); Pike's; Powell's (J.); Rather's; Rumsfeld's; Weaver's; Wilson's (W.); Yolen's; Zellar's*
Press Secretary (Presidential): *Nessen's; Powell's (J.); Ross's (C.); Salinger's*
Price: *Craditor's*
Principle: *Evans's; Shaffer's*
Probabilities: *Fourth; Gumperson's (Law)*
Problem-Solving: *Abrams's; Accuracy; Allen's (Axiom); Anderson's; Berkeley's; Billings's (Phenomenon); Booker's; Boob's; Boren's; Boyle's; Bucy's; Bureaucracy; Bureaucratic Laws; Burns; Cliff-Hanger; Cooke's; Crane's (Rule); Dijkstra's; Displaced; Dobbin's; Dror's (First); Epstein's; Evvie Nef's; Murphy's; Optimum; Peers's; Pratt; Rowe's; Rural; Sattingler's; Sevareid's; Shelton's; Short's; Skinner's; Wolf's; Zymurgy's (First)*
Procedures: *Chisholm*
Procrastination: *Inertia*
Production/Productivity: *Gammon's; Luten's; Perversity (of Production); Rogers's; Scientific*
Products: *Boyle's*

Professors: *Lenin's*
Profits: *Hale's*
Programming: *Brooks's; Computer Programming; Dijkstra's; Gilb's; Gray's (Law of Programming); Halpern's; Hoare's; Logg's; Weinberg's*
Progress: *Bustlin'; Butler's; Issawi's; Nienberg's*
Projects: *Bureaucratic Laws; Serendipity*
Prominence: *Galbraith's (Law of Prominence)*
Prototype: *Bye's*
Proverbs: *Proverbial*
Psychology: *Maier's*
Public: *Gummidge's*
Public Opinion: *Politician's*
Public Relations: *Public Relations (Client); Public Relations (Prime Rule); Rogers's; Ross's (C.); Salinger's; Ubell's*
Public Service: *Branch's*
Public Speaking: *Public Speaking*
Public Works: *Cleveland's*
Publishing: *Froben's; Murphy's*

Q

Quality: *Herblock's; Perversity (of Production)*

R

Racial Integration: *Simmon's*
Raffles: *Gumperson's (Law)*
Reality: *Sprague's*
Reform: *Reform*
Reliability: *Gilb's*
Religion: *Vique's*
Renovation: *Phelps's (Law of Renovation)*
Repairmen: *Schenk's*
Reports: *Cohn's; Mesmerisms*
Republicans: *How To*
Research and Development (R&D): *Extended; Gordon's; Lubin's; Murstein's; NASA; Parkinson's; Patrick's; Phases; Price's (Law of Science); Scientific; Wilson's (J.Q.)*
Resignation: *Galbraith's (Law of Political Wisdom)*
Restaurants: *Algren's; Calkins's; Chinese; Germond's; Harris's (Restaurant); Restaurant; Tipper's*
Results: *Riddle's*
Retirement: *Mosher's*
Revenge: *Dirksen's (Three)*
Rhetoric: *Dunne's*
Right: *McKenna's*
Risk: *Katz's (Maxims)*
Roller Skates: *Rapoport's*
Romance: *Jacoby's*
Routine: *Evelyn's*
Routing Slips: *Melcher's*
Rules: *Boquist's; Ginsberg's; Golden; Thoreau's (Rules)*
Rural: *Rural*

S

Salaries: *Mesmerisms; Riesman's*
Salesmen: *Drucker; Schenk's*
Sample: *Sells's*
Sanity: *Kreidt's*
Schedules: *Cheops's; Corcoroni's; Finagle; Ninety; Ross's* (S.)
Schemes: *Howe's*
Schools: *Boozer's; Mankiewicz's; Murphy's*
Science and Technology: *Allen's (Axiom); Ashley-Perry; Asimov's; Berkeley's; Billings's (Phenomenon); Blaaw's; Booker's; Bowie's; Boyle's; Bustlin'; Carson's; Chisholm's; Clarke's; Compensation; Computability; Coomb's; Edington's; Extended; Finagle; First; Fudge; Futility; Gall's; Golden; Gordon's; Harvard; Katz's (Other); Kohn's; Levian's; Lowrey's; Lubin's; Maier's; NASA; Nobel; O'Brien's (Law); Parkinson's; Patrick's; Phases; Pratt; Price's (Law of Science); Purina; Riddle's; Sattingler's; Schumpeter's; Science; Scientific; Technology; Woodward's*
Scriptural: *Scriptural*
Second-Ratedness: *Second-Ratedness*
Secrecy: *Cohen's (Law of Politics); Long's*
Security: *Security; Wing-Walker; Wober's*
Self-Importance: *Fifth*
Serendipity: *Serendipity*
Sex: *Algren's; Beifeld's; Bonafede's; Fischer's; John Cameron's*
Show Business: *Hartley's*
Side-Effects: *Commoner's; Hardin's* (G.)
Simplicity: *Occam's*
Sin: *Emerson's*
Slides: *Slide Presentation*
Smoking: *Dhawan's; Pipe*
Soap Operas: *Davis's (Laws)*
Social Class: *Hall's*
Social Engineering: *Robertson's*
Social Sciences: *Computability; Dawes-Bell; Finagle; Issawi's; Murstein's*
Society: *Everitt's; Gardner's; Instant; Technology; Thermopolitical*
Sociology: *Dibble's; Hart's*
Sound: *Culshaw's*
Space: *Hersh's*
Spaghetti: *Morley's*
Spare Parts: *Spare Parts*
Specialists: *Donsen's; Freemon's*
Speeches: *Bagdikian's*
Sports: *Ade's; Andrew's; Avery (Sayings); Barber's; Berra's; Bicycle; Bicycling; Frisbee; McCarthy's; Metz's; Mudgeeraba; Runyon's; Smith's (Laws); Terman's; Yolen's*
Station Wagons: *Hogg's*
Statistics: *Ashley-Perry; NASA; Perelman's; Stamp's*
Stocks and Bonds: *Crane's (Law); Stock Market; Stockbroker's*
Stress: *LeChatellier's*
Style: *Brown* (S.)
Subways: *Meditz*

Success: *Boyle's; Brien's; Brown's (Law of Business Success); Einstein's; Fourth; Heller's; Hollywood's; Instant; Paturi; Pike's; Sod's*
Supermarket: *Bombeck's (Principles); Ettorre's*
Supply and Demand: *Sadat's*
Support: *Evelyn's*
Surveys: *Fiedler's; Perelman's*
Survival: *Halberstam's*
System (The): *Goodfader's*
Systems: *Gall's; Gilb's; Martin's (Basic); Shaw's; Waldo's*

T

Talent: *Boyle's*
Taxes: *Diogenes's (First and Second); Eternity; Gumperson's (Proof); Lani's*
Taxis: *O'Doyle's; Taxi; Weaver's*
Tchaikovsky: *Short's*
Teachers and Teaching: *Boozer's; Herrnstein's; Kerr-Martin; Lenin's; Martin's (Laws); Waffle's*
Telephone: *Lawyer's (Law); Parkinson's*
Television: *Avery (Sayings); Boultbee's; Gresham's; Kitman's; Lindy's, Pastore's; Schickel's; Sahlit's*
Temper: *Hagerty's*
Testimony: *Otten's (Law of Testimony)*
Theories: *Berkeley's; Fiedler's; Finagle; Woodward's*
Thinking: *IBM*
Time: *Belle's; Character; Cohn's; DeCaprio's; Dunn's; Engineer's; Extended; Golub's; Hersh's; McLaughlin's; Meskimen's; Nienberg's; Ninety; O'Neill's; Otten's (Law of Testimony); Paul; Professionals'; Segal's*
Time (Magazine): *Galbraith's (Law of Prominence)*
Tinkering: *Ehrlich's*
Tips: *Tipper's*
Tires: *Fishbein's*
Titles: *McGovern's*
Toll-Booth: *Ettorre's*
Tomfoolery: *Gallois's*
Tools: *Anthony's (Law of Force); Anthony's (Law of the Workshop); Dobbins's; Gardening; Jake's; Johnson's (First); Kaplan's; Plotnick's; Spare*
Towns: *Steinbeck's*
Toys: *Christmas*
Traffic: *Bruce-Brigg's; Cleveland's; Road*
Trains: *Ross's* (S.)
Transistors: *Froud's*
Transportation/ Travel: *Airplane; Corcoroni's; Durrell's; Ear's; Finagle; Hogg's; Meditz; Mills's (Law of Transportation Logistics); Ross's (S.); Sprague's; Travel; Witzenberg's*
Trash: *Orben's*
Truth: *Avery (Sayings); Clopton's; Comin's; Marshall's (Universal); Short's*
Typesetting: *Otten's (Law of Typesetting)*

U

Ultimate Laws: *Ultimate (Law); Ultimate (Principle)*
Umbrellas: *Umbrella*
Unanimity: *Levy's*
Uncertainty: *Gall's*
Understanding: *Hacker's (Law)*
Unexpected: *Peter Principle*
United: *United*
United States: *Hart's*
Universe: *Haldane's*
Urban Planning: *Wood's*

V

Vacation: *Luten's*
Vagueness: *Committee*
Variables: *Osborn's*
Vices: *Paige's*
Volunteers: *Zymurgy's (Law)*
Voters: *Connolly's (Rule)*

W

Wage and Price Controls: *Connally's*
Waking: *Long's*

War: *Bustlin'; White*
War of 1812: *Short's*
Warranty: *Graditor's*
Washington: *Dean's; Rumsfeld's*
Watches: *Segal's*
Water: *Nations*
Watergate: *Colson's; Dean's; Galbraith's (Law of Political Wisdom); Nixon's*
Wealth: *Cohen's (Law of Politics)*
Weight-Watchers: *Weight-Watcher's*
White House: *Rumsfeld's*
Wickedness: *Levy's*
Winning: *Ade's; Chamberlain's; Ginsberg's; Merrill's*
Wisdom: *Cohen's (Law of Politics); Long's; Lynott's*
Women: *Human; Jacoby's; Nyquist's; Woman's*
Words: *Smith's (Principles)*
Work: *Becker's; Belle's; Boyle's; Coolidge's; Crane's (Rule); Einstein's; Extended; Gammon's; Katz's (Maxims); Labor; Miles's; Ninety; Pastore's; Peter Principle; Phases; Pierson's; Rodovic's; Rudin's; Sam's; Spare; Third; Tom Sawyer's; Vail's; Westheimer's; Woman's; Work*
Writing: *Considine's; Davis's (Law); Faber's*
Wrong: *McKenna's*

Z

Zoning: *McClaughry's (Iron)*

The Official Explanations

A

● **Abercrombie's Theory of Parallel Universes.** There exists a parallel universe into which all our lost objects are sucked, never to be seen again.

(Denis Abercrombie, from Larry Groebe.)

● **Abourezk's First Eight Laws of Politics.** (1) Anybody who really would change things for the better in this country could never be elected president anyway. (2) Don't worry about your enemies, it's your allies who will do you in. (3) In politics people will do whatever is necessary to get their way. (4) The bigger the appropriations bill, the shorter the debate. (5) If a politician has a choice between listening and talking, guess which one he will choose. (6) When voting on the confirmation of a presidential appointment, it's always safer to vote against the son of a bitch, because if he is confirmed, it won't be long before he proves how wise you were. (7) If you want to curry favor with a politician, give him credit for something that someone else did. (8) Don't blame me, I voted for McGovern.

(Senator James Abourezk, from his article "Life Inside the Congressional Cookie Jar," *Playboy,* March 1979.)

● **Acheson's Comment on Experts.** An expert is like a eunuch in a harem—someone who knows all about it but can't do anything about it.

(Dean Acheson. *TCA.*)

● **Ackley's Axiom.** The degree of technical competence is inversely proportional to the level of management.

(Bob Ackley, T.Sgt., USAF, Plattsmouth, Neb. He adds,

"Originally defined—in 1967—as 'The level of intelligence is inversely proportional to the number of stripes,' then I had to modify it as I accrued more stripes.")

● **Adams's Axiom.** It doesn't matter what you say, as long as you keep talking.
(Harold "Buck" Adams, Capt., USAF, c. 1974, from Bob Ackley, Plattsmouth, Neb.)

● **Adams's Law of Gossip.** Ninety-two percent of the stuff told you in confidence you couldn't get anyone else to listen to.
(Journalist, poet, and humorist Franklin Pierce Adams.)

● **Adams's Political Discovery.** Practical politics consists in ignoring facts.
(Historian Henry Adams.)

● **Ade's Reminder.** A bird in the hand may be worth two in the bush, but remember also that a bird in the hand is a positive embarrassment to one not in the poultry business.
(Humorist George Ade.)

● **Adenauer's Advice.** An infallible method of conciliating a tiger is to allow oneself to be devoured.
(Dr. Konrad Adenauer.)

● **Adlai's Axiom.** He who slings mud generally loses ground.
(Adlai Stevenson, 1954. *MLS.*)

● **Agrait's Law.** A rumor will travel fastest to the place where it will cause the greatest harm.
(Gustavo N. Agrait, Rio Piedras, P. R.)

● **"Ain't": Why Americans Say It.** (1) Because there ain't no reason not to. (2) Because there ain't no easy way to prove there're not reasons to. (3) Because at times it serves the purpose in communicating.

> (Editor Lucy Catherine Bowie, in the *Madison County* [Va.] *Eagle* when she learned that the government was about to issue a grant of $121,000 to find out why many Americans say "ain't.")

● **Air Force Law.** Two percent don't get the word. *(U/GT.)*

● **Albert's Law of the Sea.** The more they are in a fog, the more boats (and people) toot their horns.

> (Bernard L. Albert, M.D., Scarsdale, N.Y.)

● **Albinak's Algorithm.** When graphing a function, the width of the line should be inversely proportional to the precision of the data.

> (Marvin J. Albinak, Professor of Chemistry, Essex Community College, Baltimore, Md.)

AIR FORCE LAW

● **Alderson's Theorem.** If at first you don't succeed, you are running about average.

(M. H. Alderson, from the *Lawrence County*[Mo.] *Record.*)

● **Alfalfa's Observation.** Another day, another zero!

(From T. A. Moore III, M.D., New Orleans, who recalls it from "a memorable scene in the Our Gang comedies when Spanky, Buckwheat, and Alfalfa are descending the steps of their school after another day of intellectual disaster." Moore adds, "This is certainly a universal sentiment and could not be more succinct.")

● **Alicat Shop Generalization.** The more gushing they do, the less they buy.

(Florenz Baron, Yonkers, N.Y. Named for the Alicat Bookshop run by Florenz and her late husband, Oscar.)

● **Alice's Law.** The purpose of Presidential office is not power, or leadership of the Western World, but reminiscence, best-selling reminiscence.

(Roger Jellinek, *The New York Times Book Review,* March 10, 1968.)

● **Allan's Theorem.** In any group of eagles, you will find some turkeys.

(Allan B. Guerrina, Woodbridge, Va.)

● **Allen's Circus Axiom.** If a circus is half as good as it smells, it's a great show.

(Radio with Fred Allen.)

● **Allen's Motto.** I'd rather have a free bottle in front of me than a prefrontal lobotomy.

(Fred Allen. *DRW.*)

● **Anderson's Maxims.** (1) Colleges and universities are immune to their own knowledge. (2) You can't outthink a person who isn't thinking.
    (Phil Anderson, Assistant Professor, College of St. Thomas, St. Paul, Minn.)

● **Anderson's Observation.** Institutions tend to treat their employees as they do their clients. Schools, prisons, uptight corporations, etc., structure time for their clients and employees as well. Laid-back free clinics, certain mental health units, universities, etc., do not structure time for their clients; thus they do not structure time for their employees.
    (E. Frederick Anderson, Assistant Dean, San Diego State University.)

● **Anonymous's Bodily Discovery.** Whatever doesn't stick out is hanging down.
    (Name withheld by request.)

● **Apartment Dweller's Law.** One person's floor is another person's ceiling.
    (U/Ra.)

● **Aquinas Axiom, The.** What the gods get away with, the cows don't.
    (DRW.)

● **Armor's Axiom of Morality.** Virtue is the failure to achieve vice.
    (John C. Armor, Baltimore.)

● **Arnofy's Law of the Post Office.** The likelihood of a letter getting lost in the mail is directly proportional to its importance.

(Andrew G. Aronfy, M.D., Seabrook, Md. Aronfy's proof: "I sent the IRS a substantial check for estate taxes. A month and a half later they sent us a bill for an additional $207.00 for interest and penalties. Needless to say, they never got the original.")

● **Arnold's Square Wheel Theory.** A prevalent form of decision-making holds that if three out of four schools, firms, or whatever, are using square wheels then the fourth will follow.
(Richard Arnold, Keezletown, Va.)

● **Astor's Economic Discovery.** A man who has a million dollars is as well off as if he were rich.
(John Jacob Astor.)

● **Augustine's Plea.** Give me chastity and self-restraint, but do not give it yet.
(Saint Augustine.)

● **Aunt Emmie's Laws.** (1) A cigarette placed in an ashtray will go out if you stay in the room; if you leave the room, the cigarette will topple to the table, burn through, and drop to the floor, where it will smolder until it descends to ignite the drapes in the room below. (2) A clever remark is one you don't make at the appropriate moment but compose immediately after. (3) A pair of scissors should be a true pair; the second pair is to be used in place of the pair that is never where it is always supposed to be.
(Owen Elliott, Ridgefield, Conn. Aunt Emmie was the youngest of his mother's eight sisters.)

● **Austin's Law.** It tastes better in somebody else's house.
(Mabel Austin, New York City. Submitted by Mrs. Mariquita P. Mullan.)

B

● **Baber's Rule.** Anything worth doing is worth doing in excess.

(Susan Baber, St. Louis.)

● **Bacchanalian Conclusion.** One can get just as drunk on water . . . as one can on land!

(Eldred O. Schwab, Ojibwa, Wisc.)

● **Backus's Law.** All water is one inch over your boot tops. (Named for Dr. Richard Backus of Woods Hole and reported by Ken S. Norris, Professor of Natural History, Santa Cruz, Cal. Norris, who says, "No law I know is more completely immutable," adds that he and Backus have sighted a rock south of Cape Horn that offers a silhouette close to that of Backus with water sloshing over his boots.)

● **Bair's Rule of Lighting.** Fuses never blow during daylight hours. *Corollary:* Only after the fuses blow do you discover the flashlight batteries are dead and you're out of candles, or matches, or both.

(Penny Bair, Austin, Tex.)

● **Baker's Byroad.** When you are over the hill, you pick up speed.

(U/DRW.)

● **Baker's Secrets of Losing Politics.** (1) Address yourself to the issues. (2) Identify as closely as possible with politicians.

(3) Be a loyal party person. (4) Invoke the memories of your party greats. (5) If you are squeamish about your partisanship, at least have the good grace to refer to the accomplishments of your party's major officeholders. (6) Take the high road. (7) Never criticize your opponent's absenteeism on votes if you are seeking his congressional seat. (8) Never criticize your opponent for spending too much time in the district. (9) Avoid squandering huge amounts of money in media markets where only a fraction of the television audience is made up of your potential voters. (10) Forget about the endorsements of Hollywood celebrities and sports figures.

> (Ross K. Baker, Professor of Political Science, Rutgers University. First revealed in *The New York Times,* December 5, 1978.)

● **Ballweg's Discovery.** Whenever there is a flat surface, someone will find something to put on it.

> (Col. Lawrence H. Ballweg, USAF [retired], Albuquerque, N.M.)

● **Balzer's Law.** Life is what happens to you while you are making other plans.

> (Robert Balzer.)

● **Banacek's Law.** When the owl shows up at the mouse picnic, he's not there to enter the sack race.

> (TV character "Banacek" [George Peppard]. *MLS.*)

● **Barber's Rule of Uniformity.** If it sticks out, cut it off.

> (Linda Marsh, barber, Portland, Ore., from Gary M. Knowlton.)

● **Barilleaux's Observations on Eating Out.** (1) The price of the meal varies directly with the accent of the waiter. (2) If you need help to translate the menu, you can't afford the meal. (3)

If a salad is served with the meal, the portions will be smaller. (4) If soup is also served with the meal, the portions will be even smaller.

(Ryan J. Barilleaux, Lafayette, La.)

● **Barnes's Law of Probability.** There's a 50 percent chance of anything—either it happens or it doesn't.
(Michael R. Barnes, Dallas. *JS.*)

● **Barnum's Dictum.** Every crowd has a silver lining.
(P. T. Barnum.)

● **Baron's Law.** The world is divided between victims and predators, and you have to defend yourself against both.
(Florenz Baron, Yonkers, N.Y.)

● **Barrymore's Conclusion.** The thing that takes up the least amount of time and causes the most amount of trouble is Sex.
(John Barrymore.)

● **Bartel's Law.** When someone is kicking your ass, at least you know when you are out in front.
(Donald E. Bartel, Palo Alto, Cal.)

● **Bartlett's Observation of Input/Output.** The problem with pulling names out of a hat is that it is possible that you'll end up with a size.
(H. A. Bartlett, East Norwalk, Conn.)

● **Battista's Explanation.** The fellow who says he'll meet you halfway usually thinks he's standing on the dividing line.
(O. A. Battista, *The Philadelphia Bulletin.*)

● **Bax's Rule.** You should make a point of trying every experience once—except incest and folk dancing.

(Arnold Bax, quoted by Nigel Rees in *Quote . . . Unquote,* George Allen and Unwin, 1978.)

● **Beckmann's Lemma.** Where there is no patrol car, there is no speed limit.

(Petr Beckmann, from Richard Stone, Stanford, Cal., who insists his friend's name is actually spelled Petr.)

● **Bedard's Laws of Fossil Fuel.** (1) The last gas station for 50 miles will be closed when you get there. (2) At the moment of any departure, the level of gas in your tank depends entirely on how late you are. (3) You only run out of gas after your wife tells you to stop for gas before you run out.

(Patrick Bedard, *Car and Driver* magazine.)

● **Beebe's Law for Teachers and Preachers.** Heads should be weighed, not counted.

(Rev. Richard K. Beebe, Litchfield, Conn.)

● **Beiser's Brass Tack.** Facts without theory is trivia. Theory without facts is bullshit.

(U/RA.)

● **Belknap's Fat Flow Formula.** Fat is lost where it is wanted the least. *Corollary 1:* Fat is lost first from areas of high desirability. *Corollary 2:* With time fat flows from areas of high to low desirability.

(Hal R. Belknap, M.D., Norman, Okla.)

● **Bell's Law of Frustration.** When responding to an urgent message requesting an immediate return call, you will get: (1) a wrong number, (2) a busy signal, or (3) no answer.

(Named for Ma and Alexander Graham Bell by Joseph P. Sullivan, Indianapolis.)

● **Bell's Rules.** (1) The average time between throwing something away and needing it badly is two weeks. This time can be reduced to one week by retaining the thing for a long time first. (2) Linear objects (such as wire, string, etc.), when left to their own devices, occupy time by twisting themselves into tangles and weaving knots. (3) Tiny objects, when dropped, run and hide. (4) There is an updraft over wastebaskets.

(Norman R. Bell, Associate Professor of Engineering, North Carolina State University.)

● **Benchley's Travel Distinction.** In America there are two classes of travel—first class, and with children.

(Robert Benchley.)

● **Bendiner's Election Rule.** No matter how frighteningly the campaigners warn you that the salvation of the world depends on their winning, remember that on November 9, half of them will be wiring congratulations to the other half on their great victory and promising to co-operate fully in the predicted disaster.

(Robert Bendiner, from his article "How to Listen to Campaign Oratory If You Have To," *Look*, October 11, 1960.)

● **Bennett's Accidental Discoveries.** (1) Most auto accidents are caused by people with driver's licenses, so I tore up my license. (2) According to the latest statistics most auto accidents happen within 8 miles of your own home, so I moved.

(William S. Bennett, San Mateo, Cal.)

● **Berg's Constant.** Every time you learn a new word, you hear it five times the next day.

(Stephanie Berg, *Johns Hopkins Magazine*, May 1978.)

BENCHLEY'S TRAVEL DISTINCTION

● **Berger's Economics for the Masses.** The more there are of anything, the less they cost. Exclusivity has its price.
(Martin Berger, Mount Vernon, N.Y.)

● **Berkeley Beatitude.** The real world is just a special case of the theoretical.
(Don Smith, MBA, University of California Berkeley.)

● **Berliner's Law of Mineral Propagation.** Wire coat hangers multiply in dark closets.
(The late Josephine Mitchell Berliner, Washington, D.C., from her daughter Joie Vargas, Reno, Nev.)

● **Bernstein's Book Principles.**
Set I. Acquisition by Purchase. (1) If you buy a hardcover edition of a book, the paperback edition will appear next week, at a much lower price. (2) If you buy a paperback edition of a book, the hardcover will be remaindered next week, at a much lower price. (3) If you buy a paperback edition, or a hardcover edition, or a remaindered copy of a book, the next week you will find that a copy in excellent condition will be available in a used-book shop—at a much lower price than any of the other three. (4) If you buy a used hardcover copy of a book, a new edition that will make all previous editions obsolete will appear in hardcover next week. (5) A publisher will allow a book to go out of print just in time for you to begin looking for it. . . .
Set II. Borrowing from a Library. (1) If you go to the library for a book, the library will probably not have it in its collection. (2) If it does have the book in its collection, it will be checked out, or overdue, or lost, or stolen. (3) If it does have the book at hand, the pages you need to consult will be torn out. (4) If the book is available, at hand, and undamaged, it will probably be outdated and therefore useless. (5) If the book is available, at hand, un-damaged, and current, it will probably be too useful to be

used effectively in the library away from your other materials, and it will not be in the circulating collection. . . .
(Richard B. Bernstein, *Harvard Law Record,* Cambridge, Mass. From his larger collection of Book Principles.)

● **Bernstein's Law of Declining Progress.** One begins to lose interest in any given task and slacks off just as one is beginning to get somewhere in accomplishing that task.
(Richard B. Bernstein again.)

● **Berra's Rule of Attendance.** If the people don't want to come out, there's no way you're gonna stop 'em.
(Yogi Berra, from Steven D. Mirsky, Ithaca, N.Y.)

● **Beshere's Formula for Failure.** There are only two kinds of people who fail: those who listen to nobody, and . . . those who listen to everybody.
(Thomas M. Beshere, Jr., Charleston, S.C.)

● **Bethell's Iron Law of Washington.** The laws of supply and demand do not apply to Washington, they are turned inside out. Problems elsewhere in the country merely contribute to the wealth of Washington.
(Tom Bethell in *Harper's* magazine.)

● **Bialac's Conclusion.** Statistics are no substitute for common sense.
(Richard N. Bialac, Cincinnati, Ohio.)

● **Big Mac Principle, The.** The whole is equal to more than the sum of its parts. The whole is equal to less than the sum of its parts.
(Robert J. Samuelson, *The National Journal,* August 12, 1978. This apparently contradictory Principle bears some explanation. In Samuelson's own words, "Anyone can

understand the relationship of these truths to the real-life Big Mac. A Big Mac, of course, is 'two all-beef patties, special sauce, lettuce, cheese, pickles, onion on a sesame seed bun.' Depending on your taste, these few ingredients produce one of the magnificent gastronomical delights of American civilization *[the whole is equal to more than the sum of its parts]* or an insult to the sensitive stomach *[the whole is equal to less than the sum of its parts]*." He says that the Principle explains a lot about what is going on in Washington as things fall on one side or the other of the more-than/less-than scale. It explains, for instance, why as Congress becomes harder working and better educated, it falls in public esteem and contributes to the general creakiness of government. Congress then is equal to less than the sum of its parts.)

● **Bilbo's Proverb.** Never laugh at live dragons.
(U/GT.)

● **Billings's Advice (a smattering).**   (1) Don't ever prophesy; for if you prophesy wrong, nobody will forget it; and if you prophesy right, nobody will remember it. (2) Never work before breakfast; if you have to work before breakfast, get your breakfast first. (3) There are two things in this life for which we are never fully prepared and that is—twins. (4) I don't care how much a man talks, if he only says it in a few words.
(American humorist Josh Billings, 1818–85.)

● **Bing's Rule of Oblique Logic.** Don't try to stem the tide; move the beach.
(Wallace Bing, Mill Valley, Cal.)

● **Bishop's Theorem.** When you have accumulated sufficient knowledge to get by, you're too old to remember it.
(Columnist Jim Bishop.)

●   **Bismarck's Laws.** (1) The less people know about how sausages and laws are made, the better they'll sleep at night. (2) When you say that you agree to a thing in principle, you mean that you have not the slightest intention of carrying it out in practice.

(Bismarck.)

●   **Bixby's Law of Theater Seating.** In any given row the people with seats on the aisle always arrive first. *Corollary:* The probability that someone in the middle of the row will leave during the performance is directly proportional to the number of persons to be climbed over in reaching the aisle.

(Sandra W. Bixby, Chicago.)

●   **Blattenberger's Marital Principle.** Marriages are like union contracts in that six weeks after the fact, both parties feel that they could have done better if they had held out a little longer.

(Larry A. Blattenberger, Martinsburg, Penn.)

●   **Blewett's Rules for Dealing with Difficult Personalities.** (1) Identify the bears. (2) Tree the bears. (3) Stroke the bears. (4) Never forget how many bears you've treed. (5) Never let on to the bears who the other bears are. For that matter, never let any of the other creatures in the forest know who the bears are.

(Lt. Col. John H. Blewett, U.S. Army.)

●   **Blick's Rule of Life.** You have two chances, slim and none.

(*U/* From J. Patricia Reilly, New York City.)

●   **Blumenthal's Observation on Government.** The difference between business and government is that the government has no bottom line.

(Secretary of the Treasury W. Michael Blumenthal. *TCA.*)

● **Bobbitt's Law of TV.** Television network trouble never occurs except during the most exciting part of your favorite TV show.

    (Larry D. Bobbitt, Amarillo, Tex.)

● **Boettcher's Attribution.** If you have a bunch of clowns, you're going to have a circus.

    (R. J. Boettcher, Bridgewater, N.J. Letters to the Editor, *Time,* March 19, 1979. Boettcher attributes the maxim to the late W. L. Gilman.)

● **Bone's Labor Discovery.** Unlimited manpower can solve any problem except what to do with the manpower; e.g. if a man can dig a hole in a minute, why can't sixty men dig a hole in one second?

    (Jonathan Bone, Chicago.)

● **Boorstin's Observation.** Two centuries ago, when a great man appeared, people looked for God's purpose in him; today we look for his press agent.

    (Daniel J. Boorstin, from *The Image, or, What Happened to the American Dream,* Atheneum.)

● **Borklund's Law.** Communications is equal to the square root of the mistakes times confusion times contradictions.

    (C. W. Borklund, from a November 1966 editorial in *Armed Forces Management* magazine.)

● **Boroson's Conclusion.** There is always a professor of astronomy at a major Ivy League university who believes that the world is flat.

    (Warren Boroson.)

● **Borstelmann's Rule.** If everything seems to be coming your way, you're probably in the wrong lane.

    (U/DRW.)

● **Boucher's Corollary to Murphy's Law.** Murphy's Law holds no more than 80 percent of the time; unfortunately, it is impossible to predict when.

> (Wayne Boucher, from his article "A Practical Guide for Perplexed Managers," *MBA Magazine,* August/September 1978.)

● **Boyd's Criteria for Good County Fairs.** (1) A really good fair must have enormous traffic jams and lousy parking. (2) Good carnivals must have plenty of overpriced junk food. (3) Good fairs must have nauseating rides. (4) Top-drawer fairs must have ridiculous come-ons. (5) Good country fairs must have a "serious" side to them. (6) A four-star carnival must have plenty of "toughs" around. (7) An excellent fair must separate you from your money faster than OPEC and the IRS combined.

> (Ronald Wray Boyd, in his review of the Pinellas County Fair for *The St. Petersburg Times,* March 14, 1979. This article also contains Boyd's tips on fair etiquette, offering such timeless bits of advice as, "Don't ask for four cheese dogs, six large Pepsis, three caramel apples and then try to charge it on your Carte Blanche card," and "Don't feel as though you should tip 'The Slime Man.' ")

● **Bradley's Reminder.** Everything comes to him who waits—among other things, death.

> (English writer Francis H. Bradley. *ME.*)

● **Brauer's Warning.** He who tries to pick all the flowers is sure to get some poison ivy.

> (David F. Brauer, Orlando, Fla.)

● **Brecht's Hierarchy of Needs.** Grub first, then ethics.

> (Bertolt Brecht. *RS.*)

● **Brenne's Laws of Life.** (1) You never get it where you want it. (2) If you think it's tough now, just wait.

(From Carol Pike, Mesa, Arizona, who heard them from her father at least once a week during her formative years. She says, "These laws can be applied to anything.")

● **Bressler's Law.** There is no crisis to which academics will not respond with a seminar.

(Professor Marvin Bressler of Princeton University, from Arnold Brown, New York City.)

● **Brewster's Exception.** Every rule has its exceptions except this one: A man must always be present when he is being shaved.

(Eugene V. Brewster, from his 1925 work, *The Wisdom of the Ages.*)

● **Dr. Brochu's Professorial Discourse.** A "full professor" is not an assistant professor, an associate professor, an adjunct professor, or a part-time professor. He has been a professor for a long time, has filled all of his memory circuits with absolutely essential information; he is full of knowledge. *1st Consequence:* He cannot learn anything new without losing some knowledge essential to his position. *2d Consequence:* If he does learn something new, the essential information forgotten as a result of consequence #1 will be requested by the Dean the next time they meet. *3rd Consequence:* If he protects essential knowledge by not learning anything new, a student will ask for the unlearned new knowledge the next day. *4th Consequence:* When the students and administration find out how full he is, he will be promoted to Dean.

(Frank Brochu, M.D., Professor of Surgery, Salem, Va.)

● **Brodie's Law of the Consumption of Canapes.** As many as are served will be eaten . . . if left long enough.

> (Robert N. Brodie, New York City, who points out, "This law applies equally to social and business affairs but operates with special force at new office openings and functions where it is understood that the food costs no individual money.")

● **Brogan's Rules.** (1) When in doubt, blame the schools. (2) Also blame the press.

> (Patrick Brogan, Washington correspondent of *The Times* [London] in a January 14, 1979, article for *The Washington Post.*)

● **Bronx Law of Dominance.** No matter what year it is or how many teams are in the league, the odds are 1:2 that the Yankees will win the pennant. (You could look it up.)

> (Steven D. Mirsky, Ithaca, N.Y.)

● **Brothers's Distinction.** The biggest difference between men and boys is the cost of their toys.

> (Joyce Brothers, quoted in *Bennett Cerf's The Sound of Laughter,* Doubleday, 1970.)

● **Brown's Law of Issues.** Issues are the last refuge of scoundrels.

> (Governor Jerry Brown. *MBC.*)

● **Brozik's Law.** Never ask a question you *really* don't want to know the answer to.

> (Dallas Brozik, Braidwood, Ill.)

● **Bryant's Law.** The toughest stitch on a pair of trousers is that which affixes the price tag.

> (Larry W. Bryant, Arlington, Va.)

BROZIK'S LAW

● **Buchwald's Sans Souci Rules.** (1) Any rumor which survives forty-eight hours is most likely true. (2) When any cabinet officer comes to dine, everyone's lunch is tax deductible.

> (Art Buchwald, who formulated them over soft-shell crabs at the Sans Souci Restaurant. They were quoted by Hugh Sidey in his column in *The Washington Star,* February 11, 1979.)

● **Budget Analyst's Rule.** Distribute dissatisfaction uniformly.

> (A. A. Lidberg, Tempe, Ariz.)

● **Buechner's Principle.** The simplest explanation is that it doesn't make sense.

> (Professor William Buechner, from Richard Stone, Stanford, Cal.)

● **"Bugs" Baer's Perception.** You can always judge a man by what he eats, and therefore a country in which there is no free lunch is no longer a free country.

(Arthur "Bugs" Baer. *ME.*)

● **Bulen's Advice.** Don't put off until tomorrow what you can put off until the day after tomorrow.

(E. H. Bulen, Los Angeles.)

● **Bunuel's Law.** Overdoing things is harmful in all cases, even when it comes to efficiency.

(U/DRW.)

● **Burdg's Philosophy.** It's not the time you put in, but what you put in the time.

(Henry B. Burdg, Auburn, Ala.)

Special Section 1

Bureaucratic Survival Kit. Essential Items.

1. Credo of a Bureaucrat.
You start by saying no to requests. Then if you have to go to yes, okay. But if you start with yes, you can't go to no.

(Mildred Perlman revealed this secret when she retired in 1975 as director of classification for New York City's Civil Service Commission.)

2. The Bureaucrat's Ten Commandments.

I Don't discuss domestic politics on issues involving war and peace.

ODE TO BUREAUCRATIC IMMORTALITY

   II   Say what will convince, not what you believe.
  III Support the consensus.
  IV Veto other options.
   V Predict dire consequences.
  VI Argue timing, not substance.
 VII Leak what you don't like.
VIII Ignore orders you don't like.
  IX Don't tell likely opponents about a good thing.
   X Don't fight the consensus and don't resign over policy.
    (Widely quoted set of instructions by Leslie H. Gelb and
    Morton M. Halperin.)

3. Ode to Bureaucratic Immortality. When Senator Lawton Chiles of Florida discovered that among the 4,987 forms used by the federal government was one that would be sent to city officials after a nuclear attack asking how many citizens survived, he was moved to comment, "The implication is that even if nothing else survives a nuclear blast, the bureaucracy will rise from the ashes."

4. Useful Motto.
  Do not fix the mistake—fix the *blame.*
    (George Barbarow, Bakersfield, Cal.)

5. Confessions of an IRS Agent (McCoy's Laws).
  (1) If all line sections of government ceased to function, the administrative staff sections would function for three years before they discovered the other sections were gone. (2) Bureaucracy goes beyond the Peter Principle: When someone reaches his highest level of incompetence in a bureaucracy, the only way to get rid of him is to promote him. This continues until he retires or reaches the top of the ladder.
    (Michael P. McCoy, Special Agent, Internal Revenue Service, Criminal Investigation Division, Spring, Tex.)

6. Bureaucrat's Lament.

> I had a little document,
>   As pure as driven snow,
> Yet everywhere that paper went,
>   It wandered to and fro.
>
> I thought that people gladly
>   And swiftly would concur,
> But while I waited sadly,
>   They'd cavil and demur.
>
> Some thought the paper much too short;
>   Others much too long.
> Some thought the language much too weak;
>   Others much too strong.
>
> So by the time that document
>   Came dawdling back my way
> It made no difference where it went—
>   The issue was passé!

(*///* Found in a file at the National Aeronautics and Space Administration.)

7. Deliverance.

God told Moses he had good news and bad news.

"The good news first," said Moses.

"I'm planning to part the Red Sea to allow you and your people to walk right through and escape from Egypt," said God, adding, "And when the Egyptian soldiers pursue, I'll send the water back on top of them."

"Wonderful," Moses responded, "but what's the bad news?"

"You write the environmental-impact statement."

(Oft-told Washington parable, c. 1977.)

8. Brownian Motion Rule of Bureaucracies.

It is impossible to distinguish, from a distance, whether the bureaucrats associated with your project are simply sitting on their hands or frantically trying to cover their asses.

(*U/* Submitted by Paul Martin to *DRW.*)

● **Burgess's Law of Best Sellers.** A book will sell best if it is very long and very unreadable, since then the buyer feels he is buying a durable commodity. If he races through the book he buys in a single sleepless night, he will feel cheated.

(Anthony Burgess, in *The Washington Post Book World,* April 8, 1979.)

● **Burns's Estimating Formula.** Things cost about a dollar a pound.

(From Martin Berger, Mount Vernon, N.Y., who explains, "Burns was a college professor from whom I first heard this law. He was also the inventor of the ferrous wheel . . . pictured at right. It has been my observation that this law was surprisingly true over a very long period of time. However, inflation has finally caught up with it; in today's world, two dollars a pound seems closer to the mark.")

● **Burton's Party Laws.** *I. Children's Birthday Parties.* (1) Any birthday party of more than seven male children under the age of eleven will inevitably end in a fight. (2) Any child's birthday party in which the number of guests exceeds the number of the actual age of the child for whom the party is being given will end in disaster. *II. Adults at Parties.* (1) If a party is scheduled to run from 4 to 7 P.M., then that party will run from 5:30 to 10 P.M.

(2) If twenty-two people are invited to a party commencing at 9 P.M., one person will invariably turn up at 9 P.M. (3) At any party lasting more than three hours and twenty-two minutes, at least one woman will be crying. (4) At any party catering to more than ten people, at least two glasses will be broken. (5) At any party catering to more than seventeen people, at least four glasses will be broken. (6) At any afternoon party in which the guests stay until after midnight, all glasses will be broken. (7) A wife who has had two drinks on being offered a third will decline it. She will then drink half of her husband's drink. She will then change her mind and say that she would like a third drink. Her husband will drink this drink. (8) Exactly fourteen minutes and seventeen seconds after the host announces that there is nothing more to drink, all guests will leave, no matter what the hour is.

(Pierre Burton, from his book *My War With the 20th Century,* Doubleday, 1965.)

● **Busch's Law of the Forty-Hour Week.** The closer a day is to a weekend, holiday, or vacation, the greater the probability of an employee calling in sick. *Corollary:* No one gets sick on Wednesdays.

(Walter Busch, St. Louis. *EV.*)

Special Section 2

Business Maxims. Signs, real and imagined, that belong on the walls of the nation's offices (credits follow the maxims).

* * *

1.   Never Try to Teach a Pig to Sing; It Wastes Your Time and It Annoys the Pig.

*   *   *

2.   Sometimes the Crowd Is Right.

*   *   *

3.   Customers Want ¼" Holes—Not ¼" Drills.

*   *   *

4.   Dollars Become What You Label Them.

*   *   *

5.   The Real World Is Only a Special Case, Albeit an Important One.

*   *   *

6.   The Easiest Way to Make Money Is to Stop Losing it.

*   *   *

7.   Auditors Are the People Who Go in After the War Is Lost and Bayonet the Wounded.

*   *   *

8.   Criticize Behavior, Not People.

*   *   *

9.   Give More Than They Ask for. More Is Less, but It Looks Like More.

*   *   *

10.   If You Don't Measure It, It Won't Happen.

*   *   *

11.   There Is More Than One Way to Skin a Cat; but Be Sure the Boss Likes Cat.

*   *   *

12.　If You Can't Get Your Day's Work Done in Twenty-four Hours—Work Nights.

* * *

13.　Whom you Badmouth Today Will Be Your Boss Tomorrow.

* * *

14.　Remember, the Key to Success Opens Many Doors.

* * *

15.　To Err Is Human—To Forgive Is Not Company Policy.

* * *

16.　No Matter How Long the Day May Be, You Cannot Shingle a Roof with Prunes.

* * *

17.　Fish Die by Their Mouth.

* * *

18.　The Best Way to Get Credit Is to Try to Give It Away.

* * *

19.　It Takes Two, but Give Me the Credit.

* * *

20.　Even Monkeys Fall from Trees.

* * *

(Many of these maxims were inspired by a collection of business maxims that appeared in *MBA Magazine*. The first four maxims originally appeared in *MBA*. The sources of the other maxims are: number 5, Barry Keating, Assistant Professor of Business Economics, Notre Dame University; 6–8, Paul Rubin, Toledo; 9, Sal Rosa,

New York City; 10, Boake A. Sells, Chagrin Falls, Ohio; 11, B. J. Carroll, Lake Forest, Ill.; 12, Alfred deQuoy, McLean, Va.; 13, S. M. Oddo, San Diego; 14, Seth Frankel, Chicago; 15, E. H. Bulen, Los Angeles; 16, Andrew Weissman, New York City; 17, Ron Wilsie, Solana Beach, Cal.; 18, business leader Charles Hendrickson Brower, quoted in *Reader's Digest,* March 1971; 19, T. Camille Flowers, Cincinnati; 20. Arthur E. Klauser, Washington, D.C.)

● **Butler's Expert Testimony.** The function of the expert is not to be more right than other people, but to be wrong for more sophisticated reasons.

(David Butler, *The Observer,* London.)

● **Butler's Marketing Principle.** Any fool can paint a picture, but it takes a wise man to be able to sell it.

(Samuel Butler.)

● **Buxbaum's Law.** Anytime you back out of your driveway or parking lot, day or night, there will always be a car coming, or a pedestrian walking by.

(*U/JW.*)

● **Byrne's Law of Concreting.** When you pour it rains.

(*U*/Donald Kaul's column in *The Des Moines Register,* December 11, 1978.)

C

● **Caffyn's Law of According To.** The rosier the news the higher ranking the official who announces it.
(H. R. Caffyn, New York City. *AO.*)

● **Callaghan's Answer to the Balance of Payments Problem.** In the 19th century when Britain had defense responsibilities all around the globe, didn't she have balance of payments problems? No, there were no statistics.
(British Prime Minister James Callaghan, in reply to a question at the National Press Club. *TCA.*)

● **Campbell's Constant.** The telephone never rings until you are settled in the bathroom.
(Constance E. Campbell, Keokuk, Iowa.)

● **Campbell's Law.** Nature abhors a vacuous experimenter.
(U/DRW.)

● **Canning's Law.** Nothing is so fallacious as facts, except figures.
(British Prime Minister George Canning, 1770–1827.)

● **Cannon's Razor.** Guys who chew on unlit cigars have a tough time convincing me they're telling the truth.
(Sportswriter Jimmy Cannon.)

● **Capon's Perception.** The world looks as if it has been left in the custody of a pack of trolls.

(Robert Farrar Capon from *The Supper of the Lamb,* Doubleday, 1969. *RS.*)

● **Carlisle's Nursing Keystone.** If you treat a sick child like an adult and a sick adult like a child, everything works out pretty well.

(Ruth Carlisle, quoted in *Reader's Digest,* January 1969.)

● **Carlisle's Rule of Acquisition.** The purchase of any product can be rationalized if the desire to own it is strong enough.

(Carlisle Madson, Hopkins, Minn.)

● **Carlson's Law.** Don't ever try to eat where they don't want to feed you.

(Phil Carlson, long-time Chief of Staff of the Government Operations Committee. It was recited to Jack Sullivan in 1960, when Carlson and Sullivan entered a restaurant in the Canal Zone that refused to serve them. Sullivan suggested they demand to be fed, but Carlson knew better. Sullivan, now a high-ranking State Department official, adds, "I have found many subsequent occasions on which Carlson's Law has seemed quite appropriate.")

● **Carmichael's Law.** For every human reaction there is an over-reaction.

(U/Ra.)

● **Carolyn's Corollary.** A penny saved isn't a hell of a lot.
(David M. Hebertson, Sandy, Utah, who named this for a former girl friend "who did not revel in an 'evening out' at Burger World.")

● **Carroll's Law of Black Box Mechanisms.** If you leave them alone long enough, they will fix themselves. *Corollary 1:*

If they haven't fixed themselves, you haven't left them alone long enough. *Corollary 2:* If you open them up, they will take longer to fix. *Corollary 3:* If you try to fix them, they will be hopelessly beyond repair. *Corollary 4:* If you try to have someone else fix them, it will cost more than a new one.

   (B. J. Carroll, Lake Forest, Ill.)

● **Carson's Comedic Laws.** (1) If they buy the premise, they'll buy the bit. (2) Don't do more than three jokes on the same premise.

   (Johnny Carson, who has mentioned these laws several times on the *Tonight* show. *MLS.*)

● **Carson's Law of Singularity.** There's only one fruitcake in the whole world.

   (Johnny Carson. *MLS.*)

● **Carson's Travel Law.** There is no Gate #1 at any airport.

   (Johnny Carson, the *Tonight* show, May 22, 1979.)

● **Carswell's Law of Productivity.** Work smarter, not harder.

   (Ron Carswell, Texas State Technical Institute, Waco.)

● **Carter's Rule.** If there is a single puddle in your front yard, the newsboy will hit it, but only on those days when the paper is unwrapped.

   (Nelson Carter, Aptos, Cal.)

● **Cason's Laws.** (1) *For Plant Operation:* When in doubt, blame the Maintenance Department. (2) *For Economic Analysis:* The assumption you make without realizing you are making it is the one that will do you in. (3) *For Speed Limitation:* They will remember how poorly the job was done long after they have forgotten how quickly it was done. (4) *For Meetings:* Regardless of the length of the meeting, all important decisions will be made in the last five minutes before lunch or quitting time.

(Roger L. Cason, Wilmington, Del.)

● **Catch-22 Revisited.** A 1969 District of Columbia Court of Appeals decision on Breathalyzer tests rules that for the test to be valid the drunk-driving defendant must be sober enough to give voluntary, informed consent to letting the test be administered.

(Reported in *The Washington Star,* April 16, 1979.)

● **Cavanaugh's Postulate.** All kookies are not in a jar. *(U/DRW.)*

● **Chadwick's Observation on Book Loaning.** The only thing stupider than loaning a book is returning one.

(Clifton Chadwick, Santiago, Chile.)

● **Charlemagne's Rule.** It's smarter to be lucky than it's lucky to be smart.

(Charlemagne, in the musical *Pippin.* Richard Stone, Stanford, Cal.)

● **Cheshire's Law of Social Climbing.** Everything that goes up must come down.

(Maxine Cheshire, *The Washington Post. MLS.*)

● **Chesterton's Discovery.** The only way of catching a train I ever discovered is to miss the train before.

(G. K. Chesterton.)

● **Chesterton's Warning.** Never invoke gods unless you really want them to appear. It annoys them very much.

(G. K. Chesterton, from Sarah Risher, Bethesda, Md.)

● **Chilton's Theological-Clerical Rule.** If you work in a church office you have to keep all your equipment locked up, because nothing is sacred.

(Vee Chilton, Easton, Md.)

● **Christmas Eve, The Primary Myth of.** "So simple that a child can assemble it."

(Side-panel of a toy box that also says, "Some assembly required.")

● **Cicero's Constant.** There is no opinion so absurd but that some philosopher will express it.

(Cicero. *ME.*)

● **Civil Service Maxim. (a.k.a. The Law of the "New Army.")** The pension is mightier than the sword.

(Anonymous. Unsigned note sent to the Murphy Center.)

● **Clark's Law of Leadership.** A leader should not get too far in front of his troops or he will get shot in the ass.

(Senator Joseph S. Clark. *MBC.*)

● **Clarke's Partners Pact Paradox.** You, as one partner, will do 90 percent of the research and 99 percent of the actual term paper. While "he," your partner, will contribute 10 percent of the research and 1 percent of the actual term paper. *Corollary 1:* Of course, the 1 percent of the paper is the title page, and your partner will have spelled your name wrong. *Corollary 2:* In typing the title page your partner will give himself top billing. *Corollary 3:* Your teacher, not knowing of the injustice being done, will give your partner a higher grade than the one he gives you.

(Milo M. Clarke, Cortland, N.Y.)

● **Clay's Conclusion.** Creativity is great, but plagiarism is faster.

(Frederick A. Clay, Anaheim, Cal.)

● **Clayton's Universal Law of Social Evolution.** Bridges prohibit the progress they promote.

(John S. Clayton, Rockville, Md., who says, "This applies to all churches, school systems, automobiles, television, governments, religions, legal systems, agricultural systems, transportation, modern math, scientific theory, housing development, organizations, social reform, communications systems, political theories, industrial development, labor movements, and the invention of the zipper.")

● **Cliff's Catalog of the Least Credible English Quotations.** (1) The check is in the mail. (2) I'm from the government and I'm here to help you. (3) Of course I'll respect you in the morning.

(U/GT.)

● **Cloninger's Law.** In a country as large as the United States, it is possible to find at least fifty people who will believe/buy/try/or practice anything.

(Dale O. Cloninger, Associate Professor of Finance and Public Affairs, University of Houston at Clear Lake City.)

● **Close's Clever Cue for Clashing Couples.** If I can prove I'm right, I make things worse.

(Rev. Henry Close, Fort Lauderdale, Fla., Letters to the Editor, *Time,* March 19, 1979.)

● **Coan's Law.** If it looks complicated, lose interest.
(Nonnee Coan, Houston.)

● **Coccia's Barbecue Law.** Regardless of where you sit, the wind will always blow the smoke from a barbecue in your face.

(James R. Coccia, Glens Falls, N.Y., Letters to the Editor, *Time,* March 19, 1979.)

● **Coffin's Revision.** Some folks say the squeaking wheel gets the grease, but others point out that it is the first one to be replaced.

(Harold Coffin, Associated Press.)

● **Cohen's Laws** . . . *Of Candidates:* Many people run for office only because someone they know and don't like is running for the same office. *Of Government Salaries:* Few members of the news media have ever seen a justified pay raise, or even discovered the right time to raise pay or ever learned the right method to raise pay. *Of Political Polling:* Sometimes those who lead in the public opinion polls win the election. *Of Recollections:* Recollections of personal animosities generally last longer than the recollections of the effects of public policies.

(Mark B. Cohen, member, House of Representatives, Commonwealth of Pennsylvania.)

● **Cohodas's Law.** If it looks too good to be true, it is too good to be true.

(Howard L. Cohodas, Marquette, Mich.)

● **Colby's First Rule.** Never burn an uninteresting letter is the first rule of the British aristocracy.

(Frank M. Colby, editor.)

● **Collins's Law of Control.** Businesses exert the tightest controls over the easiest things to control, rather than the most critical.

(Kenneth B. Collins, CBS Publications, New York City.)

● **Collins's Law of Economics.** The cost of living will always rise to exceed income.

(Roger W. Collins, St. Louis. *EV.*)

● **Combs's Laws.** (1) A lot of people who complain about their boss being stupid would be out of a job if he were any smarter. (2) If you think OSHA is a small town in Wisconsin, you're in trouble.

> (M. C. "Chuck" Combs, Director, Minnesota Department of Agriculture, Marketing Services. St. Paul, Minn.)

● **Computer Programming Principles.** (1) The computer is never wrong. (2) The programmer is always wrong.
> *(U/JS.)*

● **Congress, Universal Law of.** Neither the House nor the Senate shall pass a law they shall be subject to.
> *(U/Ra.)*

● **Conner's Food Laws.** (1) Whatever the person at the next table orders, it always looks better than yours. (2) All avocados in all stores will always be rock-hard the day you want to make guacamole.

> (Caryl Conner, Washington, D.C., Letters to the Editor, *The Washingtonian,* December 1978.)

● **Connor's Restaurant Rule.** The amount of a waiter's or waitress's tip is inversely proportional to the number of people at a table times the amount of time the party occupies the table.

> (Kevin Connor, manager, The Man in The Green Hat Restaurant, Washington, D.C. Although Connor admits that this rule is not immutable, he says that it is true enough to prove true at least once or twice on any given day.)

● **Conrad's Rules.** (1) The person who misses the meeting is generally assigned to the work committee. (2) Conscience is that small, inner voice that tells you someone is watching you.

(3) The problem drinker is the one who never buys. (4) One advantage of old age is that there are more younger women all the time.

(Charles Conrad III, Racine, Wisc.)

● **Conservative/Liberal Razor.** A conservative sees a man drowning 50 feet from shore, throws him a 25-foot-long rope, and tells him to swim to it. A liberal throws him a rope 50 feet long, then drops his end and goes off to perform another good deed.

(U/TCA.)

● **Cooch's Law.** (See *Joe Cooch's Law.*)

● **Cook's Theorem.** If you can't solve a problem forward, it can usually be solved by working it backward.

(From Ronald F. Amberger, Staff Chairman, Mechanical Engineering Technology, Rochester Institute of Technology, who says it is named for Professor Cook, his machine-design professor at Rensselaer Polytechnic Institute.)

● **Cooke's Fundamental Theorem of Political Economics.** If you can only cover costs, capitalism is irrelevant.

(Ernest F. Cooke, Chairman, Marketing Department, University of Baltimore.)

● **Cooke's General Business Laws.** (1) Managers with an accounting or legal mentality will take no risk, bend no rules, and the firm will stagnate. (2) The entrepreneur who finds a remarkable new way of financing a company or putting together a conglomerate will be the most surprised when it all falls apart. (3) Just because it works doesn't mean it's right. (4) Just because the industry leader does it that way doesn't mean it's the best way of doing it.

(Ernest F. Cooke again.)

● **Coolidge Collection.** (1) If you don't say anything, you won't be called on to repeat it. (2) Make do, or do without. (3) I've traveled around this country a lot and I'm convinced that there are so many s.o.b.'s in it that they are entitled to some representation in Congress. (In response to an aide's suggestion that Senator so-and-so had gone too far and the president ought to take steps to prevent his renomination.)

(President Calvin Coolidge. *TCA, ME,* Louise Curcio.)

● **Cooper's Law.** All machines are amplifiers.
(U/DRW.)

● **Cooper's Metalaw.** A proliferation of new laws creates a proliferation of new loopholes.
(U/DRW.)

● **Corcoran's Laws.** *Popcorn:* It is impossible to properly salt the lower half of a box of popcorn without oversalting the top half unless you take the saltshaker into the theater with you. *Of Shrinkage:* Everything from your past seems smaller when you see it again except your old flame. *First Law of Sex Laws:* It is more fun trying to think up sex laws than any other laws. *Of Visiting People Who Own a Poodle:* (1) Never visit people who own a poodle. (2) If you do visit people who own a poodle, never throw a ball or small squeak toy to the poodle if you wish to be left alone during the remainder of the visit. *Of Nonsense:* (1) There is no law of nonsense since laws are logical and nonsense is not. Therefore a logical law of nonsense is nonsense and thus not a law. (2) Since the previous law is nonsense, ignore Corcoran's First Law of Nonsense. (3) If you don't like the first two Laws of Nonsense, come up with your own damn Law of Nonsense.

(John H. Corcoran, Jr., Washington, D.C., television personality who also writes good. See also his *Duffer's Laws.*)

● **Corey's Law.** You can get more with a kind word and a gun than you can with a kind word.

(Professor Irwin Corey. *MLS.*)

● **Corporate Survival, First Law of.** Keep your boss's boss off your boss's back.

(U/RA.)

● **Corry's Law.** Paper is always strongest at the perforations.

(U/DRW.)

● **Cossey's Advice.** Instead of starting at the bottom and working up, people should start at the top and work down. Only when one knows the job above can the one below be done correctly.

(Clarence Cossey, Austin, Tex.)

● **Cost Effectiveness, Three Important Points.** (1) The question was raised as to which was the best: (A) a broken watch, or (B) one that ran ten seconds slow per day. A Pentagon cost-effectiveness analysis showed that the broken one was far better. The slow watch will be correct only once every 118 years, whereas the broken one is correct twice per day. (2) The son of a cost-effectiveness specialist bragged to his father that he had saved a quarter by running behind the bus all the way to school. His father complained, "Why didn't you run behind a cab and save $2?" (3) Just before being blasted off into orbit Astronaut Walter Schirra was asked by Dr. E. R. Annis, "What concerns you the most?" Schirra thought and then replied, "Every time I climb up on the couch [in the capsule] I say to myself, 'Just think, Wally, everything that makes this thing go was supplied by the lowest bidder.' "

(FSP.)

COST EFFECTIVENESS: THIRD IMPORTANT POINT

● **Cotton's Explanation.** One can usually tell from the degree of formality with which one senator refers to another what the nature of their personal relations may be. If the reference is made casually as "Senator Jones," they are probably close friends. If someone refers to a colleague as "the Senator from Michigan," one may infer that they have a cordial relationship. If a senator refers to another as "the distinguished Senator from Indiana," one may assume he does not particularly like him. And if he refers to him as the "very able and distinguished Senator from California," it usually indicates that he hates his guts.

   (Senator Norris Cotton from his book *In The Senate,* Dodd, Mead, 1978.)

● **Court's Laws.** (1) In any country on any given television network or station the quantity and quality of locally produced programs will vary in an inverse proportion to the quantity and quality of old motion pictures transmitted over the same given network or station. (2) If the media are given the opportunity to get the facts wrong, they probably will. (3) When the media make a mistake, the correction will be inversely related to the size and importance of the error.

(Clive Court, Halifax, Nova Scotia.)

● **Craine's Law of Simplicity.** For every simple solution there are a number of complex problems. *Corollary:* For every simple problem there are a number of complex problems.

(Lloyd Craine, Professor and electrical engineer, Pullman, Wash. "This law," he says, "was devised to explain some of the fundamental relationships that escape many laymen and was used during training sessions for persons interested in understanding the energy problem better.")

● **Cramer's Law of the Sea.** You're not really seasick when you are afraid you'll die, but when you're afraid you'll live.

(Les Cramer, Arlington, Va.)

● **Cramer's Law of Teaching.** When you threaten to send the next kid that talks to the office, the next kid that talks will be the best kid in the class.

(Roxanne Cramer, Arlington, Va.)

● **Creamer's Ten Steps to Learning.**
1. To Learn Is to Hear.
2. To Hear Is to Listen.
3. To Listen Is to Speak.
4. To Speak Is to Think.
5. To Think Is to Question.
6. To Question Is to Ponder.
7. To Ponder Is to Observe.
8. To Observe Is to See.
9. To See Is to Be Born.

10.   To Be Born Is to Be Screwed.
Moral: Any way you look at it, you've got to get screwed at least once before you learn.
(William P. Creamer, San Ramon, Cal.)

● **Crisp's Creed.** Don't keep up with the Joneses: Drag them down, it's cheaper.
(Quentin Crisp. From Richard Isaac, M.D., Toronto.)

● **Cruickshank's Laws.** *Government:* We have met the enemy: in fact we elected him. *Consumerism:* Never buy a used car from a guy who can talk. Never shop in a place that has "bargain" in its name. *Committees:* If a committee is allowed to discuss a bad idea long enough, it will inevitably vote to implement the idea simply because so much work has already been done on it. *Gambling:* My old Scottish grandfather used to say: "The only game that can't be fixed is peek-a-boo." *Gimme Mine:* No matter how bad the idea, or how poor the results, a program will always be considered a howling success at the local level as long as federal funds continue to pay for it. *Sociology:* Never argue with the bouncer. *Corollary 1:* Never argue with a regular customer—the bouncer always decides in his favor. *Corollary 2:* Stay out of joints that need bouncers unless you plan to be a regular customer.
(Ken Cruickshank, *The Florida Times-Union,* Jacksonville, from his June 25, 1978, column.)

● **Cummings's Rule.** The fish are either shallow, deep, or somewhere in between.
(L. L. Cummings, Professor and Director, Center for the Study of Organizational Performance, University of Wisconsin, Madison.)

● **Cuppy's Evolution of the Species.** All modern men are descended from wormlike creatures, but it shows more on some people.
> (Humorist Will Cuppy.)

● **Cureton's Advice.** Avoid jackrabbit starts.
> (Stewart Cureton, Jr., Houston.)

● **Custodiet's Complement.** The human hand is made complete by the addition of a baseball.
> *(U/RA.)*

● **Czusack's Law of Design Changes.** Every advantage has a corresponding disadvantage.
> (Charlie Czusack, from Ronald F. Amberger, Rochester Institute of Technology.)

● **Daniels's Discovery.** The most delightful advantage of being bald—one can *hear* snowflakes.

(R. G. Daniels, from *Quote . . . Unquote* by Nigel Rees, George Allen and Unwin, 1978.)

● **Darby's Dicta.** (1) If you have to "take it or leave it"— leave it! (2) Every time I finally get an iron in the fire—the fire goes out.

(*U*/From Mike O'Neill, Citrus Heights, Cal.)

● **Daugherty's Law.** Temporary things tend to become permanent.

(Richard D. Daugherty, Professor of Anthropology, Washington State University. From Gerald H. Grosso, Port Orchard, Wash.)

● **Daum's Law of Cuckoo Clocks.** At any given party, the cuckoo will always cuckoo at the most embarrassing moment in a conversation.

(Michael J. Daum, East Chicago, Ind.)

● **Davis's Dictum.** Problems that go away by themselves come back by themselves.

(Marcy E. Davis, Philadelphia.)

● **Deborkowski's Laundry Law.** If you come out of the Laundromat with an even number of socks, you have somebody else's laundry.

(*U/Ra.*)

● **DeCicco's Law.** More policemen die in their autos daydreaming about gunfights than die as a result of gunfights.
(Alexander DeCicco, Deputy Sheriff, DuPage County, Ill.)

● **Denenberg's Laws.** *Of Rhetorical Effectiveness:* I would measure how effective my speech was by how many hours it took the audience to complain to my employer. *Of Inescapable Elements:* You can't escape death, taxes, or life insurance.
(Herbert S. Denenberg. *MBC.*)

● **DeQuoy's Catalog of Statements People Will Blindly Accept as Proof of Validity.** (1) It has been computerized. (2) It has been war-gamed.
(Alfred deQuoy, McLean, Va.)

● **DeRoy's Political Rule.** A politician solves every problem before election but very few after.
(Richard H. DeRoy, Hilo, Hawaii.)

● **Desk Jockey, Songs of the.** (1) The federal government spends enough in one hour to wire the entire population of North Dakota—and the houses, too. (2) Discriminate as little as you can and still comply with federal regulations. (3) Make the new administrator feel welcome in a Saturday afternoon ceremony. As of Monday morning, he will be behind in his commitments to group X. (4) The principle allegiance of modern man is to his group, which differs from a gang chiefly in that gangs rumble in the streets while groups rumble in the courts and on Capitol Hill. (5) A dresser is a kind of bureau that doesn't tell you how to run your life. (6) The fascination of paper clips grows inversely with the appeal of the work at hand.
(Ryan Anthony, Tucson.)

● **De Tocqueville's Law.** The lower the calling is and the more removed from learning, the more pompous and erudite is its appellation.

> (Alexis De Tocqueville, *Democracy in America*. From Kevin G. Long, Quebec.)

● **Dial's Discovery.** No matter what you do to instant coffee, it always tastes like instant coffee.

> (Thomas H. Dial, Baltimore.)

● **Dianne's Observation.** If a motel advertises itself as "modern," it isn't.

> (Dianne D. Farrar, Sacramento, Cal.)

● **Dickson's Rules.** *Auto Repair:* If you can see it, it is not serious. If you can hear it, it will set you back some. If you can neither see nor hear it, it will cost you a fortune. *Collecting:* Anything billed as "destined to be a collector's item" (commemorative plates, spoons, Bicentennial kitsch, records sold on late-night TV, etc.) won't be. *Corollary:* Things that aren't, will be. *Telecommunications:* A defective pay phone will find your last dime. *Turnpike Cuisine:* The quality of roadside food decreases in direct proportion to the number of lanes on the road in question. *Insomnia:* (1) Noises, particularly drips and creakings, intensify during the night but abate at dawn. (2) Birds make the most noise at dawn. (3) At the *precise moment* that you *must* get out of bed, there will be absolute quiet. *Transportation:* The bigger the terminal, the worse the public address system. *American Studies:* There is no phenomenon so small that some professor, writer, or politician will not latch on to it and declare that it signifies a turning point in American history. *Defense Language:* The more innocuous the name of a weapon, the more hideous its impact. (Some of the most horrific weapons of the Vietnam era were named BAMBI, INFANT, Daisycutter, Grasshopper, and Agent Orange. Nor is the trend new: From the past we have Mustard Gas, Angel Chasers (two cannonballs linked with a chain

DICKSON'S RULE OF COLLECTING

for added destruction), and the Peacemaker, to name a few.) *Roadside Economics:* Places with the suffix "-tronics" or the word "systems" in their name will charge more for the same goods or service than places with "Mr." or "City" in their name (as in Mr. Carwash or Clean City.) But forced K's (as in Kwick and Klean) aren't as cheap as they look. If you really want to overpay for something, try an antique shop with a crude, hand-lettered sign with the "n" written backward. Stores with first names (John's, Fred's, Maxine's) are generally cheaper than those with last names (Bloomingdale's, Tiffany's, Brooks Brothers, etc.). *Suburban Development:* The more trees a developer cuts down, the woodsier the name of the resulting housing development.

(Paul Dickson, Director, The Murphy Center.)

● **Disney World Rule.** Children under twelve must be accompanied by money.

(James Dent, Charleston [W. Va.] *Gazette.*)

● **Disraeli's Maxims.** (1) A precedent embalms a principle. (2) In politics, nothing is contemptible.

(Benjamin Disraeli.)

● **Dmitri's Epigrams.** (1) Nobody can ever get too much approval. (2) No matter how much you want or need, *they,* whoever *they* are, don't want to let you get away with it, whatever *it* is. (3) Sometimes you get away with it.

(John Leonard, who sometimes calls himself Dmitri in his *New York Times* columns. From his column.)

● **Dochter's Dictum.** Somewhere, right now, there's a committee deciding your future; only you weren't invited.

(U/NDB.)

● **Don Marquis's Advice to Writers.** If you want to get

rich from writing, write the sort of thing that is read by persons who move their lips when they are reading to themselves.

(Don Marquis, quoted by Franklin P. Adams in his book *Overset,* Doubleday, 1922.)

● **Donna's Law of Purchase.** If you want it, and can afford it, buy it—it won't be there when you go back.

(Donna P. H. Day, Rock Hill, Mo.)

● **Dowd's Bath Principle.** It takes more hot water to make cold water hot than it takes cold water to make hot water cold.

(Larry G. Dowd, Columbia, Mo.)

● **Dowling's First Law of Hollywood Moviemaking.** No truly bad movie gets that way without consciously attempting to join (or initiate) a trend.

(Tom Dowling, *The Washington Star,* July 30, 1978.)

● **Drogin's Mealtime Maxim.** A balanced meal is whatever gets hot all at the same time. A snack is what doesn't.

(Marc Drogin, Roanoke [Va.] *World-News,* March 23, 1965.)

● **Drunk, Rules for Getting.** (1) Not too often. (2) In good company. (3) With good wine.

(From *In Praise of Drunkenness* by Boniface Oinophilus, published in London in 1812. The author marshals strong proof for each of his rules. For instance, in support of the second rule, he says, "A man in former times would have done very ill to get drunk with Heliogabalus, whose historian reports that, after having made his friends drunk, he used to shut them up in an apartment, and at night let loose upon them lions, leopards, and tigers, which always tore to pieces some of them.")

● **Duffer's Laws.** (1) No matter how bad a round of golf you play, there will always be at least one stroke so perfect, so on target, and so gratifying that you will come back to play again. (2) The best way for a Duffer to go around a tree standing directly in his line is to aim directly at the tree, since you never hit where you're aiming anyway. (3) The only time you'll hit the ball straight is when you're applying Duffer's law #2. (4) Never carry more clubs than you can afford to break. (5) It is a myth that playing an old ball guarantees you will carry the lake. (6) Nobody cares what you shot today, except you.

(John H. Corcoran, Jr., Chevy Chase, Md.)

● **Dukes's Law.** The most powerful words in marketing are "Watch this!"

(From James A. Robertson, El Paso, who learned it from Carlton Dukes, Dallas.)

● **Dumas's Law.** Most general statements are false, including this one.

(Alexander Dumas. From John C. Armor, Baltimore.)

● **Dyer's Observation.** It all boils down to two words: "Send money," or "Raise dues," or "Increase taxes."

(Professor John M. Dyer, director, International Finance and Marketing Program, University of Miami, Coral Gables.)

● **Earle's Law of Relativity.** The shortest period of time is that between when the light turns green and when the guy behind you blows his horn.

(M. Mack Earle, Baltimore.)

● **Edison's Axiom.** We don't know one-millionth of one percent about anything.

(Thomas Alva Edison. *GT.*)

● **Editorial Laws.** (1) When you proudly publish a . . . significant article and expect a large reader response, you'll get one letter telling you about a typo in the third paragraph. (2) A dangling participle deserves dangling. (3) The poorer the writer the greater his resistance to editorial changes. (4) The author best qualified to write a special article on a hot topic is always away on a three-month overseas assignment. (5) During an interview with an important . . . official, the point of your pencil will break off at the most quotable quote. (6) If you create a magazine that is so good that subscribers refuse to part with it—that's bad. If, however, you put out a magazine that means so little to each individual that it gets passed from hand to hand, that's good. For advertisers, that is. (7) Never expect a good writer to be a good editor; never expect a former English teacher to be a good writer; or a former typing teacher to be a good manuscript typist. (8) When an article reference and page number are given on your magazine cover, the page number will change before the magazine goes to press.

(Selected from *Edpress News,* published by the Educational Press Association of America. Laws 1–6 are by the

Edpress editor Ben Brodinsky, the next is by "Editorial Experts," Washington, D.C., and the final law is by Walter Graves, *Today's Education.*)

● **Edwards's Laws.** (1) A telephone number is not recorded on the message unless you already know it. (2) Always carry a pen. (3) . . . .

> Go Ivy League?
> I sure won't
> My shirts taper
> But I don't.

(Robert V. Edwards, Washington, D.C.)

● **Edwards's Tautology.** Fat men are good-natured because good-natured men are usually fat.
(Canadian editor/humorist Bob Edwards.)

Special Section 3

On Efficiency.

An Efficiency Expert Reports on Hearing a Symphony at the Royal Festival Hall in London.

For considerable periods, the four oboe players had nothing to do. The number should be reduced and the work spread more evenly over the whole of the concert, thus eliminating peaks of activity.

All the twelve violins were playing identical notes; this seems unnecessary duplication. The staff of this section should be drastically cut. If a larger volume of sound is required, it could be obtained by electronic apparatus.

Much effort was absorbed in the playing of demi-semi-quavers; this seems to be an unnecessary refinement. It is recommended that all notes should be rounded up to the nearest semiquaver. If this was done it would be possible to use trainees and lower-grade operatives more extensively.

There seems to be too much repetition of some musical passages. Scores should be drastically pruned. No useful purpose is served by repeating on the horns a passage that has already been handled by the strings. It is estimated that if all redundant passages were eliminated, the whole concert time of two hours could be reduced to twenty minutes and there would be no need for an intermission.

The conductor agrees generally with these recommendations, but expressed the opinion that there might be some falling off in box-office receipts. In that unlikely event it should be possible to close sections of the auditorium entirely, with a consequential saving of overhead expenses, lighting, attendance, etc. If the worst came to the worst, the whole thing could be abandoned and the public could go to the Albert Hall instead.

(The Murphy Center has received a number of versions of this report, which was obviously created in England. One Fellow says he first saw a copy in London in 1955.)

● **Einstein's Explanation of Relativity.** Sit with a pretty girl for an hour, and it seems like a minute; sit on a hot stove for a minute, and it seems like an hour—that's relativity.
(Albert Einstein. *ME.*)

● **Einstein's Three Rules of Work.** (1) Out of clutter find simplicity. (2) From discord make harmony. (3) In the middle of difficulty lies opportunity.

(Albert Einstein, quoted in *Newsweek,* March 12, 1979.)

● **Eisenstein's Laws of Tourism.** (1) If you go during the season with the best weather, it will be the worst weather in forty-nine years. (2) No matter where you sit, the view out the other side will be better. (3) If you move from a room into another one because something is wrong, something will be worse in the new room. (4) The best trips are the unplanned ones; this way, you won't worry about fouling up your timetable. Conversely, the tighter the timetable, the more you'll worry and the later you'll be.

(Edward L. Eisenstein, University City, Mo.)

● **Eldridge's Explanation of War.** Man is always ready to die for an idea, provided that idea is not quite clear to him.

(Paul Eldridge, quoted in *Reader's Digest,* February 1963.)

● **Emergency Rule.** IN CASE OF ATOMIC ATTACK, THE FEDERAL RULING CONCERNING PRAYER IN THIS BUILDING WILL BE TEMPORARILY SUSPENDED.

(Sign [handwritten] found posted in a federal office building, Washington, D.C.)

● **Emery's Law.** Regulation is the substitution of error for chance.

(Fred J. Emery, Director, *The Federal Register,* Washington, D.C.)

Special Section 4

Energy Matters.

1. How You Can Save with a Wood Stove.

Stove, pipe, installation, etc.	$458.00
Chain saw	149.95
Care and maintenance for chain saw	44.60
4-wheel-drive pickup, stripped	8,379.04
4-wheel-drive pickup maintenance	438.00
Replace rear window of pickup (twice)	310.00
Fine for cutting unmarked tree in state forest	500.00
Fourteen cases Michelob	126.00
Littering fine	50.00
Towing charge—truck from creek	50.00
Doctor's fee for removing splinter from eye	45.00
Safety glasses	29.50
Emergency-room treatment (broken toes— dropped logs)	125.00
Safety shoes	49.95
New living room carpet	800.00
Paint living room walls and ceiling	110.00
Log splitter	150.00
Fifteen-acre woodlot	9,000.00
Taxes on woodlot	310.00
Replace coffee table (chopped up and burned while drunk)	75.00
Divorce settlement	33,678.22
Total first year's cost	54,878.26
Savings in conventional fuel first year	(72.33)
Net cost of first year's woodburning	$54,805.93

(From ME.)

2. Best One-Liner on the Energy Crisis.
   If God had meant for us to have enough oil he never would
      have given us the Department of Energy.
         (Robert Orben.)

●   **Epperson's Law.** When a man says it's a silly, childish
game, it's probably something his wife can beat him at.
         (Don Epperson, quoted in Bill Gold's District Line column
         in *The Washington Post,* September 11, 1978.)

●   **Epstean's Laws.** (1) Man always tends to satisfy his needs
and desires with the least possible exertion. (2) If self-preserva-
tion is the first law of human conduct, exploitation is the second.
         (Edward Epstean, from Albert Jay Nock's *Memoirs of a
         Superfluous Man,* Regnery, 1964. *JMcC.*)

●   **The ERDA Law of Materials Procurement.** Never use
lead when gold will do.
         (U/GT.)

●   **Erickson's Law of the Sea.**
      When in doubt, go fast;
      When in danger, go faster.
         (L. Bruce Erickson. *MLS.*)

●   **Ertz's Observation on Immortality.** Millions long for
immortality who do not know what to do with themselves on a
rainy Sunday afternoon.
         (Author Susan Ertz.)

Special Section 5

Explanations. A small catalog of previously eluded truths.

1. Why America's Bicentennial was not more spectacular.

Because the late Wernher von Braun's suggestion to the Senate Space Committee was not adopted. In September 1969 he proposed putting the President of the United States in orbit to celebrate the two-hundredth anniversary of the Republic.

2. Why one should not be too afraid of the Internal Revenue Service.

Recently the IRS demanded that Elizabeth R. Tunnel of Norfolk, Va., pay tax on the many automobiles that the government had determined were in her possession. Ms. Tunnel is the Elizabeth River Tunnel that runs beneath the Elizabeth River. The cars are not hers.

3. Why metric conversion is going to take a lot longer than previously anticipated.

As one radio preacher is reported to have stated, "If God had meant for us to go metric, why did he give Jesus twelve disciples?"

4. Why the United States uses humans in space.

"Man," says a 1965 NASA report on manned space, "is the lowest-cost, 150-pound, nonlinear, all-purpose computer system which can be mass-produced by unskilled labor."

5. Why television is not living up to its promise as an educational medium.

The following was actually edited out of the Nixon-Frost TV interviews:

RN: . . . We were sitting in the bow of the yacht. I'm an old Navy man. The bow is the rear-end, isn't it?

DF: . . . I, ah, . . . probably.

RN: That's right. No. The stern. We were sitting in the stern.

DF: Let's say end.

RN: All right. We were sitting down at the end of the yacht.

6. Why the government has such a hard time getting out of things it has gotten into.

Here is how the term "exit" has been defined by government experts:

An exit is a means of egress and has three component parts.

First, an exit access: Exit access is that portion of a means of egress which leads to an entrance to an exit.

Second, the exit itself: Exit is that portion of a means of egress which is separated from all other spaces of the building or structure by construction or equipment as required in this subpart to provide a protected way of travel to the exit discharge.

Third, the exit discharge: That portion of a means of egress between the termination of an exit and a public way.

F

● **Fadiman's Law of Optimum Improvement.** In the realm of objects, as well as in the realm of ethics, there can be an excess of refinement as well as a defect of crudity. It is my further conviction that a proper technological society is not the one capable of endlessly improving its artifacts, but the one able to see at what point it is best, from the point of view of the whole human being (and indeed of the whole human race), to stop the improvement.

> (Clifton Fadiman, from *This Is My Funniest,* edited by Whit Burnett, Perma Books, 1957. In his essay of the same title as the law, Fadiman gives many examples of "excessive refinement," but one that serves as well as any is book wrapping. He notes that books used to come wrapped in a piece of paper tied with a piece of cord. "In no time you could be reading the book." Now he points out, they come in "cardboard iron maidens, suitable to the transportation of safes or pianos" or in "thick bags" that are almost impossible to open without ripping. When ripped, "Out flies a bushel of ancient furry shredded gray paper, the perfect stand-in for mouse dirt.")

● **Family Law.**
Where there's a sibling
There's quibbling.
(Selma Raskin. It originally appeared in *The Wall Street Journal* and is quoted in Charles Preston's *The Light Touch.*)

● **Fannie's Ganif Theory.** (1) Most politicians are thieves. (2) Most politicians are slow learners. (3) Therefore, never vote for an incumbent. While the challenger's natural inclinations are equally bad, it will take him time to learn how to achieve his goals.

> (From Carl T. Bogus, Philadelphia, who attributes it to his Aunt Fannie, Mrs. Fagel Kanev.)

● **Faraday's Lecture Rule.** One hour is long enough for anyone.

> (Scientist Michael Faraday.)

● **FCC "Policy."** Any sufficiently promising technology must be regulated or it will succeed.

> (R. W. Johnson, from his *Ham Radio Humor,* 1977.)

● **Feather's Discovery.** Loneliness is something you can't walk away from.

> (William Feather. *RS.*)

● **Feazel's Rules:** *Travel.* Don't Go Back! It isn't there anymore. Exception: Switzerland. *Family Life:* Once you have trained your children to be an efficient team, they go away. (Examples: haying, sailing, fence building, automotive maintenance, cooking, bridge, firewood procurement.) *Experience:* You never learn anything useful from your mistakes because you never get a chance to make the same one twice. *Jogging:* All hilly courses are uphill both ways.

> (Betty Feazel, Pagosa Springs, Colo.)

● **Feline Frustration, Rule of.** When your cat has fallen asleep on your lap and looks utterly content and adorable, you will suddenly have to go to the bathroom.

> *(U/DRW.)*

● **Field's Advertising Observation.** People who think that newspaper advertisements are not read should watch a man sitting in a streetcar where women are standing.

(Chester Field, Jr., from his *Cynic's Rules of Conduct* [1905].)

● **Fields's Panaceas.** (1) If at first you don't succeed try, try again. Then quit. There's no use making a fool of yourself. (2) The best cure for insomnia is to get a lot of sleep.

(W. C. Fields.)

● **Fields's Revelation.** If you see a man holding a clipboard and looking official, the chances are good that he is supposed to be doing something menial.

(Wayne C. Fields, Jr., Newcastle, Cal.)

● **Figley's Law.** The price of a hamburger is in inverse proportion to its state of assembly.

(Preston Figley, Rudder & Finn, Texas. *AO.*)

● **The First Time—Each Time Is Like—Law.** No matter how many times you have felt miserable because you stayed up too late, drank too much, ate too much, etc., the next time you have the opportunity to stay up late, drink too much, etc., you will be unable to recall and anticipate, as anything more than an abstraction, how miserable you felt/will feel when you did/if you do. Exception: anything that resulted in carsickness.

(Hilde Weisert, Teaneck, N.J.)

● **Fitzmaurice's Law.** When you come to a stop sign and can't decide whether to turn right or left, any decision will be wrong.

(Richard Fitzmaurice, KCBS, San Francisco.)

● **Flak Diversion Theorem.** A published remark by any congressman that irritates a lobbying association or the White

House is automatically labeled by his office as "taken out of context."
(*The Washington Star* editorial, February 18, 1979.)

● **Florio's Travel Suggestion.** If you will be a traveler, have always the eyes of a falcon, the ears of an ass, the face of an ape, the mouth of a hog, the shoulders of a camel, the legs of a stag, and see that you keep two bags very full, one of patience and another of money.
(A man named John Florio, who wrote the above in 1591. Quoted in the Summer 1978 issue of *J. D. Journal.*)

● **Followers' Creed.** The lemmings know something we don't.
(Alvin W. Quinn, Arlington Heights, Ill.)

● **Fonda's Cinematic Distinction.** If a man and a woman go into the woods with a picnic basket and a blanket and have a picnic, that's a G. If they go into the woods with a picnic basket and crawl under the blanket, that's a PG. And if they go into the woods without a basket or a blanket and have a picnic anyway, that's an R.
(Jane Fonda, 1978 Academy Awards ceremony.)

● **Forbes's Rule of Parenting.** Let your children go if you want to keep them.
(Malcolm Forbes, *The Sayings of Chairman Malcolm,* Harper & Row, 1978.)

● **Fortune-Seeker's Law.** Cast your bread on the water and you get soggy bread.
(U/Ra.)

● **Fowler's Note.** The only imperfect thing in nature is the human race.
(U/DRW.)

● **The Fox Epiphenomenon.** If you do nothing, nothing will happen. If you do something, something will happen—but not what you intended.
   (James F. Fox, New York City.)

● **France's Law of Law.** The law, in its majestic equality, forbids the rich as well as the poor to sleep under bridges, to beg in the streets, and to steal bread.
   (Anatole France.)

● **Frankel's Principle.** Always think of something new; this helps you forget your last rotten idea.
   (Seth Frankel, Hillsdale, N.J.)

● **Franklin's Infallible Remedy for Toothache.** Wash the root of the aching tooth in vinegar, and let it dry half an hour in the sun.
   (Benjamin Franklin.)

● **Fresco's Discovery.** If you knew what you were doing, you'd probably be bored.
   (Catherine B. Fresco, Winston-Salem, N.C.)

● **Fri's Laws of Regulatory Agencies.** (1) If any agency can regulate, it will. (2) Regulation drives out broad-gauged, long-term thinking.
   (Robert Fri, former Environmental Protection Administrator. *AO.*)

● **Fried's Third Law of Public Administration.** If it's logical, rational, reasonable, and makes good common sense, it's not done. *Corollary:* If it's logical, rational, reasonable, and makes good common sense, don't you do it!
   (Steve Fried, Ohio Department of Economic and Community Development, Columbus.)

● **Friedman's Law of Elevators.** The amount of time an elevator takes in arriving is directly proportional to the lateness of the person waiting for it, and inversely proportional to the amount of weight in that person's arms. *Corollary:* In a crowded elevator, the person getting off first is at the back of the elevator.
(Robert J. Friedman, Lansdale, Pa.)

● **Frost's Working Rule.** By working faithfully eight hours a day, you may eventually get to be a boss and work twelve hours a day.
(Robert Frost.)

● **Fuchs's Warning.** If you actually look like your passport photo, you aren't well enough to travel.
(Sir Vivian Fuchs. *MLS.*)

● **Fuller's Historical Explanation.** In some cases, people were as much a part of the problem as anybody else.
(A professor of the same name who uttered this and other statements of this type, thereby causing Steve Cohen, Ithaca, N.Y., to drop the class.)

● **Fullner's Rules:** *Consumerism:* Regardless of who or what is responsible for inflationary increases in the cost of goods and services, the consumer pays. *Social Investment:* A male altering his personal behavior, mannerisms, grooming, etc., to accommodate a female of his attention will, subsequent to the termination of the relationship or acquaintance, meet another receptive female whose preferences concur with his characteristics prior to transformation. *Weekends:* Whenever the only time available to complete a task is on weekends, all suppliers of necessary parts, material, and equipment will be open for business Monday through Friday.
(Randall Fullner, San Jose, Cal.)

● **Galbraith's Law of Human Nature.** Faced with the choice between changing one's mind and proving that there is no need to do so, almost everybody gets busy on the proof.

(John Kenneth Galbraith, quoted in Andrea Williams's *Economics, Peace and Laughter,* Houghton Mifflin.)

● **Ganci's Advice.** You can tell a person they're ugly. You can tell a person their feet smell. You can even insult their mother, but never, never, never tell them they're stupid.

(Jerome G. Ganci, Brooklyn, N.Y.)

● **Gandhi's Observation.** There is more to life than increasing its speed.

(Mahatma Gandhi.)

● **Garland's Law.** One man's tax break is another man's tax increase.

(Virginia legislator Ray Garland, quoted in *The Washington Post,* February 12, 1979.)

● **Generalization.** Generally speaking, it is dangerous to generalize.

(Michael J. Wagner, St. Albert, Alberta, who says, "I have been told that this truth originated in one of the general organizations, i.e., General Motors, General Electric, General Tire . . .")

● **Gerrold's Law of Book Publishing.** You always find teh one typo in print that you missed in galleys.

(David Gerrold, Hollywood, Cal. See also *Short's Quotations.*)

● **Getty's Lament.** In some ways a millionaire just can't win. If he spends too freely, he is criticized for being extravagant and ostentatious. If, on the other hand, he lives quietly and thriftily, the same people who would have criticized him for being profligate will call him a miser.
(J. Paul Getty, quoted in *Forbes,* November 13, 1978.)

● **Getty's Second Law.** If you know how much you are worth, you are not worth much.
(J. Paul Getty, from Clifton Chadwick, Santiago, Chile.)

● **Giamatti's Rule of Choice.** It is my experience, in planning a course of study or anything else, that the person soonest sad, and who laments the longest, is the person who has only the courage of other people's convictions.
(Angelo Bartlett Giamatti, President, Yale University, quoted in *The Boston Globe,* November 12, 1978.)

● **Gillette's Principle.** If you want to make people angry, lie. If you want to make them absolutely livid with rage, tell the truth.
(Robert D. Gillette, M.D., Director, Riverside Family Practice Center, Toledo.)

● **Gingras's Distinction.** There is a difference between bending over backward and bending over forward.
(Armando R. Gingras, Boulder, Colorado.)

● **Ginsburg's Law.** The team you root for will always have a better season the year after you stop rooting for it.
(Phil Ginsburg, Concord, N.H.)

● **Glass's Law.** Enough money is always $5,000 more than I make.

   (U/Ra.)

● **Gleason's Advice to Public Administrators.** When leaving office, give your successor three sealed envelopes and instructions to open them in order as crises occur in the new administration. The message in the first should read "blame it on your predecessor," the second should read "announce a major reorganization," and the third should say, "write out three envelopes for your successor."

   (James Gleason, on leaving the post of County Executive, Montgomery County, Md. Quoted in *The Montgomery Journal,* November 24, 1978.)

● **Gloom of Night Law.** Checks are always delayed in the mail; bills arrive on time or sooner.

   (*U/*Donald Kaul's column in *The Des Moines Register,* December 11, 1978.)

Special Section 6

Glossary of Important Business Terms. *(For anyone who works in an office.)*

● *Activate.* To make carbons and add more names to the memo.
● *Advanced Design.* Beyond the comprehension of the ad agency's copywriters.
● *All New.* Parts not interchangeable with existing models.
● *Approved, Subject to Comment.* Redraw the damned thing.

FORWARDED FOR YOUR CONSIDERATION

- *Automatic.* That which you can't repair yourself.
- *Channels.* The trail left by interoffice memos.
- *Clarify, To.* To fill in the background with so many details that the foreground goes underground.
- *Conference, A.* A place where conversation is substituted for the dreariness of labor and the loneliness of thought.
- *Confidential Memorandum.* No time to mimeograph/photocopy for the whole office.
- *Consultant.* Someone who borrows your watch to tell you what time it is—then walks away with the watch.
- *Coordinator.* The person who has a desk between two expediters (see *Expedite*).
- *Developed After Years of Intensive Research.* Discovered by accident.
- *Expedite.* To confound confusion with commotion.
- *Forwarded for Your Consideration.* You hold the bag for a while.

● *FYI.* Found Yesterday, Interested?

● *Give Someone the Picture, To.* To make a long, confused and inaccurate statement to a newcomer.

● *Give Us the Benefit of Your Present Thinking.* We'll listen to what you have to say as long as it doesn't interfere with what we've already decided to do.

● *In Conference.* Nobody can find him/her.

● *In Due Course.* Never.

● *Infrastructure.* (1) The structure within an infra. (2) The structure outside the infra. (3) A building with built-in infras.

● *It Is in Process.* So wrapped up in red tape that the situation is almost hopeless.

● *Let's Get Together on This.* I'm assuming you're as confused as I am.

● *Note and Initial.* Let's spread the responsibility for this.

● *Policy.* We can hide behind this.

● *Program, A.* Any assignment that cannot be completed by one telephone call.

● *See me.* Come down to my office, I'm lonely.

● *Sources.*

■ *Reliable Source*—The person you just met.

■ *Informed Source*—The person who told the person you just met.

■ *Unimpeachable Source*—The person who started the rumor originally.

● *Top Priority.* It may be idiotic, but the boss wants it.

● *Under Active Consideration.* We're looking in the files for it.

● *Under Consideration.* Never heard of it.

● *We Are Making a Survey.* We need more time to think of an answer.

● *We Will Look into It.* By the time the wheel makes a full turn, we assume you will have forgotten about it too.

● *Will Advise in Due Course.* If we figure it out, we'll let you know.

(Compiled from several sets of "Office Definitions" retrieved from real offices.)

● **Godin's Law of the Sexual Revolution.** Sex is here to stay but it will never be the same.

(Guy Godin, Université Laval, Quebec. From his unpublished paper, "The Five or Six Ages of Sex.")

● **Goldberg's Law.** If anything can be misconstrued about the Jews, it will be . . . and has been.

(M. Hirsh Goldberg, author of *Just Because They're Jewish,* Stein & Day, 1978. Quoted in an interview in the *Baltimore News American,* January 31, 1979. *ME.*)

● **Golden Rule Revised I.** Do unto others . . . then split. *(U/Ra.)*

● **Golden Rule Revised II.** Whatsoever you would laugh at in others, laugh at in yourself.

(Harry Emerson Fosdick, from his book *On Being a Real Person,* Harper, 1943.)

● **Goldwynism, Tenets of.** (1) Every director bites the hand that lays the golden egg. (2) If you can't give me your word of honor, will you give me your promise? (3) Why only *twelve* disciples? Go out and get thousands! (4) Who wants to go out and see a bad movie when they can stay at home and see a bad one free on TV?

(Attributed to Samuel Goldwyn, various sources.)

● **Golfing: Observations, Theories, and Additional Rules.** (1) Rail-splitting produced an immortal president in Abraham Lincoln; but golf, with 29,000 courses, hasn't produced even a good A-Number-1 congressman. (2) Man blames fate for other accidents but feels personally responsible for a hole in one. (3) Golf is a form of work made expensive enough for rich men to enjoy. It is physical and mental exertion made attractive by the fact that you have to dress for it in a $200,000 clubhouse. Golf is what letter-carrying, ditch-digging, and carpet-beating would be if those tasks could be performed on the same hot afternoon in short pants and colored socks by gouty looking gentlemen who required a different implement for each mood. (4) In arriving at a judgment on whether or not ground is under repair for purpose of lifting a ball unpleasantly situated without penalty, the player shall toss a coin. If it falls, the ground may be deemed under repair. (5) A ball striking a tree while in flight shall be deemed not to have struck a tree unless the player making the stroke declares that he was deliberately aiming for it. In this case, play shall cease momentarily while his partners congratulate him on his marksmanship. But if the player attests in good faith that it was in no sense his intention to strike the tree, then it is obviously a piece of bad luck that has no place in a scientific game. No penalty shall accrue to the player, who is thereupon permitted to estimate the distance his ball would have traveled, but no more than half the distance to the goal line, or two bases.

> (Various sources: [1] Will Rogers. [2] *Horizons* magazine. [3] *Essex Golf and Country Club News.* [4 and 5] Mimeographed unattributed "Rules of Golf" from *ME.*)

● **Gomez's Law.** If you don't throw it, they can't hit it. ("Lefty" Gomez.)

● **Gonzalez's Laws.** (1) The easiest way to change a typewriter ribbon is to go out and buy a new typewriter. (2) If you call and they say "the check is in the mail," be prepared to call them a week later and the week after that. (3) Your enemies always photograph better than you.

> (Gloria Gonzalez, West New York, N.J.)

● **Goodman's Resolution.** To keep a little more "less" in this new year.

> (Ellen Goodman, from her nationally syndicated column of September 12, 1978.)

● **Gooen's Laws of Lost Energy.** (1) If it takes one person one hour to do a specific job, it will take two hours for two people to do the same job. (2) If it takes one person an hour to hike 2 miles on a trail, it will take two people an hour and a half to cover that same distance.

> (Irwin Gooen, Oneonta, N.Y.)

● **Gordon's Law.** If you think you have the solution, the question was poorly phrased.

> (Robert Gordon, East Granby, Conn.)

● **Gotwald's Law of Behavior Modification.** When a kick in the ass doesn't work, create envy.

> (Rev. Frederick G. Gotwald, Syracuse, N.Y.)

● **Gould's Two-Shirt Theory of Arctic Exploration.** Wear the first shirt until it becomes unbearable; then switch to the second shirt. Wear the second shirt until *it* becomes unbearable (by which time the first shirt will look pretty good again). This process may be repeated indefinitely.

> *(U/GT.)*

● **Governor's Rule.** Everyone at the executive end of Pennsylvania considers everyone at the congressional end an s.o.b. and vice versa. The governors consider anyone from Washington an s.o.b. no matter which end of the avenue he comes from.

> (Discovered by *TCA* when representing the Executive Branch at the Governors' Conference in Colorado Springs, 1949.)

● **Gracy's Axiom.** Don't pay duty. It is such a waste; the government has got more money than is good for it already and would only spend it.

> (A lady in P. G. Wodehouse's novel *The Luck of the Bodkins* [London, 1935], explaining why she wants an expensive necklace smuggled through customs. Used by columnist George Will to explain the passage of Proposition 13 in California.)

● **Grammatical Exclusion Principle.** If it can be said clearly, plainly, and in English it has just as logical and valid a claim for being examined as any other similarly constructed statement.

> (From an unsigned article of the same name in the July 1963 issue of *Air Force/Space Digest*. The gist of the article is that the author came up with this conclusion after making a tongue-in-cheek but well-worded proposal regarding an Air Force satellite. Later he found the Air Force had adopted his idea—in fact, it had become central to their planning.)

● **Grant's Musical Distinction.** I know two tunes: one of them is "Yankee Doodle," and the other isn't.
(Ulysses S. Grant.)

● **Grants Chant.**

> Pull up your socks!
> Hitch up your pants!
> Get in there and fight for
> Your Federal grants!

(Senator Harry F. Byrd, Jr., recited this on the floor of the U.S. Senate on October 3, 1974. He was protesting the hundreds of thousands of dollars in research money going to Harvard and Yale and suggested that this be used as a cheer at the Harvard-Yale football game.)

● **Gray's Theorems:** *Of N+2.* The number of referred papers required to obtain tenure in an American university is N +2, independent of the number N that have already been published. *Of the Sacrificial Victim.* Nothing gets done in America until somebody dies.

(Paul Gray, Professor, School of Business Administration, University of Southern California. He explains, "The first is based on watching tenure review committees for a number of years. The second has some classic examples: drug safety legislation was required by the Thalidomide disaster; exact fare was put in on buses after several drivers were killed; the FAA's R&D budget goes up after each major crash and then declines; pollution became a seriously recognized problem after Donora.")

● **Great, Rule of the.** When someone you greatly admire and respect appears to be thinking deep thoughts, they are probably thinking about lunch.

(U/DRW.)

● **Great American Axiom.** Some is good, more is better. Too much is just right.

(U/Ra.)

● **Greenfield's Rule of Practical Politics.** Everybody is for democracy—in principle. It's only in practice that the thing gives rise to stiff objections.

(Meg Greenfield, *The Washington Post,* in an article entitled "The People's Revenge," June 14, 1978.)

● **Greenhaus's Summation.** I'd give my right arm to be ambidextrous.

(U/DRW.)

● **Greenyea's Advice.** Learn to clip your fingernails with your left hand because you might not always have your right.
> (Writer John Greenyea, Kensington, Md., who learned this from his late father.)

● **Griffith's Maxim.** If it makes you nervous, don't watch.
> (Jean Sharon Griffith, Vice President of Student Services, Richland College, Dallas.)

● **Grizzly Pete's Philosophy.** (1) Don't do nothin' too much. (2) When a man gives you his reason for an act, just remember the chances are, nine out of ten, the reason is a trail blinder. (3) The most successful liar is the one who lies the least. (4) If there is anything in the theory of the survival of the fittest, a lot of people we know must have been overlooked.
> (Grizzly Pete of Frozen Dog, alter ego of Col. William C. Hunter, who appears in Hunter's *Brass Tacks,* published in 1910.)

● **Groebe's Law.** The more complex the problem, the sooner the deadline.
> (Larry Groebe, San Antonio.)

● **Grosso's Second Law.** Education cannot be substituted for intelligence.
> (Gerald H. Grosso, Port Orchard, Wash.)

● **Gruber's Laws.** (1) Common sense and common knowledge are the two most uncommon things in the world. (2) Everybody has to be a somebody. (If not, why get up in the morning?) (3) If you can be intimidated, you will be.
> (John F. Gruber, Oak Creek, Wisc.)

● **Guinther's Law of Problem Solving.** It is better to solve problems than crises.

(John Guinther, in *The Malpractitioners,* Doubleday, 1978. *MBC.*)

● **Guinzburg's Warning.** If you ever find yourself quixotic enough to lie down with a vampire, don't be surprised if you get a love bite on your neck.

(Thomas Guinzburg, former president of Viking Press, after being ousted by its conglomerate owner. Quoted in Hillary Mills's "Publishing Notes," *The Washington Star,* May 13, 1979.)

● **Guppy Law.** When outrageous expenditures are divided finely enough, the public will not have enough stake in any one expenditure to squelch it.

(Fred Reed, columnist for *The Federal Times,* explaining how the bureaucracy minimizes popular resistance to a government program. *AO.*)

● **Gwen's Law.** Do not join encounter groups. If you enjoy being made to feel inadequate, call your mother.

(Liz Smith, from *The Mother Book,* Doubleday, 1978.)

● **Haber's Hypothesis.** For an employee, the number and length of coffee breaks varies directly with the amount of un-completed work.

(Meryl H. Haber, M.D., Professor and Chairman of the Department of Laboratory Medicine, University of Nevada, Reno. First published in *The Pathologist,* 1970.)

● **Hakala's Rule of Survival.** Pack your own parachute.
(T. L. Hakala, Mesa, Ariz.)

● **Hall's Law of Return.** The nail that you drive flawlessly into a piece of wood without it buckling will be the same nail that you had previously singled out to show the salesperson how flimsy the nails are that he sold you.

(John Hall, from William C. Callis, Falls Church, Va.)

● **Hall's Observations.** (1) The word *necessary* seldom is. (2) Most business decisions are based on one critical factor: which method will cause the least paperwork? *Janet's Corollary:* In government, the opposite is true.

(Keith W. Hall, Harrisburg, Penn.)

● **Handel's Proverb.** You cannot produce a baby in one month by impregnating nine women!

(Sally Handel, New York City.)

● **Hanson's Law of Progress.** Any new form is always longer and more complicated than the one it replaces.

(Mark D. Hanson.)

● **Harris's Discoveries.** (1) Candy bars are smaller, but candy-bar wrappers are bigger. (2) A probable event is something good that ought to happen but doesn't. An unlikely event is something bad that should not happen but does. (3) If they catch you playing with a deck with more than four aces never admit you were cheating. Tell them you thought the game was canasta. (4) No one will ever say no to the question "You know what I mean?"

> (Roger Harris, Newark *Star-Ledger,* November 15, 1978.)

● **Harris's Law.** If a thing isn't worth doing, it isn't worth doing well.

> (Syndicated columnist Sydney J. Harris, whose father promulgated it as a cardinal rule of life. "I have made this a lifelong principle," says Harris, "and avoided dozens of onerous tasks.")

● **Hartka's Theorem.** You usually end up eating more cake after deciding to have only one thin piece than if you started with a bigger piece.

> (Thomas J. Hartka, Severna Park, Md. *Johns Hopkins Magazine,* May 1978.)

● **Harum's Theory of Fleas.** A moderate amount of fleas is good for a dog; it keeps him from broodin' on bein' a dog.

> (David Harum, the title character of E. N. Westcott's 1898 novel.)

● **Hasselbring's Law.** Never remember what you can afford to forget.

> (Andrew S. Hasselbring, Chillicothe, Ohio.)

● **Hassett's Third Law of Minutiae.** The intensity of interest in trivia is in reverse proportion to the magnitude of real-life problems encountered.

(W. Gilbert Hassett, Fairport, N.Y. This law came from his study of a retirement community where he found that the less people had to do, the fewer their real problems, the more they were concerned with little things. Why the Third Law of Minutiae? "The first two are inconsequential," says Hassett.)

● **Hazlitt's Observation.** The right thing to say always comes to mind after you've said the wrong thing and have no opportunity for rebuttal.
(John M. Hazlitt, South Bend, Ind.)

● **Health, Three Rules of.** One of the ancient natives has just confided to me a pearl of his ripe wisdom. Through 80 years of hard work, hard cider, strong tobacco, and simple food, he has only observed three rules of health, viz:
(1) Feet warm.
(2) Head cool.
(3) Bowels open.
(Richardson Wright, in *The Gardener's Bed Book,* J. B. Lippincott, 1929.)

● **Healy's Law of Distance.** The promised land always looks better from a distance.
(Pat Healy, reporter, *The Boston Globe. MBC.*)

● **Hebertson's Law of Budgets.** Don't be overly concerned with the cost of paper clips and other office supplies—fire people, and the paper clips will take care of themselves.
(David M. Hebertson, Sandy, Utah.)

● **Heifetz's Law.** No matter what you believe, you always find some people on your side that you wish were on the other side.
(Jascha Heifetz. From Earl M. Ryan, Birmingham, Mich.)

● **Hell's Angels Axiom.** When we do right you forget. When we do wrong you remember.
(From Hunter Thompson's *The Hell's Angels*, Random House, 1967.)

● **Hellman's Product Development Rule.** If you drop something and it doesn't break, mark it heavy duty.
(Mitch Hellman, Baltimore, learned while in new-product development.)

● **Hellrung's Law.** If you wait, it will go away. **Shavelson's Extension to Hellrung's Law.** . . . after having done its damage. **Grelb's Addition.** If it was bad, it will be back.
(Loretta Hellrung, Alton, Mo. *EV.*)

● **Hempstone's Dictum.** When the federal cow wanders into the paddock, somebody's going to milk it.
(Syndicated columnist Smith Hempstone, from his column of March 13, 1979.)

● **Henderson's Absolute.** There is nothing more cranky than a constipated gorilla.
(Dr. J. Y. Henderson, chief veterinarian for Ringling Brothers and Barnum & Bailey Circus. Quoted in the *Los Angeles Times* by David Larsen.)

● **Hendrickson's Law.** If a problem causes too many meetings, the meetings eventually become more important than the problem.
(U/GT.)

● **Henry's Law of Annual Reports.** The more rewrites a draft of an annual report is put through, the more the final, accepted draft for printing will match the original draft developed prior to administrative review.

> (C. Henry Depew, Tallahassee, Fla. "Last year," he says, "the annual report I am responsible for producing . . . had thirteen partial and five full rewrites. The end draft . . . almost matched the initial draft.")

● **Herbst's Laws of Military Survival.** (1) Never annoy a finance clerk. Garbage in, garbage out. (2) Have a friend in personnel, finance, supply, the hospital, and the Orderly Room. It's not what you know but who you know. (3) So conduct yourself that when your name is mentioned in the Orderly Room, everyone says "Who?" The invisible man is never on the detail list. (4) There is no way you can get through a day without violating a regulation; therefore, choose the one nobody knows. A mob is the best camouflage. (5) As far as the military is concerned, a person's IQ is in direct ratio to his pay grade. There are more dumb airmen than dumb generals. (6) The detail list is always made the day before you put in for leave, and everyone who could replace you is going on leave the day of your detail. (7) Never assume anything. Thule AB Greenland is manned by the clowns who didn't read the small print. (8) You're never that "short" that someone wouldn't try to get your butt. Wait until you're out the gate before you tell them what you think of them. (9) Never listen to an officer who always says, "I was an enlisted man myself." If he knew what it was all about, he'd still be enlisted. (10) Crap seldom rolls uphill. It rolls down and spreads out.

> (Anita M. Herbst, T. Sgt., USAF, San Antonio.)

● **Herman's Law.** Put your last change in a coffee machine or soft-drink dispenser, and have it run out of cups. Then watch the machine drink your coffee or soft drink.

> (Michael P. Herman, Fox Point, Wisc.)

● **Herman's Rule.** If it works right the first time, you've obviously done something wrong.
(Pat [Mrs. Herman] Jett, Hillsboro, Mo.)

● **Herth's Law.** He who turns the other cheek too far gets it in the neck.
(U/Ra.)

● **Hickey's Law.** When one is looking at the bank clock for the temperature, the time will always show up.
(James K. Hickey, Washington, D.C.)

● **Highrise Golden Rule.** Do over Others as You Would Have Them Do over You—Remember One Person's Floor Is Another's Ceiling.
(U/Ra.)

● **Hildebrandt's Plotting Principle.** If you don't know where you are going, any road will get you there.
(John Hildebrandt, Market Research Specialist, Durham, N.C. From Gary Russell, New London, Minn.)

● **Hill's Pet Law.** The life expectancy of tropical fish is in direct, but opposite, proportion to their purchase price. *Corollary:* Expensive breeds of dogs always run away and get lost; mongrels never do.
(Pierre Allen Hill, York, Penn.)

● **Hinds's Observation.** Man is planned obsolescence.
(Alan Hinds, Marion, Ohio, who wrote shortly after throwing his back out of joint.)

● **Hoadley's Laws:** *Decision-making:* People will take tough decisions only when not taking them is tougher. *Inflation:* The roots of inflation are human. Everybody wants more for less work. The political response is axiomatic. It is more blessed to give than to receive, when it is somebody else's money.
> (Walter Hoadley, Executive Vice President and Chief Economist, Bank of America, at a seminar for senior executives, January 9, 1979. *TCA.*)

● **Hoffman's Law of Hilarity.** A true friend will not laugh at your joke until he retells it.
> (Henry R. Hoffman, Jr., Dallas.)

● **Hoffman's Rule of the Road.** After you have spent $375 to make sure your car is in top shape, invariably three cars will pass you on the turnpike and the drivers will sound their horns and point at your rear wheels.
> (Jon Hoffman. *MLS.*)

● **Holcombe's Law.** When everything appears to be going in one direction, take a long, hard look in the opposite direction.
> (Alfred D. Holcombe, Elmira, N.Y.)

● **Holistic Revelation.** In order to cover up a hole, you've got to dig a new one.
> *(U/Ra.)*

● **Hollander's Computing Laws.** (1) The most important data will be lost due to parity errors. (2) Two "standard" interfaces are about as similar as two snowflakes. (3) The program that never failed on your last computer will never run on your current computer.
> (Howard R. Hollander, Roy, Utah.)

● **Holloway's Rule.**

> It is impossible
> to overestimate
> The unimportance
> of practically everything.

(Clark Holloway, Pittsburgh, Penn.)

● **Holmes's Law.** Once you have eliminated the impossible, whatever remains, however improbable, must be the truth.
(Sherlock Holmes. *MLS.*)

● **Hooligan, Third Law of.** The ratio of south ends of northbound horses to the number of horses is always greater than one.
(Edward H. Seymour, New York City. *AO.*)

● **Horomorun Paradox.** The more one earns, the smaller becomes the proportion of one's salary one is allowed to spend.
(From *The Yam Factor,* by Martin Page, Doubleday, 1972.)

● **Horowitz's Laws.** (1) It is impossible to be a participant in the march of time and not get a few blisters. (2) There is hope for everything in nature except for the petrified forest.
(Stanley Horowitz, Flushing, N.Y.)

● **Horowitz's Rule.** A computer makes as many mistakes in two seconds as twenty men working twenty years.
(U/DRW.)

HOLMES'S LAW

● **Horton's Law.** For difficult Yes/No decisions (especially regarding the opposite sex) you'll always wish you did if you didn't, but you'll rarely wish you didn't if you did.

(Joseph A. Horton, M.D., Philadelphia, who adds that this is also known as "the Ah Posteriori Law.")

● **Hovancik's Wait till Tomorrow Principle.** Today is the last day of the first part of your life.

(John Hovancik. South Orange, N.J.)

Special Section 7

How to:

■ *Avoid Any Educational Problem (Applicable in Many Other Fields.)*

• Profess not to have *the* answer. This lets you out of having any answer.

• Say that we must not move too rapidly. This avoids the necessity of getting started.

• For every proposal set up an opposite and conclude that the "middle ground" (no motion whatever) represents the wisest course of action.

• Point out that any attempt to reach a conclusion is only a futile "quest for certainty." Doubt and uncertainty promote growth.

• When in a tight place say something that the group cannot understand.

• Say that the problem "cannot be separated" from other problems; therefore no problem can be solved until all other problems are solved.

• Point out that those who see the problem do so by virtue of personality traits; e.g. they are unhappy and transfer their dissatisfaction to the area under discussion.

• Ask what is meant by the question. When it is clarified there will be no time left for the answer.

• Retreat from the problem into endless discussion of various techniques for approaching it.

• Retreat into analogies and discuss them until everyone has forgotten the original problem.

• Point out that some of the greatest minds have struggled with the problem, implying that it does us credit to have thought of it.

• Be thankful for the problem. It has stimulated our best thinking and has, therefore, contributed to our growth. It (the problem) should get a medal.

> (From Mark Griesbach, Des Plaines, Ill., who credits it to "Dietrich, University of Chicago.")

■ *Differentiate Liberals from Conservatives.*

(1) Liberals want to solve the marijuana problem by making it legal. Conservatives want to solve the wife-beating problem by making it legal.

(2) Liberals want to continue the ban on prayer in the public schools, as they consider religion to be personal and private. They favor compulsory sex education. Conservatives want to ban sex education. They favor compulsory prayer.

(3) Liberals want to strike down the abortion laws, so that unwanted babies can be killed off before they are born. Conservatives want to strike down the welfare laws, so that unwanted babies can be starved to death after they are born.

(4) Conservatives want to outlaw pornography. Liberals want to outlaw handguns.

(5) The conservative would prevent rape by locking up his wife and daughters. The liberal would prevent rape by legalizing prostitution. Neither considers locking up rapists, because the liberal says it is society's fault and the conservative says it costs too much money.

(6) When it comes to equal rights for women, the conservative doesn't want to monkey with the Constitution. When it comes to a balanced federal budget, the liberal doesn't want to monkey with the Constitution.

(7) Conservatives curb their dogs. Liberals keep cats. They curb other people's dogs.

> (The work of N. Sally Hass, Sleepy Hollow, Ill. She developed this scale when she discovered, "Many people think that liberals are permissive and conservatives are strict. Not so. Liberals are both permissive and strict. Conservatives are both permissive and

strict. But they are permissive and strict about different things.'')

■ *Learn to Write Goodly.*
(1) Don't use no double negatives.
(2) Make each pronoun agree with their antecedent.
(3) Join clauses good, like a conjunction should.
(4) About them sentence fragments.
(5) When dangling, watch your participles.
(6) Verbs has to agree with their subject.
(7) Just between you and I, case is important to.
(8) Don't write run-on sentences they are hard to read.
(9) Don't use commas, which aren't necessary.
(10) Try to not oversplit infinitives.
(11) It is important to use your apostrophe's correctly.
(12) Proofread your writing to if any words out.
(13) Correct spelling is esential.
   (From the newsletter of the Naval Supply Systems Command, *What's SUP.*)

■ *Name Things Impressively.*
I. General Purpose Argot Generator.
When in need of an authoritative phrase for a concept, project, or whatever, pull a three-digit number out of the air and select the corresponding words from the three columns. The number 982, for example, yields "Balanced Third-Generation Flexibility."

A	B	C
(0) Integrated	Management	Options
(1) Total	Organizational	Flexibility
(2) Systematized	Monitored	Capability
(3) Parallel	Reciprocal	Mobility
(4) Functional	Digital	Programming
(5) Responsive	Logistical	Concept
(6) Optional	Transitional	Time Phase

(7) Synchronized	Incremental	Projection
(8) Compatible	Third-Generation	Hardware
(9) Balanced	Policy	Contingency

(This guide to impressive but fuzzy words is known by a number of names including "The Baffle-Gab Thesaurus," "The Buzz Phrase Projector," and "The Handy Obfuscator." It has been widely mimeographed, photocopied, and published in trade magazines. It reputedly came out of some office of the Royal Canadian Air Force and was popularized in Washington by Philip Broughton, an HEW official.)

II. Medical Argot Generator.

Like the previous generator, this device requires random three-digit numbers. The only difference is that the user is to fill in column B with the accepted buzz words of the specialty or sub-specialty that he or she is involved in.

A	B	C
(1) Diagnostic	———————	Prevention
(2) Chronic	———————	Screening
(3) Systematic	———————	Evaluation
(4) Limited access	———————	Management
(5) Clinical	———————	Follow-up
(6) Ancillary	———————	Outreach
(7) Therapeutic	———————	Placebo
(8) Prospective	———————	Service pattern
(9) Retrospect	———————	Encounter
(10) Prognostic	———————	Incidence
(11) Preventive	———————	Intervention
(12) Life-threatening	———————	Trauma

(Writer John Paul Kowal, *Medical Dimensions,* December 1977.)

● **Howard's First Law of Theater.** Use it.
   (U/GT.)

● **Howe's Verities.** (1) When you're in trouble, people who call to sympathize are really looking for the particulars. (2) When in doubt in society, shake hands. (3) Everyone hates a martyr; it's no wonder martyrs were burned at the stake. (4) A good many of your tragedies probably look like comedies to others. (5) Put cream and sugar on a fly, and it tastes very much like a black raspberry. (6) Families with babies, and families without babies, are so sorry for each other. (6) Where the guests at a gathering are well acquainted, they eat 20 percent more than they otherwise would.
   (E. W. Howe, from his *Country Town Sayings* [1911].)

● **Hubbard's Credos.** (1) If a man says to you, "It isn't the money; it's the principle of the thing," I'll lay you six to one it's the money. (2) The fellow who owns his own home is always just coming out of the hardware store. (3) Everything comes to him who waits, except a loaned book. (4) There is somebody at every dinner party who eats all the celery.
   ("Kin" Hubbard, humorist and cartoonist, from various sources.)

● **Huffmann's Reminder.** Remember, it's everywhere.
   (William Huffmann, from Martin E. Shotzberger, Arlington, Va.)

● **Huguelet's Law of Systems Design.** Frozen specifications are like the abominable snowman, both are myths and both melt with the slightest application of heat.
   (Thomas V. Huguelet, President, Huguelet Systems Corp., Chicago.)

● **Huhn's Law.** You're not late until you get there.
(U/Ra.)

● **Human Ecology, The Three Laws of.** (1) There is no such thing as an independent individual, no such invention as an isolated technology, no such thing as a single resource, and no such place as an independent nation-state. (2) Humankind is an organized ecosystem of flows and stocks of transformed and reconstructed materials, money, energy, and information. (3) One generation's, community's, or culture's answers, solutions, or opportunities become other people's problems.
  (From Don G. Miles, the Feeding People Programme Fund, Australia.)

● **Hunter's Rule.** You see a lot when you haven't got your gun.
(U/Ra.)

● **Huster's Law.** Software "bugs" are always infectious.
  (Dwight A. Huster, State College, Penn.)

● **Hutzler's Refutation.** Desperation, not necessity, is the Mother of Invention.
  (Thomas L. Hutzler, T. Sgt., USAF, Fort Fisher, N.C.)

I

- **Iannuzzi's Universal Law of Justice.** Truth is trouble. (*U/* From a column in *Car and Driver* by Patrick Bedard.)

- **Ike Tautology, The.** Things are more like they are now than they have ever been before.
    (Dwight D. Eisenhower. From Paul Martin to *DRW.*)

- **Inch, Law of.** In designing any type of construction, no overall dimension can be totaled correctly after 4:30 P.M. on Friday. *Corollary 1:* Under the same conditions, if any minor dimensions are given to 1/16 of an inch, they cannot be totaled at all. *Corollary 2:* The correct total will become self-evident at 8:15 A.M. on Monday.
    (From an unsigned list of laws brought to the Center's attention by Ray Boston.)

- **Inge's Natural Law.** The whole of nature is a conjunction of the verb to eat, in the active and passive.
    (Nineteenth-century clergyman/writer William Ralph Inge.)

- **Institutional Input, Law of.** The wider the inter-departmental consultation on a problem, the less will any agency accept responsibility for the final report.
    (*The Washington Star* editorial, February 18, 1979.)

- **Institutions, Law of.** The opulence of the front-office decor varies inversely with the fundamental solvency of the firm.
    (U/DRW.)

● **Intelligence, Laws of.** (1) Intelligence is simple; all you have to do is find the needle in the haystack. (2) Don't forget to recognize the needle when you see it.

(Gen. William Davidson, head of the Office of Strategic Services [OSS] during World War II, to *TCA.*)

● **Inverse Peter Principle.** Everyone rises to his own level of indispensability, and gets stuck there.

(Dr. Barry Boehm, TRW, during a speech before the Special Interest Group on Aerospace Computing, March 19, 1979. *RS.*)

● **Iron Law of Consulting.** If I make the decision and I am right, you will never remember. If I make the decision and I am wrong, you will never *forget*.

(From *Operations Research for Immediate Application: A Quick and Dirty Manual* by Robert E. D. Woolsey and Huntington S. Swanson, Harper & Row, 1975. *RS.*)

Special Section 8

Irregular Verbs.

I am firm; You are obstinate; He is a pig-headed fool.

I am an epicure; You are a gourmand; He has both feet in the trough.

I am sparkling; You are unusually talkative; He is drunk.

I am farseeing; You are a visionary; He's a fuzzy-minded dreamer.

I am beautiful; You have quite good features; She isn't bad-looking, if you like that type.

I have reconsidered; You have changed your mind; He has gone back on his word.

I dream; You escape; He needs help.

I am at my prime; You are middle-aged; He's getting old.

I am a liberal; You are a radical; He is a communist.

I am casual; You are informal; He is an unshaven slob.

I am in charge of public relations; You exaggerate; He misleads.

I am a camera; You are a copycat; He is a plagiarist.

I am righteously indignant; You are annoyed; He is making a fuss about nothing.

I am a behavioral researcher; You are curious about people; He is a Peeping Tom.

I am nostalgic; You are old-fashioned; He is living in the past.

> (The game of "Irregular Verbs" or "Conjugations" was created quite a few years ago by philosopher Bertrand Russell on the BBC program *Brains Trust* when he declined "I am firm," the first example on our list. Ever since, people have been discovering new examples of how we approach self, present company, and those beyond earshot. The examples used here have come from a number of sources including *The New Statesman, The Nation, Harper's, Time, Isaac Asimov's Treasury of Humor,* Houghton Mifflin, 1971, and Ralph L. Woods's *How to Torture Your Mind,* Funk & Wagnalls, 1969.)

● **Irreversible Law of the Toe Holes.** No matter which side of the toe of the sock a hole is in, you will always put the sock on so that your big toe protrudes through the hole.

(Tom Eddins, Harding University, Searcy, Ark.)

● **Irving's Inquiry.** Who ever hears of fat men heading a riot?

(Washington Irving.)

● **Isaac's Law of Public Transportation.** No matter which direction you are going, the bus/streetcar going in the other direction will come first. *Corollary:* If you are in a hurry, at least three buses/streetcars going in the other direction will come first. (Richard Isaac, M.D., Toronto.)

J

● **Jackson's Economic Discovery.** If a young man or woman goes to any state university in this country for four years, it will cost less than $20,000. But if he or she goes to the state penitentiary for four years, it will cost slightly more than $50,000.
(Jesse Jackson, quoted in *Newsweek,* July 10, 1978.)

● **Jackson's Food Physics Laws.** (1) When stale, things innately crisp will become soft and things innately soft will become crisp. (2) The temperature of liquids gravitates toward room temperature, at which those drinks served hot are too cool and those served cold are too warm.
(Julie S. Jackson, Laurel, Md.)

● **Jackson's Laws.** (1) The next war can't start until the generals from the previous one have had time to write their memoirs. (2) Shopping centers are for people who don't have to go to the bathroom. (3) Baseball players must spit when the TV camera closes in on them.
(Michael Jackson, KABC Radio, Los Angeles.)

● **Jackson's Observation on Fame.** Fans don't boo nobodies.
(Reggie Jackson.)

● **Jacob's Laws of Organization.** (1) Never put anything away temporarily. (A dish that is taken in from the dining room and put on the sink, instead of directly into the dishwasher, ends up being put away twice.) (2) Take pity on your poor biographer (. . . organize and date your diaries and albums). (3) Why are people always complaining about being behind when all you have to do to keep up is a little every day? (4) Throwing things away is as great a joy as acquiring things. (5) If it's worth going, there's something worth taking with you. (6) If you are no good at this, give up—and cherish the nearest organized person.

(From Judith Martin's article "Organized!" in the Weekend section of *The Washington Post,* December 29, 1978. Jacob Perlman was her father.)

● **Jane's Gospel.** When there are two or more identical articles to be built or repaired, difficulty will be encountered, but only while attempting to build or repair the second (or last) one. *Corollary 1:* When both the hot and cold water faucets are leaking, the knob of the first one will be removed, the washer replaced, and the knob put back on with no complications. While attempting to repair the second, however, one will encounter (a) a permanently welded knob, (b) a screw-head stripped bare, (c) a knob that fit until removed but cannot possibly be reused, or (d) all of the above. *Corollary 2:* If the first article is dismantled again in order to determine why it went back together so easily, it will not.

(Jane L. Hassler, Marina del Rey, Cal.)

● **Jefferson's Ten Commandments.** (1) Never put off till tomorrow what you can do today. (2) Never trouble another for what you can do yourself. (3) Never spend your money before you have earned it. (4) Never buy what you don't want because it is cheap. (5) Pride costs more than hunger, thirst, and cold. (6) We seldom report of having eaten too little. (7) Nothing is troublesome that we do willingly. (8) How much pain evils cost us that have never happened! (9) Take things always by the smooth handle. (10) When angry, count to ten before you speak; if very angry, count to a hundred.

(Thomas Jefferson. Found in B. C. Forbes [ed.] *Thoughts on the Business Life* [1937].)

● **Jenkins's Rules for Football Betting.** (1) Never take a tip from a guy eating in a luncheonette. . . . (2) Find a team whose players' wives have an abundance of mink coats. Wait until the mink coats are favored by ten or more against a team playing under .500, then load up on the dog. The dog could win the whole game. (3) A team with too many members in the Fellowship of Christian Athletes can draw up to three delay penalties a game. Too much praying in the huddle. (4) Go with a good passing team against defensive backs who collect art. (5) A team with its entire offensive line living within a block of a drugstore could go all the way. (6) Finally, keep an eye out for the Ivy Leaguer in a key position if the Dow takes a sudden dip.
(Dan Jenkins, adapted from his his article "Getting in on a Zurich," in *Sports Illustrated.*)

● **Jesuit Principle.** It is better to ask for forgiveness than permission.
(Richard Molony.)

● **Jigsaw's Searching Conclusion.** You are standing on the piece that has to go in next.
(Elizabeth W. Jefferson, Roanoke, Va.)

● **Jinny's Second Law.** At a party, if you run out of ice, the guests stand around and bitch; if you run out of liquor, they go home.
(Virginia W. Smith, who is *MLS*'s mother.)

● **Jinny's Sister's Legacy.** Be careful what you give people as gifts; you may get it back when they die.
(Margaret W. Carpenter. *MLS.*)

● **Joachim's Explanation.** Nonsmokers create a vacuum and draw the smoke toward themselves.
(Gary Joachim, a smoker, who told it to Dianne Coates, a nonsmoker from Reseda, Cal.)

Job Performance Evaluation.

(The Center has received half a dozen variations on this important personnel rating system—all unattributed. This particular version was sent by *ME. FSP* collected the next item.)

Performance Level

Performance Factor	Outstanding	High Satisfactory
Quality	Leaps tall buildings with a single bound.	Needs running start to jump tall buildings.
Timeliness	Is faster than a speeding bullet.	Only as fast as a speeding bullet.
Initiative	Is stronger than a locomotive.	Is stronger than a bull elephant.
Adaptability	Walks on water consistently.	Walks on water in emergencies.
Communication	Talks with God.	Talks with the angels.
Relationship	Belongs in general management.	Belongs in executive ranks.
Planning	Too bright to worry.	Worries about future.

Satisfactory	Low Satisfactory	Unsatisfactory
Can only leap small buildings.	Crashes into buildings.	Cannot recognize buildings.
Somewhat slower than a bullet.	Can only shoot bullets.	Wounds self with bullets.
Is stronger than a bull.	Shoots the bull.	Smells like a bull.
Washes with water.	Drinks water.	Passes water in emergencies.
Talks to himself.	Argues with himself.	Loses those arguments.
Belongs in rank and file.	Belongs behind a broom.	Belongs with competitor.
Worries about present.	Worries about past.	Too dumb to worry.

Job Performance, What the Descriptions Mean. The military uses fitness reports in the evaluation of personnel performance. The following comes from the U.S. Navy but applies to general use.

Average: Not too bright.

Exceptionally well qualified: Has committed no major blunders to date.

Active socially: Drinks heavily.

Zealous attitude: Opinionated.

Character above reproach: Still one step ahead of the law.

Unlimited potential: Will stick until retirement.

Quick thinking: Offers plausible excuses for errors.

Takes pride in his work: Conceited.

Takes advantage of every opportunity to progress: Buys drinks for superiors.

Forceful and aggressive: Argumentative.

Indifferent to instruction: Knows more than his seniors.

Stern disciplinarian: A bastard.

Tactful in dealing with superiors: Knows when to keep his mouth shut.

Approaches difficult problems with logic: Finds someone else to do the job.

A keen analyst: Thoroughly confused.

Not a "desk" man: Did not go to college.

Expresses himself well: Speaks English.

Spends extra hours on job: Miserable home life.

Conscientious and careful: Scared.

Meticulous in attention to detail: A nitpicker.

Demonstrates qualities of leadership: Has a loud voice.

Judgment is usually sound: Lucky.

Maintains professional attitude: A snob.

Keen sense of humor: Has a vast repertory of dirty jokes.

Strong adherence to principles: Stubborn.

Gets along extremely well with superiors and subordinates alike: A coward.

NOT A "DESK" MAN

Slightly below average: Stupid.
Of great value to the organization: Turns work in on time.

● **Joe Cooch's Law.** (1) If things are military and make sense, coincidence has entered the picture. (2) To hell with the content, let's get the format straight. (3) Personnel officers exist primarily for the purpose of screwing up other people's careers. (4) The most complicated problems always arise at the most remote locations. (5) Writing a directive and getting people to pay attention to it are two entirely different operations. (6) Staff studies should always be written in support of foregone conclusions; assumptions will be furnished later. (7) The more esoteric the presentation, the thicker the accent of the person presenting it. (8) Generals must be kept busy or their subordinates will be. (9) Greatest consideration in personnel matters is given to those individuals who are the least efficient and the most troublesome; or, if you want top-level support, screw up. (10) It is illegal for any headquarters to admit error. (11) Planners are people who take implausible assumptions, apply these to conditions that could not possibly exist, using resources that will undoubtedly not be available, to produce a plan of action that is inconceivable to be followed out. (12) One thousand guesses added together are not necessarily more accurate than one big guess. (13) The longer you work on a casualty estimate, the less accurate it becomes. (14) If people don't obey a Regulation, write another more complicated. (15) Invariably, the least knowledgeable of individuals is the most vocal.

(We don't know who Joe Cooch is and wonder aloud if he might be a new incarnation of Murphy—or, at least, a figure created in Murphy's image. Whatever, his wisdom in the form of the multipart "Cooch's Law" is starting to show up with Murphy-like frequency. Examples of adaptations of Joe Cooch's code to fields outside the military [scientific research, for one] are beginning to appear. Our guess is that Joe Cooch is on his way to household-name status. Timothy J. Rolfe of the University of Chicago was the first to bring the Cooch contribution to the attention of the Center.)

● **Johns Hopkins Miraculous Secret for the Early Recovery of Patients, The.** Inflation.
    (*U*/ Nurse/*Ra.*)

● **Johnson's Creative Caveat.** No man but a blockhead ever wrote except for money.

(Samuel Johnson.)

● **Johnson's Law of Indices.** Any subject, no matter how abstruse or unlikely, will be found in an index, except the subject for which you are searching, no matter how common or likely.

(Rita Johnson, Stanley, N.D.)

● **Jones's Law of Authority.** The importance of an authority figure in a field is inversely proportional to the amount that is known about the subject.

(Don Jones, from James S. Benton, Los Angeles. The same Don Jones is responsible for the next set of laws.)

● **Jones's Laws of Innovation and the Organization.** (1) Organizational strength increases with time. (2) Innovative capacity is inversely proportional to organizational strength. *Corollary 1:* The least likely organization to make a significant improvement in a concept is the one that developed it. *Corollary 2:* The first step in developing a new concept is to bypass the existing organization. *Corollary 3:* Organizing for innovation is a contradiction in terms.

● **Jones's Mathematical Law.** Twice nothing is still nothing.

(Cyrano Jones, *Star Trek,* "The Trouble with Tribbles." *JS.*)

● **Jones's Rule of the Road.** The easiest way to refold a road map is differently.

(Franklin P. Jones, in *The Wall Street Journal.*)

● **Jones's Static Principle.** In a static organization, one accedes to his level of comfort.

(From J. Thomas Parry, Rockford, Ill., who attributes it to

Hugh Jones, manager of the Minneapolis *TV Guide* office. Parry says, "Mr. Jones, having been in an unchanging job for many years, developed this corollary to the Peter Principle.")

● **Jones's 3:00 A.M. Theory.** Truly important information should be retained and ready even if the boss calls at 3:00 A.M. and wakes you from a deep sleep.
(Kenneth J. Jones, Hunt Valley, Md.)

● **Jordan's Laws.** *Of Survival:* You can get over anything but a gravel in your shoe. *Of Technology:* Invention is the mother of necessity. (How long did mankind get along satisfactorily without the telephone?) *Of Psychiatry:* The client already knows all the answers, but he won't tell. The psychiatrist is lucky to guess the right questions.
(D. Wylie Jordan, M.D., Austin, Tex.)

● **Juall's Law on Nice Guys.** Nice guys don't always finish last: (a) Sometimes they don't finish. (b) Sometimes they don't get a chance to start.
(Wally Juall, East Lansing, Mich.)

● **Juhani's Law.** The compromise will always be more expensive than either of the suggestions it's compromising.
(U/DRW.)

● **Juliet's Advice.** (1) Never start before you are ready. (2) People will do to you what you let them.
(Juliet Awon-Uibopuu, River Edge, N.J.)

K

- **Kagan's Principle of Operational Verisimilitude.** You don't test something to see if it will work if you think it won't work.

  (Susan Kagan, from Shel Kagan, New York City.)

- **Kagle's Rule for Winning Stock Car Races.** Keep to the left, and get back here as soon as you can.

  (Reds Kagle, late-model sportsman champion, Old Dominion Speedway, 1976–77, Manassas, Va. *JCG.*)

- **"Kamoose" Taylor's Hotel Rules and Regulations.** (A selection.)

A deposit must be made before towels, soap, or candles can be carried to rooms. When boarders are leaving, a rebate will be made on all candles or parts of candles not burned or eaten.

Not more than one dog allowed to be kept in each single room.

Quarrelsome or boisterous persons, also those who shoot off without provocation guns or other explosive weapons on the premises, and all boarders who get killed, will not be allowed to remain in the House.

When guests find themselves or their baggage thrown over the fence, they may consider that they have received notice to quit.

The proprietor will not be accountable for anything.

Only regularly registered guests will be allowed the special privilege of sleeping on the Bar Room floor.

Meals served in own rooms will not be guaranteed in any way. Our waiters are hungry and not above temptation.

All guests are requested to rise at 6:00 A.M. This is imperative as the sheets are needed for tablecloths.

To attract attention of waiters or bellboys, shoot a hole through the door panel. Two for ice water, three shots for a deck of cards, and so on.

> (Rules posted September 1, 1882, at the MacLeod Hotel in Alberta by Henry "Kamoose" Taylor, proprietor. This important piece of Canadian lore appears in *Columbo's Little Book of Canadian Proverbs, Graffiti, Limericks and Other Vital Matters* by John Robert Columbo, Hurtig Publishing, 1975.)

● **Kaplan's Dictum.** If you are unable to decide between two things, do whichever is cheapest.

> (*U*/Fred Bondy, Wilmette, Ill.)

● **Karni's Law of Telephones.** The cessation of ringing of a phone is *not* a function of the responder's distance, velocity, or time of access. (It will stop ringing just when you reach for it, no matter how far you have to come, how fast—or slowly—you have traveled to cover the distance between you and said phone.)

> (S. Karni, Professor, University of New Mexico, Department of Electrical Engineering and Computer Science. Karni supports his discovery with this statement: "[It] is truly empirical, having been tested in the field for over twenty years [a total of some 40,000 experiments]. No theoretical proof is known to exist at this time, although some of the best brains are involved in its pursuit.")

● **Kass's Truth.** If you plan a pot luck for a club of thirty-seven members, you will end up with a meal of thirty-seven jars of dill pickles.

> (Connie Kass, St. Paul.)

● **Kathleen's Hypothesis of Earth-Water Kinesis.** The lighter the color, the higher the heel, and the more the cost of the

shoes, the deeper the mud in the puddle just outside the car door.
(Kathleen, known to Michael L. Lazare, Armonk, N.Y.)

● **Katz's Laws.** (1) No new theory is recognized until some expert claims it was plagiarized. (2) Never send your new theorem to a specialist in counterexamples.
(Robert Katz, Rockport, Mass.)

● **Kaufman's Laws.** (1) A policy is a restrictive document to prevent a recurrence of a single incident, in which that incident is never mentioned. (2) A roadblock is a negative reaction, based on irrelevant assumption.
(J. Jerry Kaufman, Dallas.)

● **Kaul's Collection.** (1) It does not rain on water-resistant materials. (2) The only thing alike in all cultures is the police. (3) A sinking ship gathers no moss. (4) Abstinence makes the heart grow fonder. (5) Do not try to solve all life's problems at once —learn to dread each day as it comes. (6) Crime doesn't pay unless you write a book about it. (7) A fool and his money are welcomed everywhere. (8) Don't bake cookies; the children will only eat them. (9) A man can have more money than brains, but not for long. (10) Suicide is the sincerest form of self-criticism. (11) A coward dies a thousand deaths, a hero dies but one—but which one?
(Donald Kaul, *The Des Moines Register.* These are laws and observations sent to Kaul by readers of his "Over the Coffee" column.)

● **Kautzmann's Law of Negativism.** Whatever you propose to do can't be done. *Corollary:* If they do what you propose, it won't work.
(Gary E. Kautzmann, Allentown, Penn.)

● **Kaye's Duplicate Bridge Players' Rule of Thumb.** The

laws of chance positively ensure that you will always play the most difficult contracts against the most competent opponents, and the "laydowns" against the beginners. *Corollary:* Whenever a partnership has lost a match by a very few points, each partner will invariably remember (and be willing to discuss ad nauseam) his own brilliant plays and his partner's errors.

(Joan C. Kaye, Los Gatos, Cal.)

● **Keller's Law of the Theater.** A whisper backstage will be heard with greater intensity than a line spoken in a normal voice on stage.

(William S. Keller, Streamwood, Ill.)

● **Kellough's Laws of Waiting.** (1) The amount of time you must wait is directly proportional to the uncomfortableness of the settings you must wait in. (2) The magazines in a doctor's, dentist's, or barber's place of business are always at least three months old. The boringness of those magazines is directly proportional to the length of time you have to wait.

(David Kellough, Chillicothe, Ohio.)

● **Kelly's Run-Around Theorem.** (1) To get published, one should get a literary agent. (2) To get a literary agent, one should be published.

(William W. Kelly, Hollywood, Fla.)

● **Kener's Law.** Tape doesn't stick where (or when) you want it. Tape only sticks to itself.

(Reed Kener, from Larry Groebe, San Antonio.)

● **Keokuk, First Law of.** The ability and adeptness of the towboat captain varies inversely with the rapidity of the approach of 8:30 A.M. and 4:30 P.M.

(Constance E. Campbell, Keokuk, Iowa. She explains: "Keokuk . . . is a river town on the Mississippi River.

There is a swing-span toll bridge connecting Keokuk and
Hamilton, Illinois, at the foot of Main Street. . . . The times
a new, inexperienced towboat captain seems always to
be trying unsuccessfully to maneuver his towboat into our
lock is invariably the times people are trying to get to
work, or to get home from work.")

● **Kerouac's Admonition.** Walking on water wasn't built in
a day.

(Jack Kerouac.)

● **Kerr's Three Rules for a Successful College.** Have
plenty of football for the alumni, sex for the students, and parking
for the faculty.

(Clark Kerr. *MLS.*)

● **Key to Happiness.** You may speak of love and tender-
ness and passion, but real ecstasy is discovering you haven't lost
your keys after all.

(U/Ra.)

● **Khomeini Corollary.** Take the revolution to where the
reporters want to be and you'll get worldwide coverage.

(Charles Peters, in *The Washington Monthly.* Peters says
that this discovery is owed to the Shah of Iran, who
landed the Ayatollah Khomeini in Paris. "Now reporters
who would never dream of going to Meshed, Tabriz, or
Zahidan could cover the main issues of the Iranian revolution from Paris.")

● **King's Religious Observation.** The shorter the gospel,
the longer the sermon.

(Donald King, Philadelphia.)

● **Klawans-Rinsley Law.** Large projects require more time,
small projects require less time.

(Alan J. Klawans and Donald B. Rinsley, M.D.)

● **Kneass's Law.** If you are a writer, editor, publisher, or affiliated with an advertising agency, everyone knows more about your business than you do.
(Jack Kneass, Huntington Beach, Cal.)

● **Knowles's Law.** The length of debate is in inverse proportion to the importance of the subject.
(Robert P. Knowles, New Richmond, Wisc., twenty-two-year veteran of the state legislature. He writes, "At one point the Wisconsin Senate spent an entire day debating the proper construction of a doghouse. The bill finally failed to pass. The next day a highly complex bill having to do with a three-phase formula for corporate taxation passed without a word of debate or a dissenting vote.")

● **Knowlton's Law of Involvement.** Fight to the death for anything in which you truly believe—but keep those kinds of commitments to a bare minimum.
(Gary Knowlton, Portland, Ore.)

● **Koolman's Laws of Physics.** [As expounded to an unfortunate student over several years by many professors, based on the original premise learned in high school: PHYSICS IS AN EXACT SCIENCE.]
(1) If it gives you trouble, get rid of it. If you can't get rid of it, ignore it.
(2) If you can't understand it, it is intuitively obvious.
Corollary: If it works, use it.
(3) Occam's razor is invalid (and dull).
Corollary: If you think it's confusing now, wait till you find out what it's really about.
Corollary: Logical constructs are only used to make the picture of the universe more confusing than before.

Corollary: Use generalities wherever possible, as it makes things more difficult to understand.

Corollary: Always introduce an arbitrary constant to confuse the issue.

(4) All fundamental particles (constants, rules, etc.) of the same kind are identical, except those that are different.

Corollary: Anything that breaks a general rule is either totally correct and the rule wrong, or is to be ignored.

(5) A meaningful concept is one that violates every rule possible.

Corollary: A meaningful concept is usually meaningless and confusing, unless your instructor or boss formulated it, in which case you'd best learn it anyway.

(6) A physicist cannot relate to his environment.

Corollary: If you want to prove something, remake the universe so that it is true.

(7) All inconsistencies are consistent with recognized theories.

(8) Contradiction is the essence of all physical theorems.

(9) In any calculation, a constant of "π," "e," or "-1" is always lost.

(10) Always use ideal constructs with no real analogues to explain them.

Corollary: Everything is useless.

Corollary: Reality doesn't work.

Corollary: If you prove it can't exist, it does, and vice versa.

Corollary: See *Law* 6.

    (Ron Koolman, Cincinnati, Ohio.)

● **Korzybski's Warning.** God may forgive you your sins, but your nervous system won't.

    (Alfred Korzybski, scientist and writer. *ME.*)

● **Kottmeyer's Ring-Around-the-Tub Principle.** Telephones displace bodies immersed in water.

    (Martin S. Kottmeyer, Carlyle, Ill.)

● **Krafft's Scale of Dumb (a.k.a. The Seven Deadly Dumbs).** [Created for military application but may be tailored to fit the particular needs of any type of organization or endeavor by removing and substituting the italicized words.]

Adjectival	Category	Application
Gross Dumb	1	Common dumb, frequently found at *squad or platoon level.*
Public Dumb	2	Less common than a gross dumb; frequently seen amongst the leadership at *company level.*
Gross Public Dumb	3	The all-emcompassing "combination of ingredients" dumb.
Incredible Dumb	4	Also known as "aggravated dumb." Causes the *Post Commander* to sit up and take notice. May have visibility at *higher headquarters.*
Congenital Dumb	5	Encountered most frequently in *other units.* We all know folks like this, but Category 5's can be excused with, "It ain't their fault—they were born that way."

Contagious Dumb	6	Frequent and prolonged exposure to *certain staff officers at the installation* causes this. Incubation period: 24 to 30 months. Temporary relief of symptoms by avoiding all staff meetings and *hot-line calls.*
Terminal Dumb	7	What happens to a victim of contagious dumb unless the condition is treated immediately.

(Maj. Gary R. Krafft, U.S. Army, Fort Meade, Md.)

● **Kramer's Law of Ploygraphy.** Whenever someone says he is being perfectly frank, he is being less than perfectly frank.
(Victor H. Kramer, from Andrew Jay Schwartzman, Washington, D.C.)

● **Krause's Discovery.** In the jungle, a press card is just another piece of paper.
(Charles Krause, *The Washington Post.*)

● **Krupka's Observation.** When you see an individual wearing a white lab coat, you can be sure he thinks he is a scientist.
(*U*/From an unpublished paper, "Famous Laws and Principles of Science," by Ray S. Hansen, Corvallis, Ore., and Robert A. Sweeney, Buffalo.)

● **Krutch's Indictment.** The most serious charge that can be brought against New England is not Puritanism but February. (Naturalist Joseph Wood Krutch.)

L

● **Lada's Commuter Corollary.** As soon as construction is complete on the fastest, most convenient expressway route from your home to your place of work, you will be transferred to another place of work.

(Stephen C. Lada, Detroit.)

● **Landers's Law of the Pinch.** Usually when the shoe fits —it's out of style.

(Ann Landers, in her column for February 6, 1977.)

● **Landon's Law of Politics.** It's a sin in politics to land a soft punch.

(Alf Landon, in an interview with David Broder, *The Washington Post,* December 14, 1977.)

● **Lansburgh's Observation.** There's no column on the scorecard headed "remarks."

(Sidney Lansburgh, Jr., quoted in Julius M. Westheimer's column in *The Baltimore Evening Sun,* March 22, 1979.)

● **Larson's Conclusion.** Shunning women, liquor, gambling, smoking, and eating will not make one live longer. It will only seem like it.

(M. Sgt. Robert V. Larson, USAF [retired], Golden Valley, Minn.)

● **Latecomer's Rule.** If you are impatiently waiting for someone to arrive who is late, go to the bathroom and that person will arrive instantly in your absence.

(A. S. Boccuti, Baltimore.)

● **Laur's Advice to Negotiators and Traders.** You've got to let the monkey *have* the banana every once in a while.
(Ed Laur, Amarillo, Tex.)

● **Laura's Law.** No child throws up in the bathroom.
(U/DRW.)

● **Law Laws.** (1) Aphorism is better than none. (2) In the beginning Murphy condensed the human condition into twelve laws. The rest of us want to get into somebody's book.
(Ryan Anthony, Tucson.)

● **Lawrence's Laws.** (1) Paperwork is inversely proportional to useful work. (2) In any bureaucracy, the triviality of any position can be derived by counting the number of administrative assistants.
(Bob Ackley, T. Sgt., USAF, Plattsmouth, Neb.)

Special Section 10

Lawyer's Language. Toward a better understanding of the law . . .

"As Your Honor Well Recalls." Tip-off by a lawyer that he is about to refer to a long-forgotten or imaginary case. (Adapted from a similar definition by Miles Kington, *Punch,* November 12, 1975.)
Basic Concept. Murder—don't do it; Theft—don't do it; Fraud —don't do it; etc. (G. Guy Smith, Media, Penn.)

Brief. Long and windy document. Should be at least 10,000 words long to qualify.

Costs. Amount required to bankrupt the acquitted. (Miles Kington.)

Duty of the Lawyer. When there is a rift in the lute, the business of the lawyer is to widen the rift and gather the loot. (Arthur Garfield Hays.)

Equality Under the Law. ". . . forbids the rich as well as the poor to sleep under bridges, to beg in the streets, and to steal bread." (Anatole France.)

Incongruous. Where our laws are made. (Bennett Cerf.)

"It has been long known that . . ." "I haven't been able to find the original reference."

"It might be argued that . . ." "I have such a good answer for this argument that I want to make sure it is raised."

Lex Clio Volente. The client is always right—particularly when he has further causes to entrust. (Del Goldsmith, *American Bar Association Journal.*)

Nine Points of the Law, The. (1) A good deal of money. (2) A good deal of patience. (3) A good case. (4) A good lawyer. (5) A good counsel. (6) Good witnesses. (7) A good jury. (8) A good judge. (9) Good luck.

Proper Pronoun. Louis Nizer has pointed out that most lawyers on winning a case will say, "We have won," but when justice frowns on the case the lawyer customarily remarks, "You have lost."

Plea Bargaining. Ending a sentence with a proposition.

Res Ipsa Loquitur. Latin for "the thing speaks for itself." Anything that speaks for itself is an abomination to the law and reason enough for a lawyer to be paid to speak for something that speaks for itself. (Adapted from Miles Kington.)

Will. Where there's a will, there's a lawsuit. (Oliver Herford.)

"With All Due Respect." Introductory phrase for a disrespectful statement.

"Yes, Your Honor." Witty rejoinder by lawyer to judge.
(Miles Kington.)

● **LAX Law.** Flying is not in itself dangerous, but the air is like the sea, very unforgiving of those who make mistakes.
(Sign seen in a hangar at the Los Angeles International Airport. William C. Young, Ballston Lake, N.Y.)

● **Le Bon's Mot.** Science has promised us truth. It has never promised us either peace or happiness.
(Gustave Le Bon.)

● **Le Carré's Assumption.** When in doubt about something like this, assume a screw-up.
(John le Carré, quoted in the *Los Angeles Times,* April 8, 1974. *RS.*)

● **Lec's Immutables.** (1) The first requisite for immortality is death. (2) All gods were immortal. (3) Even a flounder takes sides.
(Stanislaw J. Lec, from *Unkempt Thoughts,* St. Martin's Press, 1962.)

● **Lee's Law.** Mother said there would be days like this, but she never said there'd be so many.
(Jack Lee, WLAK Radio, Chicago.)

● **Lender's Law.** The law of lending is to break the borrowed article.
(U/Ra.)

● **Lennie's Law of the Library.** No matter what you want, it's always on the bottom shelf.

LE CARRÉ'S ASSUMPTION

(Lennie Bemiss, Assistant Librarian, Estes Park Public Library, Estes Park, Colo.)

● **Leo's Laws.** (1) Small talk drives out meaningful talk. (2) If a song sounds like a commercial, it will become a hit. (3) The less the product the bigger the ad.

(Doug ''Leo'' Hanbury, Des Moines.)

● **Leonard's Constant.** There are many changes in one's life, but there is one rule that remains constant: In a men's room incoming traffic has the right of way.

(Hugh Leonard, from his play *Da.*)

● **Leveut's Cause for Rejoicing.** There is always more hell that needs raising.

(Lauren Leveut. *RA.*)

● **Levine's Declaration.** Long delays on crowded expressways are due to rubbernecking by passersby observing insignificant events. However, when I finally reach this particular point, I feel that I deserve to take time to participate in the distraction.

(Kenneth C. Levine, Doraville, Georgia.)

● **Levinson's Law No. 16.** If you check your coat at the theatre, there will be ten empty seats around you when you sit down.

(Leonard Louis Levinson, from his book *Webster's Unafraid Dictionary,* Collier Books, 1967.)

● **Lewandowski's Air Turbulence Principle.** An airline flight will remain smooth until beverage and/or meal service begins. A smooth flight will resume when beverage and/or meal service ends.

(J. A. Lewandowski, Parma, Ohio.)

● **Lewin's Deduction.** The age of our universe is a function of time.

> (Walter Lewin, Professor, MIT. Richard Stone, Stanford, Cal.)

● **Lichtenberg's Insights.** (1) If life were "just a bowl of cherries" . . . we would soon die of a deficiency disease. (2) We can never get to the Promised Land, for if we did, it would no longer be the Promised Land. (3) We say that the plow made civilization but for that matter, so did manure. (4) The zoning laws in most American neighborhoods would not *permit* the construction of a Parthenon. (5) There is no occupation as practical as love; theories are useless in bed.

> (Benjamin Lichtenberg, Verona, N.J., from his book *Insights of an Outsider,* Jaico Publishing, 1972.)

● **Liebling's News Constant.** The people who have something to say don't talk, the others insist on talking.

> (A. J. Liebling, *Holiday* magazine, February 1950.)

● **Lightfoot's Lament for Collectors of (fill in the blank).** The one time you *don't* visit a dealer, flea market, auction, or whatever, is the one time that there is an abundance of rare, fine-quality (fill in the blanks).

> (Fred Lightfoot, Greenport, N.Y.)

● **Lin's Maxim.** Happiness is a state of minimum regret.
> (Wallace E. Lin, Hartford.)

● **Lincoln's Rule of Return.** When you ask from a stranger that which is of interest only to yourself, always enclose a stamp.

> (Abraham Lincoln.)

● **Lindsay's Law.** When your draft exceeds the water's depth, you are most assuredly aground.
> *(U/ME.)*

● **Lindsey's Law.** The more complex a problem is, the more simple it is to resolve—in that more assumptions are available.

(Ron Lindsey, Media, Penn.)

● **Linus's Law.** There is no heavier burden than a great potential.

(From Linus, *Peanuts.* Gerald M. Fava, Lake Hiawatha, N.J.)

● **Lippmann's Law of Conformity.** When all think alike, no one thinks very much.

(Walter Lippmann. *MBC.*)

● **Lippmann's Political Rule.** [A] democratic politician had better not be right too soon. Very often the penalty is political death. It is much safer to keep in step with the parade of opinion than to try to keep up with the swifter movement of events.

(Walter Lippmann, in *The Public Philosophy,* New American Library.)

● **Lipsitt's Law.** In matters of adversity, whatever you have the most of you are going to get more of.

(Lewis P. Lipsitt, Professor of Psychology and Medical Science, Brown University. Lipsitt points out that this law is a more sophisticated version of his original discovery, which is that "One goddamned thing leads to another goddamned thing." Of his law, Lipsett says, "I have found that living by this expectation not only helps to explain for me what to others is inexplicable, but that I can proceed in my life with the clear and soothing expectation that nothing surprisingly terrible or terribly surprising is likely to happen.")

● **Liston's Dictum.** Everything eventually becomes too high priced.
(Robert A. Liston, Shelby, Ohio.)

● **Liston's Law of Gift Wrapping.** No matter how many boxes you save, you will never have one the right size.
(Jean Liston, Shelby, Ohio.)

● **Litt's Paradox of Deadlines.** The reason for the rush is the delay, and, conversely, the reason for the delay is the rush.
(Lawrence Litt, Executive Editor, *The Fugue,* Miami.)

● **Livingston's Adjuration.** You can't win. Shoot for a tie.
(E. A. Livingston, Richmond Hill, N.Y.)

● **Lloyd George's Razor.** A politician is a person with whose politics you don't agree; if you agree with him he is a statesman.
(David Lloyd George.)

● **Lobenhofer's Law.** Any emergency sufficiently well planned for—will not happen.
(R. W. Lobenhofer, *Modern Casting* magazine, January 1979.)

● **Lockwood's Long Shot.** The chances of getting eaten up by a lion on Main Street aren't one in a million, but once would be enough.
(John Lockwood, Washington, D. C.)

● **Loderstedt's Rule.** Measure twice because you can only cut once.
(Bob Loderstedt, Mendham, N.J.)

● **Loewe's Rules of Governance.** (1) If the government

hasn't taxed, licensed, or regulated it, it probably isn't worth anything. (2) The ability of the government to create money is likened to a child's desire to change the rules of a game he is losing.

    (Donald C. Loewe, Chicago.)

● **Lone Eagle Law.** Before you fly make sure you're on board.

    (Sign in the Lone Eagle Saloon, Minneapolis–St. Paul Airport.)

● **Long's Law of Hyphens.** In any paragraph, the number of hyphenated words is inversely proportional to the author's understanding of the relationship between the words thus hyphenated. (Examples: Indo-European, Hindu-Arabic, politico-theological, socio-economic, mathematico-physical, Judeo-Christian, and Anglo-Saxon.)

    (Kevin G. Long, Quebec.)

● **Longworth's Philosophy.** Fill what's empty. Empty what's full. And scratch where it itches.

    (Alice Roosevelt Longworth.)

● **Looney's Rule of Potato Chips.** You don't eat potato chips before noon.

    (Douglas S. Looney, from an article on potato chips in *The American Way* magazine, December 1978.)

● **Los Angeles Dodgers Law.** Wait till last year.

    (Johnny Carson, the *Tonight* show, August 2, 1979.)

● **Loughrige's Lesson.** The middle of the road is the best place to get run over.

    (Alan Craig Loughrige, Springfield, Mo.)

● **Lowell's Constant.** Whatever you may be sure of, be sure of this: that you are dreadfully like other people.
(James Russell Lowell, quoted in *Catchwords of Worldly Wisdom,* [1909].)

● **Lowell's Formula.** Universities are full of knowledge; the freshmen bring a little in and the seniors take none away, and knowledge accumulates.
(Educator Abbott Lawrence Lowell.)

● **Lowell's Law of Life.** Life is a hypothesis.
(Poet Robert Lowell. *MBC.*)

● **Lubarsky's Law of Cybernetic Entomology.** There's always one more bug.
(U/DRW.)

● **Lucy's Law.** The alternative to getting old is depressing.
(U/DRW.)

● **Lynes's Law.** No author dislikes to be edited as much as he dislikes not to be published.
(Russell Lynes, from Adrian Janes, Urbana, Ill.)

- **Ma Bell's Public Relations Principle.** We don't care. We don't have to.

    (Bumper sticker cited by John Stephen Smith, Lincoln, Neb.)

- **Ma's Rule.** No matter how many pencils or pens there are in the house, none will ever be within fifteen feet of a telephone.

    (U/Ra.)

- **McCabe's Law.** Nobody HAS to do anything.

    (Charles McCabe, *San Francisco Chronicle. RS.*)

- **McCarthy's Adage.** The only thing that saves us from the bureaucracy is inefficiency. An efficient bureaucracy is the greatest threat to liberty.

    (Eugene McCarthy, quoted in *Time,* February 12, 1979.)

MA'S RULE

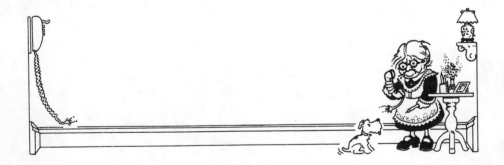

● **McGarr's First Law.** Whatever government does, it does more or less badly.

> (Judge Frank J. McGarr, U.S. District Court of Northern Illinois, from his commencement address at Loyola University Law School, June 13, 1976.)

● **McGlinchey's Law of Trust.** Never trust a world leader.

> (Herbert J. McGlinchey, former U.S. Congressman, Pennsylvania State Senator, Philadelphia ward leader from 1934 to 1976. *MBC.*)

● **McKinley's Memorial Dictum.** The worst time to ignore possible future events of high negative impact is when you are successfully building an empire and you are loved by the people.

> (In honor of William McKinley, Wayne Boucher in his article "Finding the Future," *MBA Magazine,* August/September 1978.)

● **McLaren's Motto.** Sic Transit Gloria Tuesday!

> (Jack McLaren, from *Columbo's Little Book of Canadian Proverbs, Graffiti, Limericks and Other Vital Matters* by John Robert Columbo, Hurtig Publishing, 1975.)

● **McLaughlin's Law of Walking on Railroad Ties.** They're too far for one step, but too close for two.

> (Brian McLaughlin, recorded by John Hall [c. 1953] and submitted by Hilde Weisert, Teaneck, N.J. Ms. Weisert insists that it has wide application.)

● **MacLeish's Literary Law.** If you write a novel about fruitcakes, you will hear from fruitcakes.

> (Rod MacLeish, quoted in *The Washington Post,* May 24, 1979. The discovery was occasioned by his novel, *The Man Who Wasn't There,* Random House, 1976, about a man being driven insane. He got a call from a

man in Idaho, claiming he had stolen his life story and demanding a check for $9 million.)

● **MacPherson's Working Formula.** The number of interruptions received during a work period is proportionate to the square of the number of employees occupying an office—thus, one person in an office = one interruption per hour; two in an office = four interruptions per hour; three people = nine per hour, etc.

(Ian MacPherson, Regina, Sask.)

● **Madison's Question.** If you have to travel on a *Titanic,* why not go first class?

(U/DRW.)

● **Mahr's Law of Restrained Involvement.** Don't get any on you.

*(U/*Norton Mockridge's syndicated column, February 14, 1979. *ME.)*

● **Mann's Rules.** In a corporate take-over of a well-liked cleaning product: (1) It *must* be "improved" by adding an obnoxious odor, and (2) It *must* be wrapped in a slick foil-like wrapper, to more readily slip from a wet hand.

(Mrs. Henry Mann, Holliston, Mass. *AO.*)

● **Manske's Maxim.** It doesn't matter what you do: It only matters what you say you've done and what you say you're gonna do.

(Nancy Manske, Winter Park, Fla.)

● **Mantel's First Great Law of Economics.** If two lines on a graph cross it must be important.

(U/ Ernest F. Cooke, Chairman, Marketing Department, University of Baltimore.)

● **Marguccio's Absolute.** Never buy the last item on the shelf.

(Thomas Marguccio, New York City.)

● **Marshall's Memorandum to Vice-Presidential Aspirants.** There were two brothers: One ran away to sea, and the other was elected to vice-president—and nothing was ever heard from either of them again.

(Vice-President Thomas R. Marshall.)

● **Marsolais's Law of Worst Possible Timing.** During the course of a meal, the waitress will drop by no fewer than ten times to inquire whether everything is all right; nine of those ten times your mouth will be full.

(Maurice Marsolais, Fairfax, Va.)

● **Martindale's Proverbial Logic.** [Developed from a premise stated by Dereck Williamson in *Saturday Review:* Since one picture is worth a thousand words, one word must be worth .001 of a picture.] (1) If you can lead him to water, and force him to drink, he isn't a horse. (2) The worst part of valor is indiscretion. (3) If it boils and is watched, it can't be a pot. (4) The second best policy is dishonesty. (5) If you refuse to eat the pudding, what proof have you? (6) If you are marketing a five cent cigar of high quality, you are serving admirably this country's needs.

(Canadian writer Herb Martindale, in his book, *The Caledonia Eye Opener,* Alive Press, Guelph, Ontario.)

● **Marxist Law of the Distribution of Wealth.** Shortages will be divided equally among the peasants.

(John W. Gustafson, Chicago.)

● **Mary Louise's Law.** You can't tell from where you sit when the man in the balcony will drop his program.

(Mary Louise Gabauer. *MLS.*)

● **Mary Principle, The.** If many individuals remain too long at their level of incompetence, they will destroy the organization because their presence demonstrates to others that competence is not a prerequisite for success.

(*U/*J. Thomas Parry, Rockford, Ill.)

● **Masefield's R&D Rule.** The principle function of an advanced design department nowadays is to keep up with the public relations department.

(Peter Masefield, British Aircraft managing director, quoted in Leonard Louis Levinson's *Webster's Unafraid Dictionary,* Collier Books, 1967.)

● **Maslow's Maxim.** If the only tool you have is a hammer, you treat everything like a nail.

(Abraham Maslow, the noted psychiatrist, from Sydney J. Harris, the noted columnist. It is Harris's "favorite modern saying.")

● **Masson's Admonition.** "Be yourself!" is about the worst advice you can give some people.

(Tom Masson, American humorist and editor.)

● **Masterson's Law** (or "The Iron Law of Wagers"). If a guy wants to bet you that he can make the Jack of Diamonds jump out of a deck of cards and spit apple cider in your ear, *don't* take that bet. Sure as shootin', you're gonna wind up with an earful of cider.

(Sky Masterson to Nathan Detroit in *Guys and Dolls. MLS.*)

● **Matheson's Law.** Structure commands function. If you could breed an oyster the size of a horse, it wouldn't take first place in the Kentucky Derby no matter who rode it.

(Joan Matheson, from Robert F. Tatman, Wynnewood, Penn.)

● **Matthews-Butler Principles of Plagiarism.** In the case of the first person to use an anecdote, there is originality; in the case of the second, there is plagiarism; with the third, it is lack of originality; with the fourth, it is drawing from a common stock; and in the case of the fifth, it is research.

(Professors Brander Matthews and Nicholas Murray Butler, both of Columbia University, from *Man in the Street,* J. S. Ogilvie, publisher.)

● **Mattuck's Law.** In any given problem, difficulty is conserved, i.e., there are no true "short cuts."

(Professor Arthur Mattuck, MIT, from Richard Stone, Stanford, Cal.)

● **Maugham's Advice.** Death is a very dull, dreary affair, and my advice to you is to have nothing whatsoever to do with it.

(Somerset Maugham.)

● **May's Law.** The quality of the correlation is inversely proportional to the density of the control (the fewer the facts, the smoother the curves).

(U/DRW.)

● **Mead's Law of Human Migration.** At least 50 percent of the human race doesn't want their mother-in-law within walking distance.

(The late Margaret Mead explaining rural migration to a symposium on the phenomenon. Submitted by Paul Martin to *DRW.*)

● **Mead's Law of Problem Solving.** All major problems will be worked upon diligently until they are split into two less major problems. These will be worked on, less enthusiastically, until they are divided into four less important problems. With even less enthusiasm these four will be worked on until they are now divided into eight, again, less important problems. This subdividing of problems will continue until such time that a new major problem appears, whereupon the 32, 64, 128, or whatever now very minor problems that remain are superseded by the new "major" problem. Thus problems are never really solved, they are just broken down into minor and rather ignorable problems until such time as a new one appears.

(R. H. Mead, Ithaca, N.Y., who developed it "after some twenty-seven years in the engineering profession.")

● **Medes and Persians, Law of.** One man's Mede is another man's Persian.

(George S. Kaufman.)

Special Section 11

Medical Principles. Insights into the workings of a great profession. All but a few of these special laws were discovered/written by members of the medical community. Those with the notation *RM* were originally quoted in Dr. Robert Matz's article "Principles of Medicine," which appeared in the January 1977 issue of the *New York State Journal of Medicine.*

○ *Aronfy's Rule.* All earaches start Saturday night.
(Andrew G. Aronfy, M.D., Seabrook, Md.)
○ *Barach's Rule.* An alcoholic is a person who drinks more than his own physician.
(U/RM.)

MEAD'S LAW OF PROBLEM SOLVING

o *FDA Law.* A drug is that substance which when injected into a rat will produce a scientific report.

(U/RM.)

o *Gillette's Law.* Most medical mistakes occur not from ignorance but because a physician fails to do something he or she knows should be done.

(Robert D. Gillette, M.D., Toledo, Ohio.)

o *Jordan's Medical Rules.* (1) Don't make two diagnoses at the same time on the same patient if you can help it; you'll probably be wrong twice. (2) They call it practicing because when you get it right, you can quit.

(D. Wylie Jordan, M.D., Austin.)

o *Loeb's Laws of Medicine.* (1) If what you're doing is working, keep doing it. (2) If what you're doing is not working, stop doing it. (3) If you don't know what to do, don't do anything. (4) Above all, never let a surgeon get your patient.

(U/RM.)

o *Lord Cohen's Aphorism.* The feasibility of an operation is not the best indication for its performance.

(U/RM.)

o *Marsh's Law.* Pain is always worse at night (after office hours).

(Wallace S. Marsh, M.D., Lompoc, Cal.)

o *Matz's General Laws.* (1) No amount of genius can overcome a preoccupation with detail. (2) Textbooks of a previous generation were as large as the textbooks of today, but contained a different body of misinformation. (3) New equipment and new procedures may improve medical care, but seldom decrease the cost. (4) Every psychoneurotic ultimately dies of organic disease.

(From Dr. Matz's "Principles of Medicine.")

o *Patient's Rule* (concerning his symptoms). It is not a matter of life and death—it's much more important than that.

(U/RM.)

o *Rogawski's Laws of Medical Science.* (1) A paper supporting any claim can be found somewhere in medical literature. (2) For any published paper, there is a paper giving opposite conclusions.

> (Michael A. Rogawski, Department of Pharmacology, Yale University.)

o *Shem's Laws of the House of God* (a selection). (1) At a cardiac arrest, the first procedure is to take your own pulse. (2) The patient is the one with the disease. (3) If you don't take a temperature, you can't find a fever.

> (From the novel *The House of God,* by Samuel Shem, M.D., Richard Marek, 1978. Shem is the pseudonym for a young physician.)

o *White's Rule.* The effectiveness of a therapy for a disease is inversely proportional to the number of therapies available to treat the disease.

> (Robert I. White, Jr., M.D., The Johns Hopkins University School of Medicine. Dr. White amplifies, "Instead of therapy, one might substitute drugs, etc. Good examples of this would be the wide variety of non-narcotic pain medicines or common cold remedies. The reverse, of course, is that if a patient has appendicitis, there is only one therapy, namely, appendectomy, which is extremely effective.")

● **Meller's Six Sociological Laws.** (1) Anyone who can be exploited will be. (2) If you understand the direction of the flow of money, you can predict human conduct. From this it follows that if you can control the direction of the flow of money, you can control human conduct. Man is like a sailboat and the flow of money is the wind. (3) Anything based on greed and avarice is on a firm foundation and will prevail. (4) Everyone feels that he is underpaid and overcharged. (5) For every human act there are two reasons—the stated one and the real one. These two have a correlation coefficient that varies from one to zero. (6) We have more to fear from the bungling of the incompetent than from the machinations of the wicked.

> (R. L. Meller, M.D., Minneapolis. From J. Thomas Parry, who states: "Dr. Meller is a psychiatrist and after many, many years of practice developed these laws. Dr. Meller states with conviction that these are the only laws necessary to understand human behavior.")

Memorandum.

From: Author
To: Reader
Subject: Meaning in Memos

1. In large organizations, memos are rewritten at each major hierarchical level.
2. Each rewrite changes the meaning of the memo . . .
3. . . . until it is either (a) meaningless, (b) silly, or (c) both of the above.
4. Case in point: In 1977 President Carter penned a memo to the effect that more federal money should be spent at the retail level with minority businesses. A year later, when the memo got to a small government group in Baltimore, the people in the office were told (a) they should fill out a report every time they bought gasoline with government money and note whether or not it was from a minority-owned station, and (b) they could not ask if a member of a minority owned the station for fear of offending.

● **Mencken's Rule of Unanimity.** When everyone begins to believe anything it ceases to be true; for example, the notion that the homeliest girl in the party is the safest.
(H. L. Mencken.)

● **Mendoza's Laws of Purchasing.** (1) When shopping, never look for something specific, you won't find it. (2) Always shop for nothing, you'll always come back with something. (3) After a heavy day's shopping, the perfect purchase is in either the first or the last place you've looked.
(Liz Mendoza, Fargo, N.D.)

● **Merrow's Law.** Optimism tends to expand to fill the scope available for its exercise.
(Edward Merrow, RAND Corp. economist, who uses his law to describe synthetic fuel enthusiasts. *RS.*)

● **Metropolitan Edison's Variation on Murphy's Law.** Anything that man makes will not operate perfectly.
(Walter M. Creitz, President of Metropolitan Edison, the company that operates the Three Mile Island nuclear plant. Quoted in *The New York Times,* March 30, 1979.)

● **Metzger's Maxim.** You're only as old as you feel— the next day.
(Daniel J. Metzger, Belleville, Ill.)

● **Miazga's Discovery.** Death is nature's way of telling you the FDA was right.
(Robert Miazga, Danbury, Conn.)

● **Midas's Law.** Possession diminishes perception of value, immediately.
(John Updike, *The New Yorker,* November 3, 1975.)

● **Mikadet's Cardinal Rule for Parents of Adult Children.** An eighteen-year-old can: (a) vote, (b) rebuild an automobile engine, (c) swallow a guitar pick.
(T. K. Mikadet, Lompoc, Cal.)

● **Miles's Political Prayer.** Yea, even though I graze in pastures with Jackasses, I pray that I will not bray like one.
(William Miles, Anna Marie, Fla.)

● **Miller's Corollary.** Objects are lost because people look where they are not instead of where they are.
(Henry L. Miller, London.)

● **Miller's Distinction.** There is a thin line of distinction between the avant-garde and *The Gong Show.*
(U/Ra.)

● **Miller's Law.** All costs walk on two legs.
(Arjay Miller. From Hal Hoverland, Dean, California State College, San Bernardino.)

● **Mills's Law.** The ease by which a man can be convinced, by artful manipulation of language, of something contrary to common sense, is directly proportional to his advance in philosophy.
(J. S. Mills, *A System of Logic, Book 3.* From Kevin G. Long, Quebec.)

● **Mills's Law.** There is no task so great that it cannot be done in one night.
(This law—created by Patty Mills, Mount Holyoke College, 1964, and submitted by Hilde Weisert—points out that it seems to work better in college than in "life after college.")

● **Mirsky's Law of Auditioning.** If they say "Thank you," you've got a shot. . . . If they say "Thank you very much," forget it.

(Steven D. Mirsky, Ithaca, N.Y.)

Special Section 12

Miseries of 1806. In the early days of the 19th century, a cluster of half a dozen or so books appeared in England with the key word "miseries" in their titles. Each small volume was written pseudonymously and contained a series of "groans" attesting to the conspiracy of events, objects, and other humans that kept the authors in, as one put it, "a frenzy of vexation."

These books are desperately hard to find today, but through the Library of Congress two classics of the genre—both published in 1806—have been found and will shortly be quoted from. The importance of rediscovering these miseries is simply that the books give us clear proof that the so-called curses of modernism predate the Modern Era and the knowledge of the inherent perversity of things has been a constant for longer than we commonly realize. Enough preamble. Let us move on to some of the specific miseries cited in two early Murphylogical classics, *The Miseries of Human Life or the Groans of Samuel Sensitive and Timothy Testy* by Samuel Sensitive and Timothy Testy (Wm. Miller, London, 1806) and *More Miseries!! Addressed to the Morbid, the Melancholy and the Irritable* by Sir Fretful Murmur (H. D. Symonds, London, 1806).*

---

*Some scholarly scratching leads to the conclusion that Sensitive and Testy were one man, James Beresford of Merton College, Oxford, and that Murmur was a writer named Robert Heron.

MISERIES OF 1806

■All your acquaintance telling you, that a portrait which you are aware is *rather flattering,* is not at all like you.

■Being requested by a foreigner who understands very little of the English language, to hear him read Milton.

■Calling on a sultry day upon a friend who has the mania for planting upon him; who marches and countermarches you three or four miles to see his plantations, after which he irresistibly presses you to ascend a *considerable eminence of ground,* about half a mile off, to see a couple of pines which he planted on the day his first child was born.

■Attempting, at a strange house, to take down a book from a high, crowded shelf, bringing the library upon your nose.

■As an author—those moments during which you are relieved from the fatigues of composition by finding that your memory, your intellects, your imagination, your spirits, and even your love of the subject, have all, as if with one consent, left you in the lurch.

■Writing with ink of about the consistency of pitch, which leaves alternatively a blot and a blank.

■Writing upon a thin sheet of paper, very small crumbs of bread under it.

■Looking for a good pen (which is your personal destiny never to find, except when you are indifferent about it), and having a free choice among the following varieties:

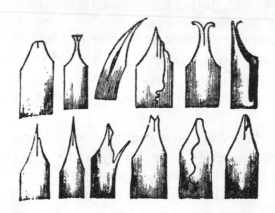

■Having a pimple on your chin, covering it with sticking plaster, and just as you enter the drawing room, discovering that it curls on all sides.

■Being bored by a man whom you don't like, to dine with him, and being nailed by his begging you to fix your own day.

■Living in chambers under a man who takes private lessons in dancing.

■Sitting at dinner next to a man of consequence with whom you wish to ingratiate yourself, being told that he has superstitious horror of the salt being spilt, and from excess of caution sending the contents of the salt cellar into his plate.

■Whilst you are making a sketch, having a number of impertinent persons staring behind you, until the crowd increases to that degree that you are obliged to abandon your subject.

■Asking a lady to permit you to look at a beautiful string of very small pearls, breaking it in two, scattering them over the floor, and crushing several under your feet in endeavouring to collect them.

■Toasting a bit of bread at the end of a short dessert fork, before a good brisk fire, and burning the ends of your fingers without being able to toast it to your liking.

■Having succeeded in fixing yourself in a most seducing, and graceful attitude, letting your cocked hat fall.

■Knocking at a door, and by a horrible and unaccountable lapse of memory, forgetting the name of the master or mistress of the house.

■Upon paying the first visit after the funeral of a relation, a distant cousin for instance, to the immediate friends of the deceased, finding them all in tears from some unaccountable counteraction of nature, and not being able to look grave upon the occasion.

■Upon returning from a Tour to the Continent, being asked by everyone you meet for *your private opinion of things in general.*

■Trying to pass a man who waddles.

■Being requested to say something to entertain the party.

■Sitting for your portrait to a subordinate painter who renders the likeness with such exasperating exactness, that every pimple, blotch and blemish in the face are faithfully represented.

■Striking your foot against another step after you had concluded that you had reached the top of the stairs.

■Being seized with a violent bowel complaint, whilst you are riding on horseback with two young ladies, to one of whom you are paying your addresses, being obliged to alight in great confusion, telling your fair companions, that there is an exquisite bit of scenery round a hedge, and which you should like very much to sketch, assuring them that you will return in five minutes, and remembering afterwards that it was well known that you never drew in your life.

> (These are but a few of hundreds of miseries catalogued by these pioneers. It boggles the mind to consider what they could have come up with if they had been alive for the coming of the telephone, IRS Form 1040, computer, television, automobile, superhighway, and other elements of human progress.)

● **MIST Law** (Man in the Street). The number of people watching you is directly proportional to the stupidity of your action.

(U/DRW.)

● **Mitchell's Rustic Rule.** Changing barnyards will not transform a turkey into a golden goose.

(Kevin Mitchell, Eden Prairie, Minn.)

● **Miz Beaver's Summation of Walt Kelly's Philosophy.** He allus said, don't take life too serious . . . it ain't nohow permanent.

(Miz Beaver, in the *Pogo* comic strip, the Christmas following Walt Kelly's death.)

● **Mockridge's Major Maxim.** If an idea is successful, the first person to claim credit for it will be the person who contended all along that it wouldn't work!
(Syndicated columnist Norton Mockridge.)

● **Modell's Laws.** (1) Nothing is so serious that it can't be teased until it is ragged at the edges. (2) Nothing is so simple that it cannot be made too complex to work.
(U/GT.)

● **Momma's Rule.** If you can't stand to eat, get out of my kitchen.
(From the comic strip *Momma* by Mell Lazarus.)

● **Money Maxim.** Money isn't everything. (It isn't plentiful, for instance.)
(Bill Woods, *DRW*'s father.)

● **Montgomery's Explanation of the Facts of Life.** All normal young people want to do this thing. It is natural, like fighting.
(Attributed to Lord Montgomery.)

● **Montore's Maxims.** (1) A true environmentalist will use both sides of a piece of paper in presenting a position paper. (2) Every journey, great and small, begins with unrealistic expectations. (3) Love expands to fill the available hearts. (4) Man's superiority to the rest of the animal kingdom is due primarily to his imagination. He imagines he is superior. (5) No balls, no blue chips.
(R. J. Montore, Henderson, Ky.)

● **Moore's Constant.** Everybody sets out to do something, and everybody does something, but no one does what he sets out to do.

(Irish novelist George Moore.)

● **Moore's Law.** The degree to which a topic is understood is inversely proportional to the amount of literature available on it. *Corollary:* That which seems vague is frequently meaningless.

(Terry C. Moore, Indianapolis, Indiana. Moore finds widespread application of this law and corollary in fields as diverse as child rearing, business management, macroeconomic theory, and Transactional Analysis.)

● **Morford's Rule.** Nothing fails like success.

(Ida B. Morford, Glassboro State College, Glassboro, N.J. Submitted by Rose Primack, one of Dr. Morford's colleagues, who says it came out of a postmortem on a "highly successful environmental education program that was almost universally applauded" when it was discontinued.)

● **Moriarity's Secret for Financial Success.** BLASH.

(Named for a highly successful investment broker named Morton P. Moriarity, who was once one of the biggest failures on Wall Street. When destitute and reduced to sleeping on park benches he had a dream in which a bearded holy man handed him a piece of paper with the word BLASH on it. Moriarity ran all around New York in search of a bearded holy man who could tell him what BLASH meant; finally, after a year-long search, he found his man, who told him it stood for "Buy Low and Sell High." This, from Carl Winston's book *How to Run a Million into a Shoestring and Other Shortcuts to Success,* G. P. Putnam's Sons, 1960.)

● **Morley's Advice to Travelers.** Avoid plays acted in a foreign language, and buildings entirely rebuilt since the war.

Beware of government-sponsored stores and light operas. Limit yourself to one cathedral, one picture gallery, and one giant Buddha a week.

> (Actor Robert Morley, from *A Musing Morley,* edited by Sheridan Morley.)

● **Morris's Law.** When writing in ink, you never make a mistake until you are at least three-fourths of the way through.

> (John C. Morris, Jr., Old Greenwich, Conn. Morris, believed to be the youngest of all Murphy Center Fellows, is a fifth-grade student in the Greenwich public schools. The law was forwarded by Annie C. Harvey, one of his teachers.)

● **Morris's Laws of Animal Appeal.** (1) The popularity of an animal is directly correlated with the number of anthropomorphic features it possesses. (2) The age of a child is inversely correlated with the size of the animals it prefers.

> (Desmond Morris from *The Naked Ape,* McGraw-Hill, 1967.)

● **Morris's Tips for Beginning Writers (a selection).** (1) Although most magazines maintain that they pay so much a word, virtually none of them will buy words submitted individually. Keep this in mind, and your mailing costs will nose-dive. (2) To sell inspirational pieces and "cute" poems, you *must* have a three-part name, preferably Elyse McBride Sensenbrenner. (3) The placing of Happy Face stickers on or about your manuscript does not measurably enhance its appeal.

> (Edward Morris, in his article "Keeping the Crayons Sharp," *Writer's Digest,* December 1977.)

● **Morrison's Last Theorem.** If you hang in there long enough and grit your teeth hard enough, your orthodontist bill will go up.

(Stan Morrison, retired basketball coach, University of the Pacific, quoted in *Sports Illustrated*. From Michael L. Lazare, Armonk, N.Y.)

● **Morrison's Second-Sheet Law.** When you are doing two copies of anything, the carbon always turns out better than the original.
(Vivian M. Morrison, Shreveport, Louisiana.)

● **Moutsatson's Law.** If you don't do anything—you can't do anything wrong.
(Pete Moutsatson, Chairman, Business Studies Department, Montcalm Community College, Sidney, Mich.)

● **Moynihan's Maxim.** Whenever any branch of the government acquires a new technique which enhances its power in relation to the other branches, that technique will soon be adopted by those other branches as well.
(Senator Daniel P. Moynihan. *AO.*)

● **Muir's Golden Rule of Menus.** If you can't pronounce it, you can't afford it.
(Frank Muir, in *The English Digest.*)

● **Muir's Law.** If it's right and you've checked that it's right, you can be sure someone will come along and correct you.
(Georgette Muir, New York City.)

● **Muldoon-Becker Rules.** (1) Software, when left unattended, rots! (2) Thank God it's Friday—only two more working days this week.
(Ed Muldoon and Nick Becker, Des Plaines, Ill.)

Murphylogical Research, Recent Findings. (An interview with the Director of the Murphy Center.)

Q. The Center's interest in the prophet Murphy and the many laws attributed to him and named in his honor is, of course, keen. Yet there still seems to be some question as to who Murphy actually was or is. Do you have any new discoveries to report?

A. Yes. As you may recall from the Center's last report *(The Official Rules,* Delacorte, 1978) it was tentatively concluded that the great Murphy was a military man, Capt. Ed Murphy, who first announced the basic law of "If anything can go wrong it will" in 1949. Other Murphylogical scholars came to the same conclusion. But now new evidence has come to the Center's attention posing some intriguing new possibilities.

Q. The suspense is too much. What are they?

A. The first comes from Theodore C. Achilles. I shall quote directly from his letter to the Center:

Many people believe that the real author was the late Ambassador Robert Murphy. During his career of more than forty years in the Foreign Service during which he served, in addition to many other trouble spots, in Hitler's Germany, Laval's France, immediate postwar Germany, he accumulated monumental evidence of its validity. I suspect he formulated it definitively at the end of the 1930s. In the late 1920s as a young Vice Consul in Munich, he and his friend Msgr. Pacelli, Apostolic Delegate to Bavaria, spent an evening in a *bierstube* listening to the ranting of a young man named Adolf Hitler. After the speech and a few steins they agreed to report to their respective authorities that the young man was merely a blowhard who was unlikely to have any significant effect on events in Germany or anywhere else. Some years later, after Pacelli had become Pope Pius XII, Bob gently reminded him of their consensus. "Ah yes," replied His Holiness, "that was before I became infallible."

Another body of evidence has reached the Center to the effect that the basic law and Murphy's name were well known during the early days of World War II. Charlie Boone, of the incomparable Boone-Ericson radio show in Minneapolis, testifies to this point: "The inspiration may go back to the training camps of World War II or earlier. At the Infantry Training School at Fort Benning, Georgia, in 1942, almost every demonstration group included a Private Murphy. In the serious business of training officers, Private Murphy provided comic relief, for he never failed to take the wrong action, make the wrong decision. His negative action often reinforced the instructor's teacher better than any school solutions or field manuals could."

Still another batch of suggestions come from those who insist that, regardless of who Murphy was, the basic principle dates back centuries to a number of sources including Julius Caesar, who once said, *"Quod malum posset futurum,"* which turns out to be Murphy's Law roughly translated. Others suggest that Murphy lies within our collective ages-old consciousness and that variations and corollaries of Murphy's Law can be found in the proverbs of many cultures: "The spot always falls on the best cloth" (Spanish), "The hidden stone finds the plow" (Estonian), and "One always knocks oneself on the sore place" (English).

Q. Fascinating. Are there more?

A. Just one. But the one I think is the best explanation to date. James V. Stewart of St. Petersburg, Florida, is the person who uncovered it. Let me quote from his letter:

> Murphy's Law was first formulated by Samuel Beckett in his novel named, of course, *Murphy,* which was first published in 1938.
>
> As I'm sure you are aware, there is no way I would be

able to know if Beckett's book is, in fact, the origin of Murphy's Law; nevertheless, Beckett's reference to "If anything can go wrong, it will" is earlier than any other that you cite as possible origins, so I thought you might appreciate being placed on notice.

For this wonderful bit of scholarship, the Center is bestowing on Mr. Stewart the coveted title of Fellow.

Q. Now that we've settled that issue . . .

A. Hold on. No research center worth its salt ever truly settles an issue, because if it did, it would soon run out of issues and put itself out of business. As befits a modern American think tank, the only true conclusion we have reached is that the need for further research is indicated.

Q. Pardon me. On to other matters. Has the Center discovered any new variations and corollaries to Murphy's Law?

A. Scores of them—some universal and some that have been adapted to the realities of a certain profession or pursuit. For instance, the Center has received so many computer-related variations on Murphy's Law that it has decided against buying one. Here are some of our new acquisitions:

o *Mrs. Murphy's Law.* Anything that can go wrong will go wrong WHILE HE IS OUT OF TOWN.

  (Mrs. Murphy, Valrico, Fla., quoted in Ann Landers's column of May 9, 1978.)

o *Murphy's Constant.* All constants are variables.

  (U/Ra.)

o *Murphy's Hope.* Today's "hopefully" is tomorrow's "It had been hoped."

  (Sal Rosa, New York City)

o *Murphy's Law of Product Geography.* The extent of problems with any new product varies directly as the distance between buyer and seller.

  (ME.)

o *NBC's Addendum to Murphy's Law.* You never run out of things that can go wrong.

> (Associated Press Television writer Peter J. Boyer, in his column for August 3, 1979, on NBC's problems.)

One of the most comprehensive codifications we have ever seen has to do with Murphy and marketing, which appeared in *Mainly Marketing: The Schoonmaker Report to the Electronics Industry* published by Schoonmaker Associates of Coram, N.Y., and which contains approximately sixty-five Murphylogical dictums. A small sampling:

o *Advertising*

. . . The longer management delays in approving a radically new campaign, the greater the odds that a competitor will preempt the basic concept.

. . . The larger the group and the higher the rank of agency members pitching a prospect, the lower the rank and the smaller the team serving the account after the contract has been signed.

o *Market Planning*

. . . In planning a related product family, the least amount of attention will be paid to the model that will prove most popular. It will prove to be impossible to meet the demand by modifying other members of the family.

. . . The more smoothly a complicated plan runs at the start, the deeper and more intricate the problems will be once the point of no return has been passed.

o *Market Research*

. . . The most academically sound survey design will yield findings in terms that are least usable (such as sales in dollars when units are needed).

o *Sales*

. . . Psychological testing that is 80 percent accurate will assign members of the 20 percent group to the most sensitive territories and accounts.

. . . The more cordial the buyer's secretary, the greater the odds that competition already has the order.

Q. Is there any evidence to show that the force of Murphy's Law is growing?

A. You jest. How else can one find any suitable explanation for the recent past—Watergate, the Department of Energy, the swine flu vaccine, OPEC, the "vast promise" of nuclear energy, metric conversion, tax reform, the WIN program, the gas line, the Aya-tollah, and so much more. On a more workaday level it is the only way that one can explain the fact that if you left here and went to a supermarket, you would immediately gravitate to a shopping cart with either a square wheel or a wheel that is pointed in a direction that is precisely 90 degrees from the other three.

One of the things that the Center is working on right now is a collection of incidents that perfectly illustrate the law in action. Frank S. Preston of the University of North Carolina has discovered an example that fits this category of "perfect." As he reports, "One of the best cases I know of involves a World War II German airplane that was hung from the ceiling of the Smithsonian Institution for exhibit. Although this airplane survived World War II unscratched, it has crashed twice inside the Smithsonian. . . ."

Now, one of my pet instances is contained in this little clipping I carry around in my wallet. Listen to this, "Brian Chellender, twenty-nine, a bricklayer, was bending down to pick up a pin for good luck, whereupon he was knocked unconscious by a falling brick . . ."

Q. Hold on a second. This strikes me as somewhat depressing —downright depressing, actually—all of this dwelling on things that backfire.

A. Not so. You have missed the point of the Law and the Center. The very fact that there is a Center that sorts, studies, and helps formalize all of this is as uplifting as—and I hate to admit this—a Jaycee Awards dinner or—more painful to admit—those silly smile faces that some people stick on their letters. You see that laying off all of these gaffs, flubs, and mis-cues on universal law is ultimately reassuring and comforting.

In all of our lives, there is the raw material to prove Murphy's Law or one of its corollaries, an amazing example of shared humanity. Rather than deny all of this, the Center celebrates the universal and unlimited imperfectibility of people, organizations, and objects.

Q. Is the Center doing research on this?

A. Of course, one of the things we're working on right now is the "Theory of the Perverse Wind." Specifically, we have evidence that we think will eventually prove there is a particular wind that dies the minute you try to launch a kite, starts up when you drop a $20 bill, and gives off a tiny puff when you are taping something, thereby forcing the tape to stick to itself.

Q. Very interesting. Anything else?

A. Much more. Just to give you an idea of some of the things under investigation here, I'll quickly list some of the specific elements of the Center's research agenda:

Zipper behavior.

Telehydrotropism (or, in lay language, the ability of wrong numbers to ring when one is taking a bath).

The reproductive ability of wire coat hangers.

The aerodynamics and camouflage of the contact lens.

Child-proof aspirin bottles that have the ability to incense adults with hangovers and refuse to open for them.

Calculators that only go out during final exams and the day before taxes are due.

Pocket genetics—trying to unlock the secret that will explain why your grandfather's fountain pen leaked in his pocket, why your father's ballpoint pen leaked in his pocket, and why your marker pen leaks in your pocket.

Key telekinesis—the supernatural process by which everyone gets a mystery key on their key ring that doesn't fit anything.

The origin of that wonderful, universal hospital custom whereby patients are wakened from a sound sleep to take a sleeping pill.

Finally, I should mention that we have one large-scale research project which has just started. Called "Project Hercules," it is a

PROJECT HERCULES

worldwide effort enlisting all of the Center's Fellows. We are trying to see if anyone, anywhere, has actually performed certain fabled superhuman feats. For instance, we're combing the globe to find someone who has actually opened a detergent box by following the instructions, "Press flap gently, lift and pull back." Tests at our secret lab have required a minimum of one chisel, a heavy rock, and an electric saber saw to manage this. Another top priority is finding someone who has completed one of those "easy weekend" projects in the home-oriented magazines in less than a month of Sundays.

● **Murray's Laws.** (1) Cars with the lucky pieces hanging off the rearview mirror will always seem to star in bad accidents. (2) You can fool all of the people all of the time—if you own the network. (3) If everything else fails, throw it away.

(Jim Murray of the *Los Angeles Times,* from his column of November 23, 1978.)

● **Mykia's Law.**

Has anyone, since the birth of the nation,
On dropping the bathroom soap,
Retrieved it not in need of depilation?

(Mykia Taylor, Glenside, Penn.)

● **Napier's Discovery.** In the past 200 years, America has manufactured close to 100 billion pencils—and we still can't keep one by the phone.

(Arch Napier, from *The Wall Street Journal.*)

● **NASA Skylab Rule.** Don't do it if you can't keep it up.
(Johnny Carson, the *Tonight* show, August 2, 1979.)

● **Nathan-Dommel Law of Federal Grants.** Given the chance, governments will spread benefits so as to provide something for everybody.

(Richard Nathan and Paul Dommel, "Understanding the Urban Predicament," *The Brookings Bulletin,* 14:1–2, 1977.)

● **Nelson's Law.** Negative thinking never got nobody nothing.

(Bert Nelson, Los Altos, Cal.)

● **Nelson's Theory of the Dead End.** Everybody at a party will sift into the room that has only one door, no matter how small or cramped.

(Designer George Nelson, quoted in *The Washington Post,* July 2, 1978. *JCG.*)

● **Nevitsky's Observation.** If a tedious job requires a certain rhythm so that it can be performed quickly and efficiently, that rhythm will be broken immediately upon psychological realization of the rhythm.

(William C. Callis, Falls Church, Va.)

● **Newell's Truisms.** (1) Whenever possible analyze planned performance—actuals are too elusive. (2) A cumulative impact never equals the sum of its increments.
(Roger Newell, Webster, N.Y.)

● **Newman's Law.** Hypocrisy is the Vaseline of social intercourse.
(U/DRW.)

● **Nock's Grim Truth.** In proportion as you give the State power to do things for you, you give it power to do things to you; and the State invariably makes as little as it can of the one power, and as much as it can of the other.
(Albert Jay Nock from his *Memoirs of a Superfluous Man,* Regnery, 1964. *JMcC.* Nock is also the author of the next item.)

● **Nock's Sad Reminder.** The hope for any significant improvement of society must be postponed, if not forever, at any rate to a future so far distant that consideration of it at the present time would be sheer idleness.

● **Nolan's Law.** If you outsmart your lawyer, you've got the wrong lawyer.
(Attorney John T. Nolan, Iowa City, Iowa.)

● **Nonreciprocal Law of Expectation and Results.** Positive expectations yield negative results. Negative expectations yield negative results.
(*U*/Richard B. Bernstein.)

● **Norris's Advice.** Always err on the side of truth.
(Ken S. Norris, Professor of Natural History, Santa Cruz, Cal.)

● **North's Law of Investment Advisors.**
There are some extremely sharp investment advisors who can get you in at the bottom of the market.
There are some extremely sharp ones who can get you out at the top.
They are never the same people.
Corollary: You will act on the advice of the wrong one at least 50 percent of the time.
(Gary North, Executive Director, American Bureau of Economic Research, Durham, N.C.)

● **Norvell's Reminder.** If you would be remembered, do *one* thing superbly well.
(Saunders Norvell. *ME.*)

● **Notes from a Life in Progress (A Selection).** ■ Science has proven that within the breast of every organism of field mouse rank or higher there beats the desire someday to shout "Stop the presses!"■ Money in a wallet tends to be spent.■ The best and the worst make history. The mediocre breed.■ Saints always muck up the demographics.
(Ryan Anthony, Tucson.)

● **Novinson's Revolutionary Discovery.** When comes the Revolution, things will be different—not better, just different.
(Ronald M. Novinson, Alexandria, Va.)

● **Novotney's Law of Correctives.** Whenever a practice or procedure is finally seen to be irrational and intolerable, the practice or procedure instituted to correct the situation will be equally irrational. *Corollary:* Every practice or procedure is actually irrational; it is only a matter of time until it is seen to be so.
(Andrew J. Novotney, S.J., Rockhurst College, Kansas City, Mo.)

● **Nursing Mother Principle.** Do not nurse a kid who wears braces.

(Johnny Carson, the *Tonight* show, August 2, 1979.)

● **Nye's Maxim.** Kind words will never die—neither will they buy groceries.

("Bill" Nye, nineteenth-century American humorist.)

● **Obis's Law.** Someone else probably has the same idea —so (a) get started, (b) plan to do it better.
  (Paul Obis, Jr., Milford, Conn.)

● **O'Brien's Law of Take-out Food.** No matter what or how much you order, it always takes twenty minutes.
  (Edward L. O'Brien, Washington, D.C.)

● **Obvious Law.** Actually, it only *seems* as though you mustn't be deceived by appearances.
  (Donald R. Woods, Stanford, Cal.)

● **O'Connor's Dicta.** (1). In any classroom, the question is always more important than the answer. *Corollary:* The necessity of providing an answer varies inversely with the amount of time the question can be evaded. (2). In any piece of electronic equipment, it is foolhardy to assume that jiggling "X" will not diddle "Y", however unlikely.
  (Vincent D. O'Connor, Winona, Minn.)

● **Oddo's Axiom.** *Never* say you don't know—nod wisely, leave calmly, then run like hell to find an expert.
  (S.M. Oddo, San Diego, Cal.)

Special Section 14

Official Diagrams. Important concepts rendered graphically.

1. One Round Tuit.

CUT OUT AND KEEP! At long last we have a sufficient quantity of these for all personnel to have their own. Guard it with your life. Never lose it, and don't let anyone take it away from you.

These tuits have been hard to come by, especially the round version. We are glad to have them because the demand has been great, and now many of our problems concerning reports and really getting things accomplished in this organization will be solved.

We look for productivity to double in every section now that each of you has his own round tuit. As so many of you have said, "I will get started on this just as soon as I get a round tuit." Others have complained, "I know the job should be done, but I just haven't been able to get a round tuit."

2. Hanging a Swing—Educational Version.

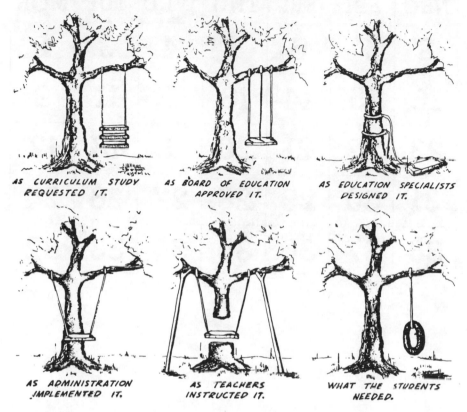

AS CURRICULUM STUDY REQUESTED IT.

AS BOARD OF EDUCATION APPROVED IT.

AS EDUCATION SPECIALISTS DESIGNED IT.

AS ADMINISTRATION IMPLEMENTED IT.

AS TEACHERS INSTRUCTED IT.

WHAT THE STUDENTS NEEDED.

(There are many variations on the swings diagram. In the business version, for instance, the swings are labeled [*left to right*]: "As marketing requested it," "As sales ordered it," "As engineering designed it," "As production manufactured it," "As plant installed it," and "What the customer wanted.")

3. Rush Job Calendar.

1. Every job is in a rush. Everyone wants his job yesterday. With this calendar, a customer can order his work on the *seventh* and have it delivered on the *third*.

NEG	FRI	FRI	THU	WED	TUE	MON
8	7	6	5	4	3	2
16	15	14	13	12	11	9
23	22	21	20	19	18	17
31	30	29	28	27	26	24
38	37	36	35	34	33	32

2. All customers want their jobs on *Friday* so there are *two Fridays* in every week.

3. There are seven days at the end of the month for those end-of-the-month jobs.

4. There will be no first-of-the-month bills to be paid, as there isn't any "first." The "tenth" and "twenty-fifth" have also been omitted in case you have been asked to pay them one of those days.

5. There are no bothersome nonproductive Saturdays and Sundays. No time-and-a-half or double-time to pay.

6. There's a new day each week called negotiation day.

4. Organization Chart: Heaven.

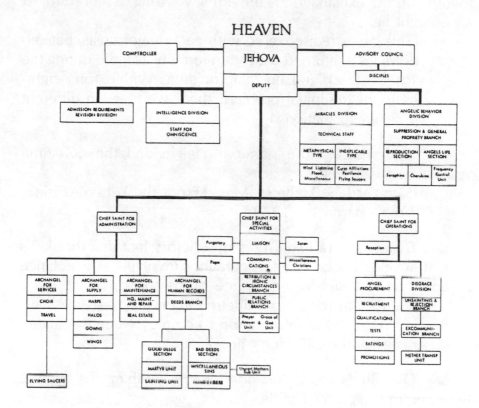

HEAVEN

COMPTROLLER — JEHOVA — ADVISORY COUNCIL

DEPUTY

DISCIPLES

ADMISSION REQUIREMENTS REVISION DIVISION | INTELLIGENCE DIVISION | MIRACLES DIVISION | ANGELIC BEHAVIOR DIVISION

STAFF FOR OMNISCIENCE

TECHNICAL STAFF | SUPPRESSION & GENERAL PROPRIETY BRANCH

METAPHYSICAL TYPE | INEXPLICABLE TYPE | REPRODUCTION SECTION | ANGELS LIFE SECTION

Wind Lightning Flood, Miscellaneous | Cures Afflictions Pestilence Flying Saucers | Seraphins | Cherubins | Frequency Control Unit

CHIEF SAINT FOR ADMINISTRATION | CHIEF SAINT FOR SPECIAL ACTIVITIES | CHIEF SAINT FOR OPERATIONS

Purgatory | LIAISON | Satan | Reception

Pope | COMMUNI-CATIONS | Miscellaneous Christians

RETRIBUTION & IRONIC CIRCUMSTANCES BRANCH

ARCHANGEL FOR SERVICES | ARCHANGEL FOR SUPPLY | ARCHANGEL FOR MAINTENANCE | ARCHANGEL FOR HUMAN RECORDS | PUBLIC RELATIONS BRANCH | ANGEL PROCUREMENT | DISGRACE DIVISION

CHOIR | HARPS | HQ. MAINT. AND REPAIR | DEEDS BRANCH | Prayer Answer Unit | Grace of God Unit | RECRUITMENT | UNSAINTING & REJECTION BRANCH

TRAVEL | HALOS | REAL ESTATE | QUALIFICATIONS | EXCOMMUNI-CATION BRANCH

GOWNS | GOOD DEEDS SECTION | BAD DEEDS SECTION | TESTS

WINGS | MARTYR UNIT | MISCELLANEOUS SINS | Unwed Mothers Sub Unit | RATINGS | NETHER TRANSP UNIT

FLYING SAUCERS | SAINTING UNIT | PROMOTIONS

● **Official Explanations, Law of.** When the word "Official" is used in conjunction with an explanation, it can only follow that the explanation is unwittingly wrong, a half-truth, or an outright lie.

> (This law is rediscovered with each major crisis, but seldom has it returned with such ferocity as it did during the Three Mile Island nuclear incident. Within forty-eight-hours of the initial problem there were seven different official explanations.)

● **Ogden's Law.** The sooner you fall behind, the more time you have to catch up.

> (Sam Ogden, Amherst, Mass. From the Letters section, *Time,* March 19, 1979.)

● **Olbers's Paradox.** The contradictory fact that the sky is dark at night, although by all calculations involving star radiance it should be as bright as the surface of the sun.

> (German astronomer Wilhelm Olbers [1758–1840]. This is a useful bit of information to employ when calculated reality and reality don't jibe.)

● **Old Boy's Law.** You don't learn anything the second time you're kicked by a mule.

> *(U / Ra.)*

● **Old's Conclusion.** The peaking of the output of a committee versus the number of committee members [is] seven-tenths of a person. Obviously one must conclude that either further research is required or that people are no damned good.

> (Bruce S. Old, in his 1946 *Scientific Monthly* article "On the Mathematics of Committees, Boards and Panels.")

● **Old Doc Moos's Law.** When it is necessary to choose between ignorance and stupidity, choose ignorance. It is curable.

> (Phil Moos, M.D., St. Cloud, Minn.)

LAW OF OFFICIAL EXPLANATIONS

● **Old Fraternity Meeting Rule.** The time spent at a fraternity meeting discussing any matter is inversely proportional to the significance of the matter discussed. For example, the theme for the next house party will be discussed for hours, whereas whether the fraternity should abandon its charter will occupy only a few minutes of discussion.
(A. S. Boccuti, Baltimore.)

● **Olly's Observation.** The tap water is always coldest after you have finished your drink.
(W. A. "Olly" Herold, Islington, Ont.)

● **Olmstead's Law.** After all is said and done, a hell of a lot more is said than done.
(Clark Olmstead, Hanau, West Germany.)

● **Olsen's Necktie Law.** The only way to prevent getting food on your necktie is to put it in the refrigerator.
(U | Ra.)

● **Omar's Maxim.** The smaller the country, the greater the passport formalities.
(Margaret K. Omar, U.S. Embassy, Tunis.)

● **O'Neill's Observation.** Nobody is too old to learn—but a lot of people keep putting it off.
(William O'Neill, Diamond Bar, Cal.)

● **Orben's Ornithological Statistic.** There are 40 million pigeons in the United States—30 million are birds, and the rest are people who pay $40 for designer blue jeans.
(Bob Orben, Arlington, Va.)

● **Organizational Parable.**
Once upon a time there was a handsome young lion. He

was captured in the African jungle and brought to America, where he was put on display in a zoo. This made the lion very unhappy because he preferred the freedom of his wild native land and the companionship of other jungle beasts. But after a time he became resigned to his fate and made up his mind that if he had to live behind bars he would be the best zoo lion around.

In an adjoining cage there was another lion, an old and lazy one with a negative responsibility and no signs of ambition or capability of any kind. He lay all day in the sun, aroused no interest from visitors. In sharp contrast, the young lion paced for hours back and forth in his cage. He acted the true King of Beasts, rolling his maned head, snarling, and baring his teeth. The crowds loved him. They paid no attention to the indolent old lion asleep in the next cage.

The young lion appreciated the attention he was getting, but he was annoyed by his failure to win adequate reward. Each afternoon the zoo keeper came through the cages to feed the animals. The lazy old lion, who made no effort to please the spectators, was given a big bowl of red horsemeat. The young lion, now a star attraction, was given a bowl of chopped-up oranges, bananas, and nuts. This made him very unhappy.

"Perhaps," he mused, "I am not trying hard enough. I will improve the act." So he strutted longer and more spectacularly. To the snarls and gnashing of teeth he added frequent roars that shook the bars of his cage. The crowds got bigger. Thousands of citizens came to see his performance, and he was pictured on page one in the local newspaper.

But the diet did not change. Still the lazy lion got the red meat, and the young lion stayed on a vegetarian diet. Finally he could endure it no longer. He stopped the keeper with a challenge.

"I am getting sick and tired of this," he complained. "Each day you give that no-good lazy type next door a big bowl of meat, and you feed me oranges, bananas, and nuts. It is grossly unfair. Why do you think all these people come to the zoo? They come to see me. I'm the star attraction, the lion that's doing all the work, and the one that gets the results. Why am I not entitled to meat for dinner?"

The keeper did not hesitate with his reply.

"Young man," he said, "you don't know how lucky you are.

"Our Table of Organization in this zoo calls for one lion. You are being carried as a monkey."

(FSP.)

● **Ormerod's Rule.** Don't try to think like the top until you are the top.

> (David Ormerod, Middletown, Ohio.)

● **Oshry's Laws.** (1) It only snows on sale days. (2) Memorandums say less than memos. Memos say less than picking up a phone. (3) No name, no matter how simple, can be understood correctly over the phone.

> (James B. Oshry, Elizabeth, N.J.)

● **O'Toole's Rule.** It is far better to play Hamlet in Denver than to play Laertes in New York.

> (Actor Peter O'Toole. *MLS.*)

● **Otten's Revision.** The wages of sin are royalties.

> (Jane Otten, in *The Washington Post,* February 12, 1978, *re* Richard Nixon, Wilbur Mills, Margaret Trudeau, etc.)

● **Owens's Law.** All humans will defend, on moral grounds, that which fattens their pocketbooks.

> (Gwinn Owens, in *The Baltimore Evening Sun,* May 9, 1979. *ME.*)

● **Oxford Rule.** It's is not, it isn't ain't, and it's it's, not its, if you mean it is. If you don't, it's its. Then too, it's hers. It isn't

her's. It isn't our's either. It's ours, and likewise yours and theirs.
(A very useful rule from Oxford University Press that
appeared in *Edpress News,* April 1979.)

● **Ozard's Rain Rule.** The amount of rain is directly proportional to the length of time your raincoat is at the dry cleaner.
(Bill Ozard, Calgary, Alberta.)

● **Ozian Deception.** Pay no attention to the man behind
the curtain.
(The Wizard of Oz to Dorothy and friends. From Larry
Groebe, San Antonio.)

● **Palmer's Law.** The only thing better than a lie is a true story that nobody will believe.
(Joe Palmer.)

● **Pancoast's Periodical Discovery.** The part of a magazine cover that you especially want to see has been covered with the address label.
(Charles Pancoast, Akron, Ohio.)

● **Pangraze's Secret.** PLAN BACKWARD!
(Joe Pangraze, Lynn, Mass.)

● **Paper's Law.** If a museum owns one cuneiform tablet, the likelihood is very high that it will be displayed upside down.
(Herbert H. Paper, Dean, School of Graduate Studies, Hebrew Union College, Cincinnati, from his letter in *The Biblical Archaeology Review,* May/June 1979. Paper adds in a letter to the Center that the law is applicable to any unfamiliar script—for instance, a recent U.S. government poster in which Korean script is displayed upside down.)

● **Pardieck's Laws of Commencement.** (1) The amount of ceremony, pomp, and circumstance involved in a commencement program is in inverse proportion to the level of education. (2) The value of the graduation gift received is in inverse proportion to class rank.
(Robert L. Pardieck, Director of Placement, Bradley University, Peoria.)

● **Parry's Law of Weather Forecasting.** When the weatherman predicts 30 percent chance of rain, rain is twice as likely as when 60 percent chance is predicted.

(J. Thomas Parry, Rockford, Ill.)

● **Parson Weems's Law.** Historical fancy is more persistent than historical fact.

(*American Heritage,* April 1971. A law that explains Washington and the cherry tree, Pilgrims leaping onto Plymouth Rock, Lincoln courting Ann Rutledge, and more.)

● **Parsons's Rule.** At whatever stage you apologize to your spouse, the reply is constant—"It's too late now."

(Denys Parsons, London.)

● **Patton's Law of Sacrifice.** You don't win wars by dying for your country; you win wars by making the other poor bastard die for his country.

(Gen. George Patton, from Joseph A. Horton, M.D., Philadelphia.)

● **Paula Principle.** In a hierarchy women are not allowed to rise to their level of incompetence.

(This discovery was announced in a paper "The Paula Principle and Women's Liberation," by Benjamin Mittman, Evanston, Ill. Mittman examined the Peter Principle ["In a hierarchy every employee tends to rise to his level of incompetence"] and asked the following: "[If] the Peter Principle were universally true, why has not society crashed into the chasm of incompetence? How can institutions, governments, and business survive? What has prevented the Peter Principle from destroying civilization? What mitigating influence has saved us?" The answer is the Paula Principle, which has "sustained society." *RS.*)

● **Paulg's Law.** Remember: In America it's not how much the item costs, it's how much you save.
(Sale ad for Kroch's & Brentano's Bookstores, the *Chicago Tribune,* December 7, 1978.)

● **Pearson's Principle of Organizational Complexity.** The difficulty in running an organization is equal to the square of the number of people divided by the sum of their true applied mentalities.
E.g.: Normal Individual:

$$\frac{1^2}{1} = 1$$

Family of four (one teen, one child):

$$\frac{4^2}{1 + 1 + .5 + .3} = 5.71$$

Government:

$$\frac{\text{Many}^2}{13.2} = \infty$$

(Carl M. Pearson, Dallas.)

● **Peary's Preachment.** Many are cold, but few are frozen.
(Attributed to the Arctic explorer by Col. William C. Hunter in his *Brass Tacks* [1910].)

● **Peer's Theorem.** The person you're leaving a note for always appears just as you finish writing it.
(Mrs. Clifford R. Peer, Palos Verdes Estates, Cal.)

● **Penner's Principle.** When the math starts to get messy —QUIT!
(*U*/From an unsigned, typewritten paper entitled "Handbuch Für Uplousen das Laboratorywerke und Ubercovern das Grosse Goofups." *TJR.*)

● **Perfection Unmasked.** If your own performance of a job looks perfect to you, it isn't because you've done a perfect job. It's only because you have imperfect standards!
(U/ME.)

● **Perlsweig's Law.** People who can least afford to pay rent, pay rent. People who can most afford to pay rent, build up equity.
(U/DRW.)

● **Peters's Principle of Success.** Get up one time more than you're knocked down.
(Country singer Jimmie Peters, quoted in the *San Antonio Express News,* January 19, 1979.)

● **Peterson's Admonition.** When you think you're going down for the third time—just remember you may have counted wrong.
(Rolfe Peterson, quoted by Bennett Cerf in *The Laugh's on Me,* Doubleday, 1959.)

● **Petroff's 27th Law of Hierarchical Behavior.** Humility decreases with every promotion, and disappears completely at the vice-presidential level. *Corollary.* Arbitrariness increases with every promotion, and becomes absolute at the vice-presidential level.
(John N. Petroff, Dhahran, Saudi Arabia.)

● **Petronius Arbiter's Observation.** We trained hard, but it seemed that every time we were beginning to form up into teams, we would be reorganized. I was to learn later in life that we tend to meet any new situation by reorganizing, and a wonderful method it can be for creating the illusion of progress while only producing confusion, inefficiency, and demoralization.
(Attributed to Petronius Arbiter, Greek naval officer, A.D. 66. From Bob Burkhart.)

● **Philanthropy, First Law of.** It is more blessed to give than to receive, and it's deductible.
(The Wall Street Journal. TCA.)

● **Pi R Rule.**
$$\pi r^2$$
πr^2—Pie are square.
$\pi r^{\not 2}$—Pie are not square!
πr^0—Pie are round.
Cr^2—Cornbread are square.
(From Wayne C. Fields, Jr., Newcastle, Cal., who found it on the wall of the library men's room at the California State University, Sacramento.)

● **Pietropinto's Peter Pan Principle.** Marriages peter out or pan out.
(Anthony Pietropinto, M.D., in *Husbands and Wives,* Times Books, 1979.)

● **Pilot's Report.** I am lost but I'm making record time.
(Anonymous pilot somewhere over the Pacific, World War II. Andrew Weissman, New York City.)

● **Pipeline Pete's Observation.** The Lord's Prayer has 56 words; at Gettysburg, Lincoln spoke only 268 long-remembered words; and we got a whole country goin' on the 1,322 words in the Declaration of Independence. So how come it took the federal government 26,911 words to issue a regulation on the sale of cabbages?
(Mobil Corp. ad in *Parade* magazine, April 10, 1977.)

● **Pitt's Hypothesis.** When things go wrong, there are always two faults, the second of which becomes apparent only after the first has been rectified.
(*U/Adhesives Age* magazine, March, 1979. *ME.*)

PITT'S HYPOTHESIS

● **Plato's Distinction.** Man is a two-legged animal without feathers.
(Plato.)

● **Pogo's Dictum.** A long run of good luck is a sure sign of bad luck.
(Pogo. From Michael L. Lazare, Armonk, N.Y.)

● **Poker, Iron Law of.** The winners tell funny stories; the losers cry, "Deal!"
(U/MLS.)

● **Political Law of Nature.** To err is human; to blame it on the other party is politics.
(From *The Light Touch,* edited by Charles Preston, Rand McNally and Co., 1965.)

● **Political Leadership, The First Law of.** Find out where the people want to go, then hustle yourself around in front of them.
(James J. Kilpatrick, in *Nation's Business,* January 1979.)

● **Politico's Law.** No one ever lost an election for a speech he didn't make.
(MLS.)

● **Polsby's Law of Families.** The children of your parents' friends are always nurds.
(Presidential scholar Nelson Polsby. *AO.*)

● **Pop's Law.** Watched boils never pop.
(Paul Seabury, who submitted this law on his stationery from the highly regarded Hoover Institution on War, Revolution, and Peace, Stanford, Cal.)

● **Porter-Givens's Perception.** The delay and expense involved in any action soar in perpendicular proportion to the number of approvals essential to take that action.

(Columnist Sylvia Porter and Attorney Richard A. Givens, from Porter's August 11, 1978, column.)

● **Porter's Home Rule.** Home is where your garbage is.
(David Porter. From Ian MacPherson, Regina, Sask.)

● **Poulsen's Law.** When anything is used to its full potential, it will break.
(U/DRW.)

● **Powell's Variation on Murphy's Law.** We have found over and over that if any statement can be screwed up and reported in a way that is disquieting to the public and the economy, it will be screwed up.

(Jody Powell, quoted in *The Washington Post,* June 6, 1979.)

● **Prentice's Congressional Constant.** There are two periods when Congress does no business: one is before the holidays, and the other after.

(American journalist and humorist George D. Prentice.)

● **Preudhomme's Law of Window Cleaning.** It's on the other side.
(U/DRW.)

● **Price's Advice.** It's all a game—play it to have fun.
(C. Kevin Price, Plymouth, Minn.)

● **Price's Rule.** A fool and his money get a lot of attention from headwaiters.

(Roger Price from *In One Head and Out the Other*, Simon and Schuster, 1951.)

● **Procrastination, Laws of.** (1) Procrastination shortens the job and places the responsibility for its termination on someone else (the authority who imposed the deadline). (2) It reduces anxiety by reducing the expected quality of the project from the best of all possible efforts to the best that can be expected given the limited time. (3) Status is gained in the eyes of others, and in one's own eyes, because it is assumed that the importance of the work justifies the stress. (4) Avoidance of interruptions including the assignment of other duties can be achieved, so that the obviously stressed worker can concentrate on the single effort. (5) Procrastination avoids boredom; one never has the feeling that there is nothing important to do. (6) It may eliminate the job if the need passes before the job can be done.

(U/DRW.)

● **Proposal-Writing Rules.** (1) Never mention money. "Resources" is the prime substitute, although "allocations" and "appropriations" are also popular. (2) Fluff up a proposal with the sort of euphemisms that bestow an aura of importance without revealing anything specific.

(Louis Kaplan, planner, quoted in *Newsweek,* May 6, 1968.)

● **Propriis's Bottom Line.** A man should be intelligent enough to wish he were more so.

(U/RA.)

● **Proverbs in Need of Revival.** (1) An emperor may have the measles. (2) The man who breaks his eggs in the center is a fool. (3) Shave with a file, if you like, but don't blame the razor. (4) The hasty man drinks his tea with a fork. (5) New milk is not got from a statue.

(From an old British almanac, quoted in *Comic Almanac* edited by Thomas Yoseloff, A.S. Barnes and Co., 1963.)

● **Public Relations Truism.** There's nothing neither good nor bad that can't be made more so.

(Earle Ferris, public relations counsel, quoted in *The Care and Feeding of Executives* by Millard C. Foeght and Lawrence Hammond, Wormwood Press, 1945.)

● **Putt's Law.** Technology is dominated by two types of people: those who understand what they do not manage, and those who manage what they do not understand.

(Archibald Putt [pseud.], in *Research/Development* magazine, January 1976. *ME.*)

● **Q's Law.** No matter what stage of completion one reaches in a North Sea (oil) field, the cost of the remainder of the project remains the same.

(U/GT.)

● **Quality of Life Constant.** Each time in your life when you think you are about to be able to make both ends meet, somebody moves the ends.

(U/Ra.)

● **Quigley's Laws.** (1) If you take off your right-hand glove in very cold weather, the key will be in your left-hand pocket. (2) Any system that works perfectly will be revised. (3) Backfire hurts only those who get behind things. (4) Courage of conviction results in the conviction of courage.

(Martin Quigley, editor of the *Midwest Motorist. EV.*)

● **Quin's Postulate.** A man must sometimes rise above principle.

(Representative Percy Edwards Quin, Mississippi, 1921.)

● **Quinn's Creed of the Follower.** Lemmings know something we don't.

(A. W. Quinn, Arlington Heights, Ill.)

● **Quirk's Zipper Discovery.** Zippers tend to fail at crucial moments simply because they are treacherous, back-stabbing little fiends.

(''Dr. Emory Quirk, the Cleveland Institute of Inanimate

Hostilities,'' quoted in a column by Dan Myers, the *San Francisco Chronicle,* June 3, 1979.)

● **Quixote's Conclusion.** Facts are the enemy of truth. (Don Quixote, in *Man of La Mancha.* From William C. Young, Ballston Lake, N.Y.)

R

● **Rabinow's Law.** If the top man is no good, all the people below him will be no good in the same way.

(Jacob Rabinow, National Bureau of Standards. *FSP.*)

● **Radovic's Rule.** In any organization, the potential is much greater for the subordinate to manage his superior than for the superior to manage his subordinate.

(Igor Radovic, in *How to Manage the Boss; or, The Radovic Rule,* M. Evans, 1973.)

● **Rafferty's Laws of Education.** (1) Educational research that flies in the teeth of common sense is for the birds. (2) In any election, the candidate supported by the teachers' union is always the one to vote against. (3) Every educational problem is caused by (a) stupidity or (b) unwillingness to work. (4) Fifty percent of all school administrators are superfluous. (5) Sixty percent of the things schools do have nothing to do with education. (6) Any educational area supported by federal funds deteriorates in quality and output in exact proportion to the amount of said federal aid.

(Conservative educator/columnist Max Rafferty. *ME.*)

● **Ranger's Rule.** We have done so much with so little for so long, that now we can do anything with nothing.

(This came from U.S. troops in Vietnam and has been applied widely since.)

● **Rangnekar's Modified Rules Concerning Decisions.** (1) If you must make a decision, delay it. (2) If you can authorize someone else to avoid a decision, do so. (3) If you can form a committee, have them avoid the decision. (4) If you can otherwise avoid a decision, avoid it immediately.

(U/GT.)

● **Ranthony's College Notebook.** (1) A liberal education teaches what is possible. Experience teaches what is not. (2) Songs of the tenured immovable object: (a) I teach to have something to test. I test to have something to grade. (b) Publish the thought or perish the thought. (3) Remember that one advantage of a very good college is that you leave behind the sort of person who functions best in chaos. You will not be at his mercy again unless you are drafted, sent to jail, or teach school. (4) Motto carved over every university's main gate: *Ici e Collegium in mundus bunchum juvenalia de primer stratum passum, et alumni cum cupiditas becommen, Dei Gratia.* (5) Just as starlight seen from Earth shows the stars as they were in the past, so does a university's reputation in the lay community reflect the accomplishments of an earlier time—and for the same reason: distance. (6) The college fraternity is dedicated to the study and celebration of the various liquids and solids that—either naturally or by force —go in and come out of the human body. (7) Two rules of housekeeping: (a) Treat bedsheets like litmus paper: leave them alone until they change color. (b) That part of the room which is within one inch of the floor (three inches beneath the bed) is the province of dust, and the rest is yours. Dust, in return for being granted sanctuary, will stay where it is, not rolling in a big ball out to the middle of the room to beg for pennies and paper clips, embarrassing you in front of guests.

(Ryan Anthony, Tucson.)

● **Ranthony's Observation on Cussing.** The English language has so few cuss words that, much like the flag, they should not be displayed day after day, but kept inside, lovingly rolled up and stored away, to bring forth proudly, unfaded, and effective on special occasions.

(Ryan Anthony, Tucson.)

● **Raper's Rules.** (1) Hit the ball over the fence and you can take your time going around the bases. (2) Don't claim too much. The manufacturer of hair restorer never advertises that it will grow hair on the back of the neck. (3) The proof of the pudding is in the demand for it. (4) Patience is fine, but it never helped a rooster lay an agg.

(John W. Raper, in *What This World Needs,* World, 1945.)

● **Raymond's Rule on Junk Mail.** If it doesn't look as if there is a check or a personal letter in it, there's nothing in it—so throw it out.

(Columnist John Raymond, *The Atlanta Constitution,* March 13, 1979.)

● **Reasons Why Not (50 Handy-Dandy Excuses).** (1) We've never done it before. (2) Nobody else has ever done it. (3) It has never been tried before. (4) We tried it before. (5) Another company (person) tried it before. (6) We've been doing it this way for 25 years. (7) It won't work in a small company. (8) It won't work in a large company. (9) It won't work in our company. (10) Why change—it's working OK. (11) The boss will never buy it. (12) It needs further investigation. (13) Our competitors are not doing it. (14) It's too much trouble to change. (15) Our company is different. (16) The ad dept. says it can't be done. (17) The sales dept. says it can't be sold. (18) The service dept. won't like it. (19) The janitor says it can't be done. (20) It can't be done. (21) We don't have the money. (22) We don't have the personnel. (23) We don't have the equipment. (24) The union will scream. (25) It's too visionary. (26) You can't teach an old dog new tricks. (27) It's too radical a change. (28) It's beyond my responsibility. (29) It's not my job. (30) We don't have the time.

(31) It will obsolete other procedures. (32) Customers won't buy it. (33) It's contrary to policy. (34) It will increase overhead. (35) The employees will never buy it. (36) It's not our problem. (37) I don't like it. (38) You're right, but . . . (39) We're not ready for it. (40) It needs more thought. (41) Management won't accept it. (42) We can't take the chance. (43) We'd lose money on it. (44) It takes too long to pay out. (45) We're doing all right as it is. (46) It needs committee study. (47) Competition won't like it. (48) It needs sleeping on. (49) It won't work in this department. (50) It's impossible.

> (This list has been popular in engineering circles for years. The earliest published appearance was in *Product Engineering,* July 20, 1959. It was supplied to the magazine by E. F. Borisch of the Milwaukee Gear Co.)

● **Reik's Razor.** If you see a snake coming toward you in a jungle, you have a right to be anxious; if you see it coming down Park Avenue, you're in trouble.
> (Theodore Reik.)

● **Reis's Law of Airplane Travel.** Whatever airline you fly and whatever airport you fly to, you always land at Gate 102.
> (Harold Reis, AO.)

● **Remusat's Reconciliation.** (1) You must pay for your sins. (2) If you've already paid, please disregard this notice.
> (Jeanne Remusat, Forest Hills, N.Y. This appeared originally in a "New York Magazine Competition," *New York,* November 28, 1977.)

● **Repartee, First Rule of.** Better never than late.
> *(U/Ra.)*

● **Retsof's Rush Hour Blizzard Law.** If there is a suitable morning snowstorm, an employee will leave after the storm to go to work. Given an equivalent afternoon snowstorm, the employee will leave before the storm to go home.

(John C. Foster, Columbus, Ohio. For reasons unclear, Foster spells his name backward when composing laws.)

Special Section 15

Revised Proverbs. Nothing hangs on quite like an old proverb, which is one reason they require occasional scrapping and updating. The list of those that should be abandoned is long—starting with such inanities as:

—A picture is worth a thousand words. (Leo Rosten has rebutted this with, "OK. Draw me a picture of the Gettysburg Address.")

—Handsome is as handsome does. (A notion that is wrongheaded beyond belief.)

—You can't make a silk purse out of a sow's ear. (First of all, who would want to. Secondly, some years ago a Boston research firm actually made such a purse distilling a silky substance from a pot of sow's ears.)

—As for revisions the possibilities are limitless. For instance, all of these collected updates of one old saw are more to the point than the original:

—A fool and his money are some party.

—A fool and his money are soon spotted.

—A fool and his money are soon mated.

—A fool and his money are invited everywhere.

—A fool and his money are the prime-time television target audience. *(MLS.)*

—A Pool. And your money is soon parted.

In no special order, here are some other relevant revisions:
—Many hands want light work.
—The early worm, on the other hand, gets eaten by the bird.
—If you give a man enough rope, he'll hang you.
—Perversity makes for strange bedfellows.
—The wages of sin vary considerably.
—A word to the wise is superfluous.
—Counting your chickens before they've hatched is sensible long-range planning.
—Familiarity breeds.
—People who live in stone houses shouldn't throw glasses.
— Early to bed and early to rise and you'll be groggy when everyone else is alert.
—Out of the mouths of babes comes Gerber's strained apricots.
—Every silver lining has its cloud.
—If at first you don't succeed, you've got one strike against you.
—A bird in the hand is inconvenient.
—Lots of Jack makes all work play.
—A milligram of prevention is worth a kilogram of cure.
—A rolling stone angers his boss.
—Poets are born not paid.
—Some are born great, some achieve greatness, and some have a great thirst upon them.
—He who hesitates is bossed.

● **Revisionist's Rule.** The easiest way to change history is to become a historian.

   (Unattributed quote, NASA file.)

● **Rhodes's Law.** When any principle, law, tenet, probability, happening, circumstance, or result can in no way be directly, indirectly, empirically, or circuitously proven, derived, implied, inferred, induced, deducted, estimated, or scientifically guessed, it will always for the purpose of convenience, expediency, political advantage, material gain, or personal comfort, or any combination of the above, or none of the above, be unilaterally and unequivocally assumed, proclaimed, and adhered to as absolute truth to be undeniably, universally, immutably, and infinitely so, until such time as it becomes advantageous to assume otherwise, maybe. (The full impact of this fundamental law may be invoked by use of the following symbolic logical operator, commonly referred to as "Charlie's Loop":

> (Charles E. Rhodes, Allison Park, Penn. Rhodes, who has been working on his law for some time, states that the original discovery was made c. 1971 in its original, less scientific form: "When in doubt, fake it.")

- **Rice's Rule.**
  No matter when you turn on the TV, there is *always* an ad showing.
  (Edith K. Rice, East Boothbay, Maine.)

- **Rigsbee's Law of Priorities.** Given the choice between doing something for which one is well-prepared and paid, or doing something for which one is ill-prepared and not paid, most individuals will choose the latter.
  (Ken Rigsbee, Bartlesville, Okla. His proof for this law: "I have just written you this letter on company time.")

- **Rigsbee's Principle of Management.** Your brightest, sharpest new employees are the first to leave your organization —as the cream rises to the top it will be skimmed off.
  (Ken Rigsbee, again.)

● **Rizzo's Reassurance.** The streets are safe in Philadelphia, it's only the people who make them unsafe.
(Philadelphia Mayor Frank Rizzo.)

● **Robbins's Law of Student Enrollment.** In required courses, failures create their own demand.
(Stephen P. Robbins, Professor, Department of Management, Concordia University, Montreal.)

● **Robert's Paradox.** My teacher says strangers are people we don't know. But that can't be true, because there are people who don't know us and we're not strangers.
(Robert, son of Arnold R. Isaacs, cited in Arnold's "The Rules of the Game" in *The Baltimore Sun,* December 31, 1978.)

● **Robert's Rules of Home and Garden.** (1) If at first you don't succeed, hire a contractor. (2) Two plus two equals four—unless you're talking about inches in a two-by-four. (3) Mulch is ado about nothing. (4) An idle mind should not mess around in a power workshop. (5) We must all hang together or assuredly the pictures will be crooked. (6) Somebody said it couldn't be done. I'll go along with that.
(Bob Herguth, the *Chicago Sun-Times. RS.*)

● **Robertson's Rules of Lunch.** (1) If it isn't deductible, don't. (2) There are no free lunches, but usually the IRS will pay for a part. (3) Everyone has to eat. (4) When there are no other ways to minimize the cost of the meal, most diners try to stiff the waiter.
(James A. Robertson, El Paso, Tex.)

● **Rochester's Theorem.** Before I got married I had six theories about bringing up children; now I have six children and no theories.
(Lord Rochester.)

● **Rogers's Advice.** Think like a hare, but act like a turtle. (Kenneth J. Rogers, Pontiac, Mich.)

● **Rogers's Sure-fire Formula.** The best way to make a fire with two sticks is to make sure one of them is a match. (Will Rogers.)

● **Rosa's Buzz-off Theory.** After completing that memo or report, substitute each buzz word with an everyday word. All on distribution will feel self-congratulatory at having for once understood a piece of writing in total. You will make friends. (Sal Rosa, New York City, who also discovered the next item.)

● **Rosa's Good Lord Willing Law.** If all causes of mishaps are insured against except "Acts of God," the good Lord will invariably oblige.

● **Rosalynn's Rule.** Don't worry about polls—but if you do, don't admit it. (Rosalynn Carter, quoted by Donnie Radcliffe in *The Washington Post,* October 5, 1978.)

● **Rose's First Law of Investments.** One should never invest in anything that must be painted or fed. (Showman Billy Rose, from William M. Mills, Hutchinson, Kans.)

● **Rosenblatt's Laws.** (1) The duration of a modern marriage is in direct proportion to the distance from one's relatives. (2) A basic law of modern education states that the further east one's university, the more honored he is the further west he travels. (3) A politician who doesn't swear at all is either an imposter or under indictment. (Roger Rosenblatt, from his columns for *The Washington Post.*)

● **Rover's Law.** A dog always wants to be on the other side of the door.

(*U/Ra.*)

● **Royal's Rule.** Think lucky. If you fall in a pond, check your hip pockets for fish.

(University of Texas football coach Darrell Royal.)

● **Rubin's Reminder.** Never confuse brilliance with a bull market.

(Paul Rubin, Toldeo, Ohio.)

● **Rubman's Law.** You always find something the first place you look the second time.

(Barbara Solonche, who named it for a relative who has proven the law.)

● **Ruby's Principles on Close Encounters.** The probability of meeting someone you know increases when you're with someone you don't want to be seen with.

(Walter Busch, St. Louis. *EV.*)

● **Ruination, Three Rules of.** There are three ways to be ruined in this world: first is by sex, second is by gambling, and the third is by engineers. Sex is the most fun, gambling is the most exciting, and engineers are the surest.

(*U/* Commonly found printed on cards passed out at engineering conferences.)

● **Russell's Classroom Rules.** (1) No working not permitted. (2) The tardy student will always want to leave early. (3) The size of the grade marked on a paper will be inverse to its importance (small A's and large F's).

(Gene H. Russell, Director, The Emperor Norton Society, Orland, Cal.)

● **Russell's Rule of Industrial Genetics.** The darker your skin pigmentation, the nearer you sit to the front window.
(Jim Russell, from his book *Russell on Murphy's Law,* Celestial Arts, 1978, as is the next item.)

● **Russell's Seismological Discovery.** Everything east of the San Andreas Fault will eventually plunge into the Atlantic Ocean.

● **Rutherford's Rule.** The more you don't know how to do, the less you have to do.
(Larry Rutherford, Virginia Military Institute.)

ROSE'S FIRST LAW OF INVESTMENTS

S

● **Sachar's Observation.** Some people grow with responsibility—others merely swell.

> (Abram Sachar, Chancellor of Brandeis University. From Richard S. Luskin, Needham, Mass.)

● **Safire's New Law of Who/Whom in Headlines.** When "whom" is correct, use some other formulation.

> (William Safire, *The New York Times Magazine,* March 25, 1979. From Rabbi Wayne Allen, Staten Island, N.Y.)

● **Sally's Law of Beauty.** In any given beauty salon, the total beauty of the operators exceeds that of the customers by a factor of 4:1. The sex of the operators and customers is immaterial.

> (N. Sally Hass, Sleepy Hollow, Ill.)

● **Sally's Rule of Aquatic Relativity.** The neatest thing that can happen to a girl at the pool is to have two guys take her hands and feet and throw her into the water, unless the two guys are her brothers, in which case it is the worst thing that can happen to a girl.

> (Sally, a teen-ager known to Michael L. Lazare, Armonk, N.Y.)

● **Samuelson's Corollary.** Public bureaucracy breeds private bureaucracy.

> (Robert J. Samuelson, *The Washington Post,* June 6, 1978. As he explains, "The more government expands, the more it stimulates a vast supporting apparatus of trade

associations, lawyers, lobbyists, research groups, economists, and consultants—all trying to shape the direction
of new federal regulations and spending programs.'')

● **Sanders's Law.** You never get walked on unless you
throw yourself on the floor.
(Chicago radio personality Betty Sanders.)

● **Sandy's Theory.** Depression and lack of inspiration are
in equal proportion to the lack of involvement and inspiration.
(Ellie Saraquese, Carmichael, Cal.)

● **Sans Souci Rule.** You are where you eat.
(Named for the Washington restaurant of the same name.
The rule was given to Art Buchwald by Pierre Salinger
when Buchwald first arrived in Washington.)

● **Santayana's Philosophical Reminder.** It is a great advantage for a system of philosophy to be substantially true.
(George Santayana.)

● **Sartorial Homogeneity, The Law of.** If you are called on
to speak at a gathering of your superiors and you are wearing
brown, everyone else is wearing blue. If you are wearing blue,
everyone else is wearing gray.
(Michael L. Lazare, Armonk, N.Y., from his own empiri-
cal studies.)

● **Schapiro's Logical Explanation.** The grass is always
greener on the other side, but that is only because they use more
manure.
(Ken Schapiro, Montclair, N.J.)

● **Scheussler's Rule of Four.** In a group of four people, one will always be honest, one will always be crooked, and the other two must be watched.

(R. W. Scheussler, Pittsburgh, Penn.)

● **Schinto-Bacal's Four Steps to Becoming a Legend in Your Time.** (1) Start a fad or religion. (2) Charm birds off trees. (3) Build an empire. (4) Never volunteer.

(Gene Schinto and Jules Bacal from their book *How to Become a Legend in Your Own Lifetime,* Abelard-Schuman, 1966.)

● **Schlegel's Two-Student Theory.** Of two students, one will begin immediately working on a difficult problem set (or other homework) while the other fools around. The night before the homework is due, the "fooler" will seek out the "worker" and will want to find out how to do the problems. The "fooler" will then: (1) Gleefully point out all the errors in the "worker's" solution; (2) Get a better grade on the homework.

(Eric M. Schlegel, Bloomington, Ind.)

● **Schonfeld's Law of Cameras.** The best shots occur: (1) When you are out of film; (2) when you don't have your camera; (3) when you are looking the other way.

(Jerry Schonfeld, Portsmouth, Va.)

● **Schorr's Laws of Economics.** (1) If there are imperfections in the structure of the marketplace, entrepreneurs will make lots of money. (2) If there are no imperfections in the structure of the marketplace, entrepreneurs will make imperfections in the structure of the marketplace.

(Kenneth L. Schorr, Little Rock, Ark.)

● **Schroeder's Admonition.** Don't ask questions you don't want answers to.

(Capt. Schroeder, USCG, from W. R. Jurgens, Bowie, Md.)

SCHONFELD'S LAW OF CAMERAS

● **Schulze's Restatement.** Always stop along the way to smell the roses—your competitors will be happy to get you out of their way.

    (Paul Schulze III, Chicago.)

● **Schwartz's True View of Life.** Don't look for your real success until you're past fifty. It takes that long to get over the distractions of sex.

    (Eddie Schwartz of Minneapolis, quoted in *A Couple of Cards* by Alfred McVay and Ed Hickey Associated Marketing Enterprises, 1973.)

● **Schwemer's Pontification.** The number of variables required to define completely a system or process will always exceed by one the number of experiments performed, regardless of the number of experiments performed.

    (Warren Schwemer, Ashland, Ky.)

● **Science, Basic Definitions.** (1) If it's green or wiggles, it's biology. (2) If it stinks, it's chemistry. (3) If it doesn't work, it's physics.

    (U/TIR.)

● **Scott's Do-It-Yourself Code.** (1) Any tool left on top of a ladder will fall off and hit you in the head. (2) Any rope left dragging from any object in any location will catch on something. (3) For the successful completion of any task requiring tools, it is necessary to bleed at least once.

    (Bill Scott, Tujunga, Cal.)

● **Scott's Hypothesis.** If it doesn't play in Peoria—it probably will in Dubuque.

    (Sid Scott, former Peoria resident, now living in Dubuque.)

● **Seligson-Gerberg-Corman Rule of Sexual Sameness.** Having bad sex with someone you care about is the same as having bad sex with someone you don't care about.

(Marcia Seligson, Mort Gerberg, and Avery Corman, from their book, *The Everything in the World That's the Same as Something Else Book,* Simon and Schuster, 1969.)

● **Sgt. Preston's Law of the Wild.** The scenery only changes for the lead dog.

(Curt Heinfelden, Baltimore.)

● **Shanebrook's Law.** If you do a job twice, it's yours.

(J. Richard Shanebrook, Chairman, Mechanical Engineering Department, Union College, Schenectady, N.Y.)

● **Shannon's Law.** Nothing is simple.

(Stan Shannon, Dallas.)

● **Shannon's Observation.** Nothing is so frustrating as a bad situation that is beginning to improve.

(William V. Shannon. *ME.*)

● **Shapiro/Kaufman Law.** The lag in American productivity is directly related to the steady increase in the number of business conferences and conventions.

(Walter Shapiro and Aleta Kaufman in their article "Conferences and Conventions: the $20-Billion Industry That Keeps America from Working." *The Washington Monthly,* February 1977.)

● **Sharples's Philosophy.** (1) A rolling stone gathers momentum. (2) Progress is nondirectional. (3) Don't be taken by the vitamin itself.

(Virginia M. Sharples, Houston.)

● **Shaw's Axiom.** For every problem science solves, it creates ten new ones.

   (George Bernard Shaw, from Sydney J. Harris.)

● **Shaw's Golden Rule.** Do not do unto others as you would that they should do unto you; their tastes may be different.

   (George Bernard Shaw, quoted by Joseph Wood Krutch in his essay "The Best of Two Worlds." *RS.*)

● **Sheehan's Law of Rational Government.** Using logic to deal with government is illogical; using illogic to deal with government is logical.

   (Raymond J. Sheehan, Springfield, Mass.)

● **Shelton's Law of Bill Paying.** The bill was due before you got it.

   (John Shelton.)

● **Sheppard's Laws of Organization.** (1) If a surface is flat, pile things on it. (2) If a pile grows to more than one foot tall, start a new pile.

   (Jeffrey Sheppard, in *The Washington Post,* January 5, 1979.)

● **Shick's Problematic Laws.** (1) Small problems have deep roots (a zero variance normally indicates that errors of + 1000 and − 1000 have occurred simultaneously and canceled one another.) (2) Large problems are the cause of small problems (an error in judgment in the beginning brings on an awful lot of judgment for error in the end). (3) There is no problem a good miracle can't solve.

   (Harry R. Shick, San Bernardino, Cal.)

● **Shields's Eternal Questions.** (1) How does Yassir Arafat constantly maintain a two-day growth of beard? (2) Who does

Anita Bryant's hair? (3) Why does Menachem Begin always look like he's eaten a bad meal?
>(Political consultant Mark Shields, who asked these on his WRC radio show.)

●   **Shore's Absolute Law.** Any unexpected and undesirable negative quantities or results may be rectified by the judicious insertion of absolute-value signs and prayerful interjections (e.g. ''Dammit!'').
>(*U*/from Warren Schwemer, Ashland, Ky.)

●   **Short's Quotations (A New Selection).** (1) The hardest lesson to learn is that learning is a continual process. (2) The only thing worse than learning the truth is not learning the truth. (3) The human brain is the only computer in the world made out of meat. (4) A human being is a computer's way of building another computer: usually a better one. That's why computers will never decide to replace human beings. We are their sex organs. (5) One fact can change your whole point of view. For instance, did you know King Kong was a lesbian? (6) If the opposite of *pro* is *con,* then what is the opposite of progress? (7) The more you treasure the object, the more noticeable the flaw. (8) Even Murphy's Law goes wrong sometimes.
>(David Gerrold, a.k.a. Solomon Short, from his work in progress *Quotebook of Solomon Short.* See also *Gerrold's Law.*)

●   **Sieger's Law.** You will have the same amount of money left at the end of the month, no matter how many raises, bonuses, or windfalls occur during the month.
>(*U/Ra.*)

●   **Sign at the Pentagon.**
THEY TOLD HIM THE JOB COULDN'T BE DONE.
HE ROLLED UP HIS SLEEVES AND WENT TO IT.

HE TACKLED THE JOB THAT COULDN'T BE DONE
—AND HE COULDN'T DO IT.
(*U/* Department of Defense.)

● **Sissman's First Twenty Rules of Reviewing.** Never review the work of a friend.

(Critic L. E. Sissman, quoted by Johnathan Yardley in *The Washington Star,* March 11, 1979. *JCG.*)

● **Sit, Whittle, and Spit Club Rules.** (1) Don't sit in the sun. (2) Don't whittle toward yourself. (3) Don't spit against the wind.

(Reported by Clyde W. Wilkinson, in his article "Backwoods Humor" in the *Southwest Review,* January 1939.)

● **Skinnell's Rule.** You don't start traditions, traditions start.
(K. W. Skinnell, Bethel Park, Penn.)

● **Skinner's Law.** Anyone who owns a telephone is at the mercy of any damn fool who knows how to dial.

(Jean Skinner Ostlund, Willmar, Minn., who learned it from her father, the late Arthur Z. Skinner.)

● **Sklenar's Second Rule.** No time is a convenient time for a meeting.

(Leslie James Sklenar, Chicago.)

● **Skole's Hotel Law.** When, through hard work, chance, position, or other fortuitous circumstances, you finally can stay in a hotel you could only dream of in your youth, it has deteriorated into a dump.

(Bob Skole, Stockholm, Sweden, written on the stationery of a famous New York hotel.)

● **Slavens's Discoveries.** (1) The toilet paper never runs out on the other guy. (2) Never let a drunk friend drive—especially if the party was at *his* place. (3) People with strong minds have weak eyes. (4) A good newspaper column cannot be written unless there is a can of beer on one side of the typewriter and a bag of Doritos on the other.
> (Larry M. Slavens, Publisher, *The Fontanelle Observer,* Fontanelle, Iowa.)

● **Slim's Law.** Any significant military action will occur at the junction of two or more map sheets.
> (Field Marshal Viscount Slim of Burma. Richard J. Keogh, Honolulu.)

● **Smith's Fourth Law of Inertia.** A body at rest tends to watch television.
> (G. Guy Smith, Media, Penn.)

● **Smith-Johannsen's Secret of Longevity.** Stay busy, get plenty of exercise, and don't drink too much. Then again, don't drink too little.
> (Herman "Jackrabbit" Smith-Johannsen, 103-year-old Canadian cross-country skier, quoted in *Sports Illustrated,* August 21, 1978.)

● **Smith's Laws.** *Small Appliance Axiom:* If it doesn't break immediately it can never be fixed. *2d Small Appliance Axiom:* If it breaks immediately, by the time it's fixed it will be too late to fix it if it breaks again. *Marketing:* You can never buy the new improved version because a new improved version is already replacing it.
> (Jerry Smith, Florissant, Mo.)

● **Smith's Observation.** There is nothing so trivial, so eso-

teric, so unique, or so commonplace, but someone will spend time and effort in an attempt to codify it.
(John Stephen Smith, Lincoln, Neb.)

● **Smith's Writing Rule.** In composing, as a general rule, run your pen through every other word you have written; you have no idea what vigor it will give your style.
(English clergyman and essayist Sydney Smith, 1771–1845.)

● **Smock's Travel Observations.** (1) Every country is a "land of contrast." (2) Wherever you travel, the weather is "unusual for this time of year."
(Ruth J. Smock, Silver Spring, Md.)

● **Smolik's Law.** Anything highly publicized needs to be.
(Richard C. Smolik, St. Louis.)

● **SNAFU Principle.** Communication is only possible between equals.
(From *Illuminatus* by Robert Shea and Robert Anson Wilson. From John W. Gustafson, Chicago.)

● **Socio-Genetics, Second Law of.** The law of heredity is that all undesirable traits come from the other parent.
("Morning Smile" column, *The Toronto Globe and Mail,* February 21, 1979. From Richard Isaac, M.D., Toronto.)

● **Solis's Amendment.** There is no such thing as a free lunch . . . the lunch gets more expensive each year.
(L. L. Solis, Columbus, Ohio. Letter to *The Wall Street Journal,* November 11, 1974.)

● **Somary's Fifteenth Law.** The less protection the State provides for its citizens, the more it charges for the job.

(Swiss banker Felix Somary; one of his twenty social laws from *Crisis and the Future of Democracy.* Quoted by Brian Crozier in *The National Review,* March 1979. *JCG.*)

● **Spaatz's Three Rules for the Conduct of Air Force Officers Before Congressional Committees.** (1) Don't try to be funny. (2) Don't lie. (3) Don't blurt out the truth.
(Gen. Tooey Spaatz, Chief of Staff, USAF, from Brig. Gen. William J. Becker, USAF.)

● **Spats's Restatement.** Every silver lining has a cloud.
(The character "Spats" Baxter in *Movie Movie.*)

● **Speculating on Margin, Three Good Rules for.** (1) Don't! (2) Do not! (3) If, after careful perusal of the two forementioned Rules, you are still resolved upon Folly, go to your Bank, Cracked Teapot, Old Stocking, or other financial depository where your hard-earned Cash is kept, and, having therefrom taken One Thousand Dollars . . . roll them carefully in strong, brown wrapping-paper and seal the ends. You are now ready for the next step. Placing the Roll in your inside vest pocket proceed briskly to the nearest Ferry slip and take the first boat which leaves. When midway between the termini, walk to the stern of the boat, take out the Roll, and heave it far into the troubled waters. Your money will have then arrived at its terminus, and you should calmly proceed to yours. By following this method of Deposit for your Margin, you not only save Brokers' commission and Interest, but many anxious days and sleepless nights, besides having anticipated by a few hours the Sinking of your Money.
(Gideon Wurdz [Charles Wayland Towne] in *Foolish Finance* [1905].)

● **Spindel's Motivator.** Aim at nothing and you will hit it.
(Donald T. Spindel, St. Louis.)

● **Stanley's Rules of the Road.** (1) The later you are, the greater the length of the red light. (2) The least-traveled roads have the longest green lights.
(Randall L. Stanley, St. Charles, Mo. *EV.*)

● **State Service Syndrome.** Never ask a business question during lunch hour.
(James Brown, former state employee. From Gary Knowlton, Portland, Ore.)

● **Steckel's Rule to Success.** Good enough isn't good enough.
(Paul W. Steckel, Gainesville, Fla.)

● **Steele's Fifth Law of Water Beds.** Bodies tend to oscillate at the same rate that they accelerate.
(Ashley H. Steele, Toledo, Ohio.)

● **Steele's Law of Excellence.** Only 10 percent of anything can be in the top 10 percent.
(Guy L. Steele Jr., Cambridge, Mass.)

● **Stengel's Law.** Good pitching will always stop good hitting and vice versa.
(Casey Stengel. From Steven D. Mirsky, Ithaca, N.Y.)

● **Stephen's Law of Averages.** Based on the summation of parts, divided by the number of samples, the *average* human has one breast and one testicle.
(Stephen J. Grollman, Hartsdale, N.Y.)

● **Stevenson's Presidential Paradox.** By the time a man is nominated for the Presidency of the United States, he is no longer worthy to hold the office.
(Adlai Stevenson, 1956, from Sydney J. Harris.)

● **Stock's Observation.** You no sooner get your head above water than someone pulls your flippers off.
(U/DRW.)

● **Strout's Law.** There is a major scandal in American political life every 50 years: Grant's in 1873, Teapot Dome in 1923, Watergate in 1973. Nail down your seats for 2023.
(Richard Strout, quoted in *Time,* March 27, 1978.)

● **Stults's Situation Report.** Our problems are mostly behind us—what we have to do now is fight the solutions.
(Banker Alan P. Stults, quoted in the *Chicago Tribune,* July 11, 1975.)

● **Sukhomlinov Effect, The.** In war, victory goes to those armies whose leaders' uniforms are least impressive.
(Roger A. Beaumont and Bernard J. James, *Horizon* magazine, Winter 1971.)

● **Sullivan's Law.** All great organizations were built on the backs of blind mules on treadmills. *Corollary:* No great organization was ever built with one-eyed mules.
(J. M. Sullivan, Creve Coeur, Mo.)

● **Sullivan's Proverbial Discovery.** Proverbs usually read just as well backwards, or jumbled up. Fine words do not a parsnip make nor iron bars a summer.
(Humorist Frank Sullivan, from his essay "It's Easy to Quote a Proper Proverb.")

● **Swartz's Maxim.** Live every day as if it were your last
. . . and some day you'll be right.
(U/Ra.)

● **Sweeney's Laws.** (1) The joy that is felt at the sight of a new-fallen snow is inversely proportional to the age of the beholder. (2) Today's society will ignore almost any form of public behavior except getting in the express line with two extra items. (3) Never trust a skinny cook.

> (Paul Sweeney, in *The Quarterly,* which he writes for the Defense Mapping Federal Credit Union.)

● **Swinehart's Definition.** The lecture is that procedure whereby the material in the notes of the professor is transferred to the notes of the students without passing through the mind of either.

> (Donald F. Swinehart, Department of Chemistry, University of Oregon. *TJR.*)

● **Sybert's Law of the Workshop.** Whenever a project is undertaken, the least expensive but most important item for its completion will be forgotten (i.e. sandpaper, paintbrushes, etc.).

> (Christopher Sybert, Lutherville, Md.)

● **Szymcik's Universal Law of Experts.** An expert is not someone who is often right, as opposed to a nonexpert; each is wrong about the same percent of the time. But the expert can always tell you why he was wrong; so you can always tell the difference.

> (Rev. Mark Szymcik, Leominster, Mass.)

T

● **T. Camille's Axioms.** (1) You are always doing something marginal when your boss drops by your desk. (2) You've made a decision whether or not you decided. (3) Title distinctions are functions of everything they shouldn't be. (4) It is easier to do it the hard way. (5) You'd always rather be doing something else when you are doing what you thought you wanted to do. (6) The least important and the most important information gets passed on at the office copying machine. (7) If you haven't asked yourself "Why the hell did I go to college anyway?" you must be teaching. (8) You haven't not worked until you've worked for the government. (9) He's not smarter than you—he's just more convincing. (10) If you feel incompetent, you probably are. (11) If someone else's clout depends on your productivity, (s)/he'll be on your back. (12) I'll do it Monday. (13) May the odds be with you! (14) Nobody likes a smart-ass; nobody likes a dumb-ass either.

　　(T. Camille Flowers, Cincinnati, Ohio.)

● **Tansik's Law of Bureaucratic Success.** Success in a bureaucracy depends not so much on whom you please, but on whom you avoid making angry. *Corollary:* To succeed, concentrate not on doing great things but on the avoidance of making mistakes.

　　(David A. Tansik, Associate Professor, University of Arizona.)

● **Taranto's Theorem.** The amount of intelligence on Earth is finite; the population increases exponentially.

　　(Harri V. Taranto, New York City.)

420

T. CAMILLE'S AXIOM NO. 1

● **Tatman's Assumption.** Always assume that your assumption is invalid.

(Robert F. Tatman, Wynnewood, Penn.)

● **Taylor's Discovery.** In any organization there are only two people to contact if you want results—the person at the very top and the person at the very bottom.

(Warren E. Taylor, Burlington, N.C.)

● **Tennis Players' Ten Commandments.** *I.* Thou shalt have no sport other than tennis. *II.* Thou shalt remember thine appointed court time and put nothing before it. *III.* Thou shalt honor thy backhand as instructed by thy pro. *IV.* Thou shalt not bear false witness as to when thou wast last the provider of new tennis balls. *V.* Thou shalt not take the name of the Lord in vain when thy shot hitteth the tape and faileth to roll over. *VI.* Thou shalt not destroy thy racquet after having lobbed directly to thine opponent at the net. *VII.* Thou shalt not commit a double fault at set point. *VIII.* Thou shalt not steal thy partner's overhead smash. *IX.* Thou shalt not covet they neighbor's court time, nor his or her partner. *X.* Thou shalt not use four-letter expletives when thou hast caused an easy volley to be ensnared in the net.

(U/NDB.)

Special Section 16

Tests and Examinations

① *M.I.T. Graduate Qualifying Examination.*

Instructions: Read each question thoroughly. Answer all questions. Time limit—four hours. Begin immediately.

History. Describe the history of the papacy from its origins to the present day; concentrate specially but not exclusively on the social, political, economic, religious, and philosophical impact on Europe, Asia, America, and Africa. Be brief, concise, and specific.

Medicine. You have been provided with a razor blade, a piece of gauze, and a bottle of Scotch. Remove your own appendix. Do not suture until your work has been inspected. You have fifteen minutes.

Public Speaking. 2,500 riot-crazed aborigines are storming the classroom. Calm them. You may use any ancient language except Latin or Greek.

Biology. Create life. Estimate the differences in subsequent human culture if this form of life had developed 500 million years earlier, with special attention to the probable effects on the English parliamentary system. Prove your thesis.

Music. Write a piano concerto. Orchestrate it and perform it with flute and drum. You will find a piano under your seat.

Psychology. Based on your knowledge of their works, evaluate the emotional stability, degree of adjustment, and repressed frustrations of each of the following: Alexander of Aphrodisias, Ramses II, Hammurabi. Support your evaluation with quotations from each man's work, making appropriate references. It is not necessary to translate.

Sociology. Estimate the sociological problems that might accompany the end of the world. Construct an experiment to test your theory.

Management Science. Define management. Define science. How do they relate? Why? Create a generalized algorithm to optimize all managerial decisions. Assuming an 1130 CPU supporting 50 terminals, each terminal to activate your algorithm, design the communications interface and all the necessary control programs.

Economics. Develop a realistic plan for refinancing the national debt. Trace the possible effects of your plan in the following areas: Cubism, the Donatist controversy, the wave theory of light. Outline a method from all points of view. Point out the deficiencies in your point of view, as demonstrated in your answer to the last question.

Political Science. There is a red telephone on the desk beside you. Start World War III. Report at length on its socio-political effects, if any.

Epistemology. Take a position for or against the truth. Prove the validity of your position.

Physics. Explain the nature of matter. Include in your answer an evaluation of the impact of the development of mathematics on science.

Philosophy. Sketch the development of human thought; estimate its significance. Compare with the development of any other kind of thought.

General Knowledge. Describe in detail. Be objective and specific.

(U/ME.)

② *North Dakota Null-Hypothesis Inventory. NDNI.*
Instructions: Respond to each statement with one of these three answers: (1) Sometimes; (2) Always; (3) Never.
    1. I salivate at the sight of mittens.
    2. At times I am afraid my toes will fall off.

3. Chopped liver makes me laugh.
4. As an infant, I had very few hobbies.
5. Some people never look at me.
6. I sometimes feel that my earlobes are longer than those of other people.
7. Spinach makes me feel alone.
8. My sex life is A-okay.
9. I often fart in crowds.
10. Dirty stories make me think about sex.
11. I am anxious in rooms that have hairy walls.
12. Cousins are not to be trusted.
13. Sometimes I think someone is trying to take over my stomach.
14. I have never eaten a fly.
15. I cannot read or write.
16. As an infant I hated chopped liver.
17. I have killed mosquitos.
18. My teeth sometimes leave my body.
19. I am never startled by a fish.
20. Plaid Stamps are better than Green Stamps.
21. I have never gone to pieces over the weekend.
22. My parents always faced catastrophe with a song.
23. Recently, I have been getting shorter.
24. I have taken shoe polish to excess.
25. I have always been disturbed by the size of Lincoln's ears.
26. Chicken liver gives me a rash.
27. I like mannish children.
28. Most of the time I go to sleep without saying good-bye.
29. I am not afraid of picking up door knobs.
30. Chiclets make me sweat.
31. I stay in the bathtub until I look like a raisin.
32. Frantic screams make me nervous.
33. It makes me angry to have people bury me.
34. I hate orgies, if nobody else is there.
35. I am afraid of Vikings.

(Shortened version of a longer NDNI. The NDNI is another classic of unknown origin that the author first came in contact with in 1964 in New York. It is, of course, a replacement for the ubiquitous Minnesota Multiphasic Personality Inventory [MMPI], which is used to create data for everyone ranging from college administrators to prison wardens. There is now an even newer test called the "No-Nonsense Personality Inventory," published for the first time in the November 1978 issue of *The Journal of Irreproducible Results,* which asks for response to such statements as: "I am often bothered by thoughts of sex while having intercourse," "God rarely answers my questions," "Weeping brings tears to my eyes," and "I often bite other people's nails.")

③ *Test Entitled "Can you follow directions?" (three-minute time test).*

1. Read everything before doing anything.
2. Put your name in the upper right-hand corner of this paper.
3. Circle the word "Name" in sentence two.
4. Draw five small squares in the upper left-hand corner of this paper.
5. Put an X in each square.
6. Sign your name under the title of this paper.
7. After the title, write "Yes, yes, yes."
8. Put a circle around sentence seven.
9. Put an X in the lower left-hand corner of this paper.
10. Draw a triangle around the X you just put down.
11. On the back of this paper, multiply 703 by 66.
12. Draw a rectangle around the word "paper" in sentence four.
13. Loudly call out your first name when you get to this point in the test.
14. If you think you have followed directions carefully to this point, call out "I have."

15. On the reverse side of this paper, add 8950 and 9850.
16. Put a circle around your answer and put a square around the circle.
17. Count out in your normal speaking voice, from ten to one backward.
18. Punch three small holes in the top of this paper with your pencil.
19. If you are the first person to get this far, call out loudly, "I am the first person to this point, and I am the leader in following directions."
20. Underline all even numbers on the side of this page.
21. Put a square around every number written out on this test.
22. Say out loud, "I am nearly finished, I have followed directions."
23. Now that you have finished reading carefully, do only sentence two.

   (Variations on this test show up from time to time on college campuses and military installations, where it is given to underscore the true meaning of following directions. This particular version appears in *Urban Folklore from the Paperwork Empire* by Alan Dundes and Carl R. Pagter, American Folklore Society, 1975.)

● **Thermodynamics of Political Gossip.** When affection for a sitting President cools down, the chatter about the senior available Kennedy heats up.

   (*Newsweek,* May 8, 1978.)

● **Thidias's Law of Ironic Fate.** (Also known as, *Thyrsus's Law, Thyreus's Law, Thydeus's Law, Thidius's Law,* and *Agrippa's Law.*) When you go down in history, they'll spell your name wrong.

   (N. Sally Hass, Sleepy Hollow, Ill.)

● **Thomas's Observation.** No child-proof bottle is absolutely "child-proof."

(John and Joyce Thomas, Grissom AFB, Ind.)

● **Thomas's Rules of the Game.** (1) No matter how well you do something, someone won't like it. (2) No matter how trivial the assignment, it is always possible to build it up to a major issue. (3) A good, illegible signature is a key to success.

(Robert H. Thomas, Farmington, Mich.)

● **Thompson's Publication Premise.** The probability of anyone reviewing a document in full diminishes with the number of pages.

(Charles I. Thompson III, Port Jefferson Station, N.Y.)

● **Thompson's Rule.** If you can't do anything about it, don't.

(William I. Thompson, West Hempstead, N.Y.)

● **Thurber's Amplification.** Love is blind, but desire just doesn't give a good goddam.

(James Thurber, in his *Further Fables for Our Time,* Simon and Schuster, 1966.)

● **Thurston's Law.** The higher the drifts, the harder to find a boy with a shovel.

("Thirsty" Thurston, in the *Hi and Lois* comic strip.)

● **Thwartz's Theorem of Low Profile.** Negative expectation thwarts realization, and self-congratulation guarantees disaster. (Or, simply put: if you think of it, it won't happen quite that way.)

(Michael Donner, editor of *Games* magazine, from the Editor's Message in the September/October 1979 issue. *DRW.*)

● **Tiberius's Law of Politicians.** Caesar doesn't want Caesar's. Caesar wants God's.
(N. Sally Hass, Sleepy Hollow, Ill.)

● **Tiller's Theory.** Car washing precipitates precipitation.
(George Tiller, Memphis, Tenn. Quoted in *Johns Hopkins Magazine,* May 1978.)

● **Tobias's Law.** The most sensible investments are mundane.

(Financial writer Andrew Tobias, who insists that it is easier, less risky, and a "better investment" to save $1,000 a year through special sales and discounts on everyday household items than it is to try to clear $1,000 in the stock market. Quoted in an interview in *The Baltimore Sun,* March 7, 1979. *ME.*)

● **Todd's Law.** In an area where the degree of confusion approaches infinite proportions—major disasters pass unnoticed.
(J. K. Todd, M.D., Calgary, Alberta.)

● **Tolkien's Reminder.** It does not do to leave a live dragon out of your calculations, if you live near him.
(J. R. R. Tolkien, quoted in *Reader's Digest,* September 1978.)

● **Tomlin's Request.** If love is the answer, could you rephrase the question?
(Lily Tomlin, quoted in *Time,* March 28, 1977.)

● **Toomey's Rule.** It is easy to make decisions on matters for which you have no responsibility.
(Jim Toomey, the St. Louis Cardinals, St. Louis, Mo.)

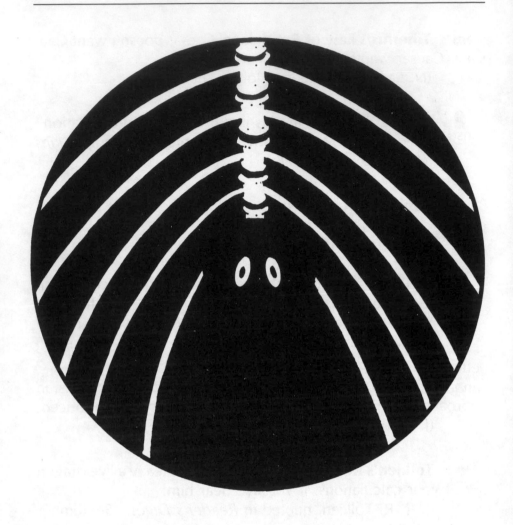

TOLKIEN'S REMINDER

● **Towson State College Rule.** If you are smart enough to fill out the application, you don't need to be here. (Towson State student/*Ra.*)

● **Trauring's Discovery.** Technical reports are expanded

from outlines, so that aides can recondense them for executive use.

> (Mitchell Trauring, Los Angeles.)

● **Treaty Ruling.** Treaties should be interpreted as to make sense, if possible.

> (U.S. Supreme Court. *TCA.*)

● **Tromberg's Laws.** (1) Oil is thicker than blood. (2) Just because you can do it doesn't mean you can make a living at it. (3) You ain't got it till you got it and even when you got it you may not. (4) When you see the word "net" in a contract, it means "nothing."

> (Sheldon Tromberg, writer/radio personality, Washington, D.C.)

● **Truman's Law of Qualifications.** Always vote for the better man. He is a Democrat. Anyone who votes for a Republican gets what he deserves.

> (Harry S Truman. *MBC.*)

● **Truman's Parental Instruction.** I have found that the best way to give advice to your children is to find out what they want, and then advise them to do it.

> (Harry S Truman. *MBC.*)

● **Tuchman's Axiom.** When something is perfect the way it is, someone will come along to improve it—and screw it up.

> (Stephan A. Tuchman, Rockville Center, N.Y., quoted in a letter to *Money* magazine on the magazine's new look. The letter appears in the February 1979 issue.)

● **Tufte's First Law of Political Economy.** The politicians who make economic policy operate under conditions of political competition.

(Edward R. Tufte, Professor of Political Science, Yale University, from his *Political Control of the Economy. TCA.*)

● **Turtle Principle, The.** If you go slow enough, long enough, you'll be in the lead again.

(Wayne Hoy, Rutgers University, Graduate School of Education. From Gerald Fava, Lake Hiawatha, N.J. Fava lists a few of the many areas in which the Turtle Principle applies:

Criminal Justice: victim's rights vs. criminal's rights.
Political Science: centralization vs. decentralization.
Physics: wave theory vs. particle theory of subatomic entities.)

● **Twain's Addendum.** Familiarity breeds contempt—and children.

(Mark Twain.)

● **Twenty-Third Qualm, The.**
The professor is my quizmaster, I shall not flunk.
He maketh me to enter the examination room;
He leadeth me to an alternative seat;
He restoreth my fears.
Yea, though I know not the answers to those questions, the class average comforts me.
I prepare my answers before me in the sight of my proctors.
I anoint my exam papers with figures.
My time runneth out.
Surely grades and examinations will follow all the days of my life,
And I will dwell in this class forever.
(U/TJR.)

● **Twyman's Law.** Any statistic that appears interesting is almost certainly a mistake.

(From Iwan Williams, London, who got it from A.S.C. Ehrneberg, Professor of Marketing, who got it from a colleague.)

● **Typesetter's Punctuation Rules.** Set type as long as you can hold your breath without getting blue in the face, then put in a comma. When you yawn, put in a semicolon. And when you want to sneeze, that's time for a paragraph.

(U/Ra.)

● **Udall's Fourth Law of Politics.** If you can find something everyone agrees on, it's wrong.

(Morris Udall, quoted in *The New York Times,* April 4, 1975.)

● **Umbrella Justice.**

> The rain it raineth on the just
> And also on the unjust fella;
> But chiefly on the just because
> The unjust stole the just's umbrella.

(Sir George Bowen, quoted by Senator William Proxmire, U.S. Senate, March 26, 1979.)

● **Unitas's Law.** If you hang around long enough, you'll end up somewhere.

(Quarterback Johnny Unitas, on being notified of his election to the Football Hall of Fame, January 29, 1979.)

● **United States Army Engineer General Orders.** (1) Measure it with a micrometer; mark it with a grease pencil; cut it with an ax. (2) If it doesn't fit, get a bigger hammer. (3) Pound to fit and paint to match.

(U.S. Army Engineer Training Brigade, Fort Leonard Wood, Mo. *MLS.*)

● **Universality of the So-Called "Rebel Yell."** Ain't nobody doesn't know to commence hollering "Yee-haw!" when circumstances dictate.

(*U/RA.*)

● **Upward-Mobility Rule.** Don't be irreplaceable. If you can't be replaced, you can't be promoted.
(Desk sign/*Ra.*)

● **Useful Refrain.** When you're down and out, lift up your voice and shout, "I'M DOWN AND OUT!"
(U/Ra.)

V

- **Van der Rohe's Explanation.** God is in the details.
  (Miës van der Rohe, from Anthony M. Cresswell, Evanston, Ill.)

- **Van Leuvan Storm Theory, The.** If it is raining now, and wasn't a little while ago, it is moving this way.
  (Jeff Van Leuvan, from his old college roommate, Earl Allen, Manhattan, Kans.)

- **Vargas's Varied Laws.** *Of Contrary Geography:* If the directions for finding a place include the words "you can't miss it," you will. *Of Free Booze:* People who hardly drink at all will imbibe stingers at 8:00 A.M. if the drinks are served on an airplane and free. *Of Paucity:* There is no such thing as a little garlic . . . or a mild heart attack . . . or a few children. *Of Jars:* A jar that cannot be opened through any combination of force, household tools, and determination will open instantly if picked up by the lid. *Of Human Statistics:* Figures don't lie, they lay.
  (Joie Vargas of Reno discovered all of these save for the last, which is from her husband, George L. Vargas.)

- **Vaughan's Rule of Corporate Life.** The less important you are on the table of organization, the more you'll be missed if you don't show up for work.
  (The late Bill Vaughan of *The Kansas City Star.*)

- **Vielmetti's Letter-into-Envelope Law.** If you think you have folded it enough, you haven't.
  (Ed Vielmetti, Michigan.)

● **Vietinghoff's Precept.** He who controls the forms controls the program.

> (William F. Vietinghoff, Space Shuttle Main Engine Systems, Rockwell International, Canoga Park, Cal.)

● **Vogel's Rules.** (1) Nothing gives more satisfaction than telling a hypochondriac how well he is looking. (2) The length of a minute depends on which side of the bathroom door you're on. (3) The simplest incentive program: One mistake and you're through. (4) To shorten the winter, borrow some money due in the spring. (5) The wrong number on a telephone is never busy. (6) You will never lock your keys in the car at home.

> (W. J. Vogel, Toppenish, Wash.)

● **Wain's Conclusion.** The only people making money these days are the ones who sell computer paper.
(U/DRW.)

● **Walker's Rule.** If you're there before it's over, you're on time.

(Politician James J. Walker.)

● **Wallace's Two-out-of-Three Theory.**
SPEED
QUALITY
PRICE
Pick any Two.
(James M. Wallace, Minneapolis. Wallace says that the dictum applies particularly to advertising, print shops, etc. He adds, "This is of course theoretical. In real life, one is usually hard-pressed to get any *one*.")

● **Warning-of-the-Century.** Do not place this Wine Brick in a one-gallon crock, add sugar and water, cover and let stand for seven days, or else an illegal alcoholic beverage will result.
(Label from a Prohibition-era product made of compressed grapes.)

● **Washington's First Law of Summer Survival.** Because so little of consequence happens here in August, whatever does occur is embellished, embroidered, and otherwise exaggerated far beyond reality.
(Political writer Robert Walters, who used the law to

explain *l'affaire* Andrew Young during the summer of 1979.)

● **Wattenberg's Law.** There is nothing so powerful as an old idea whose time has come again.
(Ben Wattenberg, quoted by Hugh Sidey in *The Washington Star,* May 6, 1979.)

● **Weiner's Wisdom.** Indecision is the key to flexibility.
(Lt. T. F. Weiner, USN, from R. J. Montore, Henderson, Ky.)

● **Weisert's Law.** If somebody will fund it, somebody will do it.
(Hilde Weisert, Teaneck, N.J.)

● **Welby's Law.** No problem is so deep or intractable that it can't be successfully overcome in the alloted time-slot.
(Named for TV's Dr. Marcus Welby. In a column by Alan M. Kriegsman in *The Washington Post,* January 19, 1979.)

● **Welch's Rule.** An apple every eight hours keeps three doctors away.
(David P. Welch, Bloomington, Ind.)

● **Wells's Law.** When in doubt, use clout.
(Stephen Wells, North Tarrytown, N.Y.)

● **Wemhoff's Law of Trade-offs.** Every advantage of any given course of action has a correspondingly equal and opposite disadvantage that, over the long run, fully offsets the advantage. *Corollary 1:* Over the short run, a specific advantage or disadvantage may predominate in any course of action. *Corollary 2:*

WEISERT'S LAW

Success in business consists in judging the short-run ascendancy of any specific advantage or disadvantage.
(Joseph A. Wemhoff, Chicago.)

● **West's Proven Facts.** (1) Man has yet to invent any substance that a Ping-Pong ball cannot get over, under, around, or through on its way to the most inaccessible spot in the playroom. (2) Electronically timed tests show that it takes a brand new tennis ball less than ten seconds to find, and stop dead-center in, the *only* puddle of water on any given tennis court. A ball that has been used until it barely bounces won't find such a puddle if you played all summer.
(Robert T. West, Minneapolis.)

● **Westheimer's Discovery.** A couple of months in the laboratory can frequently save a couple of hours in the library.
(Frank Westheimer, Harvard chemist, from Joseph A. Horton, M.D., Philadelphia.)

● **White House, First Law of Life in the.** Don't do anything you're not prepared to see in the papers the next morning.

> (Stated by a former White House staffer at the time of the Dr. Peter Bourne resignation. Quoted in *Newsweek,* July 31, 1978.)

● **White's Law.** Things are never as bad as they turn out to be.

> (Richard N. White, Director, School of Civil and Environmental Engineering, Cornell University.)

● **White's Observations of Committee Operation.** (1) People very rarely think in groups; they talk together, they exchange information, they adjudicate, they make compromises. But they do not think; they do not create. (2) A really new idea affronts current agreement. (3) A meeting cannot be productive unless certain premises are so shared that they do not need to be discussed, and the argument can be confined to areas of disagreement. But while this kind of consensus makes a group more effective in its legitimate functions, it does not make the group a creative vehicle—it would not be a new idea if it didn't—and the group, impelled as it is to agree, is instinctively hostile to that which is divisive.

> *(U/GT.)*

● **Whitehead's Injunction.** Seek simplicity—and distrust it.

> (Alfred North Whitehead to his students. From Sydney J. Harris.)

● **Whiteman's Findings.** *Wind Law for Pilots:* A head wind will reverse directions on the return flight. *First Corollary to Parkinson's Law:* Eight people will do ten people's work better than twelve people. *Measure of Success:* The measure of success

is not how much money you have in the bank, but rather how much money the bank will lend you.
(Jack W. Whiteman, Phoenix.)

● **Whitney's Second Law of the Democratic Process.** In a democracy, having been born, death ensues. Everything else is negotiable.
(Peter Whitney, Tucson.)

● **Whole Picture Principle.** Research scientists are so wrapped up in their own narrow endeavors that they cannot possibly see the whole picture or anything, including their own research. *Corollary:* The Director of Research should know as little as possible about the specific subject of research he is administrating.
(U/DRW.)

WHY THIS BOOK WILL BRING YOU LUCK

Why This Book Will Bring You Luck.

This book will bring you good luck. The luck is in your hands. Don't ruin it. You are to receive good luck within 14 days of buying this book if you follow instructions.

This is no joke.

To ensure your luck buy 20 additional copies and send them to people you think need good luck. Please do not send them money or any other book. All 20 books must be mailed within 96 hours.

Place the names and addresses of three of the 20 people at the bottom of this page along with your own name and address. Each subsequent recipient is to remove the top name when adding new names.

See what happens. It works. Accept no other chain letters. Dan G. of Denver has, at last count, 4,311 copies, and the estate of Harriet P. of Toledo has 1,406 copies (accumulated before she broke the chain and died).

Don't break the chain, and don't tell the spoilsport postal authorities about it.

_____

_____

_____

_____

● **Wickre's Law.** On a quiet night, there will always be two good movies on TV, or none at all.
(U/NDB.)

● **Wiio's Laws of Communications.** (1) Communication usually fails—except by chance. *Corollary:* If you are satisfied that your communication is bound to succeed, then the communication is bound to fail. (2) If a message can be understood in different ways, it will be understood in just the way that does the most harm. (3) There is always somebody who knows better than you what you meant by your message. (4) The more communication there is, the more difficult it is for communication to succeed. *Corollary:* The more communication there is, the more difficult it is for communication to succeed. *Corollary:* The more communication there is, the more misunderstanding will occur. (5) In mass communication it is not important how things are; the important thing is how things seem to be. (6) The importance of a news item is inversely correlated with the square of the distance.
(Professor Wiio, Director of the Institute for Communications Research at the University of Helsinki.)

● **Wilde's Maxim.** Nothing succeeds like excess.
(Oscar Wilde.)

● **Will's Paradox of Popular Government.** People are happiest when they are in a position to complain about government and they can complain with minimum confusion and maximum righteousness when they acknowledge, indeed insist, that government is not "by the people."
(Columnist George Will, in his *Washington Post* column for June 8, 1978.)

● **Williams's Critical Key.** Any critic can establish a wonderful batting average by just rejecting every new idea.

(J. D. Williams, quoted in Bennett Cerf's *The Sound of Laughter,* Doubleday, 1970.)

● **Williams's Law of Political Rhetoric.** Never underestimate the ability of a politician to (a) say something and tell you not very much, (b) do it with style, and (c) touch all the bases.
    (Robert H. Williams, in *The Washington Post.* His proof was a statement made by Senator Henry M. "Scoop" Jackson to Israel's Prime Minister Menachem Begin: "As we Christians approach the Christmas season, we can all be thankful to a Moslem and a Jew.")

● **Willis's Law of Public Administration.** In any federal management report, the recommendations that would result in actual savings will be rejected, but the rejection will be "balanced" by the enthusiastic acceptance of those which increase costs.
    (Bennett Moser Willis, McLean, Va., former Chief of Management, U.S. Department of Justice. He is also the author of the next item.)

● **Willis's Observation.** Except for courtship and travel, everything seems to take longer and cost more than: (a) it used to, (b) the estimate.

● **Willis's Rule of Golf.** You can't lose an old golf ball.
    (John Willis, WCVB–TV, Boston.)

● **Wilson's Dietary Discovery.** It is impossible to lose weight lastingly and all diets are atrocious.
    (Sloan Wilson, from *What Shall We Wear to This Party —The Man in the Gray Flannel Suit Twenty Years Before and After,* Arbor House, 1976.)

● **Winners' Law.** It isn't whether you win or lose, but how much you win by.

    (Paul J. Spreitzer, age fifteen, Chicago.)

● **Winston's Second Rule of Success.** Your greatest assets are other people's money and other people's patience.

    (Carl Winston, in *How to Run a Million into a Shoestring and Other Shortcuts to Success,* G. P. Putnam's Sons, 1960.)

● **Winter's Law of the Stranded.** The shortest distance to aid is in the opposite direction.

    (Robert F. Winter, M.D., Spring Valley, N.Y.)

● **Winters' Rule.** In a crowded place, the person directly behind you always has the loudest voice. *Corollary:* People with loud voices never have anything interesting to say.

    (Christine Winters, the *Chicago Tribune.*)

● **Woehlke's Law.** Nothing is done until nothing is done. (Richard A. Woehlke, Sutton, Mass. A few examples from the man who discovered the law: (1) Middle managers can never get the people they need for a job as long as they continue to muddle through by means of overtime, ulcers, and superhuman effort. But when enough people quit in frustration so that the job is not finished, upper management will approve the hiring of the necessary people. (2) Ditto for salaries. (3) The energy crisis [substitute your favorite crisis] will worsen until the whole house of cards collapses. Then and only then will effective measures be taken.)

● **Wohlford's Baseball Formula.** Ninety percent of this game is half mental.

(Outfielder Jim Wohlford, quoted in *Sports Illustrated,* October 24, 1977.)

● **Wolf's Law.** You never get a second chance to make a first impression.
(U/NDB.)

● **Wood's Incomplete Maxims.** (1) All's well that ends. (2) A penny saved is a penny. (3) Don't leave things unfinishe
(Donald R. Woods, Stanford, Cal.)

● **Woodruff's Work Rule.** *Everybody* works for the sales department.
(Jeff Woodruff, ABC. *MLS.*)

● **Woods's Rule for Drinking.** I always drink standing up because it is much easier to sit down when I get drunk standing up than it is to get standing up when I get drunk sitting down.
(Ralph L. Woods, from his book *How to Torture Your Mind,* Funk & Wagnalls, 1969.)

● **Woolsey-Swanson Rule of Problems.** People would rather live with a problem they cannot solve than accept a solution they cannot understand.
(Robert E. D. Woolsey and Huntington S. Swanson, from their book *Operations Research for Immediate Application: A Quick and Dirty Manual,* Harper & Row, 1975. *RS.*)

Y

● **Yoakum's Rule.** Don't put off until tomorrow what you can get done sometime next week.
(Robert Yoakum, Yoakum Features, Lakeville, Conn.)

● **Young's Law.** Nothing is illegal if one hundred business-men decide to do it.
(Andrew Young.)

● **Young's Research Law.** All great discoveries are made by mistake. *Corollary:* The greater the funding, the longer it takes to make the mistakes.
(U/DRW.)

ACKNOWLEDGMENTS

Excerpts from "This Way to the Exit" by Dr. Ross K. Baker: © 1978 by The New York Times Company. Reprinted by permission.

"Children's Birthday Parties" and "Adults at Parties" from *MY WAR WITH THE 20TH CENTURY* by Pierre Berton: Copyright © 1965 by Pierre Berton. Reprinted by permission of Doubleday & Company, Inc., and Curtis Brown, Ltd.

"Gerrold's Law" and "Short's Quotations": copyright © 1980 by David Gerrold. Used by permission.

Excerpt from "Getting In On A Zurich" by Dan Jenkins: reprinted courtesy of *Sports Illustrated,* September 4, 1978. © 1978 Time Inc.

"Murphy's Marketing Maxims": © 1971, Schoonmaker Associates, P.O. Drawer M, Coram, N.Y. 11727.

"Murray's Laws": Copyright © 1978, *Los Angeles Times.* Reprinted with permission.

"Robert's Rules of Home and Garden": Reprinted with permission from the *Chicago Sun-Times.* Excerpts from the column "Poor Robert's Almanac for Home Handymen and Gardeners" by Bob Herguth.

"Rosenblatt's Rules": Copyright © 1979 *The Washington Post.*

Time "Letters" column, March 19, 1979, for Boettcher's Attribution, Close's Law, Coccia's Law, and Ogden's Law: Copyright 1979 Time Inc. All rights reserved.

Index

A

Absolute: Marguccio's; Shore's

Abstinence: Kaul's

Academia: Anderson's; Boroson's; Bressler's; Kerr's; Lowell's. *See also:* Education

Accidents: Bennett's

Achievement: Moore's; Ormerod's

Acquisition: Carlisle's

Action: Gomez's; Grizzly Pete's; Manske's; Moutsatson's; Obis's; Porter-Givens's; Ranger's; Rogers's; Thompson's

Adversity: Lipsitt's

Advertising: Field's; Leo's

Advice: Cureton's; Ganci's; Greenyea's; Juliet's; Masson's; Raper's

Age: Conrad's; Metzger's; O'Neill's; Sweeney's

Aid: Winter's

"Ain't": "Ain't"

Airplanes, Air Transportation/Aviation: Air Force Law; Lewandowski's; Reis's; Spaatz's. *See also:* Flying

Alcohol: Medical Principles; Warning

Ambidextrous: Greenhaus's

America: Dickson's; Great American Axiom

Anger: Jefferson

Animals: Morris's

Annual Reports: Henry's

Answers: O'Conner's

Apartment: Apartment dweller's; Highrise

Aphorism: Law

Apology: Parson's

Appearance: Business Maxims; Obvious

Apple: Welch's

Appliance, small: Smith's

Approval: Dmitri's

Arctic: Gould's; Peary's

Argot: How to:

Army: Civil Service; United States

Assembly: Christmas Eve

Assumption: Cason's; Tatman's

Astronomy: Olbers's

Atomic Attack: Emergency

Attendance: Berra's

Attitude: Business Maxims

Audition: Mirsky's

Auditors: Business Maxims

Authority: Jones's

Automobile/Automotive: Bennett's; Buxbaum's; DeCicco's; Dickson's; Hoffman's; Murray's; Vogel's

Average: Stephen's

B

Backfire: Quigley's

Balance of Payments: Callaghan's

Baldness: Daniels's

Balls: West's

Baseball: Custodiet's; Gomez's; Jackson's; Los Angeles; Raper's; Wohlford's

Bath: Dowd's

Bathroom: Campbell's

Beauty: Sally's

Behavior: Maslow's; Petroff's; Sweeney's

Behavior Modification: Gotwald's

Bicentennial: Explanations

Big Mac principle: Big Mac

Bills: Shelton's

Birds: Ade's
Black Box: Carroll's
Blame: Brogan's; Bureaucratic
BLASH: Moriarity's
Blizzard: Retsof's
Boats: Albert's
Body: Anonymous's
Boils: Pop's
Books: Bernstein's; Burgess's; Chadwick's;
   Hubbard's
Boredom: Fresco's
Bosses: Business Maxims
Breathalyzer: Catch-22
Bridge: Clayton's; Kaye's
Britain: Callaghan's
Budget: Budget Analyst's; Hebertson's
Bugs: Huster's
Burden: Linus's
Bureaucracy: Desk Jockey's; Fried's; Insti-
   tutional; Institutions; Lawrence's;
   McCarthy's; Samuelson's; Tansik's;
   Vietinghoff's
Business: Blumenthal's; Business Maxims;
   Cassey's; Collins's; Comb's; Cooke's;
   Corporate Survival; Duke's; Hall's; In-
   verse; Joe Cooch's; Jones's; Mann's;
   Masefield's; Ormerod's; Russell's;
   Shapiro/Kaufman
Business terms: Glossary

C

Calculations: Tolkien's
Calendar: Official diagrams
Cameras: Schonfeld's
Campaigns: Bendiner's; Politico's
Canapes: Brodie's
Candidates: Cohen's; DeRoy's
Candy: Harris's
Cardiac arrest: Medical principles
Cards: Harris's
Carnivals: Boyd's
Carsickness: First Time, The

Car Washing: Tiller's
Cat: Feline
Chain-letter: Why this book . . .
Chance: Barnes's; Blick's
Chart: Official diagrams
Chastity: Augustine's
"Child-proof": Thomas's
Children: Benchley's; Disney World;
   Laura's; Mikadet's (adult); Rochester's;
   Twain's
Church: Chilton's
Circus: Allen's; Boettcher's
Civilization: Lichtenberg's
Claims: Raper's
Clowns: Boettcher's
Coat hangers: Berliner's
Coffee: Dial's
Collecting: Dickson's; Lightfoot's
Colleges/Universities: Anderson's; Boro-
   son's; Kerr's; Lowell's
Comedy: Carson's
Commandments: Jefferson's
Commencement: Pardieck's
Committee: Conrad's; Cruickshank's;
   Dochter's; Old's; White's
Common sense: Bialac's; Gruber's; Mills's
Communication: Air Force Law; Bork-
   lund's; SNAFU; Wiio's
Commuter: Lada's
Company policy: Business Maxims
Competence/incompetence: Ackley's;
   Mary; Paula
Competition: Bartel's; Schulze's
Complexity: Coan's; Crane's; Modell's
Compromise: Battista's; Juhani's
Computer: Computer Programming; Hol-
   lander's; Horowitz's; Short's; Wain's
Conciliation: Adenauer's
Conclusion: Old's
Concrete: Byrne's
Conduct: Spaatz's
Confidence: Adams's
Conformity: Lippmann's
Confusion: Albert's; Todd's
Congress: Big Mac; Congress; Coolidge;
   Cotton's Flak; Prentice's

D

E

F

G

H

I

Institutions: Anderson's; Institutional; Institutions

Intelligence: Ackley's; Charlemagne's; Combs's; Grosso's; Intelligence; Propriis's; Rutherford's; Taranto's

Intention: Banacek's

Internal Revenue Service: Arnofy's; Explanations

Intimidation: Gruber's

Invention: Hutzler's

Investments: Rubin's; Rose's; Tobias's

Involvement: Horowitz's; Knowlton's; Mahr's

Irony: Hall's; Thidias's

Isolation: Human ecology

Issues: Brown's

Ivy League: Edwards's

J

Jars: Vargas's

Jews: Goldberg's

Jesuit: Jesuit

Jobs: Job performance. *See also:* Work

Jogging: Feazel's

Junk Mail: Raymond's

Justice: Umbrella

K

Keys: Quigley's

Kindness: Corey's; Nye's

Knowledge: Anderson's; Bishop's; Bismarck's; Dr. Brochu's; Edison's; Lowell's; Oddo's; Old Boy's; O'Neill's

Kooks: Cavanaugh's

L

Labor: Bone's

Lament: Bureaucratic

Language: Grammatical; Lawyer's; Mills's; Oxford; Safire's

Lateness: Huhn's

Laundry: Deborkowski's

Law/lawyers: Beckmann's; Bismarck's; Cooper's; Emery's; France's; Lawyer's; Nolan's; Rhodes's

Leadership: Clark's

Learning: Creamer's

Legend: Schinto-Becal's

Legislation. *See:* Congress; Government; Politics

Lemmings: Followers'; Quinn's

Lending: Lender's

Letters: Colby's; Vielmetti's

Liberals/Conservatives: Conservative/Liberal; How to:

Library: Lennie's

Lies: Grizzly Pete's; Palmer's

Life: Balzer's; Blick's; Brauer's; Brenne's; Denenberg's (insurance); Gandhi's; Health; Hovancik's; Howe's; Larson's; Lee's; Lichtenberg's; Lowell's; Lucy's; Miz Beaver's; Quality; Schwartz's; Swartz's

Lighting: Bair's

Lobotomy: Allen's

Logic: Bing's; Martindale's; Schapiro's; Sheehan's

Loneliness: Feather's

Longevity: Health; Smith-Johannsen's

Long-Shot: Lockwood's

Loss: Miller's

Lost and found: Rubman's

Loud people: Winters's

Love: Lichtenberg's; Montore's; Thurber's; Tomlin's

Low profile: Thwartz's

Luck: Charlemagne's; Pogo; Royal's; Why this book . . .

M

Machines: Cooper's; Herman's

Mail: Arnofy's

Making ends meet: Quality

Male/Female: Field's; Fullner's; Parson's; Sally's

Man: Boorstin's; "Bugs" Baer's; Cuppy's; Eldridge's; Epperson's; Epstean's; Explanations; Field's; Hinds's; MIST (in the street); Montore's; Plato's; Quin's

Management: Ackley's; Rigsbee's

Manpower: Bone's

Maps: Jones's; Slim's

Marketing: Butler's

Marriage: Blattenberger's; Pietropinto's; Rosenblatt's

Martyrs: Howe's

Math: Jones's; Penner's

Maxims: Business

Measurement: Loderstedt's

Medes: Medes and Persians'

Media: Court's; Murray's

Medicine: How to; Medical principles; Welch's

Meetings: Cason's; Sklenar's

Memorandum: Memorandum; Oshry's; Rosa's

Memory: Hasselbring's; Hell's Angels' (novel)

Menus: Muir's

Metric: Explanations

Middle of the road: Loughrige's

Military: Herbst's; Krafft's; Slim's

Minutiae: Hassett's

Miseries: Miseries of 1806

Mistakes: Business Maxims

Money: Astor's; Barnum's; Berger's; Bryant's; Burns's; Business Maxims; Carolyn's; Dickson's; Disney World's; Dyer's; Figley's; Getty's; Glass's; Guppy's; Horomorun's; Hubbard's; Jefferson's; Johnson's; Kaul's; Meller's;

Miller's; Money maxim; Notes; Owens's; Paulg's; Perlsweig's; Price's; Sieger's; Tromberg's; Wain's

Morality: Armor's

Moses: Bureaucratic survival

Motel: Dianne's

Mothers: Lee's; Mead's (in-law); Momma's; Nursing Mother's

Motivation: Spindel's

Motto: McLaren's

Mouse: Banacek's

Movies: Dowling's; Fonda's; Goldwynism; Wickre's

Mud-slinging: Adlai's

Murphylogical Research: Murphylogical

Murphy's Law: Boucher's; Metropolitan Edison's; Powell's; Short's;

Museum: Paper's

Music: Grant's; Leo's

Myth: Christmas Eve

N

Nature: Campbell's; Fowler's; Inge's

Necessity: Hall's

Necktie: Olsen's

Needs: Brecht's

Negativism: Kautzmann's; Nelson's

Negotiation: Laur's

Nerves: Griffith's

New England: Krutch's

News: Caffyn's; Powell's; Safire's;

Newspaper: Carter's; Slaven's

Nice Guys: Juall's

Nonsense: Corcoran's

North Dakota Null-Hypothesis Inventory, NDNI: Tests and Examinations

Notes: Peer's

Nothing: Jones's; Ranger's

Nuclear Attack: Bureaucracy and

Nursing Care: Carlisle's

O

Observation: Alfalfa's; Hall's; Harris's; MIST
Obsolescence: Hinds's
Official: Field's; Official Explanations
Oil: Energy matters; Q's; Tromberg's
Operation: Medical principles
Opinion: Cicero's
Optimism: Merrow's
Organization: Jacob's; Joe Cooch's; Jones's; Mary's; Organizational parable; Pearson's; Petroff's; Petronius Arbiter's; Rabinow's; Radovic's; Sheppard's; Sullivan's; Taylor's; Upward-Mobility; Vaughan's; Whitemen's; Woehlke's
Ornithological Statistic: Orben's
Outcome: White's Law
Output: Bartlett's
Overdoing: Bunuel's
Over the hill: Baker's
Owl: Banacek's
Oz: Ozian

P

Pain: Medical principles
Paper: Corry's
Paperwork: Lawrence's
Parable: Organizational
Paradox: Olbers's
Parenting: Forbes's; Mikadet's; Truman's
Parkinson's Law: Whiteman's
Parties: Burton's; Jinny's; Nelson's
Partners: Clarke's
Passport: Omar's
Patience: Bradley's; Raper's
Patients: Medical principles
Paucity: Vargas's
Payment: Gonzalez's
Pencils: Ma's; Napier's

Penny: Carolyn's
Pension: Civil Service
Pentagon: Sign
People: Business Maxims; Cloninger's; Heifetz's; Scheussler's
Performance: Newell's; Perfection
Periodical: Pancoast's
Permanence: Daugherty
Persians: Medes and
Personality: Blewett's; Masson's
Personal Worth: Gruber's
Pets: Hill's
Phenomenon: Fox's
Philadelphia: Rizzo's
Philanthropy: Philanthropy
Philosophy: Cicero's; Longworth's; Mills's; Santayana's; Sharples's
Phrase generator: How to:
Physics: Jackson's (food); Koolman's
Pigmentation: Russell's
Pigs: Business Maxims
Pilot: Pilot's
Pi R Rule: Pi R
Plagiarism: Clay's; Matthews-Butler
Planning: Pangraze's
Poison Ivy: Brauer's
Poker: Poker
Police: DeCicco's; Kaul's
Policy: Kaufman's
Politics: Abourezk's; Adams's; Baker's; Bendiner's; Cohen's; Congress; Coolidge's; Cotton's; DeRoy's; Disraeli's; Fannie's; Flak; Governor's; Landon's; Lippmann's; Miles's; Political (law); Political (leadership); Politico's; Rosenblatt's; Strout's; Thermodynamics; Tiberius's; Truman's; Tufte's; Udall's; Washington's; White House; Williams's
Polls: Rosalynn's
Poodle: Corcoran's
Popcorn: Corcoran's
Population: Taranto's
Possession: Midas's
Postal Service: Arnofy's; Gloom of Night
Potato Chips: Looney's

Results: Nonreciprocal
Return: Hall's; Lincoln's
Reviews: Sissman's
Revolution: Khomeini; Novinson's
Right: Close's; Muir's
Roadblock: Kaufman's
Royalties: Otten's
Rubbernecking: Levine's
Ruination: Ruination
Rules: Bureaucratic Survival (Brownian);
   Mitchell's; Sit, Whittle, and Spit;
   Thomas's
Rumor: Agrait's; Buchwald's
Rush hour: Retsof's

S

Sacrifice: Patton's
Safety: Rizzo's
Saints: Notes
Sartorial Homogeneity: Sartorial
Satisfaction: Vogel's
Scandal: Strout's
Schools: Anderson's; Brogan's
Science: Le Bon's; Science; Notes; Shaw's
Scientist: Krupka's
Scissors: Aunt Emmie's
Score: Lansburgh's
Sea: Albert's; Erickson's
Seasickness: Cramer's
Seating: Bixby's
Second-chance: Wolf's
Second-sheet law: Morrison's
Seismological discovery: Russell's
Self-restraint: Augustine's
Seriousness: Modell's
Sermon: King's
Sex: Barrymore's; Corcoran's; Godin's;
   Horton's; Ruination; Seligson-Gerber-
   Corman
Shavelson's Extension: Hellrung's
Shoes: Kathleen's

Shopping centers: Jackson's
Shrinkage: Corcoran's
Sibling: Family law
Silver lining: Spat's
Similarity: Lowell's
Simplicity: Craine's; Shannon's; White-
   head's
Sin: Korzybski's; Otten's; Remusat's
Singularity: Carson's
Sinking ship: Kaul's
Skylab: NASA
Smoke: Coccia's
Smoking: Aunt Emmie's; Joachim's
Snake: Reik's
Snow: Oshry's
Soap: Mykia's
Social Climbing: Cheshire's
Social investment: Fullner's
Society: Howe's; Nock's
Sociology: Cruickshank's; Meller's
Socks: Deborkowski's; Irreversible
Solution: Gordon's; Hellrung's; Human
   ecology; Jigsaw's; Stult's; Well's
Song: Leo's
Space: explanations
Speech: Adams's; Baker's; Coolidge's;
   Denenberg's; Faraday's; Hazlitt's; Olm-
   stead's; Oxford
Sports: Ginsburg's; Lansburgh's
Square wheels: Arnold's
State service: State Service
Statistics: Bialac's; Callaghan's; Twyman's
Status: Crisp's
Storm: Van Leuvan
Strangers: Robert's
Strong mind: Slaven's
Structure: Matheson's
Style: Landers's
Suburban: Dickson's
Success: Alderson's; Bartel's; Borstel-
   mann's; Business Maxims; Field's; Mor-
   ford's; Peter's; Steckel's; Thomas's;
   Tromberg's; Whiteman's; Winston's
Suicide: Kaul's
Sum: Big Mac Principle
Supply and demand: Bethell's

Vampire: Guinzburg's
Variables: Schwemer's
Verbs: Irregular
Vice: Armor's
Vice-President: Marshall's
Victim: Baron's; Gray's
Virtue: Armor's
Vocabulary: Berg's

W

Waiting: Kellough's
War: Eldridge's; Jackson's; Sukhomlinov
Warning: Warning
Washington: Bethell's; Big Mac Principle
Water: Backus's; Kerouac's (walking on);
   Olly's
Water beds: Steele's
Wealth: Astor's; Getty's; Marxist
Weather: Parry's; Van Leuvan
Weekends: Fullner's
Weight: Lindsay's
Wheel: Coffin's
Whole: Big Mac Principle
Who/Whom: Safire's
Wild: Sgt. Preston's
Window cleaning: Preudhomme's
Winning: Livingston's; Winners'

Wood stove: Energy matters
Words: Pipeline
Work: Bernstein's; Billings's; Busch's; Business Maxims; Carswell's; Cason's; Conrad's; Cossey's; De Tocqueville's; Einstein's; Frost's; Gooen's; Haber's; Harris's; Herman's; Kagan's; MacPherson's; Mills's; Muldoon-Becker's; Nevitsky's; Penner's; Retsof's; Shanebrook's; T. Camille's; Tromberg's; Woodruff's
Workshop: Sybert's
World: Boroson's; Capon's
Worth: Harris's
Writing: Don Marquis; Editorial: How to; Kelly's; Lynes's; MacLeish's; Morris's; Otten's; Smith's

Y

Yankees: Bronx law

Z

Zipper: Quirk's
Zoning laws: Lichtenberg's

Source Code

A/C Advanced Instruments' "Compilation of Very Important but Little Known Scientific Principles." A brochure, numbered SNAFU 8695, put out by this Newton Highlands, Mass., company about 1970.

AO Alan Otten of *The Wall Street Journal.* From his files and columns on the subject.

ASF Astounding Science Fiction. From that magazine's long-running series of letters on laws. (See *Finagle File* for a fuller description.)

Co. A notation indicating *Common* — i.e., difficult to pin to any collection because it appears in so many.

DRW. Donald R. Woods, Stanford, Cal.

EV. Elaine Viets, from her columns on laws in the *St. Louis Post-Dispatch.*

FD Fred Dyer's collection.

FL "Farber's Laws." From an article of that title in *The New York Times Magazine* for March 17, 1968.

FSP. Frank S. Preston, Charlotte, N.C.

GT. Gregg Townsend, who is now in charge of the collection of laws that was begun by Conrad Schneiker and developed by Ed Logg and others. The seminal laws collection. Tucson.

HE Hans Einstein, the RAND Corp.

HW Harper's "Wraparound." Laws solicited from readers for the section of "Wraparound" items in the August, 1974, issue.

JCG. Joseph C. Goulden, Washington, D.C.

JE John Erhman computerized collection housed at the Stanford Linear Accelerator Center.

JIR The Journal of Irreproducible Results.

JMcC John McClaughry, Concord, Vt.

JS. John Shelton, Dallas.

JW Jack Womeldorf, collector-in-residence, Library of Congress, Washington, D.C.

"LSP" "Life's Simple Philosophies." A Xeroxed collection of laws that I have been unable to attribute to any person or publication. Several copies were sent to me by people who found copies circulating around their offices.

MB Malice in Blunderland, Thomas Martin's important book (McGraw-Hill, 1971.)

MBC Mark B. Cohen, Pennsylvania House of Representatives.

ME. M. Mack Earle, Baltimore.

MLS Marshall L. Smith, research director, WMAL Radio, Washington, D.C. A maker and collector of laws.

NDB. N. D. Butcher.

POR "Principles of Operations Research." From the series of articles by Robert Machol that have appeared in *Interfaces.*

PQ Peter's Quotations. Dr. Lawrence J. Peter's invaluable reference.

RA. Ryan Anthony, Tucson.

Ra. Radio. These are rules and laws that were called in to radio talk shows on which the author appeared to talk about the Murphy Center. Many of these are marked with *U* for unknown, as their authors typically did not have time or chance to give their full names.

RM. Robert Matz.

RS Robert Specht, the RAND Corp.

Scientific Collections Designation for several one-page collections of "Scientific Laws" found floating through or tacked up in such places as the National Institutes of Health and the National Bureau of Standards.

S.T.L. The Schneiker/Townsend/Logg et al. collection from the University of Arizona.

TCA. Theodore C. Achilles, Washington, D.C.

TJR. Timothy J. Rolfe.

TO'B Tom O'Brien, the Department of Labor.

2p? A two-page set of laws in my files that is unreferenced.

U Unknown, at least to the author.

Report from the Director

● **Newton's Other Law.** If I have seen further, it is by standing on the shoulders of giants.
(Sir Isaac Newton, February 18, 1676.)

Since the creation of the Murphy Center for the Codification of Human and Organizational Law, dozens of people have come forth to offer laws of their own discovery or examples which they have collected from others. In order to properly acknowledge these people, they have been appointed to positions at the Center and are listed on the following pages.

With the help of these people more than 2,000 laws have been collected to date with still more coming in. For this reason —and because it tends to prove that the Center fills a void in American life—it will remain open indefinitely continuing to collect laws for possible enlarged editions or new collections. The address:

Paul Dickson, Director
The Murphy Center for the Codification
of Human and Organizational Law
P.O. Box 80
Garrett Park, MD 20896

Two classes of position have been created by the Center, with the senior appointments reserved for those whose contributions have been truly major.

Senior Fellows

Theodore Achilles
Nancy H. Dickson
Fred Dyer
M. Mack Earle
John Ehrman
Joseph C. Goulden
Edward Logg
Alan Otten

Frank S. Preston
Conrad Schneiker
Marshall L. Smith
Robert D. Specht
Gregg Townsend
Jack Womeldorf
Donald R. Woods

Fellows

William L. Aamoth
Denis Abercrombie
Bob Ackley
Clyde F. Adams
Gustavo N. Agrait
Bernard L. Albert, M.D.
Marvin J. Albinak
Earl Allen
Wayne Allen
Patricia Altobello
Ronald F. Amberger
Vic Anapolle
E. Frederick Anderson
Joe Anderson
Phil Anderson
Ryan Anthony
John C. Armor
Richard Arnold
Andrew G. Aronfy, M.D.
Michael Atkins
Juliet Awon-Uibopuu
Susan Baber

Don Bailey
Penny Bair
Lawrence H. Ballweb
Ryan J. Barilleaux
Florenz Baron
A.J. Barton
Donald E. Bartel
H.A. Bartlett
Nick Becker
William J. Becker
Richard K. Beebe
Hal R. Belknap, M.D.
Norman R. Bell
Lennie Bemiss
William S. Bennet
James S. Benton
Martin Berger
Edmund C. Berkeley
Richard B. Bernstein
Judith deMille Berson
Thomas M. Beshere, Jr.
Richard N. Bialac

Wallace Bing
Sandra W. Bixby
James Blankenship
Larry A. Blattenberger
Murray Teigh Bloom
Larry D. Bobbit
A.S. Boccuti
Carl T. Bogus
Fred Bondy
Jonathan Bone
Warren Boroson
Bruce O. Boston
Ray Boston
Ben Bova
Charlie Boyle
David F. Brauer
Howard Bray
Nicholas Bretagna II
John Bright-Holmes
Frank Brochu, M.D.
Robert N. Brodie
Ben Brodinsky
Arnold Brown
Dallas Brozik
Larry W. Bryant
E.H. Bulen
Henry B. Burdg
Bob Burkhart
N.D. Butcher
Gil Butler
Richard Butler
Jo Cahow
William C. Callis
Constance E. Campbell
B.J. Carroll
Ron Carswell

Nelson Carter
Robert L. Cason
Terry Catchpole
Clifton Chadwick
Stephen M. Chaplin
Vee Chilton
Milo M. Clarke
John S. Clayton
Leonard R. Cleavelin
Steven Clifton
Nonnee Coan
Dianne Coates
Mark B. Cohen
Howard Cohodas
Kenneth B. Collins
M.C. "Chuck" Combs
Ray Connolly
Kevin Connor
Charles Conrad III
James E. Conrad
Robert Cook
Ernest F. Cooke
Bruce C. Cooper
John H. Corcoran, Jr.
Clarence Cossey
Carson and Clive Court
Lloyd Craine
Les and Roxanne Cramer
William P. Creamer
Anthony M. Cresswell
Don Crinklaw
Walter J. Crowell
Ken Cruickshand
L.L. Cummings
Louise Curcio
Stewart Cureton, Jr.

Michael J. Daum
James I. Davis
Donna P.H. Day
John Dean
Alexander DeCicco
Anne Denmark
C. Henry Depew
Alfred deQuoy
Dichard H. DeRoy
Raj K. Dhawan
Thomas H. Doal
Isabelle C. Dickson
Larry G. Dowd
Bob Duckles
Gov. Pierre du Pont
Tom Eddins
Robert V. Edwards
M.W. Egerton, Jr.
Bob Einbinder
Hans Einstein
James T. Evans
David and Jayne Evelyn
Doug Evelyn
Richard N. Farmer
Dianne D. Farrar
Gerald M. Fava
Betty Feazel
Edgar R. Fiedler
Wayne C. Fields, Jr.
Richard Fitzmaurice
Joyce A. Flaherty
Sally Flanzer
Edward A. Flinn
T. Camille Flowers
John C. Foster
James F. Fox

Seth Frankel
Catherine B. Fresco
Steve Fried
Robert J. Friedman
R.S. Friedman
B.A. Fuller
F. Buckminster Fuller
Randall Fullner
G.G. Gallagher
Jerome G. Ganci
Ray Geiger
Gents of East Russell Hall,
   University of Georgia
David Gerrold
G. Gestra
Robert D. Gillette, M.D.
Armando R. Gingras
Phil Ginsburg
Guy Godin
Michael F. Goff
Vic Gold
Valerie Golvig
Gloria Gonzales
Irwin Gooen
Robert Gorden
Frederick G. Gotwald
Joseph C. Goulden
Sherry Graditor
Paul Gray
Daniel S. Greenberg
John Greenya
Mark Griesbach
Jean Sharon Griffith
Larry Groebe
Stephen J. Grollman
Gerald H. Grosso

John F. Gruber
Douglas Guerette
John W. Gustafson
Meryl H. Haber, M.D.
T.L. Hakala
Keith W. Hall
Bob Hamm
Doug "Leo" Hanbury
Sally Handel
Mark D. Hanson
Sydney J. Harris
Betty Hartig
Charles D. Hartman
Annie C. Harvey
Andrew S. Hasselbring
W. Gilbert Hassett
Jane L. Hassler
Stanley H. Hayaski
John W. Hazard
John M. Hazlitt
David M. Hebertson
Curt Heinfelden
Mitch Hellman
Paul Herbig
Anita M. Herbst
Michael P. Herman
W.A. Herold
Pierre Allen Hill
Raymond M. Hill
Alan Hinds
Henry R. Hoffman, Jr.
Jon Hoffman
William G. Hogan
Alfred D. Holcombe
Howard R. Hollander
Clark Holloway

Stanley Horowitz
Joseph A. Horton, M.D.
John Hovancik
Hal Hoverland
Dwight A. Huster
Thomas L. Hutzler
Richard Isaac, M.D.
Charles Issawi
Andrew E. Jackson
Julie S. Jackson
Michael Jackson
Robert A. Jackson
Adrian Janes
Elizabeth W. Jefferson
Pat Jett
Kenneth J. Johes
M.M. "Johnny" Johnson
Rita Johnson
D. Wylie Jordah, M.D.
Wally Juall
W.R. Jurgens
Shel and Susan Kagan
Dr. James Kane
S. Karni
Connie Kass
Dr. Arthur Kasspe
Amron Katz
Robert Katz
J. Jerry Kaufman
Donald Kaul
Gary E. Kautzmann
Joan C. Kaye
Barry Keating
Eleanor W. Keller
William S. Keller
David Kellough

Richard J. Keogh
Donald King
Larry King
Arthur E. Klauser
Erwin Knoll
Robert P. Knowles
Gary Knowlton
Ron Koolman
Martin S. Kottmeyer
Gary R. Krafft
Martin Krakowski
Stephen C. Lada
Robert V. Larson
Ed Laur
Rudy Lawton
Linda A. Lawyer
Michael L. Lazare
Jack Lee
Lauren Leveut
Kenneth C. Levine
Marion Levy
J.A. Lewandowski
Mike Lewis
Benjamin Lichtenberg
A.A. Lidberg
Fred Lightfoot
Jack Limpert
Wallace E. Lin
Ron Lindsey
Lewis P. Lipsitt
Jean Liston
Robert A. Liston
Lawrence Litt
E.A. Livingston
John Lockwood
Bob Loderstedt

Donald C. Loewe
Kevin G. Long
Dale Lowdermilk
Bob Luke
Richard Luskin
John McClaughry
Michael P. McCoy
Juliet McGhie
Gerard E. McKenna
Tom W. McLeod
Ian MacPherson
Robert Machol
Carlisle Madson
Peter Maiken
Mike Manion
Frank Mankiewitz
William F. Mann
Nancy Manske
Mark Manucy
Thomas Marguccio
Michael Marien
P.W. Marriott
Wallace S. Marsh, M.D.
Maurice Marsolais
Thomas L. Martin
Frank Martineau
Robert E. Maston
Sharon Matthews
Robert Matz, M.D.
R.H. Mead
J.R. Meditz
Liz Mendoza
Donald A. Metz
Daniel J. Metzger
Robert Miazga
T.K. Mikadet

Don G. Miles
William Miles
Henry L. Miller
Joe Miller
William M. Mills
Michael T. Minerath
Steven D. Mirsky
Kevin Mitchell
Van Mizzell, Jr.
Norton Mockridge
Richard Molony
R.J. Montore
T.A. Moore III, D.D.S.
Terry C. Moore
Phil Moos, M.D.
Ronald J. Moran
John C. Morris, Jr.
Vivian M. Morrison
Pete Moutsatson
Georgette Muir
Ed Muldoon
Mariquita P. Mullan
Dr. Fitzhugh Mullen
Kent Myers
Helen Neal
Bert Nelson
Roger Newell
John T. Nolan
Ken S. Norris
Gary Novak
Ronald M. Novinson
Andrew J. Nowotney
Paul Obis, Jr.
Edward L. O'Brien
Tom O'Brien
Vincent D. O'Connor

S.M. Oddo
Ted Olbrich
Clark Olmstead
Margaret K. Omar
Bill O'Neill
Mike O'Neill
William O'Neill
Bob Orben
David Ormerod
James B. Oshry
Jean Skinner Ostlund
Bill Ozard
Charles Pancoast
Joe Pangraze
Herbert H. Paper
Robert L. Pardieck
J. Thomas Parry
Denys Parsons
Carl M. Pearson
John Peers
Layne B. Peiffer
John N. Petroff
Carol Pike
Douglas Pike
Jody Powell
C. Kevin Price
Rose Primack
Martin Quigley
Alvin W. Quinn
Dan Rapoport
Barbara and Marcus Raskin
J. Patricia Reilly
Robert E. Reynolds
Charles E. Rhodes
Edith K. Rice
Phyllis Richman

Ken Rigsbee
Donald B. Rinsley, M.D.
Sarah Risher
Stephen P. Robbins
James A. Robertson
Dan Roddick
Michael A. Rogawski
Kenneth J. Rogers
Timothy J. Rolfe
Robert E. Rosa
Sal Rosa
Jane Ross
Mike Ross
Steve Ross
Paul Rubin
George H. Rule
Gary Russell
Gene H. Russell
Patricia A. Samson
Robert J. Samuelson
Betty Sanders
Ellie Saraquse
Rick Scanlon
Ken Schapiro
R.W. Scheussler
Eric M. Schlegel
Jerry Schonfeld
Warren K. Schoonmaker
Kenneth L. Schoor
Marc A. Schuckit
Paul Schulze III
Eldred O. Schwab
Warren Schwemer
Bill Scott
Sid Scott
Paul Seabury

Boake A. Sells
J. Richard Shanebrook
Stan Shannon
Virginia M. Sharples
Raymond J. Sheehan
John L. Shelton
Martin E. Shotzberger
L.J. Skelnar
K.W. Skinnell
Robert Skole
Larry M. Slavens
Bob Smith
Don Smith
G. Guy Smith
Jerry Smith
John Stephen Smith
Robert J. Smith
Ruth J. Smock
Richard C. Smolik
Dee Solomon
Barbara Solonche
Robert Sommer
Donald T. Spindell
Paul J. Spreitzer
Jim Srodes
Paul W. Steckel
Ashley H. Steele
Guy L. Steele, Jr.
Theodore Stern
James O. Stevenson
James V. Steward
Richard Stone
Charles Suhor
Dan Sullivan
J.M. Sullivan
John H. Sullivan

Joseph P. Sullivan
Larry W. Sussman
Robert A. Sweeney
Christopher Sybert
Mark Szymcik
David A. Tansik
Harri V. Taranto
Robert F. Tatman
Warren E. Taylor
John and Joyce Thomas
Robert H. Thomas
Charles I. Thompson
William I. Thompson III
John Thornton
Claude Timblin
August A. Toda
J.K. Todd, M.D.
Jim Toomey
Mitchell Trauring
Sheldon Tromberg
Dr. Leo Troy
Marcello Truzzi
Joie and George Vargas
Ed Vielmetti
William F. Vietinghoff
Elaine Viets
W.J. Vogel
Ralph W. Voight
Jonathan Waddell
Michael J. Wagner
James M. Wallace
Robert Walters
Roy W. Walters

Sam W. Warren
Hilde Weisert
Jay Weisman
Andrew Weissman
Rozanne Weissman
David P. Welch
Nancy Wells
Stephen Wells
Josheph A. Wemhoff
Robert T. West
Richard N. White
Robert I White, Jr., M.D.
Jack W. Whiteman
Peter Whitney
Iwan Williams
Bennett Moser Willis
John Willis
Ron Wilsie
Bob Wilson
Hal John Wimberly
Robert F. Winter, M.D.
Gary Witzenburg
Wizard of FM 101
Richard A. Woehlke
George Wolfford
Donald R. Wood
Steven R. Woodbury
William K. Wright
Robert Yoakum
Will Yolen
William C. Young
Mark W. Zemansky

Murphy Center Newsletter

Volume 1. No. 1.

CENTER DENIED FOUNDATION GRANT WHICH IT DIDN'T ASK FOR IN THE FIRST PLACE: DIRECTOR HONORED

A letter from a top official of an important philanthropic foundation who was applying for a Center Fellowship ended his letter with the request that the Murphy Center *not* attempt to get a grant from his foundation. *"Our foundation,"* he explained, *"contributes only to frivolous programs, not serious ones like yours."*

The Director of the Center issued an immediate statement that said in part, "We think we are honored by this philanthropic first. As far as we can tell, we are the only research institute in the nation that not only does not have any foundation or government grants but has been peremptorily turned down for one. And for good reason."

Professor Puts Center Research to Good Use

A professor in the natural sciences, who shall remain nameless to protect his ruse, has found that the Center is a boon to his hobby of terrorizing graduate students. What this resourceful scientist does is to use oral examinations as a chance to ask hapless Ph.D. candidates to recite and explain one or two of the

Center's laws, principles, or hypotheses. Invariably, the students conclude that the law in question is a key biological concept that they somehow missed during years of relentless study.

"Whatevers" Collection Growing

For reasons unclear, people have increasingly taken to sending the Center their pet "whatevers"—odds and ends that are hard to define save by example. Our file contains such gems as:

—A copy of the text that the late Rube Goldberg allegedly asked to have put on his tombstone: "Dear God, Enclosed please find Rube Goldberg. Now that you've got him, what are you going to do with him?"

—A sign found in a Japanese hotel room: "Please to bathe inside the tub."

—A yellowed clipping—undated, unsigned, unattributed—in which the writer suggests that there is deep satisfaction to be had from going out and intentionally violating conventional, proverbial wisdom. For instance, visiting a farm and putting all your eggs in one basket and then counting all your chickens before they're hatched.

—A small item from *The Wall Street Journal* reporting that Princeton University has installed a 3" × 5" card file-system to replace a computer that kept breaking down. (Two Fellows brought this to the attention of the Center.)

—More. Cartoons, religious tracts, "simple assembly instructions" that make no sense, chain letters, etc.

The Center is proud of this collection and thanks those who have helped start what may become one of the best whatever collections around.

New Research Suggested

From time to time, Fellows suggest new areas for Center investigation. Here is the best we have ever received:

> I might also mention that I have a very large collection of instances where persons' names and either their occupations or preoccupations are in synchrony. This is an area of human lawfulness which has not been sufficiently or seriously organized. I knew that there was orderliness here when I noted that on the Brown University campus a Mrs. Record was in charge of alumni files, Mr. Banks was the Controller, and Mr. Price was in charge of purchasing. Looking a bit beyond my own campus, I found that Dr. Fish was indeed the head of the University of Rhode Island Oceanographic Institute, and he had hired one staff member named Saila and another named Seaman. I won't belabor the situation further, beyond mentioning simply that my own research area is that of sucking behavior in infants.
>
> Sincerely Yours,
> Lewis P. Lipsitt
> Professor of Psychology and Medical Science;
> Director, Child Study Center.

Center Takes Up Arms . . . Motto

Resourceful friends of the Center have been most helpful in giving it a stronger institutional identity. Robert N. Brodie of New York City has suggested a slogan: "Ain't it the truth!" and Marshall L. Smith of Washington, D.C., has researched and presented us with the "Arms of the Edsel Murphy Family with Family Motto." The slogan, arms, and motto have all been officially adopted by the Center. Here are the arms with Smith's explanation.

ARMS OF THE EDSEL MURPHY FAMILY ADOPTED FOR
THE MURPHY CENTER
FOR THE CODIFICATION OF HUMAN AND
ORGANIZATIONAL LAW

Arms: **Gules** three mismatched cogwheels, *or* two monkey wrenches salient, *or* three tack caltraps rampant.

Crest: An arm dressed, holding a broken pencil proper; spilt milk and India ink mantling.

Motto: Calamitas Necessaria Esı (Disaster Is Inevitable).